About the Author

Born in Germany, Liam Klenk is a world citizen of German-French-Italian descent. He is an incorrigible dreamer and romantic who also keeps both feet firmly planted on Planet Earth.

Liam collects life experiences and meaningful encounters with people around the world. He has traveled, lived, and worked in Europe, North America, Asia, and Africa, while making a living as a photographer, movie theater manager, English teacher, visual services artist, scuba diving instructor, hyperbaric chamber operator, show diver, theater coach, and production manager.

He currently lives in Zurich, Switzerland.

www.liamklenk.com
Follow @liamklenk on Twitter

Paralian

Not *just* transgender

Liam Klenk

Matador
9 Priory Business Park,
Wistow Road, Kibworth Beauchamp,
Leicestershire. LE8 0RX
Tel: 0116 279 2299
Email: books@troubador.co.uk
Web: www.troubador.co.uk/matador
Twitter: @matadorbooks

ISBN 978 1785891 205

British Library Cataloguing in Publication Data.
A catalogue record for this book is available from the British Library.

Printed and bound by CPI Group (UK) Ltd, Croydon, CR0 4YY
Typeset in 11pt Aldine401 BT by Troubador Publishing Ltd, Leicester, UK

Matador is an imprint of Troubador Publishing Ltd

For Frida

My beloved oma – she was born on 14th of October 1909 and passed away on the 26th of December 1996. I am quite sure that without her strength and inner peace to guide me through my early years, I would not be here today, would not be able to write these words for her, for myself and for all of you.

Contents

Introduction   ix

1. River Enz   1
2. Amniotic Fluid   10
3. North Sea   23
4. Froschteich   36
5. Swabian Ocean   46
6. Lake Monrepos   61
7. Atlantic Ocean   67
8. Schanzengraben   87
9. Northern Mediterranean Sea   105
10. River Limmat   115
11. Greifensee   132
12. Lake Zurich   137
13. River Sihl   144
14. Oma's Bathtub   160
15. Two Lakes   166
16. Columbia River   174
17. River Neckar   192
18. Southern Mediterranean Sea   199
19. Kuredu Lagoon   217
20. Puget Sound   222
21. Pacific Ocean   238
22. Lake Lucerne   257
23. Lhaviyani Atoll   266
24. Indian Ocean   276
25. South Ari Atoll   295
26. Philippine Sea   310

27. Noonu Atoll   321
28. Belgian Pool   330
29. Pearl River Delta   351
30. Macau Pool   364
31. The Mangal   377
32. South China Sea   391
33. Lake Minnewanka   405
34. Xijiang River   415
35. Untersee   423

75% – an Epilogue   435
Acknowledgements   437

Introduction

For twenty-five years, I dreamed of writing a book about my life. Life itself however, and my quest for home swept me along, not leaving me time to at the same time let my experiences flow onto paper. When I got stranded on the shores of Hong Kong in the fall of 2013, I finally took time to stop and breathe and I realized that all my life experiences in the last forty years had led me to that moment. And now I am finally mature enough to share my story with the world.

Doors have opened all along the way, leading me on an unforgettable journey. This quest for home was always shaped as well as driven by two major factors – the people I met along the way and water that carried me, both literally as well as metaphorically.

I believe I have something to give to the world, something very basic, yet precious – hope, and an unwavering passion for life. I hope with all my heart you will not be able to put down this tale. I hope you will read all or parts of it more than once. I hope it will make you smile and laugh and cry, that it will make your heart feel both heavy and light, and, above all, let you feel without a doubt that no matter what happens to you, life is precious and so much worth living!

As my unique journey continues, I hope that from now on it will become a literary journey as well. My mind is bursting with stories. I have waited too long to share them with the world.

This is for you, dear Reader, straight from my heart.

"What would an ocean be without a monster lurking in the dark? It would be like sleep without dreams."

WERNER HERZOG

1

River Enz

Our small town was a monotonous, urban forest of grey concrete high-rise buildings from the Sixties. Just as dull as the man-made surroundings were the conversations of the adults around me. They complained about their neighbor's shrieking parrots, or gossiped about those who dared hang up their freshly-washed underwear on the balcony.

Growing up in this incredibly drab but safe town in Southern Germany, I became a nomad in my mind, long before my body was ready to be one. Outwardly, I seemed a well-adjusted, quiet girl who did what was expected of me. I smiled, greeted older people on the street, held doors open for others, and happily played with Lego for hours at a time. Inwardly, a storm was raging. The turmoil started from a very young age. Who was I? What was I? Where did I come from? What was my purpose? Had my brain been a muscle, I would have experienced a constant ache. Yet I found no answers.

I observed my parents, their appearance, behavior, and constant discontent. I wasn't quite able to shake the feeling of being different from them. I was too dark-skinned, too dark-haired, too optimistic and soulful, and too much of a tomboy to belong to these people.

Confused and lost, I kept to myself and escaped into my imagination. I would explore entire continents without leaving my small room. I would accompany the heroes of my adventure books on their journeys. Or I would lie on my bed, close my eyes, ignore my screaming parents, and imagine wild adventures. Evil forces would chase me. Eventually, they would manage to catch me. They would enslave me, chain me spread-eagled to the ground and torture me to gather information from the hidden depths of my mind. I would be held captive in caverns directly underneath the safety of our house. None of my family would ever come to my rescue. I would endure and, with stubborn strength, never reveal a single precious thought to my unknown captors. Then, after months of braving torture and near starvation, I would manage to escape my bonds – free and proud to have prevailed against all odds.

Tales of loyalty and brotherhood struck a deep chord with me. I rejoiced in stories of strong warriors who never gave up, who did anything for their brethren, no matter how dangerous their quest might prove to be.

On my afternoons off of school, I would roam the forests and, more often than not, the dense underbrush on the shores of the river Enz. It was a narrow, timid river, a soothing presence in our quiet town. In my imagination, the harmless Enz grew to Amazonian proportions, wild rapids making the deep, wide river immensely dangerous for me to cross. Yet I had no choice; a tribe of merciless cannibals on the opposite shore had caught my blood brothers. I would swing on ropes and build shaky stone bridges. I would even attempt to jump from tree to tree across the torrents. On countless evenings, my parents would shake their heads at the little, muddy apparition coming home for dinner.

The more I read, the more I internalized ideals of honor, truthfulness, loyalty, persistence, integrity and compassion. I hoped to prove strong enough in real life to live up to these ideals. I dreamed of one day being able to come to someone's rescue.

As I got older, I progressed from adventure stories to philosophy. At thirteen, I admired Jung and Schopenhauer. At fourteen, my romantic heart and inquisitive mind delighted in Immanuel Kant's *Categorical Imperative*. I didn't understand half of what the man was saying, but his philosophical concepts of freedom of mind, autonomy, duty and responsibility touched my young heart.

One thought of poet and philosopher Christian Fürchtegott Gellert in particular stayed with me: "Lebe, wie du, wenn du stirbst, wuenschen wirst, gelebt zu haben." (Live, so you can die, secure in the knowledge of having lived as you desired.) I had stumbled over something very important but couldn't get past the old-fashioned sentence structure. So as not to forget, I took a big brush and painted the odd sentiment crudely on the wall of my room. Over time, I understood. Why didn't he simply say, "Live your life fully, without regrets"? I promised myself to do just that, no matter how scared I might be at times.

I was almost twenty-one years old when I was finally presented with the grand opportunity to be a knight in shining armor. I was studying in far-away Zurich at the time and only visited my dad on the weekends. Imagine my surprise when he cleaned out my childhood room and Timotei, a handsome Romanian man I had never heard him mention before, moved in with him. Konrad explained how the young man was one of a group of Romanian asylum-seekers who might soon be sent back to their country. Timotei needed a home and my dad was trying to help. I was very proud of him. Timotei became a part of our family and an anchor of hope for Konrad.

Throughout his eventually failing marriage to my mom Hildegard, my dad had been a shadow of himself. He was depressed and very rarely enjoyed life. Timotei, who was twenty years younger, granted Konrad a second adolescence. He literally seemed to shed several decades. Suddenly, he was going dancing and clubbing with his buddy. On my weekend visits, I would be in bed long before Konrad and Timotei came home from whichever hip dance establishment they had explored that night. My dad beamed with happiness and laughed more than I had ever seen him laugh before. His usual, predominantly melancholy disposition had changed.

Then, after only a few months of bliss, the harmonious life he led with Timotei and his Romanian friends ended all too quickly. I could read fear in Konrad's eyes, which evolved into outright panic. Timotei's petition to be granted asylum in Germany was inevitably denied. Since he was unable to prove to the authorities that his life had been threatened in Romania, they didn't see him as having escaped political persecution but rather as someone who had left his home country simply hoping to find a better future elsewhere. At his final official court hearing, he was informed he would shortly be deported and sent back to Romania.

My dad and I had long conversations over the phone about how we could help Timotei. Konrad was in tears. It was breaking my heart to see him so hopeless, as if the world would end the very next day. I tried my best to counsel and console him. We thought about legally adopting Timotei and then – I do not know who thought of it first, my dad or me – we began considering marriage. I remembered my adventure novels, and my readings of Jung, Gellert, Kant, Schopenhauer and their peers. My firm, romantic belief in selflessness, truthfulness, and courage in the face of adversity had only grown stronger over the years. Here was a chance to act, not just think and talk. Yes, I was ready to leap on my white steed and charge into battle.

While I brimmed with youthful enthusiasm, Konrad felt like he had let the genie out of the bottle. He was torn between my well-being and Timotei's. What made things even harder for him was his awareness of my innocence, deep trust and loyalty. He knew I was clueless and had not yet learned to read between the lines: my dad was keeping a secret from his family. If we let the momentum whisk us away and went ahead with my marriage to Timotei, my dad knew he would have no choice but to reveal his secret. Would I embrace what he needed to tell me? Or would his disclosure mar a father-daughter relationship that was more like a deep friendship? He felt like a seeker of treasures who, in order to reach the end of the rainbow, needed to sacrifice more than his goal might be worth.

One evening at dinner, as we toasted to my coming marriage, my dad said, "Cheers! And I need to tell you something: I am gay. Timotei and I are in an intimate relationship." Unbeknownst to me, he had been madly in love with Timotei long before his lover had moved in with him. Well-muscled and proportioned, with soulful, dark eyes, Timotei was admittedly quite the catch. He had a good sense of humor, coupled with sparkling intelligence and boundless self-confidence to boot.

At first, when I realized this had never been about helping a Romanian refugee, I felt betrayed and used. My dad simply wanted me to marry his lover so they could stay together. Then again, what better way could my dad help someone than by loving him?

I couldn't help but be inspired. Seeing my dad, thinking back on his behavior over the past months, I realized he had been privileged, at the age of forty, to experience a romantic love affair of the kind usually reserved for teenagers. I was truly happy for him – especially since I had witnessed my parents' catastrophic marriage, and knew it had made my dad phobic of deeper connections. Naturally, I wanted to help him stay connected, happy and rejuvenated.

After Konrad's coming out, we took every opportunity to talk on the phone and discuss our options in more detail. There weren't many. My dad couldn't marry Timotei himself. It was the early nineties: two men marrying each other was not yet possible. Only three more weeks, and a couple of police officers would be knocking on our door to escort Timotei to the airport.

This scenario was inconceivable, to both of us. A wave of boundless idealism drove us forward. We looked at each other like two alchemists on the verge of discovering the *Philosopher's Stone*. We felt united in our goal, bold and passionate. I felt oddly important, with the power in my young hands to help two people I deeply cared about. It was time to don my shining armor and prepare to sacrifice myself.

After weeks of bureaucratic preparation, our wedding day arrived. The German authorities were unaware of me only visiting on weekends. Technically, Timotei and I were supposed to share a household. On paper we would. In real life, I would continue living in Zurich.

We got married in the medieval town hall of our small community. Konrad, being a very emotional man, added real credibility to the proceedings. Tears of true joy and happiness streamed down my dad's cheeks, despite his full knowledge of our marriage being for his benefit, rather than being the celebration of a life-time commitment between his daughter Stefanie and a handsome, charismatic Romanian man. His sentimental heart must have treasured the two people he loved most in this world uniting for a common cause. Timotei, Konrad and I celebrated under the warm summer sun. During this short peaceful moment, sipping a strong coffee together under a clear blue sky, our sense of family seemed almost real.

Only two days later, it was time to return to my studies in Zurich. I hugged Konrad and his lover goodbye. I hoped for the best but mentally prepared for the worst. Planning our wedding had given me a chance to get to know my "husband" better. He was a smart man who knew how to create opportunities. I sincerely doubted his professions of love for my dad. Still, Timotei's deportation had been avoided. I was happy with what we had accomplished, no matter where it might lead.

Truthfully, I had benefitted as much as the two men in my life. Legally an adult, I had still no concept of who I was. I was lost in my body, eagerly devouring book after book to make sense of my existence. On most days, nothing made sense. Taking action, helping my dad and Timotei, helped me breathe meaning into my life. For just a brief while, chaos reverted to consonance.

Timotei opted to take our family name. Unsurprisingly, with a German name and his new visa status, it became easier for him to find jobs in his profession. He was a very talented mechanic, specializing in sports cars. With each passing month, Timotei felt safer from losing his foothold in his chosen home.

The more independent he felt, the more he broke my dad's heart. At first, he tried to hide switching back to his true sexual orientation – females, preferably long-legged, big-breasted blondes. Still unsuspecting, my dad saw less and less of his lover. Eventually, Timotei became bolder and stopped pretending. He still cared for my dad, but more as his friend and son than his lover. Konrad began to see more than he wanted to see when Timotei began bringing some of his many blondes home with him. Timotei was utterly oblivious to the emotional pain their love-making in the room next door caused my dad, who couldn't help still being madly in love with his son-in-law.

Timotei started to enjoy his life, and began frequenting rougher establishments. With each of his drug-related arrests, and ever more loan sharks circling my dad's building, I started to feel the burden of my responsibility of being married to a virtual stranger. What would I do if my spouse got himself into serious trouble?

Inevitably, my dad and Timotei grew further and further apart. They tried to switch from being in love to simply being father and son. But for Konrad, the pain of loss was too intense. He couldn't help but fluctuate between being heartbroken and love-struck. For legal purposes, my quasi-husband stayed registered at my dad's home but he came home less and less often. Soon, he moved in with one of his girlfriends. My dad reverted to his former dark, melancholy self.

I felt the futility of my sacrifice, but soothed myself with the knowledge that at least I had taken action and tried to help. The biggest worry I had was: whether Timotei would keep his word and divorce me after five years, the legally-required period we needed to stay married so he could acquire a permanent visa for Germany.

Konrad worried his heart out. He battled with his conscience and realized that he had complicated his daughter's teenage life through a peculiar marriage arrangement. At the same time, my dad had created a situation where his ex-lover might inherit half of his estate, should anything untoward happen, thus partially disinheriting his daughter.

During his frequent panic attacks, Konrad was ready to pull the plug and pleaded with me to file for immediate divorce. He had been the one who had initiated our union but for the last two years of my marriage to Timotei, it was I who kept it all together. I dealt with Timotei's unpredictable behavior while at the same time reassuring an increasingly frantic Konrad that all would be fine in the end. Naïve faith and stubbornness prevailed as I held on like a bulldog to a stinking bone, wanting to finish what we had started.

So my handsome Romanian husband and I waited until the mandatory five-year mark of our marriage was finally reached. By then, I was getting tense myself. What if he disappeared? What if he contested the divorce?

Thankfully, Timotei kept his promise to part ways amiably without any obligations. To my surprise, our divorce was swift and bureaucratically unproblematic. I was free. I promised myself never to repeat the experience and hoped Timotei would use his chance wisely and find true happiness in Germany.

Coming out of the courthouse on the day of our official separation, the three of us enjoyed a final cup of coffee together, mirroring the events of our wedding day while relief as well as a sense of happy ending flooded us.

As I walked the long way to the train station, enjoying the sunny path along the River Enz, I wondered: was this what a commercial diver perceived when stepping out of a decompression chamber? Thousands of atmospheres of pressure fell away from me instantly. I felt as light as a feather, tap-dancing in the soft, soothing afternoon light.

In Zurich once again, I pondered how life could sometimes be as wild as my imagination. More than one genie had wiggled out of the bottle while Konrad had been organizing my wedding to his lover. Apart from homosexuality, another revelation had been made.

In Germany, it is customary to have two certificates documenting a child's birth. The birth certificate divulges only the essential details of name and birthdate. The other certificate is called *Abstammungsurkunde* or parenthood certificate. It lists all the details suppressed on the birth certificate – who your parents were, and any changes to your family history that the state might have discreetly documented.

In planning the wedding, my dad had discovered that a wedding was, unfortunately, one of the few events in a German citizen's life for which the more informative document had to be unearthed from the bowels of the German filing system. The citizen who got married would see his parenthood certificate for the very first, and very likely the last, time in his life.

When the envelope arrived in my dad's mailbox, he opened it and immediately felt as if he had been handed a poisoned fruit. The official document stated it plain as day: I had been adopted. The burden of finally sharing the truth with his teenage daughter had fallen into his lap.

My parents had missed the moment during my childhood when it would have been easy to explain the adoption. As an inquisitive three-year old, I had probed my adoptive mom with questions and asked, "Mom, where did I come from?" It would have been easy to say, "We couldn't have children of our own but wanted so much to have a little girl just like you. We chose you. We are meant to be together." Instead she had answered, "Well, you came out of my tummy, of course."

Now, twenty-one years into his daughter's life, Konrad faced the choice of keeping the adoption hidden by cancelling the wedding and losing his lover, or divulging another secret and going ahead with the wedding plans. He opted for the wedding, his lover, and a revealing of the long-suppressed truth. Part of him was grateful to be forced to put an end to a string of lies that, like Pinocchio's nose, had grown longer and longer over the years.

During one of my weekend visits from college, my dad sat me down on his comfortable couch and explained how they had found me, a cute little orange girl in a Stuttgart orphanage – orange, because I was addicted to carrot purée as a baby. Besides mother's milk I would eat nothing else, until the carotene turned me into an orange-complexioned heartthrob. Konrad and Hildegard had fallen in love with me and visited every week. I had smiled at them with such vivid, soulful eyes that, after a few months, they had decided there was nothing to do but take me home. They had fostered me until I was one year old. After the official trial period was over, they legally adopted me.

I had been stunned into silence by my dad's news. Sitting there on his couch, I felt as if I was sinking into an abyss, frantically trying to swim back to the surface but being dragged downward ever further by a weight too great to resist.

For years, I had puzzled over being the only dark-haired, darker-complexioned person in our family. My emotional make-up and character didn't quite seem to fit with the rest of my family either. I had kept searching for similarities between my parents and me, as every child does, and had found none. But my mom Hildegard had been very convincing as to our shared blood. She had scared me with stories of how her multitude of hereditary afflictions would manifest themselves in me as I grew older. She had a large goiter on her neck as well as suffering from acute asthma. I had inherited both from her, she insisted, and would suffer as she did eventually. No matter how unpleasant the knowledge, no matter how lost I felt, and whatever life threw at me while growing up, at least I had always been secure in the knowledge of who my family was. It proved to be quite dysfunctional at times, but it *was* a family. But now, with my dad's revelation, the truths on which I had based my life shattered into a million pieces.

I had always been terrified of becoming my mom, as I got older. The knowledge of her multiple hereditary ailments had suffocated me. Now, despite the heaviness in my heart, I had to admit: I felt happy not to be her blood relative. I battled feelings of immense relief, guilt, utter confusion, and grief. More than ever before, I felt literally uprooted. Conflicting emotions tumbled through my heart like stubborn, prickly tumbleweeds.

2

Amniotic Fluid

Thoughts about my heritage dominated my days and nights. Back in Zurich, I buried myself in work for my projects, socialized like there was no tomorrow, and watched multiple movies each week, all in an attempt to distract myself and free my mind of the nagging doubts and confusion.

The soothing smells of stale popcorn and flat Coke in Zurich's historical movie theaters relaxed me. When the lights went out, I focused on the stories of my favorite characters and cried hot tears for their happiness. My pent-up thoughts would release like the steam from the valve on a pressure cooker. After two hours in an alternate universe, sinking ever deeper into softly-padded seats until I could hardly extract myself, I was able to see the promise of a better tomorrow. My storm of emotions would calm considerably, and the prickly tumbleweeds would come to rest for a brief time, giving me respite.

Processing the information Konrad had given me would take years. Regardless of how I intellectualized the situation, for a few months I was shell-shocked. It was as if, instead of a gentle revelation, a hand grenade had exploded on my dad's comfy couch. Nothing helped, except picking myself up and taking decisive action. I needed to start searching for the two individuals who had created me and meet them at least once so I could better understand my identity and origins.

The process of finding them, however, proved to be a long and winding road. Since I was legally an adult, the German authorities freely handed over their file on my biological parents. My excitement waned considerably when it consisted of only one page, filed in 1971, bearing the scent of withering old leaves. Printed on it was the Italian home address of my biological father. A yellowed black-and-white passport photo showed him sporting a very interesting Seventies hairdo – something between an Afro and a wildly growing bush. Last but not least, my biological mother's German address had been included as well.

I continued staring at the scant information while my brain caught up slowly. In awe, I focused on my biological father's address: Taranto, Southern Italy. So, I was half Italian.

I scanned myself in the mirror, my dark complexion, my shock of dark brown hair, and my almond eyes. A big part of the puzzle fell into place. My eyes flitted back and forth between my father's passport image and myself. I longed to dive into the picture, to see him, feel him, and smell him. We looked incredibly alike.

Stereotypes of Italians came to my mind such as temperamental, impulsive, emotional, and loud. In my imagination, I traveled to the town of Taranto. I saw a clear blue sky, and a big marketplace teeming with enthusiastically gesticulating, laughing people, burning under the hot Mediterranean sun. My eyes twinkled as I laughed out loud at my own reflection. I was impulsiveness personified. Emotional, romantic, and passionate, I longed for dazzling, warm rays of sunshine.

The German authorities let me know in no uncertain terms that locating my biological father quickly would be completely impossible. Since I didn't speak a word of Italian, I would need to learn the language *Matrix*-style, or bring an interpreter while searching the region of Apulia in Southern Italy for him. It didn't help that his name was one of the most common Italian names imaginable.

I was cautioned to be sensitive while investigating his whereabouts. My sudden appearance could wreak havoc with the conservative family life typical of Apulia. The last thing I wanted was destroy my father's life. After much deliberation, I decided to leave him alone until I had both the time and the resources to investigate subtly, without making waves. For now, just knowing about my Southern Italian genes was enough. I felt like Pixar's *boundin'* Jackalope.

My biological mother was another story. I decided to make a serious attempt at finding at least this much of my heritage. My birth mom seemed to have stayed in Germany, yet had become a veritable nomad in her early years. Each time I would track her to a city of residence, it would turn out she had moved yet again. After six months of driving all over the map on my weekends away from college, I was up to a count of twenty moves. I started to feel like a lost wanderer in the Saharan desert, stumbling from mirage to mirage in hope of shelter and water.

Only half an hour from where I grew up, I finally stood in front of a doorbell with my birth mom's name on it. By then, I felt so dehydrated from my walk through the desert that my brain needed a moment to grasp what was happening. This was no mirage. I triple-checked – but the house didn't disappear. Her printed name remained on the doorbell. It wasn't faded, but new.

I turned to look at the sleepy little village, expecting fanfare and fireworks to immortalize the moment. But nothing stirred. Closing my eyes, I snapped a picture with my heart and committed the moment to memory.

The apartment building my biological mother lived in was painted a soft blue, reminding me of a shallow lagoon. Time seemed to stand still to give me a chance to breathe and observe for a moment. I had found what I had been looking for. Now I wondered what surprises awaited me. I felt exhilarated and scared out of my wits. I wanted to both storm inside and run as far away as I could get.

I didn't ring my birth mom's doorbell that day. Instead, I walked back to my rental car across the street and sat staring at her house entrance for a while. After half an hour, a woman came out of the house. She was petite with dark blonde hair, elegant yet modest in appearance. Turning around for just an instant, she seemed to scan her surroundings. She was beautiful and held herself with dignity. At the same time, she seemed cautious and wary of the world. I knew without a doubt: this was my biological mother. But I stayed in the car, my entire body quivering with the strain of keeping myself from running after her. I watched her walk down the eerily quiet street, wondering whether she could sense the close proximity of the child she had lost so many years ago.

As soon as I arrived home, I composed a long letter to the woman I had seen, asking her if she would like to get together for a chat. Two days after receiving my letter, unable to contain her excitement and curiosity, my biological mom called me.

We set a date and I returned to the blue house. Again, I stood in front of probably the most important doorbell of my life. I was more thrilled than scared at this point. I just had to see her, and maybe, by doing so, find another piece of the puzzle.

My biological mom lived on the top floor of the four-story apartment building. There was no elevator. With every step up, my heart soared and fluttered a bit more. My legs were made of feathers and lead at the same time. Finally, I reached her floor.

In the doorway of what looked like a modest little apartment stood the same short, forty-something, elegant lady I had observed the weekend before. Her eyes were careful and guarded yet also filled with wonder. Her expression was vivid. She looked me up and down and said, "Oh my god, you are so tall and pretty!" I was instantly amused, since I am only five foot six and stood in front of her in my usual, rather boyish attire: tennis shoes, faded jeans, and an old red tank top. My hair was cut short and, as always, I wore no make-up. My biological mom took a hold of my hand and pulled me into her little rooftop domain.

We felt comfortable right away. Since I had learned about my adoption, I had never felt any anger towards her. Life happens, and often we find ourselves in positions in which we are forced to make very tough choices. I understood that my being raised by adoptive parents wasn't anybody's fault. Blame is definitely never an answer to the obstacles we encounter. Nevertheless, I had been worried how I would feel when we actually met. But now, here I was and I just felt happy – and curious to finally unveil the mystery of how our story had unfolded and, most importantly, how I had come to be.

While preparing some strong Italian coffee in her tiny kitchen, my biological mother, Sandra, couldn't stop looking at me. As soon as we settled on her couch, she poured some coffee into delicate cups, made of china, and asked me with amazing straightforwardness, "Are you angry with me?"

"No, not at all," I reassured her immediately. "I am just very glad and amazed to finally be together in the same room."

I had not arrived with any expectations – of the situation, of her, of anything. I savored the moment and treasured the opportunity to find out more about her and, maybe more about myself at the same time. Sandra hadn't started talking yet, but I already recognized impulsiveness and an emotional intensity in this woman that seemed all too familiar.

In her charming and soft Swabian accent, Sandra explained, "I thought about you every day, all my life, especially each year on your birthday. I never stopped wondering where you were and whether you were happy. I thought your parents would tell you about the adoption. And I knew the authorities don't allow adopted children to legally search for their birth parents before the age of eighteen. So when your eighteenth birthday came and went, I was on pins and needles for months – but nothing happened. That's when I finally gave up hope and figured you probably hated me and didn't want anything to do with me. You can imagine my surprise when three years later, your letter arrived in my mailbox. It was almost too good to be true. Why didn't you contact me? Are you sure you aren't upset with me?"

At this point, Sandra had tears in her eyes. I could see clearly how shaken up she was by our encounter, how hopeful and afraid she was, all at the same time. I answered gently, "My father only just told me about my adoption. I never knew. As soon as I heard, I wanted to find you. It's taken me a few months to track you down. And no, I really am not upset in any way. Honestly, I feel like I am floating on clouds right now."

I proceeded to tell her a little about my life and my current studies in Zurich. Sandra listened in fascination, hungry to hear more and more about my life. She couldn't stop herself from telling me every few minutes how happy she was to finally see me and how beautiful I was. I felt overwhelmed, happy, and a little bit helpless in the face of her emotions. Her smile was so wide it could have encompassed an entire universe.

Our words tumbled out faster and faster, like excited children spilling out of a school's front door. Finally, pouring some more of her aromatic Italian brew, Sandra sighed deeply and said, "It will hurt, but I think now the time has come for me to dig up some bitter-sweet memories and tell you the story of your origins."

1969 was the fateful year during which my birth mom's life had begun to change forever. She was seventeen years old at the time. Friday evening was disco night out with her friends. On a Friday like any other, Marcello, a charming young Italian man with a haircut closely resembling an exploded chicken began flirting with her. He was only eighteen years old and one of many Italians staying in Germany to earn money to support their families back home. Sandra felt herself instantly drawn to Marcello. He had a gentle manner, a sonorous yet calm voice, and very beautiful eyes brimming with soul and fire. His exotic masculinity paired with his gentle nature made him safe yet exciting at the same time.

My birth mom's parents were very conservative. Harsh rigidity and intolerance ruled Sandra's life while growing up. Her bristling teenage spirit welcomed a hot love affair with a charismatic Italian man. Their romance would constitute a grave rebellion against her parent's values.

What started out as an act of rebellion swiftly bloomed into a full-blown love. To avoid the wrath of Sandra's parents, all meetings between the young lovers took place in secret. Marcello's parents were just as conservative and unforgiving. Even though they lived in far-away Taranto, Marcello had to be careful to avoid other Southern Italian immigrants. There was always a risk of being recognized by someone who might report his unmarried union with a German girl to Marcello's strictly Catholic family.

While reminiscing about her parents, Sandra remembered an interesting detail about them. "I almost forgot to tell you: my mother was French. I guess this makes you half Italian, a quarter French, and a quarter German." Considering that, on a visceral level I had never been able to identify with German culture, I was far from unhappy to hear this surprising news.

Sandra's father had been raised in a very devout German family. Her mother had grown up in an isolated, catholic parish in the Pyrenees. My birth mom's parents were extraordinarily inquisitive about their daughter's movements, imposing strict curfews on her. It took all the creativity of a young soul desperately in love to continuously invent new ways to be able to see her boyfriend. Sandra and Marcello's first six months together were spent in hidden corners, on park benches, dark alleyways, and anywhere under the stars where they could find a moment of solitude. For both teenagers, it was their first intimate relationship. They explored each other and puzzled over their increasing sexual drive.

The subject of sexuality had always appalled both of their parents. It was not to be discussed. Period. Their children would live properly and hence discover intercourse after marriage before having children of their own.

As good at heart as their parents' intentions might have been, their actions left Sandra and Marcello utterly clueless and unprepared for their sexual relationship. They had overheard conversations about sperm cells leaving a man's penis at the moment of orgasm and then rushing off to… somewhere. Allegedly, the arrival of the sperm cells at their coveted destination caused women to become pregnant. This summed up the extent of my birth parent's knowledge. 1970 was still far away from the age of Internet and both teenagers were too ashamed to ask anyone or buy themselves a book explaining fertility and contraception.

Besides their painful awareness of committing a sin by having sex out of wedlock, they felt nowhere near ready to consider having a family of their own. Sandra gave me a sad smile. "Marcello was a romantic gentleman. He promised to always be there for me. If I should get pregnant despite our precautions, we would run off together."

I asked, "So what did you do to avoid pregnancy?"

She sighed, "Our naïve young minds came up with a very simple and – to us – very logical solution. We figured if Marcello's sperm cells never managed to enter my body, then they wouldn't be able to cause any trouble. Marcello promised to be cautious and always pull out before his orgasm."

"Oh," was all I could think to say. I worked hard to suppress rising giggles.

By the beginning of 1970, Sandra had had enough of the paralyzing, conservative pressures at home. With the small amount of money she earned as a sales clerk in a women's clothing store, Sandra claimed her independence. Against her parent's wishes, she moved out into a very cheap and rugged little apartment. It was located on the ground floor just next to a major traffic intersection in Stuttgart. The walls were bare and so thin you could hear someone blowing his nose farther up the street. The ancient wallpaper smelled of garlic and threatened to fall off the walls. The rough wooden floor was stained and splintered, creaking loudly with every step. For Sandra and Marcello it was heaven. They had finally found a sanctuary.

By now, their love seemed larger than life. During their many sexual encounters, Marcello kept his promise and did his very best to prevent his sperm cells from swimming on their merry way. Each time the young lovers reached consummation, he would remember to pull out as fast as he could.

Close to midnight, on a Saturday in August 1970, Sandra and Marcello were wrapped in each other's arms, in physical and romantic ecstasy. Marcello was nearing orgasm, desperately trying to keep a clear head so he would be able to react quickly when the moment came to, unfortunately, pull out once more.

Five drivers were on their way home. Four of them had enjoyed a great night with their buddies, getting drunk, flirting, and dancing their hearts out. The fifth driver was a factory worker, coming home late from a weekend shift. They all moved towards the intersection where Sandra had found her little haven. The drivers' paths were meant to cross for just an instant before seeing each other speed off towards their final destinations, leaving only the lingering roar and stinking exhaust of their engines in their wakes. All the drivers were racing along at well above the legal speed limit in an attempt to make it home before their dazed minds gave in to exhaustion and intoxication. They hurtled towards each other, each opening their windows wide to let in the cool night air, one of the drivers slapping himself hard to snap awake for yet another minute.

The factory worker had pulled a tough fifteen-hour shift. He lost the battle for consciousness at the precise moment when all five drivers converged in the intersection. His eyes closed and his hands let go of the steering wheel. Instead of speeding straight ahead, his battered Volkswagen Beetle changed course, crashing head-on into the oncoming vehicle. The remaining three drivers registered their predicament but the alcohol had reduced their reaction times to slower than the crawl of a slug. Two more cars crashed into the ruins of the first two vehicles. Metal bent and screeched. Lives unavoidably ended as the cars piled on top of each other and merged in ways they were never supposed to. Only one car escaped this mayhem. Catapulted into the air by the collision with the four other cars, it continued on a new trajectory.

Meanwhile, Sandra and Marcello were submerged in their own universe. The fifth, airborne car continued on its deadly, graceful path. At some level, the lovers' minds must have registered the sudden tumult beyond their flimsy bedroom walls. Still, Marcello and Sandra remained oblivious as they entered into the beautiful, almost suspended state of simultaneous orgasms.

Marcello felt a delightful wave of heat and energy rushing through his body just as the fifth car reached its final destination – Sandra's bedroom wall. It impacted in a cacophony of noise and falling debris. Instead of pulling away from her, he instinctively wrapped his arms around his girlfriend in the hope of shielding her from danger.

So. This was it. This was my moment. Marcello's sperm cells hurried to my mom's egg cell… and without even knowing it yet, an innocent teenage couple were on their way to becoming my parents.

Only a moment later, Marcello's penis softened inside of Sandra. My biological parents slowly gathered their courage and sat up in bed. They were dazed but unharmed. The apartment, however, was a field of destruction. Dust and debris were everywhere and sirens were blaring in the distance.

Six weeks later, they both knew without a doubt that the night of the accident had brought more than death and destruction. Sandra was eighteen and Marcello, nineteen. My biological father panicked, feeling far from ready to become a parent in a foreign country. He gave Sandra his address in Italy, and told her to contact him should she, for whatever reason, not want to raise their child. His family would take care of me. Having delivered his message, he turned and escaped home to Italy as quickly as possible.

Sandra hadn't heard half of what Marcello had tried to tell her about his family taking the child in. She was furious. The love of her life had betrayed her, running home to mamma, abandoning her and her unborn child. Without giving it any thought, she tore his address to shreds and flushed it down the toilet, destroying along with it any chance of getting in touch with Marcello or his family. Now, because of her impulsiveness, she would have to get through the pregnancy and deal with a newborn child on her own.

My birth parents were both just children themselves at the time. They were clueless, overwhelmed by what was happening to them. No one showed them kindness or helped them in making their decisions.

Following Marcello's panicked exit, a desperate Sandra went to her parents for help. They were disgusted with their daughter. In her parents' conservative eyes, the one thing worse than having sex before marriage was a woman bearing a fatherless child. They disowned her, showing neither kindness, nor forgiveness, nor understanding for her teenage digressions. Throughout the long months of Sandra's complicated pregnancy, her parents never inquired about her or her soon-to-be-born child. To them, we were both dead.

Sandra had only her work as a junior sales clerk with minimum salary. When she found herself unable to continue work due to complications with her pregnancy, with nowhere to go and no one to turn to, she was forced to approach social services. A shelter for pregnant prostitutes in Stuttgart offered my birth mom shelter. They welcomed her but made it clear that, like all the other women of ill repute harbored at the shelter, she would only be allowed to stay until she had given birth. Afterwards, she would be on her own once more. Sandra nevertheless braved the strong tide against her and was determined to bring me into this world.

Meanwhile, it seemed I was not quite so sure about entering the world, or maybe a bit too sure, depending on how you want to look at it. The great number of complications my biological mother experienced during her pregnancy culminated in an early birth – a full five weeks too early.

On the 9th of April 1971, when I struggled to come out and glimpse the light of day inside the prostitute shelter, I weighed a meager three pounds three ounces. I was immediately put in an incubator and fed with special formula to help me develop properly and give me a chance to survive. And, stubborn little me – I did.

As a developing fetus Sandra's amniotic fluid had given me shelter. I had now brusquely left this protective environment way too early, surely missing its warm embrace and easy weightlessness the moment I left it. Perhaps this explains why my entire life has revolved and developed around water. From the moment of birth until today, a terrestrial life centered on gravity has proven hard for me in many ways. Thankfully, many bodies of water accompanied me, countering gravity and grief with their transparent hues of blue, turquoise, brown, and even black. Water was where I found myself. Immersed in its warm embrace, I found my greatest passion and happiness. Water soothed me, carried me, inspired me and gave me strength.

After weeks of watching me grow in the incubator, my birth mom was delighted to finally be allowed to hold me in her arms. She felt a deep love towards me and did not regret her decision against an abortion. As soon as she and I were well enough, however, Sandra faced a cruel wall of bureaucracy.

The prostitute shelter asked her to leave. Sandra had never managed to accumulate any savings, and had no possessions of any kind. Her job and apartment had been lost. The authorities impressed upon her the urgency of her situation and the impossibility of raising me by herself. Her parents insisted on keeping their silence and stayed in the shadows. Legally, Sandra was still a minor, and as such, without her parents to support her, the authorities had the last word.

When I was one month old, I was taken away from my birth mom and transferred to a state orphanage. Sandra was given no choice. On the day the orphanage keepers whisked me away, she held me in her arms for the last time, and gave me my very first name: Corinna.

Sandra was not allowed to visit me because the officials were afraid we would become too attached to each other. They thought it best to severe all mother-child ties immediately so I would bond more easily with an adoptive family. In their eyes, a married couple with enough resources and good social standing to ensure security for my young life was far preferable to a young single mom who was barely able to take care of herself.

Soon enough, a wealthy couple visited the orphanage in search of a child. Konrad had told me it was love at first sight. At five months old, he and Hildegard took me home to foster me for a few months and see how we got along. Only the closest of relatives knew I wasn't theirs. The female fashion of the time favored very bulky garments. Their few friends and neighbors readily believed the story of my adoptive mom's "pregnancy". People congratulated my parents on their adorable offspring, ooohhh-ing and aaahhhh-ing as they went. They expressed their amazement at how much I looked like my adoptive dad. On my first birthday, the wealthy young couple legally adopted me. My first name was changed to Stefanie.

For many months after losing me, Sandra went through emotional torture of the worst kind. Nevertheless, she picked herself up, found work as a sales clerk in another clothing store and tried to move on with her life. During the first years, my biological mother held on to the irrational hope of being able to get me back if only she did well enough. She tried to locate me but, to protect the adoptive parents as well as the child, adoptions were strictly anonymous.

Over the years, our paths must have crossed many times. Sandra loved spending her weekends at the idyllic Lake Monrepos in Ludwigsburg. This same romantic playground of former kings also happened to be one of the favorite weekend getaways of my adoptive parents. I can imagine them passing each other every so often, perfect strangers, who never gave each other a second glance, unaware that the little orange-tinted toddler in the stroller connected them so intimately.

Sandra's luck never turned. She married another charming Italian man and had two daughters with him. I was delighted, hearing for the first time about my half-sisters. But my joy at learning of my growing family quickly turned to dismay when Sandra described how her husband had beaten and abused her. She had found solace in alcoholism and denial. When she wasn't drinking, she was busy lighting one cigarette after another, dulling her senses even further.

Then, one day, her older daughter, Gabi, approached her and said, "Mom, I don't want to kiss you anymore. You reek of alcohol even in the early morning. You need to sober up and help us. Daddy has raped me for years, but now he has started on Petra." Barely conscious in her alcoholic daze, Sandra lashed out at her daughter, backhanding her across the face. "You little slut! Stop lying to me like that!" Gabi stared back at her in shock. Then she nodded, turned around slowly, and went into her room to pack a small backpack. Half an hour later, she walked out the door, never to be seen again.

Sandra woke up to reality at the bang of the door. But it was too late. She had lost another child. With only her youngest daughter Petra left, Sandra finally found the strength she needed to overcome her paralyzing fears. Terrified, after twenty years of hell, she grabbed Petra and a suitcase. She moved out into the small apartment in which we now sat together, and filed for divorce.

She seemed to have escaped at last. Then one night, my birth mom heard a small noise. She woke to find her husband sitting at her bedside, pointing a gun to her head. He warned her to strongly reconsider leaving him and quietly disappeared into the night. Sandra persevered and divorced him despite her mounting fear. Exhausted, she reached the end of the line and suffered a breakdown. Child services came to collect my younger half-sister to place her in a foster family. And so, my biological mother lost her third child.

I looked at my birth mom while she poured yet more coffee into the fragile, beautifully crafted cups made of china. After five refills, my stomach cramped and struggled with a caffeine overdose. I was amazed, appalled, and at a loss of how to respond in the face of all this tragedy. Sandra told me she was nearing the end of her therapy and would soon be reunited with her youngest daughter. She clutched my hand as if letting go would make me disappear in a wisp of smoke. My birth mom and I hugged for a long time in the early evening light, and slowly parted ways with the promise to never lose sight of each other again.

After so many hours of talking, I felt as if we had just run a marathon together. I was out of breath and utterly exhausted. Life remained a mystery and seemed to become ever more complex with each passing year. Amidst all the cruelty and waves of emotion crashing over me, I sensed beauty, magic, strength, stubborn optimism, a powerful will to survive, as well as a strong wish to be a positive force no matter what obstacles life would throw at me. Giving up was not an option and never would be.

3

North Sea

My adoptive parents, Konrad and Hildegard, had tried for years to get pregnant. They had kept a menstrual calendar on their nightstand, right next to their luxurious king-sized bed. Every evening, they had brooded over numbers, trying to pinpoint the exact moment of ovulation and getting ready to make use of their small window of opportunity – all to no avail.

Becoming ever more desperate, Hildegard had pushed Konrad to undergo countless tests. When the doctors couldn't find any problem, it was Hildegard's turn to be prodded and probed. To her dismay, the specialists soon discovered that she was unable to ovulate.

This didn't bother Konrad. He was focused on his career and not quite sure if he wanted a child at this busy point in his life. But for a woman of Hildegard's generation, being unable to give birth to a child was equal to having failed to fulfill her divine purpose. Following the diagnosis, Hildegard was heartbroken as well as seething with self-hatred and loathing. As she spiraled ever deeper into a state of depression, Konrad's concerns for his wife's wellbeing took the upper hand.

He took charge and spent many long nights with Hildegard, talking about the virtues of adoption. Soon, he managed to spark his wife's enthusiasm. They visited the closest orphanage, found me, and swung into high gear – diving headfirst into the vast ocean of official adoption paperwork.

Konrad hoped my arrival in their otherwise comfortable home would give it warmth and make Hildegard realize she wasn't incomplete.

His mother Frida couldn't help but throw in the odd word of caution.

"Son, just think this through. Adoption won't be a magic potion for Hildegard. She has some serious psychological issues and those won't simply be solved with the appearance of a little girl."

Konrad didn't want to hear his mother's reasoning. More than anything, he wanted to believe in his wife and in the possibility of a bright future together.

Frida was born in 1909 and had seen her fair share of suffering. She had survived the demanding life of being the eldest daughter on a small farm and then managed to raise two children while surviving two world wars. She was wise in the ways of the world and had always been gravely worried about her son's union with his chosen wife. Her daughter-in-law was untrained in the art of housekeeping. Even more disturbing, Hildegard's neuroses and paranoia made it difficult for her to take sufficient care of others. Frida feared the worst.

But all her reservations prior to my arrival evaporated the moment she laid eyes on me. Her strong but tender hands felt the vibrations of my heartbeat and any misgivings about her daughter-in-law became irrelevant. As Frida fell in love with me and became my grandma, she knew she would never let any harm come to me and would even raise me herself, if necessary. After only one week, she couldn't remember ever having lived without her smiling, clumsy grandchild.

Frida carried herself with dignity. She was delicate, and small, but very strong. When she made *spaetzle*, a Southern German pasta delicacy, the recipe called for her to beat the dough continuously for half an hour. She did so without a problem while I barely managed five minutes before it felt as if my arm was falling off. Her skin felt like soft, warm leather with thousands of fine wrinkles. When she smiled, her entire face seemed to shine with her strong but tender soul.

My dear oma (as we lovingly call our grandmas in Germany) was modest. All of her clothes were handmade. Her kitchen was cozy and stocked with very few items for herself. The shelf dedicated for me overflowed with cookies and other delicacies she knew I loved. Oma was calm and had a German proverb for every occasion. The one I still remind myself of, whenever life seems to spiral out of control, is: "The stew is never eaten as hot as it is cooked." Sometimes Oma got upset. On those occasions she would clap her hands together above her head and exclaim,

"Ay-ay-ay-ay-ay-ay-ay-ay!" The effect would be so comical, I wouldn't know what to do – laugh at her or fold my arms around her in an attempt to comfort her. When Frida listened to me, the world stood still and gave me a chance to catch my breath. When she took me in her arms, I felt safe and loved unconditionally.

Frida was my guiding star. She was strict, yet generous. She was serious, yet had a beautiful sense of humor. Most importantly, she was loyal and had the biggest heart of anyone I have ever known. She became my knight, or rather, dame in shining armor and made it her purpose in life to make time for me whenever Konrad and Hildegard did not. She quietly saved my soul, by being an indestructible protectress who was always there no matter what happened to me, no matter what I did, no matter how devastated she felt herself. My oma became the only rock in the raging tide, keeping me sane throughout my childhood and teenage years.

For my adoptive mom Hildegard, life was like navigating through a muddy minefield in dense, gloomy fog. Even as a teenager, she had harbored multiple neuroses, unable to control her fear of germs and other questionable organisms such as people. Since adolescence she washed her hands multiple times per hour, opened cupboards and doors with her legs, and suspected malicious intent behind every sentence and gesture intended for her or her loved ones.

For a while, my arrival *did* soothe Hildegard's soul. She was delighted to finally be a mother. Despite her fragile psychological state, she loved me as if I were her own daughter and tried as best as she could to take care of all my needs.

Choosing a new first name for her little girl was the first step in an elaborate fiction. Soon she couldn't even remember being infertile.

When I curiously asked the question, "Mommy, where do I come from?" she not only omitted the fact of my adoption, but also told me the elaborate story of how I had popped out of her tummy at exactly 3:55 p.m. one sunny Sunday afternoon after an easy labor. She embellished the tale with golden rays of sunshine lighting up the small hospital room as I emerged. Konrad listened helplessly, at odds with the lie, yet willing to pay the price for anything that would make Hildegard more happy and stable.

As a baby, I was cuddled and spoiled. My oma made delicious carrot puree to keep me orange-tinted and healthy. During the world wars and their aftermath, she had experienced near starvation and extreme hardship twice. Oma vividly recalled huddling in humid, concrete bomb shelters, all the while getting weak from lack of nutrition. People had yawned a lot during those awful times. And so, no matter how sleepy I was, my concerned oma would always assume I was hungry. This led to multiple meals a day and many sweets in between. She was convinced that I needed at least four liters of milk a day to give me strong, healthy bones. Luckily, being an active child as well as a very picky eater prevented me from becoming too chubby.

My mom delighted in bathing me. In the evenings, she sang old German lullabies. Whenever she would sing *Hoch auf dem Gelben Wagen* with her strong but raspy voice, I would listen happily and drift away towards the rustling whispers of golden fields stretching all the way to the horizon.

Daytimes soon proved to be far less romantic. Hildegard's deeply ingrained paranoia led her to be over-protective. She was terrified of letting me go on any extensive crawling excursions, afraid I would fall off the edge of the Earth and disappear. On the other hand, when she needed time for herself, she would let me out on the landing connecting our and my oma's penthouse apartment. I would stand in front of my oma's door calling, "Oooommmmmmaaaaa" until she let me in. Years later, Hildegard would do the same with our Cocker Spaniel. Cora would sit in front of Frida's door, barking "Woooooooooooof!" until my oma would take pity on her and open the door.

Hildegard had never received professional help for her psychological afflictions. But by herself she was unable to control her anxiety attacks, which often led to fits of anger, leaving her sensitive husband Konrad utterly clueless. When he came home from work at night, she would launch into verbal attacks as soon as he would step through the front door, narrating her entire day and how the whole world, in this instance my grandma and me, had conspired to make her feel miserable.

No matter how abstract her claims, Konrad did his best to guide his wife through the gloominess of her existence. He often ended up defending her. What he did not grasp was the extent of Hildegard's delusion. In order to survive the scary minefield that was her daily life, she needed to transform reality and package events into endurable quasi-truths. Many tales Hildegard told him about me, Frida, and the rest of the world, had only happened in Hildegard's imagination.

My mom wasn't in control of her emotions. Our interactions became just as unpredictable to me as her mind, which was an impenetrable mist ranging from various shades of cloudy grey to frightening, hot crimson. Perfect harmony could shift to self-righteous rage in a heartbeat.

We would sit peacefully in the living room, watching cartoons together when suddenly she would start screaming, "You selfish little bitch, get out. Figure skating is on. Do you think I want to watch your crap all day long?"

Each time an outburst like this – or worse – happened, I felt as if I had just been thrown into the darkest dungeon. With tears in my eyes, I would either scream right back at her or slink away into the arms of my loving oma.

Despite the psychological catastrophe simmering beneath the surface of our safe, upper-middle class family life, my early years were filled with very positive memories. We had an enormous couch in the living room. Thirteen feet long, it was a padded playground. I remember rolling around on it with my dad in the evenings, enjoying being tickled until I was completely breathless. His laughter and kind smile made me forget the many unsettling moments I had had to endure with Hildegard during the day.

One of my favorite times during early childhood was the month of December. My dad had an elaborate miniature toy train landscape stored in our basement. He had built this little gem when he was a teenager. Early each December, he would cheerfully announce, "It's time again: let's build our own world!" and we would bring the disassembled toy train universe up into my room. The landscape was fitted out with huge mountains, green meadows, multiple railway lines and tunnels, lush pine tree forests and miniature villages. Once we had finished setting up in my room, there would barely be enough space for my bed. Dad and I would play with the toy trains during every spare moment that month. I treasured sitting next to him, helping him to conduct our railway symphony.

There was nothing better than spending time traveling through our phantasy world together. Dad would take me far away to distant lands, into a realm of eternal sunshine and possibility. After the holidays, we would return the toy train world to the darkness of our basement. Immediately, my life would seem lonely and bleak. Returning to my room would feel like entering a void. I would sense the weight of the real world creeping back onto my shoulders and, sitting down heavily, I would be unable to stem the flow of hot tears streaming down my cheeks.

We had a Steinway concert piano in our living room. My mom and dad both tried playing it but rarely got much farther than *Alle Meine Entchen*, an old German children's song like Chopsticks. I loved the piano, because it provided me with a cavernous space underneath it. When things got too crazy during the day with Hildegard, I would either hide in my room, or retreat to my Steinway hideaway with some toys.

By far my favorite sanctuary was in Frida's living room, though. From as early on as I can remember, I would spend hours on her carpeted floor, playing with Legos, constructing ships, space ships and other modes of escape. Alternately, I would crawl around on my oma's thick carpet and pick up all the needles she dropped while sewing clothes for her friends in town. She worked at home on a beautiful old Singer sewing machine that clattered reassuringly and made me feel safe.

Oma's mixed diet of carrot puree, cookies, and milk seemed to be working. I appeared healthy and strong. When I was three years old, however, a neighbor watched me tackling the stairs to our flat. Using my arms, I half crawled half climbed the short set of stairs, from the elevator door to our landing, at an agonizingly slow pace.

"I hope you don't mind my asking but, how old is Stefanie now?" our neighbor asked my mom.

I stopped mountaineering for a moment and proudly held up three fingers.

"Hmm," he said, "Shouldn't kids usually be able to walk up and down stairs on their own by the time they reach two years of age?"

Hildegard looked stunned.

"Why don't you mind your own business?"

Nevertheless, during the following days, she pondered the meaning of his observation. Was I not moving around enough for a child my age? Had her overprotectiveness slowed down my physical progress? Or was I simply a very slow developer? Hildegard had to concede that, at three years of age, I still couldn't do much more than totter along in a straight line. She eventually decided to consult a physician. The doctor diagnosed me with severe spasticity in both legs. He urged my mom to put me into physical therapy to ensure I would later be able to move like a regular adult.

Thus Mrs. Olsen entered my life. She was a very tall and voluminous lady from Hamburg. To my little three-year-old self, she looked like a giant. I didn't really have a clue what was happening. All I knew was that Mrs. Olsen was very friendly, always brought me sweets, and proceeded to move my legs in every direction for hours at a time. I had therapy sessions twice a week until I was six years old before I became almost as agile as other kids. I was still a bit stiff and would never become a yogi, but at least I could finally use my legs and they were flexible enough for me to run, jump and play with my friends.

After years of being confined to the ground, I loved climbing and took every opportunity to clamber up the branches of trees. A certain clumsiness lingered, however, and more often than not, I would fall. Hildegard was afraid to let me climb anything higher than a chair. My smallest ailment – a cough, a fever, or a scrape – would trigger my mom's stories about her asthma, her low blood pressure and her goiter. Her fragile state led her to the conclusion that I shared the same fate.

"It's only a matter of time. In fifteen years from now, your goiter will begin growing and you will find yourself struggling with chronic bronchitis. Later on it will turn to asthma. It is unavoidable." She would shrug at my terrified expression, saying, "It's hereditary."

From the very beginning, I was determined to prove Hildegard wrong. Whatever she did, I did the opposite. She would wash her hands every fifteen minutes. Just to spite her, I would wait days before even going near a bar of soap. My parents were afraid of thunder. They would close all the blinds as soon as a storm rumbled closer. So I would marvel at the dark clouds piling up on the horizon and sneak outside as soon as the first raindrops hit my window. I would run through the pelting rain, arms spread wide, inviting the lightning to come closer and strike me. Sometimes lightning would hit so close to me that, just for an instant it would look like a glowing, purple-silver column. In the face of nature's raw power, I would scream with joy rather than fear.

During my early years, we would go to the North Sea every summer for a long family holiday. I was enchanted from the first moment I laid eyes on the dark blue endlessness. My senses were alert and I felt intensely alive.

Nowhere else had I felt so invigorated. Every cell of my small body tried to absorb as much of the beauty around me as it possibly could. I breathed deeply, tasting and smelling the salty air. It seemed to be dense and alive with the power of the ocean.

The sand dunes rolled softly under my feet, making me feel rested and at home. Rabbits bounded around the tall dunes, sea gulls screamed and fiercely defended their territories. Sometimes, when we stumbled unawares into a nesting ground, we had to fend off the enraged birds by wildly swinging our umbrellas. Hildegard would be terrified, Konrad, amused, and I, delighted at the sight of these huge birds as well as the exhilarating sense of adventure. At low tide, we hiked far out into the mud flats, my young soul inquisitive about every tiny worm and crab we encountered. The mud flats felt like frozen velvet, for the North Sea water temperatures were cold even during the warmest months of the year.

Discovering the ocean changed my young life. I threw myself into the cold churning waves, balloon-like arm floats encircling my tiny arms. Goose bumps quickly covered my entire body as I savored the taste and the sensation of a living entity enveloping my body. My soul felt rested and at home while at the same time sensing danger and fragility. Whatever might happen to me in the years to come, I would always draw solace and strength from the ocean. I had discovered the love of my life. From then on, I would be drawn to any body of water no matter its size. I would soon marvel at flowing rivers and the peacefully lapping waters of our German lakes.

On our very first North Sea summer trip, when I was four years old, I began to do something very peculiar. As soon as we arrived on the small North Sea island of Sylt, I introduced myself to all the other children as Stefan.

I had a grand time roaming through the sand dunes with the boys. On the first evening of our stay, Konrad and Hildegard couldn't find me anywhere.

"Has anyone seen our daughter Stefanie? She's small. Olive skinned. Short hair. She looks like a boy."

No one had seen a girl by that description. It took my parents a few hours of frantic searching to realize that Stefan and I were the same person. Relieved to have found me, they never made a big deal out of it. They simply shrugged in helpless wonder.

Each summer, I couldn't wait to get back to the ocean. The sand dunes seemed to traverse the island like mountainous, slow-gliding golems. More than anything, I longed to reclaim my freedom. As little Stefan, tiny but sinewy and bronzed, I would sit in the sandbox for hours, baking sand cakes and building castles. Soon I would find friends and we would have sack races along the beach or explore the shores of the dark blue North Sea as pirates. The beaches gleamed as golden as if the many grains of sand under our feet consisted instead of millions of sparkling stars. We felt sure our secret treasure chest couldn't be hidden far away. For a few summer vacations, I remained the adventurous pirate Stefan, feeling free as a bird and more myself than ever before.

My adoptive parents must have had many worried chats. As for me, I simply did what felt right. The longer my switch from Stefanie to Stefan continued, the more mystified Konrad and Hildegard grew. They comforted each other.

"Well, children can have weird fantasies sometimes. She sure acts strangely, but it's just a phase. She will outgrow it."

I did not outgrow it. Hildegard kept looking forward to dressing her rugged princess in pretty pink skirts and blouses, braiding her hair, watching her play with dolls, taking ballet classes and piano lessons. I remained an altogether different creature. I liked my hair very short. Pink garments, cute dolls and other girly things mortally offended my sense of self. Hildegard and I became infamous at the local children's clothing store. She would drag me to her favorite shop on a regular basis, trying to force another pink monstrosity on me.

Before long, she would exclaim, "Oh Stefanie, you look so cute and lovely in this dress. I just love it!"

At five years old, I began fighting back.

"Nooo, I don't want the dress!" I would scream. "This isn't me! If you like it so much, then why don't you go buy it for yourself?"

Hildegard was heartbroken.

We both couldn't help it. She wasn't really a mom to a little girl at all, but how could she have known that? I would never be able to become her princess. I was following my instincts but was too young to explain this to my disappointed mom. Anything adventurous with a chance of getting covered in mud exhilarated me. I would carefully practice with a self-made bow and arrows, getting ready for a possible attack of zombies, cannibals, or clones. The large ocean-going vessels and spaceships I constructed from my imagination with Lego became ever more elaborate. I played with cars, Play Mobil cowboys and Indians, as well as children's science sets.

Trying to put me on the right path, my mom went in search of adorable dolls. I had the disconcerting habit of taking them into the bathtub with me. There, I would systematically dismember them and little plastic body parts would end up floating in the softly perfumed bathwater. After three studiously selected plastic babies, my parents stopped buying me dolls.

In another attempt to awaken my inner princess, my mother signed me up for flute lessons in primary school. I hated that blameless instrument from the very first moment. Flute lessons were held during first period. I would leave the house at 7 each school morning. For an entire year, instead of going to first period, I hid somewhere on the school grounds, drew pictures, and read comic books.

At the annual parent-teacher interviews, my mom asked Mrs. Rainer, my teacher: "So, how are Stefanie's musical skills coming along?"

The uncomprehending teacher responded, "What do you mean?"

Hildegard quickly got annoyed. "Her flute lessons, of course."

"Oh," the teacher said, "We have never seen Stefanie in that class."

Needless to say, my mom came home from the conference in quite a state. Thankfully, after lots of simultaneous screaming at one another, she didn't insist on me giving flutes another try the following year.

I loved nature and books. Not having an ocean around the corner, I substituted by spending endless hours out alone or with friends, building tree houses and caves in the thick undergrowth or rafts on the river. We treasured the rich smells of the forest, the taste of earth in our mouths, the cold refreshing water of our little river on our skin, and the soothing green light in our eyes. Our imaginations let us be whoever we wanted to be, heroes and villains, stars and underdogs. I loved to play the underdog who got captured, tortured and falsely accused, and then managed against all odds to survive and come out the biggest hero of them all.

My greatest source of inspiration was the German novelist, Karl May. His stories stimulated my sense of wonder and adventure. I would spend whole nights with a flashlight under the covers, letting Mr. May take me on journeys as *Old Shatterhand* or *Kara Ben Nemsi*. I would venture into the wild mountains of North America or into the Arabian deserts. After finishing each of his seventy-four books in fewer than three days, I would start all over again at book one.

After a few years, Hildegard became less insistent about providing a pink childhood. Oma helped me to be more myself. Creative spirit that she was, she made colorful boy's clothing with lots of patterns and stripes for me – very Seventies.

Several attempts of having me grow my hair longer ended with me taking things into my own hands – literally. Using my dull school scissors, I would try to give myself a haircut and end up looking like a newly-turned zombie in the process of losing his formerly healthy, human hair. Off we would go, to a proper barbershop and cut my hair even shorter, in an attempt to make me look at least halfway presentable.

Upon entering school-age, my life became more solitary. The girls were suspicious and gave me the cold shoulder because I wasn't a girl in any usual sense. The boys didn't know what to do with me because obviously my name was Stefanie and I was biologically a girl, yet at the same time, I was more a buddy than a sweet little creature to flirt with.

My tastes did not fit with most of my contemporaries either. Classical music floated gently through our penthouse as soon as my dad got home. I knew all the famous operas from an early age. Our living room had a ceiling-high bookshelf stacked with everything from classical to modern literature. I had no connection to popular culture. If we listened to the radio, it would only be to classical stations.

In my early school years, I was the alien of the schoolyard. No one wanted to be seen with me. I dressed strangely – colorful, checkered and striped – and never paid attention to any of the latest fashions. I talked precociously, didn't know anything about the Pop bands of the hour, and got kicked out of the girls' lavatory at least once a day because people mistook me for a boy. On top of it all, I struggled with my spasticity and couldn't hold my own out on the sports field. I spent the majority of my time in my room or hidden from view in a quiet corner, reading books and listening to Konrad's classical records.

As hard as it was to always be the odd one out, I also felt special and enjoyed being different from my contemporaries. I was content with the cultural tastes of my dad until I turned sixteen years old. Once I had my first summer job and earned my own money, I ventured out and bought my very first stereo system. That's when I started discovering much more of the musical world.

Throughout my school career the school librarians were my trusted friends. They delighted at my ability to easily devour three books a week.

Enchanted by my literary interest, the librarians asked me early on, "Do you want to be a test reader? We need someone who will read our new acquisitions and let us know if the other children would enjoy them, too."

I wasn't sure if I was the best judge of what other children might like, but I jumped at the special attention and felt safe in the presence of the few people who seemed to like me just the way I was.

Being a serious and thoughtful child, it was infinitely easier for me to connect with adults than with other children. I was a regular in the town library as well, spending hours in library corners with a stack of books by my side. Apart from reading, I reveled in painting and drawing animals.

I had created my very first more sophisticated watercolor painting at the age of four. Amazingly, even though irrelevant at the time, it depicts a scuba diver, surrounded by an indigo-colored ocean and dozens of colorful reef fish.

Whenever I felt lost, I turned to nature, be it heading outdoors or into beautiful picture books of our planet. I loved plants. My little ninety-square-foot room at home looked like a jungle by the time I was ten. I had grown my plants from offshoots my oma and her friends had given me. Over the years, the plants had grown to ceiling height. Visitors could barely walk through my door with all the foliage blocking their way.

I had a few buddies with whom I roamed the neighborhood and forests, yet none of those children grew to be good friends. Mostly, I learned to be comfortable on my own. My mind seemed to work differently from those of other children.

I vividly recall one afternoon in our courtyard. At that time, I was hanging out with three boys from our neighborhood. They all dared each other to do something extraordinary. One boy burned himself with a cigarette; the second performed a perfectly executed handstand; the third threw a rock at an apple and managed to dislodge it from the tree.

When they looked expectantly at me, I said, "I can make something out of anything."

The boys stared uncomprehendingly then started laughing. One of them squatted down and picked up a piece of trash. It was a frayed, sticky piece of gum wrapper, only about two inches long and half an inch wide. He threw it at me.

"Oh yeah? Well, here you go smartass. Create something."

I took the challenge very seriously and sat down, pondering the old, still faintly gleaming paper. I could smell an exotic mix of spearmint, old gravel, and motor oil.

In sudden inspiration, I did the simplest thing I could think of: I rolled the gum wrapper up into a tight roll then put it in the palm of my hand. It unrolled slightly, ending up being a tiny silvery-white coil.

"What's that supposed to be?" the biggest kid asked.

I gave the small object serious consideration.

"Hmmm, it could easily be a clock spring from a rare old timepiece."

The other kids laughed at me. Shouting "See Ya, moron," they ran off down the street, leaving me behind. I looked after them, feeling lonely, but somehow proud of transforming the often stepped-on, old gum wrapper into something special and beautiful.

I had only one best friend my age. His name was Markus. He lived in the same high-rise building as our family, with his parents and older sister. He and I shared a passion for adventure stories and nature. In our minds we traveled to places around our planet most human beings would be too terrified to explore. We courageously risked our lives for the sake of science and the conservation of species. During my short hours with Markus, I would feel free as a bird. I would feel like myself once again.

4

Froschteich

Living with Hildegard was getting harder with each passing year. The minefield of her emotions seemed to be getting larger. Unfortunately, with the mines frequently changing locations, it was impossible to avoid them. When my dad and grandma weren't home, I preferred staying away or behind the firmly closed door of my jungle-like room.

I was such a lonesome child. All I wanted was to be able to trust my mom and rely on her. I trusted my dad and always longed for his return home in the evenings. The only stable element about Hildegard was her instability. One moment, she would call me her darling and the next moment, her eyes would become as cold as shards of ice and she would call me anything from *Frecher Igel*, which literally translates into "naughty hedgehog" to "piece of dirt" or "bitch".

Children play. They run, they are clumsy, and if they are battling the after-effects of spasticity as I was, they trip over themselves or anything else that gets in their way. Due to my stiff legs, I stumbled far more often than other children. Sometimes, I would even trip over my mom's feet. Outraged, she would take it as an attack and hold a grudge for weeks, glaring at me hatefully.

Hildegard's grudges inevitably led to retaliation. She would lock me in my room for hours – which wasn't so bad, since there I would shut out reality and escape into my books.

My worst childhood moment with Hildegard occurred after I had once more accidentally tripped over her toes while playing in our apartment. My mom took me to my room and, with a maliciousness that

I find hard to comprehend to this day, stared me down for hours, forcing me to collect all my favorite toys, put them in garbage bags, then throw them down the garbage chute of our apartment highrise with my own hands. Even years later, I could still painfully remember favorite teddy bears and other small toys that had given me comfort throughout my often perilous childhood journey being violently ripped out of my life by our fateful standoff.

Though I wasn't one to hold grudges myself, I couldn't bring myself to forgive my mom for a very long time. Part of our connection and our trust went down the chute along with those bagfuls of toys.

I learned to tread carefully. I persevered and solved problems with sensitivity, creativity and determination. Still, no matter how careful I was, no matter how hard I tried to anticipate potential disasters, frequent clashes with my mom were inevitable. In fact, only once did I manage to escape her anger.

Konrad was fond of enormous, decorative vases. My parents would caution me, since often the huge pieces of pottery wobbled precariously as I ran past them. One evening, when my parents went to the opera, I was playing ball inside our spacious penthouse apartment.

As I bounded through the rooms, enjoying my momentary freedom, the inevitable happened: my soccer ball collided with the biggest, most expensive vase in our living room. For a moment, it seemed to simply wobble and settle back to rest in the same space. And then, in what seemed like slow motion, it fell. It hit the stone fireplace and shattered into hundreds of pieces.

I had battled with my mom over abstract trifles throughout the week. If trifles had aggravated her so much already, how would she react to her favorite vase being broken? I sprang into action and raided our house for solutions. Some minutes later, I returned to our living room armed with several packages of superglue. I checked the kitchen clock and calculated I had roughly four hours before I would have to face my parents' wrath.

The vase had been one foot six inches in diameter and approximately three feet tall. I tackled the pile of shards in front of me like a life-or-death puzzle game. As the hours passed, I felt greater urgency and redoubled my efforts. Towards midnight, I was exhausted and exhilarated as I contemplated the result of four hours of intense concentration and dedication standing in front of me. I could see what looked like hairline cracks all over the finely-sculpted work of pottery. Yet to the unsuspecting eye, my dad's most prized pottery possession would look as proud as ever.

Only minutes after cleaning up all the evidence, Konrad and Hildegard returned from their cultural outing, glowing with happiness. As they gently opened my door to check on me, I stayed as still as possible, breathing deeply and hoping they would believe my act of being sound asleep. After a few minutes, my parents retreated quietly and soon went to bed themselves.

It took them years to discover my crime. Every time one of them would buy big flowers, I feared they might fill the superglued vase with water. Luckily, for many years, they decided on other vases instead – until one Easter, five years after the soccer ball incident. Konrad came home with fresh, large willow branches for our living room. He compared branch sizes to vases and decided my superglued beauty would fit best. As he poured a big bucket of water into it, all seemed well. Then, little jets of water erupted on all sides of the vase. My dad looked on in amazement, then jumped into action and tried to remove the expensive vase-turned-fountain from our equally expensive wooden floor. As he moved the vase, it broke apart again, and water flooded our living room floor.

While we cleaned up, my dad noticed traces of superglue on some pottery shards. Turning instantly as bright red as a fire hydrant, I confessed, adding my little story of how I had spent an entire night piecing it back together. Rather than being angry, Konrad was amused and oddly proud of his daughter's achievement.

When Hildegard asked what had happened, he just shrugged his shoulders and said, "The vase must have been badly made. The glaze seems to have gone brittle over the years."

I was as relieved as a gladiator who at the end of the fight unexpectedly receives a thumbs-up from Caesar.

Unfortunately, my mom's instability and paranoia extended further and further, leaving me ever more powerless and vulnerable.

Children can be cruel. Their worldview is often a very simple black and white, an uncompromising right or wrong, in or out. I was already branded an outcast because I did not fit common parameters. Over the years, Hildegard added a whole new dimension to my loneliness.

After a long school day, the day's events resonated within me and I longed to share my experiences with an understanding soul. Every so often, I would run home from school, brimming with excitement, and tell my mom about the pictures I had drawn with my friends, or the new game of marbles I had been taught by some of the boys.

Maybe I was more excited than most children would be: it wasn't common for other kids to socialize with me. Whenever I had a positive experience at school with one or several of my classmates, I would be over the moon. I would come home talking so fast that even the best supercomputer would not have been able to keep up. I didn't have any brothers and sisters. Konrad was at work. So I told Hildegard all about my day. Oma was, of course, always a safe option, but I also wanted to talk to Hildegard because, no matter how we clashed at times, she was my mom and sometimes all I wanted to be was a trusting child.

The stories I told Hildegard were not the stories she heard. When I laughed about painting together with a friend, she would hear how this child had abused me and stolen my pens. When I burst with excitement about a new marble game I had been taught, Hildegard would conclude that the boys had used me and nicked my marbles. She would work up a dangerous level of self-righteous indignation. Then, she would pick up the phone, call the parents of the children I played with, and go into a rant about how their children had ripped me off and abused me. These parents then naturally went off on their children, punishing them and setting them straight.

The very next day, the school grapevine would buzz with rumors of my snitching and lies. It would take just one day for all kids to shun me. Multiple events added up to years with no one speaking to me at school, no one wanting to be associated with me. Former friends would look at me with contempt, some even spitting at me as I walked past. I didn't know how to make things right. My quiet protests were pushed away by my classmates. No one was interested in my side of the story. I had done nothing wrong except to trust my mom, yet I felt deeply ashamed nonetheless.

Each time my innocent ramblings led to disaster, I would battle through daily fear and despair. I would promise myself to never trust Hildegard again, to never tell her anything personal ever again. But I was only a small child longing for love and a harmonious home. Holding grudges was not in my nature. I forgot and forgave easily.

A few months after each event, my outcast status at school would be mildly revoked. Very slowly, my classmates would forget their anger and start to treat me once more as a fellow human being. Slowly, I would be included in every day social encounters in the classroom and schoolyard, which would flood me with relief. I would cautiously become more outgoing again and start talking to my peers. At first, I would remember not to talk too much with Hildegard at home, but over time I would inevitably let my guard down too much.

I couldn't win. The only cure was to tell my mom nothing about my day, share nothing about my experiences, no matter how sweetly she asked. The most innocent tale would set Hildegard off, sending her on another phone rant to right a wrong that had only been committed in her imagination.

I stopped bringing friends home as well, because Hildegard would invariably find only negative attributes in them. A few days after meeting my friends, Hildegard would break into rants first to me, then despite all my begging, arguing and screaming, to my friends' parents about how awful their children were and what atrocities they had committed.

The next day, I would be back to being everyone's favorite target for spitting practice. With each event, my peers would trust me even less, prolonging my solitary confinement. It wasn't only the other children that were disgusted with me. I was disgusted with myself for having lost control, for having trusted my mom yet again, for having stupidly brought this desperate situation upon myself again.

This vicious circle of broken trust continued throughout my early school years. Fortunately – or unfortunately – I did eventually learn my lesson as all innocence concerning my mother was finally beaten out of me. I began to carefully censor every word I spoke at home. I would warily quadruple-check every sentence in my mind before I verbally engaged with my unpredictable mom.

Through four years of primary school, my oma saved me time and again. She knew what was happening and that it was breaking my heart. Each and every school break, without fail, Oma would show up in a secluded alcove close to the main schoolyard. There we would sit together, sheltered under the trees, with birds singing all around us.

Oma would bring me milk and cookies but, much more importantly, she would bring me her kind and open heart. She was there for me and was the only person who understood that I was the victim of psychological imbalances far beyond my mother's and my control. I was a little Don Quixote, tilting at the psychological windmills of Hildegard's mind.

Every school day, I tried to brave the fallout as best I could and gritted my young teeth. I looked forward to, and for the most part told myself that I was content with, Oma's company. She never wavered, never interfered with the other children. She just gave me the quiet assurance that there was nothing wrong with me and I was worthy of being loved.

Hildegard's windmills created destructive hurricanes in my young mind, threatening to blow me far away to a place so isolated, I wouldn't even be able to find myself anymore. Everything beyond my grandma seemed to be a dark and never-ending abyss of isolation, illuminated only for brief instances by my friend Markus before I was plunged back into darkness. Had I not been born with a very strong fighter's soul and a positive, romantic heart, who knows where I would have ended up?

One of the windows of my room faced the walkway leading to our and my oma's main door. In her concern for my emotional state, Oma sometimes stood in front of my window, staring in. Every so often, I would look up from what I was doing in the privacy of my room and be startled at seeing her gently wrinkled face staring back at me. For years, her innocent efforts translated into nightmares of an evil witch, lurking behind my window and stalking me relentlessly.

Our penthouse gave me nightmares as well. It was an elegant Seventies dwelling perched atop a soulless highrise with large picture glass windows overlooking the urban desert of our neighborhood. On top of our concrete tower, my soul must have felt exposed rather than safe because for many years, I suffered through nightmares of being trapped inside our fragile glass house while terrorists or aliens surrounded our home. Our neighborhood would burst into flames as alien ships bombed buildings one by one, coming ever closer, threatening to end our lives as well. I escaped each time, braving the elevator that in my dreams plummeted towards the ground, out of control, breaking its speedy descent just in time for me to jump out into the burning streets, unharmed.

The nightmare-inducing forest of highrise buildings we lived in offered one advantage: the expansive lawns and parks, and a maze of concrete enclosures were a safe playground for children. As much as I tried to be one of the neighborhood gang, however, I still failed to connect with any of them.

One day, I tried to gain their respect by stealing a candy bar from our neighborhood store. My parents received a phone call from the storeowners faster than I could blink. It turned out the gang had reported me as soon as I left the store.

After the candy bar incident, I made one more attempt at becoming a thief. When my dad wasn't looking, I stole five Deutschmarks from his wallet. To legalize the stolen money, I waited until our next family hike, hung back playing with foliage, and then dropped the shiny coin onto the forest ground.

"Oh!" I exclaimed, answering my parents' questioning looks by pointing excitedly to my shiny find amidst crumbling leaves.

Instead of being excited at my finder's luck, my dad said, "You took that out of my wallet. I have known for days and just wanted to see what would happen. Stefanie, you are most likely the worst liar I have ever seen – and that's not a bad thing."

I grudgingly conceded to not having any criminal talent and discontinued my budding career as a thief.

Konrad and Hildegard didn't have many friends and shared my fate of being a social outcast. Their fate seemed self-inflicted even more so than mine however, since they did not socialize with people they met or even with their own relatives.

Hildegard alienated everyone she came more personally in touch with. She was convinced the whole world was conspiring to attack her and take advantage of her. She was sure of being right. In her mind, she was the only one perceptive enough to see through people's disguises and lies. No one around her had enough courage to mention therapy or medication. People simply retreated and never came back.

Thus my world was small. It continued to deteriorate over the years as Hildegard drove Konrad into an ever-growing state of despair. When I reached eight years of age, my dad reached his breaking point. Even being at work all week long, he couldn't escape the daily dramas unfolding more and more frequently in our home. Konrad wasn't equipped to deal with conflict. He increasingly reacted with hysterical shouting as well as self-destructive behavior. He ceased being my calm oasis, leaving me to brave the storms raging in my mom's mind on my own.

Day in, day out, I wondered what was wrong with me? What did I do to upset her so, to bring her to the brink of insanity? It took me decades to understand there was nothing wrong with me at all. I was not a trigger, not a monster, not a bitch, not characterized by any of the words Hildegard had called me over the years. Her state of mind was not her fault. But it had never been *my* fault, either.

It seems like such a cliché, but adversity did make me stronger. A new classmate arrived during my last year of primary school. His name was Mehtap. His family had immigrated to Germany from Turkey. Soon, all the children at school arrived each day fueled with racist sentiments they had picked up from their parents at home. They bullied Mehtap without understanding the phrases that came out of their mouths.

"Go home to your sheep, you stinking Turk." they would say. "You people can't be trusted. Surely, you are hiding a knife somewhere?" or, "Hey monkey, come here and clean my shoes."

I had endured daily attacks and seen wisdom in evading conflict for so many years, but now something snapped inside of me. I couldn't bear watching what happened to Mehtap. I took a stand and began stepping in front of him at every opportunity, defending his dignity and humanity.

We became best friends during this last primary school year. I learned about Turkish culture as I accepted Mehtap's invitations to his home and got to know his family's customs. In essence, there was no difference between us. In our humanity, we were brothers with much the same battles to fight. The relief of finally having a kindred spirit at school, accepting me as I was, lifted my spirits. Each day, Mehtap and I stood up for each other while the other children spat at us, literally as well as figuratively.

In the afternoons we would head out into the fields on the edge of town, to a small pond the locals simply called "Froschteich". No one else ever came there. Mehtap and I would relax amongst the tall reed grass and inhale the scent of algae and brackish water. The sunlight seemed warmer out here and the world much better.

Mehtap and I would jump into the muddy water on hot summer days, happily floating on our backs and gazing up at the sky. At other times we would splash each other until we were bent over with laughter and forgot all our troubles. We were too young to think of romance and simply enjoyed being able to relax in the presence of a person we trusted with all our heart. After all, who knew what challenges tomorrow might bring?

A good friend of mine once told me how, every time life threw her yet another curve ball, her dad used to say, "Cheer up sweetheart. It's just a character building experience." When my friend was twelve years old, and her dad responded to a new set of problems with still the same sentiment, she lost it and screamed at the top of her voice, "I think I have enough character now!"

Similarly, I figured I had gotten my fair share of adversity to deal with during my early years. But life was only getting started.

When I was eleven years old, I began to have very strange fainting spells. If I found myself in a closed room, combined with exhaustion or physical shock of any kind, I would start to feel a very unique, heavy, floating sensation as my world blurred and black patches appeared in my vision. Seconds afterward, I would plummet into an abyss, becoming completely unresponsive and as stiff as a log for a few minutes. Each time, I would come to in a fog of weakness and nausea, leaving me incapacitated for hours afterward.

It started happening every few weeks, leaving Hildegard bewildered and scared. Fainting spells in growing children are common, but something was off in my case. I seemed to enter a state of near-death for a few minutes, completely unresponsive, cold to the touch and seemingly in rigor. Then I would come back to life.

One afternoon, some boys at school challenged me to a stupid game. It involved charging each other with bicycles, one of us standing his ground while the other child drove at him with all his might, swerving off at the very last moment.

When the time came to stand my ground, I did, but the boy racing towards me swerved a moment too late, slamming into me on his bicycle. My arms instinctively flew up to defend myself from the onrushing metal. The bicycle's mudguard connected with my tiny hand, its sharp edges slicing into my flesh. Spiking adrenaline kept me from realizing the extent of the damage at first, yet the wound was deep and exposed internal parts of my hand I had never laid eyes on before.

When I made it home, the deep wound was still bleeding and obviously needed stitches. Hildegard reacted quickly, called a taxi, and packed me into the elevator to travel the eleven floors down to the ground floor. As soon as the elevator door closed, I felt myself drifting away in the peculiar manner I had come to recognize as the warning signal preceding one of my fainting spells. I fought the sensation, but lost the battle at the exact moment the elevator doors opened, falling face-first onto the tiled floor. My nose shattered.

The ensuing bloodbath was too much for Hildegard to bear. She decided it was time to admit me into hospital to gain a deeper understanding of what was happening to me. But even after days of thorough examination, the doctors couldn't find anything wrong with me.

Before the age of fourteen, I was admitted into hospital care three more times to get to the bottom of my fainting spells. Each time, my doctors found different symptoms and pondered their significance.

I had a funnel chest and several physicians commented on the fact that my heart had shown an irregular shape on X-rays. Due to lack of space in my chest cavity, my heart seemed to be rather flat and wide like a prime steak instead of the round and compact fist depicted in medical books.

One doctor detected an eerie whistling sound that originated inside my heart yet he was unable to follow it to its source.

All doctors seemed to agree that, at certain times, shock or exhaustion dramatically altered my blood pressure. In those moments, one of my heart valves would stop moving and stay firmly shut for a few seconds. A regular fainting spell leaves its victims with all their reflexes intact. As they pass out and fall, their arms automatically come up in front of their face to shield themselves from injury. In my case, the uncooperative heart valve caused me to lose all my reflexes, my entire body stiffening up each time I passed out.

My doctors never clearly communicated if I was dealing with a heart defect or not. They all agreed I would eventually grow out of it. But I never did.

To this day, no one is sure about what exactly is causing these abnormal fainting spells. Throughout adolescence, I toppled over at inconvenient moments, breaking my nose several more times, falling into people's laps from one moment to the next, waking up in staircases feeling sick to my stomach, or bleeding, in a puddle of my own piss without any recollection of how long I had been out. As an adult, I continued experiencing the same mysterious fainting spells occasionally. The only changing element in the equation was the interval. While as a child and teenager, I had toppled over every few weeks, the intervals lengthened to every few years, as I grew older.

Over the years, my nasal passages started to look like winding roller coasters, yet, inexplicably, no doctor ever thought to suggest corrective surgery. Checking myself in the mirror every so often, I began to appreciate the hints of imperfection. My repeatedly broken nose gave my features a rugged twist of irregularity. I looked tougher, rough-around-the-edges and almost manly. Considering I had already weathered my fair share of challenges, it seemed strangely fitting for my face to show signs of struggle.

5

Swabian Ocean

Between twelve and fifteen years of age, the failing marriage of my adoptive parents became the dark center of my life. Their ongoing battles swallowed my energy like a giant black hole. I longed for a brother or sister, an ally who would understand and share my pain.

Good moments were rare, so I felt like a little boy at Christmas when my dad surprised me one afternoon by taking me out of school with a twinkle in his eye. Then, it suddenly felt like ten Christmases all wrapped up into one when he said, "For the next week, let's tell them you're sick. Let's go to Sylt together and have a grand time. Just the two of us." He opened the trunk of our car, revealing two suitcases and lots of beach toys. After a ten-hour drive, we reached the North Sea coast. Once the ferry had brought us over to our favorite island, we relaxed in the sunshine and splashed through the salty, shallow water for the entire week. It was one of the best vacations of my life.

We never went back. My parents became too wrapped up in their depressions to find the energy to travel far anymore. Instead, we started going to a lake in Swabia, the southernmost region of Germany, for our vacations. The remote villages of Lake Constance are Germany's haven for senior citizens. Besides me, there were no children within a ten-mile radius of our village. Instead, I was forced to stay with my parents for most of the day, listening to their fights become ever more abrasive.

Whenever I could, I tried to escape from my quarreling mom and dad to inhale the fresh scent of the "Swabian Ocean" – as the locals lovingly called it. With its surface area of two hundred and nine miles and a maximum depth of eight hundred and twenty-seven feet, the large body of water, occupying a former glacier basin, surely deserved its nickname. Its gently lapping waves sang a soft lullaby for me. Listening intently, I could feel a smile playing around the corners of my mouth. Even though the Swabian Ocean was tame compared to my beloved North Sea, it *did* help me to find my balance. Sitting under swaying willows, imagining what might lurk in the unexplored depths of the seemingly peaceful loch, I felt content.

In the evening, back at our holiday home, the lingering tension of my parents' squabbling was like a punch to the gut. Slipping under my blanket, I would remember the singing waves. As sleep claimed me, my dreams would transport me deep into the Swabian Ocean, where I was free to enjoy the weightlessness of its liquid twilight. The following morning, I would open my eyes feeling refreshed and strong enough to face another day with my struggling parents.

My mom's neuroses had gotten worse with every passing year. My dad's consistent inability to confront the crisis in a constructive manner exacerbated their situation to an unresolvable standoff. The louder their shouting matches, the harder it became for me to escape into the haven of my imagination – to a point where no body of water could wash away my despair. My world became a claustrophobic, flat disk. I feared I would reach its horizon at any moment and was outright terrified of plummeting over the edge into the abyss.

Watching my parents' misery only increased my ever-growing sense of loneliness. Had I been *Eeyore*, the dark rain cloud following me everywhere would have been the size of a small country. After my traumatizing primary school experiences, I had resolved to not give up on trying to make friends nonetheless. But now, my parents launched words like missiles, destroying everything in their path. I couldn't help but to huddle in corners and hide in my books once more. What few friends I had found, disappeared. They didn't know what to make of me. I was too lost in my thoughts, too serious and intense. No one wanted to discuss Kant or Buddha with a tomboy in Birkenstocks, if instead they could dance to the latest tunes of Cool and the Gang. Not willing to simply give in and follow the crowd, I shrugged my shoulders and resigned myself to being alone.

Thankfully, I still had one friend: Markus had remained my best buddy. His parents were no strangers to child psychology. Both were teachers and easily discerned my need for a safe haven. Without needing to say a word, they let me know I was welcome in their home at any time. They always greeted me with a genuine, warm smile and open arms. I would smile back, feeling happy and safe as soon as I entered their colorful home. It seemed to be filled with laughter, creativity, and mutual respect. Half-finished art projects cluttered their living space. Often, the entire family would sit around their living room table to create mythical papier-mâché creatures together. Everyone would be covered in the gooey substance and my heart would soar at the sight. It felt good to be amongst like-minded spirits.

Still, Markus and I mostly preferred staying in the privacy of his room. We never grew tired of embarking on imaginary safaris while leafing through pictures of breathtaking wild creatures in our encyclopedias. We competed for who could collect more nature books and spent hours learning all the Latin names of animals and plants.

Markus and I both dreamed of becoming game wardens in a big national park when we grew up. We would sit on his bed, learning about the wildlife sanctuaries and uncharted territories around our planet. As we pointed to pictures of different animals, Markus and I would conjure expeditions. On one, we paddled through the Okavango Delta, carefully sneaking closer to a pack of lions. Further into the dense swampland, we managed to film a group of hippopotami while barely escaping an attack by the group's alpha male. Our next expedition took us into the vast reaches of the Pacific Ocean, where we explored the deepest trenches in our submersible. We researched sperm whales and giant squid, only surfacing here and there to spend our evenings on remote islands. There, we got settled around the local campfires and listened to enchanting tales of a life lived in harmony with nature. Our expeditions took us further and further away from home each time we dreamed together.

As soon as I left Markus' family's apartment and took the four flights of stairs up home, reality would reassert itself with a vengeance. Even *Rapunzel* couldn't have felt more imprisoned on top of her castle's tower than I did in that penthouse.

My grandma seemed to have sprung straight from a glossy fairy tale picture book of classic housewives. She embodied a level of perfection my mom was never able to reach. This left Hildegard choking on feelings of insecurity, anger, and defeat. The consummate mother-in-law living right next door to us only highlighted her own inadequacy every single day. Instead of finding and developing her own unique virtues, my mom let herself go more and more, succumbing to a state of morose resentment.

My dad found striking a balance between loyal husband and mediator ever harder to achieve. His wife asked him to change the world for her, but he couldn't. Feeling increasingly defeated, he escaped into work, and spent much of his free time in the saunas located throughout the bigger cities close to our boring town. In addition to the cleansing, hot steam, the odd glass of wine also helped him take off the edge.

I couldn't help but find myself in the line of fire on many occasions. A simple dinner could trap me between the fronts, should I dare to volunteer opinions during either my parents' brooding silences, or their forced attempts at family harmony. Nerves were thin and aggression was never far from the surface.

My mom was a struggling cook who barely managed to cook an omelet without burning it – and my comments about the food I found on my plate often served as the last drop in the bucket of my mother's temper. Her schnitzel's consistency reminded me of leathery shoe soles. I might have made this undiplomatic observation a few times too often. During one memorable lunch, I ducked instinctively as a schnitzel flew over my head and slammed into the vintage wallpaper behind my chair. Hildegard's speed had been astonishing. Thankfully, my young reflexes were well honed. I watched as the mistreated piece of meat, lubricated by thick brown gravy, slid slowly over the wallpaper, ending up in a sad heap on the floor. My teenaged response of giggles did not help lighten the mood.

Over time, other culinary delights would follow in the path of the schnitzel. Our dining room wallpaper suffered under the repeated impacts of the greasy debris. New patterns would imprint over delicate vintage designs.

Hildegard's neuroses escalated ever further. Her fear of germs had reached a level where even washing her hands after touching a door handle seemed not to be enough. Her hands looked like raw meat and bled because she washed them repeatedly after touching anything. As steam oozed through the bathroom door, my dad and I listened to my mom's bathroom ritual: the sound of running hot water, then a bar of soap hitting the wash basin again and again, for minutes on end. Before long, my body would tense every time I heard my mom opening a faucet.

She had no control over the rites she performed, and her level of self-destructiveness broke my heart. Seeing my mom's small hands, dry from the overuse of soap, cracked and bleeding, left me feeling empty, angry, and depressed. I felt for her. At the same time, I felt disgusted and overwhelmed. As a result of my negative feelings, I felt guilty, responsible, and powerless. I wanted to protect her, but knew the extent of her psychological problems was way out of my league.

As I grew older, Hildegard began to use me as a sounding board. She would often share her misgivings and conspiracy theories regarding Oma and Dad as well as random suspicious strangers. In the evenings, I would watch Dad become gradually more remote and quiet in the face of Hildegard's depressing, dark world.

Yet, even as the walls around us crumbled, we still experienced good moments. We loved playing board games and watching movies. For movie nights, my dad and I always sat on the big couch opposite to the smaller one my mom perched on. The right soundtrack, a happy moment, a sad moment, a death, a hug, a cute puppy, a happy ending – anything could set us off crying. If it resonated emotionally, my dad and I would weep openly, tears streaming down our cheeks. Hildegard would watch us with disdain. Crying over stories remote from our own experience was an outlet for my dad and I, a safe, neutral chance to shed tears and relieve the ever-increasing pressure in our elegant apartment.

As a teenager, I started to feel like a dwindling army, spread over too many fronts. Slowly but surely, I spiraled into a deep depression.

My parents were in no position to help me. Apart from me witnessing their arguments, their involvement in my daily life was minimal. They were too deeply entangled with their own demons. I never felt free to openly discuss my problems and thoughts with them. They rarely helped with homework, teenage angst and insecurities. I had no choice but to overcome all obstacles by myself.

Gradually, the stress at home, alongside my other troubles, became too much for me to handle. I became suicidal. During this phase of my life, I frequently jumped up onto bridge railings, despite being probably the worst athlete anyone had ever laid eyes on. With no sense of balance or coordination, I would teeter at the edge of the abyss. One part of me hoping I would fall and wondering who would notice or care. Another part of me shaking my heavy head at my stupidity and wanting to live, to live a full life more than anything.

Thankfully, these moments of tempting fate taught me how much I loved being alive. After only a few months of contemplating taking my own life, I dug deep and found courage. And I made a decision: whenever faced with seemingly insurmountable problems, I would do my best to stop running, stop resisting and instead choose to embrace them.

Regardless of the surrounding turbulences and testiness, I often felt love and energy burgeoning within me. Like a nuclear reactor, overheating on raw power without an available outlet, I feared an impending meltdown. I had so much to give. Maybe I needed to try and tap into this positive force to help myself first. I needed to at least give it a try and vowed to find passion in all aspects of my existence. Recognizing – and seizing – moments of beauty in everyday life would help me to cherish this one magnificent life.

I began to channel my energy so that something positive could grow from the destruction. I had been an avid reader as far back as I could remember. I had started to write at age seven. Now at thirteen, I spent hours bent over my diary, diving into my emotions. I dabbled at writing poems as well as short stories, describing the world as I saw it, or creating new worlds far better than my own. The door to my room would stay firmly locked as *Peter Gabriel* and *Genesis* blasted from shabby speakers. I would play songs like *Land of Confusion* and *Don't Give Up* over and over again. While writing, I would sing along at the top of my voice, trying to shout louder than the demons within and around me. Or I would go to the movies, favoring any romantic movie with a happy ending. Happy endings were what I craved with all my heart.

In the midst of this, I developed an obsessive crush on one of my high school teachers. He was a kind intellectual, trying hard to teach us appreciation for German literature, history, and social studies. I fiercely held on to my feelings for him and rode the wave of passion, letting it carry me through high school with top scores. I wanted him to love me back more than anything, so I excelled at everything in order to gain his approval. Like a noble knight, he did the right thing: he ignored my frequent gazes of admiration and longing, and praised my good work instead.

Teachers in general became my idols. They were far enough removed from my life to be neutral and safe. Even though I was a loner and outsider, school became my sanctuary. I fiercely invested energy into all my classes and focused on forgetting my problems, even if it was just for an instant. After years of reading adventure and philosophy books, I now turned to the old classics, in a continuing search for meaning and spiritual guidance.

I still had no idea who, or what, I was. Looking at myself was like gazing upon a mosaic, years away from completion: I couldn't see the whole picture because it wasn't yet formed.

There were so many questions. For instance, why was I terrified to go to swimming lessons with the other children? Every week, I asked Hildegard to lie for me and write me a sick leave note. Being no stranger to bending the truth, Hildegard easily complied.

At fourteen, I knew dishonesty could no longer be a part of my life. More than anything, I needed to be true to myself. My parents never faced their problems. They kept avoiding themselves and each other, always finding excuses, and thus rarely finding solutions. I needed to take control and do good in order to start seeing things change for the better within me as well as around me.

So, summoning all my courage, I started with my sports teacher. I caught her on her way to the office. Looking straight into her eyes, I said, "I have lied to you for many years to avoid swimming lessons. I am very sorry. It will never happen again." Mrs. Reber wasn't angry. She just nodded and answered, "Thank you, Stefanie. I really appreciate that."

I kept my word. From then on, every Wednesday morning during swimming lessons, I sloshed enthusiastically across the pool – and hated it with all my heart. Nevertheless, I pushed on. The lack of integrity and clarity I witnessed at home reminded me every day of how important it was to face our fears, to squarely face life.

I hated being in the locker room with the other girls and detested being at such close quarters, changing clothes. I didn't want the other children to see my naked body. This was why I had lied all those years, but I still didn't understand why.

Even during our holidays at the Swabian Ocean, I couldn't bring myself to go swimming. So I sat at the lake's mellow shores with all the senor citizens, staring out into the blue horizon. The exuberant fish I had been during my early childhood, unable to stay out of the smallest puddle of water, had disappeared. Instead, I had turned into a rigid, robed statue, afraid to move or to have my body exposed in any way.

Why did I feel like this? Why couldn't I be at home in my own body? Why could I never belong? Confusion ruled my life.

The mere thought of wearing girl's clothing made me shudder like a wet dog on a cold winter day. I opted for gender-neutral tennis shoes, jeans, and t-shirts. My breasts were developing slowly and promised to be enormous. Even before they reached their true proportions, the wobbly sacks of flesh made me feel distinctly uncomfortable. From then on, to hide them as best as I could, I resorted to buying all my sweaters and shirts at least two sizes too big.

Dad got more and more depressed, often mentioning suicide. I spent hours talking with him, listening to him and soothing him while he speculated on how he would go about ending his life. During the worst of his depression, I spent almost a year frantically searching cupboards for bleach, fertilizer, pesticides, and knives, and hiding them from him. Being only thirteen at the time, I felt desperate and wished for a magic wand, an epiphany, an act of god, a natural disaster – anything to break the vicious circle of darkness. I needed help but didn't know to whom I could turn.

My oma had too much on her plate. Hildegard had long ago turned Oma's life into a warzone, attacking her daily for the slightest reasons. The last thing she needed was hearing about her son's dreams of suicide. I decided to spare her the agony.

Due to my parents' neglect of family relationships, none of my other relatives had grown close to me. Oma had taken me a couple of times to visit her sister and her sister's many children and grandchildren. I had felt great spending time with them, but we had seen each other on too few occasions to really get to know each other. Now, it was too late. No help would be coming from that direction either.

When I finally felt completely overwhelmed by trying to keep my dad alive, I shared just fragments of what was happening in my home with my friend Markus' parents. The look of pity and shock was so evident in their eyes I never brought the subject up again. Two months later, my only friend and his parents moved away to another city. We never saw each other again. I felt more alone than ever before.

With no other option, I did the only thing possible: I gritted my teeth and faced the storm. I became the parent. I mediated, soothed outbreaks of emotion and attempted to help mend broken hearts. I listened to both Dad and Hildegard at any hour of the day and night. I felt responsible to be available for them to talk to. They asked me for advice and I gave it. Imagine that: me, a pubescent therapist, divulging her wisdoms on life and marital problems.

Around this time, my parents started talking openly about divorce. Dad spent less and less time at home. He was going to his sauna outings several times per week. Thankfully, he seemed to become more stable, and found a friend. Walter was a seemingly very conservative, god-fearing, forty-year old man who still lived with his mother. My dad and Walter went on many hikes together in their free time, listening to each other for hours. Sometimes, Dad took me along with them.

Walter was friendly at first, but seemed to grow mysteriously aggressive and jealous towards me. I felt unwanted, yet was immensely relieved: finally, my dad had found someone else to talk to about his twenty-year marriage with Hildegard, and their impending divorce. I couldn't quite see light at the end of the tunnel, but impenetrable darkness seemed to have transformed into a very dark grey. Now, at least I could stagger forward, carefully putting one foot in front of the other.

Dad was plagued by emotional pain and an urge to run from his wife, followed by immediate doubts and remorse. It took two years for my parents to make up their minds and put an end to their – and my – torture. During the entire time, they kept confiding in me. It made me feel strangely adult and important, but at the same time it broke my heart over and over again. I just wanted it to be done with, for all our sakes.

Of course, the question came up of where I would live after the divorce. The choice was an easy one. Even though Hildegard had never meant for any of this to happen, my emotional life with her had always been traumatizing to say the least. I knew it would hurt her to lose me but, for once in this drawn-out drama, I had to take a stand and look after myself. I decided to stay with my dad. It was the only possible, realistic, and bearable solution.

With Hildegard gone, family life between Dad, Oma, and myself became more relaxed. The doors between our adjacent penthouses stayed wide open for the first time in their existence, with my oma coming over to our bigger apartment often to spend time with Dad and me. The door to my room was finally able to remain open as well. I enjoyed sitting at my desk, doing my homework while listening to Frida and Konrad relaxing in the living room, laughing and talking with each other.

I felt like I had just been forced to hike through deep snow for ages and my body had come to the point of freezing. Just in time, I had reached a cabin with an open fireplace. Warmth and relief coursed through me in equal measure. At the same time though, my defrosting body tingled with thousands of pins and needles – just like my conscience when thinking of my now very lonely mom.

Even with the tension at home gone, I still felt dedicated to my schoolwork. I was on a roll and found that I enjoyed studying and was my own worst critic. If I worked as hard as I could before a test and failed it, I wasn't upset. But if I realized that failing it had been entirely my fault, due to not investing enough effort into the task at hand, I was ready to rip my own hair out.

On the upside, I felt happy and content with my work, and my teachers were enchanted with me. On the downside, my youth had evaporated. I hadn't had time for fun and games. I had been too busy babysitting my parents and trying to keep a grip on pretty much the entire universe.

As part of the weight lifted off my shoulders, I experienced a surge in creativity. Whereas before I had only dabbled in writing, recording memories, I now began writing for an audience and entered writing competitions. Simply plunging into the experience headfirst, I had no real sense of how to structure an endeavor as complex as writing a research paper or story.

The Parliament of Baden-Wuerttemberg in Germany provided five themes each year which students could choose as their topic. I would usually sign up months in advance. Then I would procrastinate until a few days before the final deadline. Three days before the deadline, I would start writing my heart out, staying awake on pure adrenaline and passion, until I was practically, physically and mentally finished. I would end up holding fifty, surprisingly cohesive, pages in my hand. Since it would be too late by then to send the manuscript by post, I would take the train to the address stated in the competition papers, managing to enter my work virtually at the very last second.

The first time, I won second prize. The following few years, I won first prize each year. Writing in a crazy, trance-like dash seemed to agree with me. I began to wonder what I might be able to achieve if I wrote a piece for a few months, instead of cramming the entire process into a span of three days.

Scholastic successes aside, I still pondered my existence and more often than not, felt like *ET*. I just wanted to phone home and reunite with the people of my planet – if only I knew who and where my people were.

In the meantime, a positive effort had proved to be the most therapeutic course of action. My search for meaning brought me to a local conservation club. At first, I joined the adults on their bird-watching expeditions. Soon after, I longed for more and founded a youth section. We became part of a nationwide German conservation society. I spent my free time organizing volunteer-events. We did cleanups in our local forests, helped frogs to cross highways during their migration, and converted people's gardens into natural habitats.

I had only just turned fifteen, but most members of my group were between the ages of ten and twelve. Having the younger children look up to me and follow my lead was an amazing experience. Within this group of environmentalist nerds who dedicated their free time to making a small difference, I suddenly didn't feel quite so odd. On the contrary, I discovered how much I treasured following my own path and carrying responsibility. Leading my group, I felt self-assured, followed my judgment, and discovered that I possessed the necessary charisma to hold the team together.

I took every opportunity to become more involved. My long summer breaks from school were spent in the mountains, staying awake all night to watch falcons' nests with night vision telescopes. Many poachers raided these nests to sell baby falcons to rich Arab sheiks. If we caught them rappelling down the steep cliff face towards the nest, we scared them away with our powerful searchlights, at the same time warning them through megaphones, pretending to be the police.

It was during those nights that I experienced my first kiss. Alfonso was the same age as me, handsome and gentle, with curly dark hair and a dazzling smile. I felt safe and excited with him, but I was unable to let go and enjoy myself. Kisses seemed to be all I was capable of. In terms of gender and sexuality, I was too confused to be able to surrender completely into romantic bliss. But the suspense of outsmarting poachers paired with innocent teenage romance did lift my spirits nonetheless.

The conservation society taught me many valuable life lessons – belonging, friendship, and caring for others being only three of many. One year, our society organized a summer camp between youth activists from Germany and Malta. We went to Liechtenstein to visit one of the world's oldest glaciers. After climbing up to the glacier, I couldn't go back down. Unprepared for the adventure, I wore only tennis shoes and kept slipping. Pippin, one of my newfound Maltese friends took off his left hiking boot and asked me to give him my left tennis shoe. Holding on to and steadying each other, we made it safely to the bottom of the valley. I was touched by his kindness and immensely grateful for the experience.

At the age of sixteen, I handed leadership of my conservationist club over to one of the other children. With a heavy heart, I moved on and concentrated on the busy last year of high school. Dad, Oma, and I were very close at this point. We were like survivors who had become inextricably linked through our shared trauma. Our renewed sense of family gave me strength to excel beyond my wildest dreams. Becoming a straight-A student, I graduated high school with distinction.

Adolescent hormones had hit me full-on by then. As my body developed ever more female curves and massive breasts, I felt increasingly stranded in my body, as though I had landed in an airport without my passport. I had been allowed to fly in, but now I was stuck in this foreign place with apparently no way out. Who was I?

Another question rattling me after graduation was, what on Earth was I going to do professionally? I wasn't without talents, but couldn't make up my mind. The guidance provided by school didn't help. During senior year, they had tested my suitability and aptitude for various professions. My test results had come back stating that I had all the makings of a midwife. Really? This evaluation did not fit well with my dreams of becoming a park ranger, archeologist, deep-sea submersible pilot, sea captain, or even a Navy Seal.

Inhabiting a female body at the time influenced my choices considerably. During a three-day internship in our town's sewage treatment plant, I experienced utter bewilderment. The sewage plant's team consisted entirely of middle-aged men. Their good-natured banter felt as alien to me as listening to Martians. My attempts to be one of the guys made them chuckle harder than ever.

Unluckily, my monthly period coincided with the internship. Being a stranger in my own body, I had always tried to pay as little attention to it as possible, with the sentiment being: if I don't touch it, then maybe it will change or disappear. So I avoided using tampons. Every month, I would bleed like a stuck pig, leaving me no choice but to buy the largest size of pad on the market.

Imagine my surprise when, on the second day of my internship, one of the men took my spare pad out of his pocket during lunch in the canteen and started handing it around. The unpackaged, diaper-like contraption must have slipped out of my jacket pocket that morning. "Look what I found guys! Seems like one of the old ladies from the neighborhood has lost her diaper." Soon all the men were having the time of their lives, joking where the pad might have come from. Even as I felt my face turning the brightest red, I attempted bravado and tried a joke of my own: "Maybe it's the luxurious bed of a wealthy, nesting bird, and it fell out of a tree." I could not claim the pad, no matter how badly I needed it. Too ashamed to do anything else, I stuffed my underpants full of toilet paper. As I worked alongside the men, the paper rustling suspiciously with every step I took, I could feel blood running down my legs. I kept looking down at my crotch, checking for blooming spots of red.

Afterwards, I felt more timid than ever, about my body as well as about entering predominantly male work environments. Everything felt twisted and wrong. I tried to walk with a swagger. In an effort to conceal my breasts, I became the *Hunchback of Notre Dame* in Birkenstocks, with a stiff cowboy gait, sporting enormous North Sea sweaters that looked like knitted teepees.

Too perplexed, and too afraid of entering the fray that was working for a living, I stood rooted to the spot. My parents kept saying, "Stefanie, you should really consider becoming a bank teller or insurance agent." I couldn't stand the thought, but since the safest course of action seemed to be to keep going to school until I saw a way out of my predicament, I went along with Konrad's idea to enroll in a three-year programme, specializing in Business.

Sitting in the school's classrooms in my large sweaters, eyed suspiciously by my fellow students, I also encountered strong differences in mentality between us. For the first time in my life, I was proud not to belong, even glad. The only classes I enjoyed were German literature and English. Everything else centered on power and money. The German business elite of the future was being groomed behind the inconspicuous walls of our institution. Clearly, I had landed on the wrong planet.

Our sports teacher was a former professional triathlete who, after a serious knee injury, had had to stop competing professionally and settle for a career as a coach. He kept his despair in check by targeting the weak athletes in his classes. He thrived on humiliating them in front of the other students.

There was a lesbian girl in my class, Annika. She and I constituted the bottom of the barrel. I couldn't move. I just couldn't. My body terrified me and made me incredibly self-conscious. My breasts had grown to a cup size other girls fantasized about. They bobbed up and down like volleyballs in a pool, no matter how tight a bra I wore. All I could think of was to hide them by standing still, walking very slowly, or hunching over. Sports made that impossible. Whenever I ran, I became painfully aware of my bouncing monstrosities.

Annika simply hated sports. Our teacher, on the other hand, hated us for denying ourselves the opportunity of using our healthy, young bodies. Often, sports training would consist of the former triathlete compelling Annika and me to perform in front of our – mostly very athletic – fellow students. He would force us to climb ropes, perform handstands, do fifty pushups, and other exercises worthy of a military academy. As the others looked on and laughed, Annika and I would inevitably crash onto our butts, weak, out of breath, humiliated and ashamed.

It never occurred to me to ask the dean of the school or my parents to intervene on Annika's and my behalf. As with everything else I had been through, I simply endured, tried to manage as best as I could alone, and vowed to survive. I tried to be unprovocative and slink into the shadows. Annika proved to be a true friend. We stuck together and accepted each other exactly the way we were, no matter what. Our friendship endured far after we both left Business College.

For two years, I labored along in an education that meant nothing to me. By the beginning of the third school year, my formerly amazing grades were just barely good enough to prevent being thrown out.

One morning, during the fifth semester, I was staring out the classroom window, on a mental quest for greener pastures. At first, I just stared blankly into space. Then my eyes came to focus on a strange new object in the distance. A white Big Top stood proudly on the banks of the River Enz, just across from our college. I couldn't wait to escape the lectures for the future economic elite and instead explore the magical new object that had appeared in our dull Southern German community.

By early evening, I was off, flying towards the Big Top on my bike. It had been erected that same day. The crew had worked fast. They were almost done. A huge banner over one side of the tent proclaimed *Phaenomena*.

I bumped into a tall elderly gentleman and asked him what *Phaenomena* was all about. It turned out that it was a science exhibition, created by a quirky Swiss philosopher and inventor. It was a creative, interactive approach to science, explaining complicated concepts in a playful manner. The exhibition had already been shown in Zurich and was now scheduled to stay in our town over the summer. As I thanked him and turned to be on my way, the grey-haired gentleman called after me and asked, "Hey, I am the local manager of the exhibition guides. We are still looking for help. Are you interested?" I didn't even have to think about it. Beaming, I answered, "I would love that! I can help out on the weekends. And during the upcoming spring break." As we shook hands, I already felt a million times lighter.

6

Lake Monrepos

Phaenomena expanded my universe. Science had always been a mystery to me, beckoning and forbidding at the same time. My high school physics teacher had shaken his head at my lack of scientific prowess. Now, the interactive experiments broadened my understanding. All of a sudden I grasped concepts I had never before been able to comprehend. Pythagoras, Newton, Einstein and many of their contemporaries became like friends instead of scary old men with crazy hair speaking an incomprehensible language.

Making money doing something I passionately enjoyed was an eye-opening experience. I gave guided tours for school classes and visitors in general. I wasn't afraid of speaking in front of people, but rather enjoyed it. My supervisor was full of praise, commending my dedication and enthusiasm. It made me recall the days of leading my group of teenage activists. A charismatic person was hiding underneath the gigantic folds of my sweater.

Slowly, my life at *Phaenomena* grew to be my main priority. I couldn't wait for the daunting college weeks to end so I could go to my beautiful, inspiring riverbank sanctuary on the weekends. Our Big Top being open to the outside provided us with a protective roof over our heads, while at the same time allowing us to work outdoors and fully enjoy the sunshine and sweet smell of fresh riverbank grass.

After two months of working part-time at *Phaenomena*, college seemed ever more like a hostile alien planet. I had a few more months before the fifth semester ended. The sixth semester would have to wait, since I had decided to spend my eighteenth year of life with a host family in the United States.

Actually, part of me had no intention of ever going back to Business College. With only three months to go for the exhibition, I realized, I had no intentions of continuing the struggle to finish my fifth semester either. Enough was enough. I would never become a business mogul, and I knew it.

From one day to the next, I dropped out of school and started working full time at *Phaenomena*. I was in heaven. I interacted, charmed, taught, and inspired. It was simply fabulous. My world and heart opened up like desert flowers reviving after the first rainfalls of spring.

Something magical I had never previously experienced happened, a sign of true contentment and happiness: time stood still and went into warp speed all at the same time.

Happier than ever before, underneath the brilliant white tarpaulin of the Big Top, I was still a confused youth who wasn't sure of anything. Outside of *Phaenomena*, I remained a social outcast. I had neither experienced love nor sexual relationships – nothing beyond my first kiss and the short period of innocent romance in the falcon trailer years before. Some boys had flirted with me and I had been at a loss of how to react. I had felt no attraction, only confusion and fear.

While working for the exhibition, I couldn't help but notice the carpenter. You could say I recognized a kindred spirit in his awkwardness. I wore my tent-like shirts, baggy pants, and Birkenstocks. Heinrich wore old-fashioned corduroy pants, fading lumberjack shirts, and battered steel-toed boots.

Heinrich was a quiet, modest, intelligent and introverted forty-year old Swiss man. With his big, gentle hands, and sad eyes behind thick glasses, he created magic from featureless pieces of wood. Heinrich had been with *Phaenomena* since its first opening in Switzerland. He unofficially took care of the entire exhibition while it was stationed in our town.

As we gradually became tongue-tied around each other, I realized we were falling in love. Easygoing conversation turned into hearts skipping a beat and sentences skipping words. I loved the crazy vibrations coursing through every fiber of my body, loved the thrill of apprehensiveness mixed with anticipation. Everything seemed perfectly aligned and at odds at the same time.

An albatross waking up on a beautiful rock in the ocean surrounded by dazzling yet treacherous seas must feel similar to how I felt back then – energized, enjoying the beauteous moment, but aware of my limitations at the same time. I loved where I had arrived. But how would I manage to get enough run up, to provide lift to soar into the skies? Would I be able to fly and overcome the inexplicable rigidity I felt during every waking moment? What was I supposed to do with this female body of mine? Would my love for Heinrich give me the momentum to finally arrive within myself and be able to enjoy a satisfying relationship with him?

I decided to ignore my mounting trepidation. I would never find the answers to my questions if I allowed fear to get the better of me. Initially, Heinrich and I were both unsure how to proceed. We sought each other's company. As soon as we found it, we stumbled and stuttered until we managed to disengage. The suspense was killing me. Did he love me or was this all just happening in my muddled subconscious? I simply had to find out.

When Heinrich next approached me on the top floor of our Big Top, my heart almost burst, it beat so hard. Out of breath and trembling with excitement and fear, I said, "I am in love with you. There is nothing I can do about it. Would you have dinner with me?" Very quietly, with a warm-hearted smile, he answered, "Sure. How does tonight sound?"

I barely functioned that day. My brain did backflips inside my skull. Finally, we were sitting at dinner, carefully making small talk until Heinrich reached over the table. He gently laid his hand over mine and confessed, "I am very much in love with you, too." At these words, the stimulating vibrations in my body intensified to almost unbearable proportions. I wanted to rip his clothes off right then and there, and slip into the warm embrace of his big, hairy body.

Heinrich would soon return to live hundreds of kilometers away in Switzerland, at home with his mother whom he had never left. I would be off to the United States in only two months and would be gone for an entire year. Our age difference was considerable. But love truly knew no boundaries. It swept us away, and we agreed to forget all fear and let it take us to where it may.

It took us to magic. The following two summer months were a blur. We worked on the exhibition grounds together. During our breaks, we spent romantic moments in the surrounding meadows.

On our days off, we often went to Lake Monrepos. It was a romantic hideaway, featuring a small castle and ancient trees. Their roots entangled to form mystical shapes. In the early mornings, my active imagination would make me see the ghosts of former kings and knights, riding on the lakeshore or meeting for early morning duels. Every now and then, Heinrich and I would rent a rowboat. We would silently glide through dark passages between trees bearing a striking resemblance to the ancient *Ents* of *Middle Earth*. Protected by these living behemoths of emerald foliage and intertwining roots and branches, we would float and lose ourselves in deep kisses. As I couldn't get enough of exploring every inch of Heinrich's mouth with my tongue, hours would pass in what seemed like merely seconds. Back at the exhibition, remembering our burning kisses, my whole body would quiver with happiness and excitement.

Heinrich's company had rented a small studio apartment for him, close to the exhibition grounds. Soon, I was only going home for a change of clothes. I would rush in, greet Dad and Oma with a cheerful wave, throw some clothes in a backpack, and run straight back out again.

I enjoyed Heinrich's company and aimed to soar. But we were both as awkward as penguins with their useless wings tied behind their backs. Heinrich was very inexperienced and shy. He was gentle and immensely patient as well. I loved him with all my heart and could feel orgasms building up inside me just by looking at him. But my body was an albatross that never took flight. My whole body would freeze as soon as we ventured beyond kissing. I would become passive, lying beneath him like a deer caught in the headlights. The romantic ecstasy I felt during the day in anticipation of his muscular body next to mine would disappear as soon as he penetrated me. While he gently caressed me, always concerned for our pleasure to be mutual, he would push his penis ever deeper into my vagina. As soon as he moaned in ecstasy, I would give it a few seconds before doing my best imitation of a woman enraptured by the most earth-shattering orgasm of her life. Indeed, no matter how much I loved Heinrich, during intercourse my lusty-sounding screams were never far from revealing the truth – excruciating pain, discomfort, and frustration. I longed for a true orgasm, but never had the heart to be honest with Heinrich and thereby shatter his illusions. He looked so happy. And he was not to blame. It was me: my body felt completely wrong.

August drew nearer and with it came my planned departure to the United States. I had looked forward to this exciting opportunity for over a year. Despite my body's refusal to cooperate, I was in despair at the thought of losing Heinrich and did not want to go anywhere without him. My teenage heart was in an uproar. Yes, I felt lost regarding my sexuality. But in all my eighteen years, I had never experienced falling in love, being in love, being loved as intimately as this. Why did it all have to happen now, just before I had to leave for twelve long months?

Our last night together arrived with the speed of a torpedo. We hung on to each other as if we were the last two people on Earth. We smiled, laughed, made another awkward attempt to reach orgasm, and cried hot tears. We exchanged presents and promised to be in touch over the entire year. Nothing would break us apart.

My flight was due to leave from Stuttgart airport at 8 a.m. and I hadn't even packed. At 5 that same morning, I stumbled into our house and hastily packed two suitcases to sustain me throughout the coming year abroad. I was functioning in a sleep-deprived daze, barely registering my surroundings. As Dad gently maneuvered us towards the parking garage, I at least remembered to hug Oma goodbye.

Somehow, we made it to the airport just in time. I knew I needed to go. I was the one who had *wanted* to go. But at that moment, all I wanted to do was hang on to one of the departure hall pillars like an overgrown chimpanzee to prevent anyone from dragging me through that departure gate. A constant advertisement banner seemed to circulate through my mind in fluorescent, loud colors – Heinrich, Heinrich, Heinrich.

With a heavy heart, I said goodbye to my ever-tolerant dad. Suddenly, my brain woke up. Shocked, I perceived my selfishness. Mesmerized by the drama of my first love, I had neglected to talk with him in weeks. Now, we wouldn't see each other for a full year. What had I done?

We hugged. Then, selfless beyond belief, tears streaming from his eyes, my dad pushed me away from him and through the gate, towards new horizons.

We had been so late, and the airplane was so full, that for the very first overseas flight of my young life, I ended up being seated on a painfully uncomfortable folding chair. The pain in my back and bum echoed the pain in my romantic heart.

A fellow traveller engaged me in conversation. Amused by my overflowing teenage emotions, he ordered whisky cokes for us throughout the flight. At New York airport, my new friend and I waved a drunken goodbye. My heart still heavy, I boarded the connecting flight to Salt Lake City. Since I was already drunk, I continued ordering whisky cokes on this next flight as well.

The third and last connecting flight in Salt Lake City was to Pasco. The plane was very small. The turbulence due to storms over the mountains was substantial. Late that night, I arrived in Pasco, thoroughly shaken and stirred. I braced for meeting my American host family. I stumbled down the stairs from the airplane onto the tarmac. This part of the planet felt very unstable. But I made it, nevertheless, to the small arrivals building.

Behind brightly-polished glass doors, four smiling and excited people awaited my arrival. For this sincere Mormon family, I was a first step towards opening up to the outside world. I was the first foreign student they had decided to welcome into their family home. I approached my host parents, their bleached-blonde teenage daughter and young, slightly chubby son. They walked towards me with open arms.

As the sincere looking, middle-aged gentleman with neatly combed hair, reached out for me, I did my best to smile. Just then, the State of Washington seemed to tilt beneath my feet. Half digested airline meals surged out of my mouth on a sea of whisky cokes – and crashed on the shores of my host dad's gleaming shoes.

7

Atlantic Ocean

After a bit of coaxing, my brave American host family managed to bundle me into their van. My host dad, Stuart, visited the airport lavatory in an attempt to clean his puke-stained leather shoes – with only moderate success. As we drove towards my new home in the beautiful pine forests of Washington State, the stench of regurgitated whisky and pasta lingered.

It was pitch black outside. We were far away from big city life and every mile brought us further out into remote wilderness. My blurry eyes tried to catch glimpses of majestic pine trees. After a while, I gave in to the jetlag and drunkenness and told myself I would say hello to those trees and whatever else was out there, the next morning.

A year earlier, Dad and I had approached an agency to organize a stay with an American host family. I had read hundreds of adventure books so, of course, I wanted to see the Wild West – preferably on horseback. After consulting many travel books, the pictures resonating with me the most were of the beautiful Cascade Mountains and Washington State. Be it the mysterious and forbidding Mount St. Helens, the gorgeous Mount Rainier, or the dense wilderness of the Pacific Northwest coast – everything seemed pristine and breathtakingly beautiful. To top it off, Washington State was called the Evergreen State. I had found my destination.

Soon after my interview process, I was sent information on the most suitable host family. Pictures showed a remote country home and a nice, smiling group of people surrounded by dogs, cats, and – oh, heaven! – two horses, in a small paddock next to an adjoining barn, situated right next to the family's house. The accompanying letter included personal information on the entire family. All sounded compatible enough. Contracts were signed and dates agreed upon.

Now, twelve months later, I awoke in my new home, nursing the biggest hangover of my young life. When I opened my eyes, the blinds were drawn. My mental state was an intriguing mix of obsession with Heinrich, sadness at being apart from him, and excitement at having arrived on the North American continent.

I opened the blinds and was greeted by… desert, as far as the eye could see. I must have stood there for ten minutes, staring out the window and comparing my image of invigorating forests with this dusty desert. As I contemplated the expanse of flat, dry space, tumbleweeds rolled past my window and cheerfully bounced up and down.

Over the next days, it became clear to me that writers of travel literature censored certain geographical areas to make their books more attractive. I found myself in a barren region I had never seen advertised in any travel literature.

It was called the Columbia Basin. The Columbia River flows through this basin, creating a belt of green along its riverbank. Otherwise, the entire place consists of dry earth, tumbleweeds and, as I was about to find out, rattlesnakes, skunks, cacti, wineries, golf courses, and irrigation installations. The Columbia Basin is surrounded by the Cascade Mountains. Rain clouds usually don't make it all the way over the mountaintops. A very unusual pocket climate is thus created in the isolated basin area, despite its location so far north of the equator.

Even though what I encountered was far from what I had expected, I loved the rugged beauty and isolated wildness of it all. I found I didn't mind swapping my imagined forests for this vast desert. There would be much to discover either way. Town was an hour's drive away. The riverbank was beautiful. Its lush green vegetation grew in stark contrast to the vivid colors of the desert. In springtime, after heavy rainfall, the desert floor would come alive with wildflowers like a magic carpet unrolling towards the horizon.

My romantic soul soon imagined drawing and painting on the riverbank for hours, or riding through the desert on my trusty steed.

Option one was made impossible by poisonous black widow spiders. They had a nasty habit of crawling up my pant legs while I practiced being a romantic artist.

Option two turned out to be a bit more adventurous than I had bargained for. Rattlesnakes would frequently spook my not-so-trusty steed named Cinnebar into a wild gallop. I was far too inexperienced a horseback rider to take control of a horse running in fear of its life. Consequently, I reverted to keeping it simple and enjoyed taking long walks instead.

Cinnebar and Mr. Bojangles were my host family's horses. Mr. Bojangles was too big and temperamental for a novice like me. With the exception of our rattlesnake adventures, Cinnebar was a kind soul who patiently endured my clumsiness. One morning, I opened the gate to the paddock and walked towards the two horses to fetch Cinnebar. She trotted over to me and I gently slipped the bridle over her head. We had done this many times before, so I was surprised at how much my presence agitated Mr. Bojangles.

As I turned with Cinnebar to walk her out of the paddock, Mr. Bojangles closed the distance between us in a few powerful strides. Shocked, I turned towards him. He reared up and kicked me in the stomach with the full force of both his hind legs. Suddenly I was on the ground, struggling to catch a breath. Excruciating pain shot through my entire abdominal region.

I had fallen very close to the fence. Instinct took over and I rolled under the wire to safety. As I slowly caught my breath, I could see my host mom, Katie, through the kitchen window, shaking her head.

Feeling sorry for myself, I walked indoors hoping for some reassuring pats on the back. "Should have stood your ground," Katie told me, in a voice hard as steel. "You should have gotten back on no matter how much it hurt or how scared you were. You'll never be able to go into that paddock again." She was right. Mr. Bojangles never respected me again. From then on, the moment I approached the fence, he would run at me, his head held high, his nostrils flaring.

The metaphorical significance of my experience didn't escape me. I had rolled under the fence too often as a child. For most of my early school life, I had stood quietly in a corner, trying to avoid bruises and flying spittle. Mr. Bojangles taught me the need to believe in myself and face my opponents, no matter how unpleasant the experience might turn out to be. I needed to respect myself enough to stand up in the face of adversity. How else would I ever manage to belong in the world?

During the first few months in Richland, I was like a knight, attempting to slay too many dragons at once. Everything surrounding me was unknown. I tried to fit into Mormon family life, high school life, and small-town American life in general. Besieged by all these new impressions, I would drop into bed at 7 or 8 p.m. This was partly due to the ongoing English-German translation whispering inside my brain. After two months, I started to dream in English. That's when I knew I had successfully breached the language barrier.

My hosts, Stuart and Katie were devout members of the Church of Latter Day Saints. They had raised four children in their secluded country home. Two had left home already and were in college. Katie ruled the remaining family of four with an iron fist. My host sister, Linda, was a high school junior. Her little brother, Greg, was fourteen years old.

I had enjoyed a very liberal upbringing. Whereas I had accompanied my parents to nude beaches, had rarely seen a church from the inside, and managed my life independently, my host family members had never seen each other naked, and their life centered on church activities.

There may have been abundant emotional turmoil in my German family, but we were liberal and unprejudiced people. Now, I had landed in an alternate universe where a narrow norm was clearly defined by the Mormon Church. My host family isolated themselves, to make upholding their strict community rules less difficult. We prayed before every meal. Sunday was the day of the Lord and was spent exclusively in church or rather, at the nearest Mormon temple. Nicotine and alcohol were forbidden. All rules and values governing daily life were strictly conservative. Movies rated anything other than PG were deemed inappropriate, as were all things that were not downright modest.

We went on long road trips to visit their relatives. My host mom read novels to all of us during the long ride there and back. I remember being very amused to hear her censor the book as she went. She did it fluidly enough, but the tiniest pause betrayed that yet another kissing scene, violent act, inappropriate opinion, or offensive expletive had been skipped over to protect the innocence of her beloved family.

Early on during my stay, I was invited to accompany my host family to the temple on a Sunday. Nothing preached that day moved me or touched my soul. Gathering my courage, not wanting to be impolite, but seeing no other way, I honestly told my host parents that I would rather do without the temple experience in the future. Surprisingly, this was readily accepted and I was never asked again.

Unfortunately, my presence alone caused problems I never imagined. My host brother had just turned fourteen. Katie caught him a few times in front of the mirror, naked, touching himself and curiously inspecting every aspect of his physique. She was outraged, and lashed out at me: "Stay away from Greg. Since you arrived, we are having problems. You are corrupting my little boy." Felling hurt and misunderstood, I looked at her in utter astonishment. "What on Earth are you talking about? I have never tried to influence Greg."

I still spent as much time as possible ignoring my own body. It never occurred to me that Greg might have been aroused by suddenly having a very big-breasted "sister" who, to make matters worse, never wore bras. I couldn't bring myself to do so. Similar to my tampon theory, I figured if I didn't acknowledge my bulging breasts, they might change or even disappear altogether. By then, I loved wearing muscle shirts. They would make me feel manly and dangerous, like my hero *John McClane* in *Die Hard*. Paradoxically, I never once realized how in these shirts, from certain angles, my bosom would be swinging in plain sight.

Thankfully, Katie's and my differences didn't get in the way. My host parents were determined to make my stay at their home a pleasant one. Husband and wife also complemented each other perfectly. Katie was impulsive, protective, harsh, and sometimes just a bit overbearing. Calm, diplomatic, and soft-spoken, Stuart was a tempering influence. He was a man with a generous, good heart and soul. He let Katie rule their world, yet when the scales tipped too much to her uncompromising side, Stuart always managed to gently reinstate balance.

I was fascinated as well as challenged by their family life in general. Growing up with Hildegard and Konrad had instilled the conviction in me of being inevitably alone. My adoptive parents had somehow missed out on Life 101 – how to fight, then forget and forgive. Every single fight we had at home seemed to shatter our existence into a million pieces. We didn't make up. Fights were never forgotten, and over the years the chasm of bad words and intentions grew so wide that no bridge would be able to reach over the abyss.

Watching my host parents and siblings quarrel regularly, then hug each other soon after, I grudgingly had to acknowledge not knowing the first thing about family dynamics or social competence in general. Under

Katie and Stuart's tutelage, I slowly overcame, and developed a new understanding. I learned how arguing and disagreeing can be as natural in human relationships as loving and breathing.

It wasn't uncommon for other foreign students to change host families three times during their year abroad. No matter how exasperating our family life got at times though, neither my host parents nor I gave up on each other. My host siblings, Greg and Linda, remained tolerant and gentle towards me at all times.

One very important attribute I discovered within myself that year was a fierce tenacity. Deep within my soul, I knew this was a valuable learning experience precisely because it was so hard and sometimes incredibly uncomfortable. My instincts clearly told me to stay put, look deeper, and aim to understand the underlying life lessons of being stranded in a home profoundly different to my own. I stubbornly held on to this faith.

Nonetheless, I often stumbled over our denominational differences. Due to further arguments with Katie, I began working up a self-righteous, opinionated theory on how Mormons were ruining my life – these Mormons in particular – and how their entire world view was simply too suffocating and exasperating for me to comprehend. We might as well originate from two separate solar systems. Stuart could feel my indignation. In his very calm, non-threatening manner, he asked me to come have a seat next to him on the porch. We watched the bouncing tumbleweeds together. After a while he gently told me this story:

"You must be wondering who we are and why we are the way we are, live the way we live," he began. "Have you considered that we are following a way of life inherited from our great grandparents, which they in turn inherited from their great grandparents?

In the very beginning of Mormon history, we were a small minority and were persecuted for our beliefs. Our ancestors went in search of a place where they could live in peace. They heard of the State of Utah. It was said to be desolate – just harsh mountains, salt flats, and infertile land. No other settlers wanted to lay claim to it. In the hope to be left alone where no one else wanted to be, our ancestors packed all their belongings and went on their long trek to Utah.

During the time it took to travel several thousand miles, they were attacked countless times. Women and children were hiding, while their men fought for their lives. When the Mormon community finally reached Utah, there were only few of them left – most of them women and children. Only a handful of men had survived. But someone had to protect the women and children. The Elders agreed that instead of letting them fend for themselves, it would be better to change the community's way of life. So from then on, they allowed the remaining men to take more than one wife."

Stuart continued, "Many generations later, my dad was born into a family with four mothers. For them, this was simply the way life was meant to be. My dad wasn't entirely sure which mother was his birth mom. To him, it didn't matter. They were all together – eleven brothers and sisters with their mothers.

As my dad grew up, the United States government outlawed polygamy. All of a sudden, his family was forced to split up. His father, my granddad, had to make choices he couldn't possibly make. He had to choose one wife and her children over the rest of his family. But he loved them all. You can imagine, there was quite a lot of heartache during that time. My dad was a child, and couldn't understand what had happened to his moms, brothers and sisters and why they couldn't be with him anymore.

What may seem wrong to people with their particular upbringing and history may seem very natural to others. There are countless ways to live a righteous life. Who will chose which way of life is more righteous or less? Will the judges be righteous enough themselves? Only few Mormon families still hold on to polygamy, but in other parts of our lives we keep practicing what our dads and granddads have taught us. We honor their memory and keep following the path they have chosen for us to follow. Most people around the world do, no matter where they come from or what they believe."

Stuart looked at me and smiled. I looked back at him for a very long time. Neither of us spoke. My universe reshaped itself during those precious moments. It expanded. After a while I smiled back, nodded, and thanked him.

I found peace within Mormon family life afterwards. I concentrated less on the differences of belief and ideology, but more on the people themselves, their personalities, actions and intentions. Stunned, I realized how easily I had fallen into the trap of judging the lives of my hosts without knowing the first thing about the personal history that shaped them. Moreover, just because my host parents had opinions different to my own, didn't make their convictions wrong. It didn't mean they didn't care. Something dawned on me: I wasn't as unprejudiced as I had thought and needed to outgrow some preconceived notions of my own. Right and wrong were not as clearly defined as I had previously imagined.

Katie and Stuart relaxed as well and, as they had done from the beginning, they continued to amaze me by treating me as one of their own. During school breaks, we all took family holidays together. One highlight was our Thanksgiving road trip to Salt Lake City. I was amazed at the sight of the largest Mormon temple. Decked out in early Christmas lights it truly looked like something out of a fairy tale.

Come Christmas 1989, I was astonished to find a stocking for me hanging over the fireplace, right next to everyone else's. All of my host family's children were home for their semester break so the number of stockings was staggering. The next morning, surrounded by smiling siblings, I unwrapped a huge present with my name on it. Amazingly, my generous American family had given me a big ghetto blaster so I could listen to music in my room. I had tears in my eyes.

Katie also included me in Linda and Greg's horseback riding lessons. We drove two hours there and back, once a week. The short road trips through the desert wilderness were magical. Colors changed from yellow to golden to brown. A dazzling blue sky held promises of a good tomorrow.

Turquoise passion struck during a host family trip to Florida in 1990. I rediscovered my deeper love of water first in *Typhoon Lagoon*, the big water park of Disneyworld. As someone who had avoided swimming since adolescence, I surprised myself by enjoying myself tremendously and, for once, not worrying about my body. I fearlessly braved the wave pool as well as mile-long water sleds.

During our visit to the Florida Keys, I went snorkeling for the first time of my life. The Atlantic Ocean was radically different from the North Sea I had known as a child. The water was soothingly warm, all shades of turquoise dazzling me with their cheerful brightness and inviting me to jump in. Even though I must have looked more like a drowning dog than a swimming human being, I felt my connection to the ocean.

Inexperienced in the use of snorkels, I managed to half-drown myself, swallowing more water than I would have swallowed *without* the plastic tube in my mouth. I paddled out to see the first coral reef of my life, instantly getting stuck on top of the shallow reef and cutting myself on beautiful yet very sharp corals. I finally managed to extract myself and swam to the edge of the reef.

Rounding the large coral blocks, I came face-to-face with an adolescent nurse shark. Neither of us had expected to see the other. We stopped in our tracks, stared at each other for a moment, then rushed off in opposite directions. I finally reached the shore, out of breath and delighted, longing for more and feeling intensely alive. I had glimpsed boundless strength and passion within myself. For just an instant out there, in the arms of the Atlantic Ocean, I had felt beautiful.

Once back home in the dry Columbia Basin desert, Katie and I grew fonder of each other. We discovered our mutual love for puzzle games and henceforth bonded over solving elaborate puzzles together. In between homework and housework, bent over thousands of small pieces for hours, Katie shared stories of her life. I told her about my life in Germany, my hopes and dreams, and my passionate love for Heinrich. It all seemed so far away.

Greg and I became best buddies. He thought I was very cool to hang out with, since I was such a tomboy. We spent many afternoons together in the seemingly boundless desert, exploring the surprisingly abundant wildlife.

The remoteness of my host family's property seemed tedious at first. Everything was at least a one-hour drive away. Slowly, I came to understand the blessing of being removed from the world. Geographic distance to other humans besides my hosts meant less awkwardness. I needed time with myself. I needed this island of peace to recuperate from the tension of previous years.

Everyone else in my host family was very busy with their professions and hobbies, so when I wasn't out exploring with Greg, I was often home alone, enjoying the company of just the cats, dogs, and horses. I watched eagles soar over our property, or went to the riverbank and watched hunters of the Yakima tribe spearfish for salmon.

Even though she was everything I was not, my host sister Linda and I became friends and shared many pleasant moments. She was a confident young woman, smart and insightful. She was bleached blond, curvaceous, and very feminine. She was also adventurous, kind, and fun to be around. We watched movies, listened to our favorite music, and talked about our lives.

Every morning, we rode to school together in Linda's car. She loved speeding and got pulled over by the police every now and then. Watching her ensuing Oscar performances amused me to no end. Linda would start crying pitifully, at the same time working her charm and giving the police officer her sweetest smile. Marilyn Monroe would have been green with envy. More often than not, we were sent on our way with just a verbal warning.

Since Linda was a junior and I was a senior at her high school, we did not cross paths during our daily school life. Much like *Groundhog Day*, I felt I was re-living the same Hollywood clichés over and over again. Imagine every US high school drama you have ever watched in an infinite loop: the long halls with lockers lining the walls; the jocks and nerds easily distinguished by the football team jackets or the ugly horn-rimmed glasses they wore; the cheerleaders sashaying through hallways; the girls exchanging make-up tips and screaming "Oh my God!" every other sentence; colorful spirit week with everyone sporting their school colors in make-up and clothing; and the fervent patriotism of teachers and students for their school and country. School assemblies left me speechless with wonder. I never quite got the concept of school pride, football stars, and cheerleaders.

It was disconcerting how close to fiction reality actually came. To this day, I never memorized the German national anthem, yet I can still recite the Pledge of Allegiance. In the early mornings, drunk with sleep, the words "I pledge allegiance, to the flag, of the United States of America. And to the republic, for which it stands, one nation under God." had become second nature. Eyes barely open, we stood there with hands pressed firmly over our hearts, too tired and young to truly grasp the meaning of the words we were reciting.

Despite giving me the feeling of being an extra in a soap opera, American high school was an invaluable gift. European children might end up with a lot more scholastic knowledge crammed into their heads at the end of their classroom life, yet here, I felt teenagers were given more space to be themselves and explore their strengths and weaknesses.

On one hand, a large number of students were unable to spell even the simplest words by their senior year. On the other hand, I witnessed excellence on a daily basis. Both amazed me. Visual Art classes were bursting with highly talented young artists. Nerds and future Einsteins populated math and physics classes.

Many teachers were living clichés. Their positive can-do attitudes were charming as well as sometimes just a little bit over-the-top. Many were inspired and truly cared. Our chemistry teacher, Mr. Hardy, wore thick glasses in an old fashioned black frame. He had lost his left hand in a science experiment as a young man. It had been replaced with a metal hook. Admittedly, I was slightly worried whenever he performed an experiment in front of us, wondering about possible explosions, but I adored his teaching style. Never before had chemistry been presented to me in such a lively manner.

In order to graduate with a high school diploma at the end of the year, I had to take certain mandatory classes like Washington State history, American history, American literature, yet I also had space in my curriculum for the subjects closer to my heart.

I took weight lifting classes first thing in the morning, hoping that maybe working up a mountain of muscle would make my breasts disappear. I threw myself into the daily early morning workouts and did gain copious amounts of muscle. My bouncy bust didn't diminish in size, however.

In my first semester, I signed up for Visual Art. My arts teacher became a very important presence in my life, and has been ever since. Mrs. Moorcroft was a very tall lady with an even taller bush of hair on her head. Her eyebrows, hidden beneath her thick bangs, were the stuff of legend – no one had ever laid eyes on them and students were speculating wildly on what her eyebrows might look like.

Mrs. Moorcroft had an amazingly strong, good character. She had a dry, politically-incorrect sense of humor that we all adored. She could be intimidating and took the Arts very seriously.

After the first semester, she invited me into her Advanced Arts class. I was over the moon. Mo, as we lovingly called her, found the perfect balance of being strict, yet letting us explore our talents by throwing paint or clay around to our heart's delight. Everyone worked hard. The artwork I saw in our small high school workshop far surpassed anything I have laid eyes on since. I had worked on visual art projects all my life. Here, finally, was someone who actively encouraged me to pursue my talents a lot more vigorously and seriously.

A beautiful side effect of my art classes was blending in effortlessly with the other art nerds. I met thoughtful, soulful, intelligent, dare-to-be-different characters that lived their outsider status to the fullest, with dignity.

School life, and life in general for that matter, had been difficult for me in Southern Germany. American high school was not much easier. But I felt liberated nonetheless. My fellow students didn't get so hung up on my mannerisms, baggy clothes, and bad posture. To them, my being German was responsible for my weirdness, and thus more exotic and excusable.

Inspired by clichéd high school life, I decided to at least try to give a female existence a shot. I let my hair grow to shoulder length and even started shaving my legs for a while. Still missing Heinrich, I began to explore myself sexually. For the very first time in my life, I touched myself. Finally, at nineteen years of age, I learned to masturbate and experienced the ecstasy of my very first orgasm.

The sensation was so new and intoxicating, I couldn't keep myself from masturbating during class. I distinctly remember sitting in chemistry class, watching my teacher perform his latest science experiments. The American style single desk covered my entire lower body from view as soon as I leaned forward. Never moving my upper body so as not to arouse suspicion, I would use a pen to masturbate, slowly and carefully. Science classes were great foreplay; they triggered my imagination and evoked a sense of adventure. I rode my orgasmic highs while listening to the intricacies of the periodic table, or observing flames shooting from beakers. Surprisingly, neither my classmates nor my teachers ever caught me.

Masturbating only once a day just didn't seem enough. I had a lot of catching up to do. Some days, I would feel like a drug addict and keep looking for a quiet corner to get my next fix. During the long ride home with either Linda or on the school bus, I would feel restless, fidgeting until we arrived at my host parents' property. I would run through the door, exchange a few words with my host mom, and then exclaim, "I need to take care of my homework! I'll be back in time for dinner." Katie would applaud my studiousness. While she would return to her dinner preparations, I would close the door to my room, and hop under the blanket for another few rounds of vigorous masturbating.

My mind would conjure elaborate phantasies to aid in the effect of my busy fingers: much like when I was a child, I imagined being captured by unknown forces. But here, all similarity ended. In a radical departure from my childhood visions, the faceless captors of my imagination proceeded to chain me spread-eagled to a wall. While I looked on in horror, unable to move more than a few inches, they prepared the tools of my undoing. But this time, I felt no urge to escape. Instead, I provoked my masters, because I wanted them to violate my vulnerable, helpless body. Angered by my taunts, my captors used ropes to restrict my movements even further, until I couldn't move a single muscle. Then, they began to tease my vagina into one climax after another. They never penetrated me but alternated between being gentle and rough, probing my vagina and every inch of my body with their fingers, until I felt like a supernova, shining more brightly than ever before and longing to escape the boundaries of my physical form.

In the reality of my small room, inside the home of my strictly religious host family, I used my free hand to clamp my mouth shut. Meanwhile, I imagined my captors forcing a gag down my throat to stifle my rising screams of unadulterated pleasure. Riding one real-life orgasm after another, I would finally manage to disengage from my phantasy-dungeon just in time to stumble out of bed for dinner.

For most of my life, my body had seemed like a prison. At nineteen, I was still trapped and just as forlorn as ever. A traveler with the wrong passport seemingly doomed to wander the hallways of the airport I had flown into until the end of time. The chains in the dungeons of my imagination transformed confinement into rapturous bliss. It was the closest my soul had come to breaking free, thus far.

My host family had built a swimming pool on their expansive property. I never went swimming during the week, but Sundays were my private day. I had the entire property to myself until nightfall. While my hosts worshipped at the temple, I spent hours in the swimming pool, masturbating naked under a bright blue sky. I enjoyed immersing myself in the water while being all by myself. I slowly began to relax.

Then, one night, Linda and I were sitting on the floor of my room. I had my back to the window. Linda sat facing it. We were listening to *Erasure* and helping each other with our homework. While she explained a math problem to me, Linda happened to look towards the window. She froze. Time stopped. Linda kept talking, but now, with paralyzing fear in her eyes, she told me there was a man standing beyond our window, staring into the room, watching us. Every muscle in me wanted to turn around, see his face, and then run. I didn't turn around. And I didn't run.

Linda whispered, "Pretend like nothing has happened. I am going to get up smiling and relaxed as if I just need to step out for a moment. But I'll get Dad to come help us. Blink once to let me know you'll be ok." Terrified, I blinked. Linda got up slowly a moment later, a frozen smile on her lips. As soon as she cleared my doorway, I heard her run down the darkened corridor to get Stuart.

It was the first time and last time I ever heard my host dad swear. Stuart grabbed a baseball bat from the playroom and ran outside, furious. He saw a man disappearing into the shadows surrounding our property, and raced after him, shouting, "You fucking sick son-of-a-bitch! Get the hell off of my property!" Fortunately, Stuart's belly was too big and the other man was too fast. As much as I admired our dad taking instant action, I was relieved our uninvited guest didn't get a chance to hurt him.

Immediately after this incident, we used flashlights to inspect the outside of the house. What we found chilled us to the bone: boot marks and cigarette butts, both in front of Linda's downstairs bedroom windows and in front of mine. The number of prints and amount of debris in the bushes indicated a stalker who had enjoyed multiple visits.

We notified the police, of course. The two officers calmly took our statements and took note of the evidence embedded in the desert sand underneath our windows. Nodding sincerely, one of them said, "I am sorry, but there isn't much we can do at this point. Stay alert and notify us at the slightest sign of the intruder. Our best bet will be to catch him in the act."

For the next few nights, Linda and I were so scared we slept together in her bed. For the rest of the year with my host family, being home alone didn't feel good anymore. I closed all the blinds, checked behind all the corners, and was afraid to venture outside without at least one other person being home.

None of us ever saw the stalker again, or found new evidence. Even if he had snuck back up on us, we never would have known because Linda and I kept our ground floor rooms hermetically sealed and covered day and night. We figured if we couldn't see out, then he wouldn't be able to see in.

I remembered all the things I had enjoyed doing while I was alone at home. How I had masturbated on the bed, on the floor and on the living room couch. How I had gone swimming naked in the backyard pool, in an attempt to befriend my body even further.

Had a stalker watched all of that? I couldn't bear thinking about it and tried to push the memory of Linda's panicked eyes, the naked fear inside of them when seeing his face in the darkness beyond our window, from my mind. Did I roll under the fence again? Yes I did. Nothing else was conceivable under the circumstances. I had lost my sanctuary.

My love Heinrich and I wrote each other every day for the entire year. Unfortunately in 1990, email and Skype were not yet a feature of our lives. It took our letters one week to reach their destination. This made our conversation drift awkwardly out of sync, but nonetheless made our efforts beautifully romantic. My host family observed my teenage obsession with Heinrich with a detached, tolerant sense of humor. Come to think of it, they were fantastic. They all were aware of him being twenty-two years my senior, which in their very strict, conservative world must have been more than controversial.

During the first six months, my year abroad had seemed like a life sentence. During the last six months, I got progressively into the swing of things. Time started to fly by. The closer the end date came, the more I realized how much good had come from this year in another world and how amazingly lucky I was to have had this opportunity. Living with my Mormon family, whose life was so contrary to my own, gave me a first glimpse into the extreme diversity of ideologies on our planet. I fell in love with our world. And I fell in love with its people.

As high school graduation beckoned on the horizon, Stuart surprised me with an immensely personal and thoughtful early graduation present. He dedicated many hours to teaching me how to drive a car. I almost gave him a heart attack when I reversed out of our garage for the first time and crashed through the fence surrounding our property. Some wild turkeys, scavenging for food, were not impressed about being disturbed and screamed in protest. My heart beating a mile a minute, I quickly learned to go easy on the gas pedal.

While I rumbled through the countryside in my host dad's old truck, my fellow high school seniors were starting to get very excited about senior prom. Waves of anxiety washed over me at the mere thought of going. Just like in the movies, prom was a conservative affair in which students were expected to honor ancient traditions. Dress code was strict and dictated ballroom dresses for girls, tuxedos for boys. I had tried, but I knew the attempt to grow into my own body had not been successful. No way in hell was I going to wear a dress! I avoided any conversations about the event like the plague, hoping the day would pass without people noticing my absence.

Over the course of the year, I had made friends with an exchange student from New Zealand, Alice. She and two other female exchange students urged me not to miss this unique experience. They planned to go together as a group. When would we have the chance again to experience an event we had seen so many times on the big screen? After much coaxing, I finally relented and we all started shopping for dresses and makeup. I had not worn a dress since I was a child and had never worn high heels. I immediately contested any notions of wearing makeup since I had never applied any and would most likely end up looking like the evil clown in Stephen King's *It*.

In the end, I arrived at the senior prom wearing one of Alice's dresses and a pair of Linda's ballroom shoes. My breasts were significantly larger than Alice's and strained to break through the thin, bright green fabric. I stayed close to the wall and wobbled slowly from table to table. I never danced, not knowing how, but mostly being afraid of breaking my neck in those high heels. I barely made eye contact with anyone all evening. Many of my fellow seniors chuckled at my awkward attempt at being a lady. As much as I tried to have fun, senior prom ranks right up there in my Top Five Most Uncomfortable Life Events.

Two weeks before the end of my stay, Konrad tackled the long journey from Germany to Washington State. We had planned for him to be there for my high school graduation ceremony, so he could get a little taste of my life abroad.

Afterwards, we planned to go traveling together for a few weeks through the United States. We were both delighted with the idea of being just us, father and daughter reunited during a classic road trip. Surely, I had inherited my romanticism from my dad.

Blood relation is by far not as important in shaping us as people want to believe. Looking back on my life now, I know without a doubt that a big part of my character got shaped through imprinting and learning from the mannerisms of those closest to me, none of them blood-related. As life continues, as I keep engaging with other people, I learn from their example. Sometimes people's actions have such a profound impact on my life, they trigger long-term shifts in my behavior, changing me permanently for the better – I hope.

Exhausted from his long trip, Dad arrived in the Pacific Northwest. Despite my leaving Germany so unceremoniously eleven months earlier, we still shared an incredibly close bond and I was excited and happy to see him again.

Almost instantly after his arrival, however, I realized my worldview had shifted. I wasn't the same person who had left Germany a year before. My experiences in the New World had been exactly that for me – a very new world. With more exposure came an ability to compare.

Over the past months, I had experienced the calm integrity and fortitude of Stuart. While I had idolized Konrad during my childhood, he symbolizing the yin to my mom's yang, I could now see the flaws in his behavior. His self-absorbedness and lack of conviction had often led to my being hurt deeply. Looking at my childhood experiences with a lot of cultural, geographical, and mental distance made me realize that, as much as I loved my dad, he was not the hero my romantic childhood eyes had perceived. Realization and disappointment hit me like a sledgehammer. By being thrown into a completely opposite universe, I had learned to value as well as question life as I knew it.

Being the intuitive, sensitive soul that he was, Konrad felt me struggling with our relationship. I guess the only thing more obvious could have been me carrying a sign around that read, "I hate you." For once acting my age, I threw all maturity overboard and became a stereotypical adolescent menace.

Looking back now, I am grateful to know my dad was smart enough to understand he was dealing with an overwhelmed teenager. He had been so caring as to fly literally across the world to be by my side for celebrations marking the end of my successful year in the United States. But I had finally, for a short period of time, arrived in the world of teenage rebellion.

Nevertheless, Dad was immensely proud of me and happy to be reunited after our long separation. With tears in his eyes, he gave in to my every whim. He even bought me my very own high school jacket, and every other little silly memento American high school students need to mark this "coming of age" moment in their lives. He loved me so much, and it made me furious. I questioned, doubted, compared, judged – and still loved him.

My frustrations found an outlet during the formal graduation ceremony. It was a very dignified event, following traditions to the letter. All involved parties were beaming with great pride. After everyone had received their diplomas, the school band went on stage to perform for the departing seniors. My friend Alice and I were on fire. Through the first rocking tunes we looked at each other, grinned, and went off. We jumped out of our chairs and danced, head-banging and screaming our hearts out. AC/DC would have immediately recruited us as professional groupies. At first, all the other students stayed in their seats. The entire assembly hall was frozen in shock. Parents, teachers, and students stared in disbelief at the two foreign teenagers who had just lost their minds. Teenagers being teenagers, however, the other seniors couldn't sit still for very long at the sight of us going wild. As the band kept playing, half of the seniors followed suit. The assembly hall started to feel more like a legendary rock concert – with people in strange robes, wearing funny hats. And the school band played on. They performed three songs. Afterwards, in the sudden embarrassed silence, we all sat back down. A few more words were said, then we all threw our hats in the air and rushed out of the hall.

Years later, I heard that due to our impulsive act of rebellion against ancient structures, the Richland school district had almost considered cancelling all future public ceremonies.

While the other seniors partied in a pre-booked venue, I hijacked my dad's rental car, and drove across the Columbia Basin with the windows open. I was needing space and wide horizons to process the intense year and my impending departure. Letting the warm night wind embrace me, I looked far ahead, wondering where life would lead me, and marveled at the unpredictability of it all. What was in store for me, once I returned to Europe?

A few days later, Konrad and I set off on a Washington State discovery tour. We drove through the Cascade Mountains and along the Pacific Coast. Halfway up Mount Rainier, I had stopped briefly to consult our map when my dad rolled down the window and cooed, cashew nuts in his hand, "Come here, beautiful little bear!" – to a fully grown grizzly. "Are you out of your mind?" I screamed, and stomped on the gas pedal, saving him from getting mauled by the furry giant. When we reached the top of Mount Rainier, we encountered ten feet of snow in the middle of July. Wearing only t-shirts and sandals, we shivered uncontrollably and didn't stay long.

Despite little mishaps, Konrad and I enjoyed this part of our trip through the wild forests of Washington State immensely. A few more days with my host family followed, then it was time for emotional goodbyes at Pasco airport – the return to the scene of the crime – where it had all begun with whisky cokes crashing onto Stuart's fine shoes.

My dad and I departed to Portland, Oregon. From there, we rented another car and explored the entire Pacific Northwest coastline. Once arrived in San Francisco, we flew to Buffalo, New York, and visited Niagara Falls. Again southward bound, we boarded another airplane from Buffalo to Las Vegas, where we rented yet another car to explore the Grand Canyon and other natural wonders.

For four memorable weeks, we explored cities and countrysides – and our changed relationship. Full of frustration and a huge amount of angst, I picked fights with my patient dad whenever I could. The truth was, I had gotten so used to my new American way of life that I was heartbroken to have lost my Richland family and whatever little balance I had found in their midst.

I had enjoyed being away from Germany, barely ever missing the country of my birth or any elements of my life therein. During the entire year, I only remembered one attack of genuine homesickness. We were watching *All Quiet On The Western Front*, a movie about a young soldier during World War I. The cruelty and disillusionment of war didn't shock me as much as seeing the familiar landscape of green, rolling hills and small, beige houses. In a *Dr. Zhivago* moment, I felt like Yuri, unexpectedly spotting his long-lost love Lara from the streetcar: my heart felt close to breaking. I had seen the familiar landscape of my youth right in front of me, but it had been unattainable. At the end of the class, staggered by the intensity of my emotions, I had found myself enveloped in the strong arms of my equally-bewildered history teacher.

Now, during our trip across several states, memories of my year on the North American continent flooded me. I couldn't bring myself to admit to my dad how sad I was to have to leave it all behind – and how scared I was to go back. Equally, I couldn't concede how much I needed him. Not even the thought of seeing Heinrich again made me feel any better. Instead of enjoying a wonderful time with my dad, I vented my insecurities wherever we went. Not even natural wonders as immense as Niagara Falls or Grand Canyon could shake me out of my funk. My moods transformed our road trip into an unforgettable, bittersweet multi-course meal – beautiful and indigestible at the same time.

Four weeks of exploring half a continent. Four weeks of a dad trying to give his daughter the "coming of age" present of a lifetime. Four weeks of said daughter mourning a life that no longer existed, and desperately trying to process a multitude of memories, ranging from her teenage-idol-dad to her life in the Wild West. Teenagers are the world's most bizarre natural wonder. Parents are the real miracle. My dad continued loving me no matter how much I struggled or how rude I got in the process, and he has never stopped to this day.

8

Schanzengraben

Dad and I returned to Germany on a hot summer day. Being back, I realized for the first time how much my year abroad had changed me. When listening to my friends chat about their daily lives, I felt strangely detached. My small hometown felt claustrophobic, and people's worries seemed far removed from my own. Listening to former high school buddies discuss bull and bear markets, their plans to buy a house, and how their neighbors had protested a cherry tree leaning too far over a fence, I was relieved that my own world had grown larger. I had finally made the metamorphosis from intellectual to practical nomad. While beholding mighty rivers and majestic oceans, the River Enz of my childhood had lost its power to carry me further. Also, after tasting life abroad, materialistic values were the furthest thing from my mind. I longed for growth and spiritual freedom as well as for different kinds of bulls and bears – the untamed kind.

Being reunited with my beloved oma was the best part of being back in Germany. Entering her modest apartment truly felt like coming home. It wasn't her place so much as her heartfelt smile of unconditional love. She immediately started bringing out cookies and milk and we spent many hours on her couch, holding hands and feeling very comfortable with each other. Only then did I realize how much I had missed her.

I saw Hildegard for a short while. I loved her and cared about her, but my visit only served to reawaken barely forgotten memories from my childhood. Looking back on our time together evoked images of a little child lost in a forest of cacti. Their long dagger-like spines had made it impossible for me to take a step forward without drawing blood. Hildegard's mind on the other hand, had conjured a past far different from the one I recalled. Since we had been separated, all her memories of our time together had turned into tender spring meadows. Where I saw spines, she saw daisies. I almost envied her ability to not only forget completely but, at the same time create memories as beautiful as Ikebana masterpieces. I stayed a few days, trying with all my might to be gentle and smiley. I left with a deep sigh and a heavy heart while Mom waved happily and called after me, "Goodbye, mein Schatz! It was so wonderful to see you. I can't wait to get together again." I hoped one day I would be able to forgive her the many hurts she had inflicted. Until then, I needed distance to sustain a balance in our relationship.

A few days after my return to Germany, over dinner, I had a confession to make.

"Dad, I will never go back to Business College. I don't belong there. I want to become an artist."

Konrad looked shocked, as if I had just said I had cancer. "Wait a minute. Let's think about this."

I stopped him short. "Dad, there is nothing to think about. I want to study art. And I won't be able to do it in Germany if I don't finish my *Abitur* at the college. No university will accept me. I'll have to look elsewhere. But that's just as well. My year in the States has been one of the best and most important experiences of my life. It will be good to go away again."

Dad saw my sincerity, and nodded, grudgingly granting the possibility. "Let me know what you find."

My American high school art teacher, Mrs. Moorcroft, had inspired me. I was determined and started to research the possibilities of studying art in other European countries. Searching through the Internet was not yet an option. It was still in its infancy, with far fewer websites and exasperatingly slow connection speeds. I called friends and traveled through Europe in search of alternative college education.

One factor influenced my search of a suitable path much more than I was ready to admit at the time: I was still madly in love with Heinrich. He lived with his mother in a tiny village close to the Swiss town of Schaffhausen. Ideally, I wanted to be based somewhere close to where he lived.

It just so happened that the Zuercher Schule fuer Gestaltung (The Zurich Academy of Visual Arts) – only one hour away from Heinrich's village – was the first art college to respond to my inquiries. I was just in time for their yearly application procedures, which were designed to give opportunities to any young artist who had talent, whether or not they had the proper accreditation. An extraordinary portfolio would help open doors for those who hadn't done their *Abitur* or any other equivalent form of higher education.

Within four months, I had prepared an extensive portfolio as well as a special project assigned by the art academy. My entire being was focused on this one goal. I remember looking at my portfolio later on and hardly recognizing any of my artwork. My yearning heart and soul, wanting nothing more than to once more leave a country tainted by depressing memories, conspired to help me create art way beyond my years.

During an intense three days in Zurich, I attended all the workshops mandatory for finalizing the application process. The Academy wanted to verify that all applicants had in fact created their own portfolios. Under the watchful eyes of academy lecturers, hundreds of us spent the three days drawing, painting, and sculpting our young hearts out.

I returned to Germany to await the Academy's decision. After a few weeks of biting my fingernails to the quick and driving everyone around me totally crazy, a letter finally arrived from the Zuercher Schule fuer Gestaltung. I sat in my room, afraid to open it. I stared at it, willing the answer to be "yes", knowing full well that the decision had already been made one way or the other. So I finally took a very deep breath and ripped open the envelope.

I jumped up, and ran into the living room, waving the acceptance letter like a flag and beaming at my dad as if I had just won a Nobel Prize.

"Dear Stefanie, we are pleased to inform you that your application has been approved," I read aloud.

Out of roughly one thousand applicants, only one hundred had been chosen for the basic training year – and I was one of the few. My whoop of joy could be heard deep into the Black Forest.

Dad couldn't help but be swept along by my enthusiasm. He wrapped his arms around me and said, "I am so very proud of you. Congratulations. But – are you sure you'll be ok? I'd be terrified, moving all by myself into a big, foreign city."

I just kept holding on to him and nodded vigorously. Yes, I was sure. In fact, I was so happy, I nearly burst like an over-ripe melon. Unknown adventures lay ahead of me. Like a meadow, cast into darkness by an eclipse, then being bathed in glowing light with the re-emergence of the sun, my life was improving and the skies seemed instantly brighter.

A few months of impatient preparations followed. I cleared out my childhood room because I couldn't imagine myself ever moving back to Germany. Together, Dad and I transformed my old room into a cozy guest bedroom for anyone, including me, who ever wanted to come visit.

Dad struggled with the thought of being apart again, this time for an indeterminate period. But I reminded him that at least this time, we would only be a three-hour drive apart.

Meanwhile, Heinrich and I were over the moon. Soon we would be able to see each other much more often. Living together was not an option I was prepared to consider, though. I craved independence.

Again, I did not have the option to search for a small room or apartment from a distance. The Internet was still a few years away from being commonly used. I had to travel to Zurich every weekend to look through newspaper classifieds and notice boards in coffee shops, colleges, and universities.

Weeks of frantic searching brought no results. Then, I heard rumors of a farmhouse in Heinrich's neighboring village. The five young people sharing this farmhouse were looking for an additional roommate. When I went to have a look, I was instantly charmed, as much by the people and their alternative lifestyle, as by their ruggedly self-renovated farmhouse. It was bright and spacious, located just at the edge of a small village with only two hundred inhabitants. My rental agreement would be for six months only, by which time the farmhouse occupants planned to convert my room into a shared study. The only disadvantage was the isolated location. The half-hour distance from the nearest train station necessitated commuting for two hours each day by a combination of bicycle, bus, train, and tram to get to the Academy and back. I didn't care. I welcomed my lucky break of finding a roof over my head just days before starting college, and six months was ample time to find a more conveniently located home.

Moving day arrived and I was on my way, driving a small van with my most treasured possessions over the border into Switzerland. My chosen destination was relatively close to where I grew up, both in geographical distance and culture, yet still far enough away and different enough to give me hope. I was in search of myself, as well as a place where I belonged.

My new housemates proved to be a family beyond my wildest dreams. These people looked beyond my hunchback posture and shy yet ever-present smile to see the hidden treasure underneath.

The closer we got to the six-month mark and my departure from the group, the sadder I became. I hadn't even started searching for a new home yet, since I couldn't imagine leaving this enchanted house. "The elephant in the room" sat at the table with us each evening. I needed someone to break the silence and give me a final deadline – a rough wake-up call to kick-start me into searching for a new home and allow me to give up hope of remaining with them.

One evening at dinner, I couldn't stand the tension anymore and blurted out, "I know I promised to move out after six months, but I really don't want to leave."

Five sets of eyes were on me. Their faces lit up with relieved smiles. One of them laughed out loud, and looking around at the others, said, "Perfect. We have discussed with each other for weeks. And we all agree we can do well without a shared study. We don't want you to leave, either."

It was one of those rare moments when time simply ceased to exist. The room seemed to grow brighter. My housemate continued, "We would have said something sooner, but we didn't want to influence your decision. So we just waited and hoped you would do exactly what you just did – let us know that you'll stay a little longer. Welcome to the family." It was one of the happiest evenings of my life.

We grew our own produce and made our own yoghurt, cream, and butter. Once every three months, we butchered some of our many rabbits. Since I loved to eat meat, I felt I needed to face the challenge and if not be a hunter, at least be able to be a butcher.

Jochen, one of my housemates and quiet leader of our small farmhouse community was usually the one who killed the fluffy animals. He then taught me how to skin and process our bunnies, separating the edible internal organs like liver and heart carefully from inedible parts like the bladder. Their little hearts were a special delicacy and had to be cooked the same day.

Helping with carefully preparing the meat for storage, I began to understand myself better. A romantic and dreamer at heart, I apparently also had a very practical, down-to-earth side to my personality and possessed the courage to make tough decisions.

Apart from producing most of our own food, we also chopped wood for our stove, which was connected to a water-circulating central heating system. In late fall, we would transport whole trees into our backyard. We would then spend several weekends together, chopping the trees into manageable logs. It was truly a team effort.

Each wood-chopping day towards noon, Sofia, Jochen's partner, would venture inside to make a healthy broth for all of us. We would enjoy our lunch break outdoors, wrapped up in blankets, sitting on the not-yet-processed tree trunks. Working hard and laughing together, we would continue into the late evening hours, finally giving in to exhaustion and dragging ourselves into our respective beds at the end of the day. It was a wonderful, happy kind of exhaustion I could never get enough of.

Each of us would cook one evening a week. At first, my culinary attempts were about as enjoyable as eating rotten restaurant leftovers from a dumpster. Meat, pasta or vegetables all looked a lot like puree and I used incompatible herbs. Everyone took it with good humor though. Looking like they had just taken their first sip of cod liver oil, they would give me a shaky thumbs-up and groan good-naturedly, "Fantastic effort!" After my first few attempts, one of my helpful housemates seemed to always materialize just in time, joining me at the stove and casually throwing in the odd additional herb or two, to prevent disaster. Within a few months, I could improvise on my own, with truly delicious results.

After dinner, our little farmhouse family enjoyed movie evenings together at least once a week. Since Sofia's room was the only one with a TV set, we would all pile up on her couch. Six people, all comfortably crowded together, would watch thrillers but also family movies, since Jochen was a single dad raising his little son Peter.

One evening we decided to watch *ET*. Steven Spielberg's sentimental science fiction fairy tale moved us all to tears. We trusted each other and felt entirely comfortable openly sharing our emotions. When *ET* lifted his long, knobbly, brown finger towards the stars and just wanted to phone home, we held on to each other. My heart opened as I realized that at least for now, unlike *ET*, I didn't need to phone home anymore – I had found a true home right there amongst my housemates.

Whenever I worked on a drawing, painting, or photo project for college, Peter would sit next to me, watching with his big round eyes. He seemed to be mesmerized by my artwork. I would share some of my paper, oil pastels, or acrylic paint with him so he could explore his own growing imagination. Sitting on the floor of my room together, we would both be fully focused on developing our creations. We enjoyed each other's company and to my astonishment, I became a role model for Peter. Can you imagine my even more profound wonder and excitement when I ran into Peter almost twenty years later and found out he had become an artist himself? I had inspired him to the extent that he had attended art school, creating comic strips and movie projects. By the time we met again, Peter was already establishing himself as a promising young cameraman within Switzerland's film scene. What a humbling, magical privilege to have had such a lasting influence on someone's life, simply by sharing what I loved.

About seven months into my studies, Heinrich and I began quarreling. He still loved me, whereas I was slowly but surely falling out of love. I had no intentions of hurting him, but my life had expanded and, with the passage of time, our paths had begun to seem incompatible to me.

Heinrich sought stability. During most of our time together, I had been grateful for the peacefulness this had given our relationship. It had grounded me and given me a degree of safety. During my first year in Zurich, I began developing into a young adult who was eager to explore. I started feeling trapped in my relationship with Heinrich. All the cells of my heart and brain seemed to unite in chanting an alluring chorus: "Go! Go and seek new adventures. There are more and better things waiting for you."

Nothing had changed with respect to my body. Concerning our sexual relationship, all I felt was agony and confusion. Due to his own timidity, Heinrich never sensed the extent of my revulsion towards our lovemaking. Not wanting to hurt him, I blamed my busy schedule and managed to limit our sexual encounters to only a few times per month. Each time, Heinrich would cherish me with his big, loving eyes while enjoying every second of entering me. I would hold him, whisper how much I loved him, and endure. It took all my energy to hide my mounting discomfort and frustration. I knew I needed to stop protecting Heinrich – for both of our sakes.

One evening, almost three years after we had first professed our love, I rode my bike to Heinrich's home for one last time. We sat in his garden having dinner. I reached over the table, took his hand into mine, and said,

"I am so sorry Heinrich, but I can't go on. I still care for you, but I don't feel as deeply as I used to."

Heinrich had always been a gentleman. Even now, as I broke his heart, he nodded understandingly, and said, "It's okay. I understand."

I was relieved, when suddenly he began crying. Tears quietly streaming down his face like water from a faucet, he whispered, "All the best. I will miss you terribly."

As I rode through manicured Swiss forests towards my farmhouse home, I cried as well. Despite my heavy heart, I knew I had done the right thing, and hoped Heinrich would find happiness.

My life with Jochen, Sofia and our group at the farmhouse had a strong impact on my developing social life. While growing up, I had witnessed my parents' heaviness whenever they were around other people. On the rare occasions when they invited someone into our home, my mother would become hysterical two days before our guests arrived. She would attempt to clean our house, getting increasingly resentful with the fact that she had to clean and cook for other people. It never occurred to her that socializing should, in essence, be a positive experience both for herself and for her guests.

My childhood birthday parties were the rare exception. Hildegard would get a grip on her neuroses once a year, and do her best to let me have a good time with my few buddies and friends.

In the sunny afternoon, we would set up a garden-hose-shower on our terrace for us kids to play in. I would whittle long sticks I had found in the forest. Later on, my friends and I would make campfire twists in our fireplace and do our best to outdo each other with spooky stories.

Even after these quiet evenings around the softly crackling fire, my mom would start ranting about the other children as soon as they left our house. As a result, I never quite learned what it really meant to be a casual host, let alone a laid-back friend.

Living with my Mormon host family had been an eye-opener, but had been unusual as well, since Katie and Stuart essentially valued being isolated from anyone but their fellow parishioners.

More than any prior social experience, my Swiss farmhouse family brought an enlivening breeze into my life. A warm-hearted, welcoming atmosphere prevailed. Our kitchen was downstairs and we would only close its folding glass doors during the night. Every day, friends would show up unannounced, bearing a bottle of wine as a present. We often ate dinner on a large handcrafted wooden table, sitting on benches in front of our house. Villagers would walk past and would always be invited to sit down and enjoy a glass of wine with us.

I got a rousing glimpse into how fulfilling sharing a home and getting to know other people can be. Guests were nothing special to my housemates, but rather a natural extension of our household and patchwork family. No one would go into a frantic dash to clean beforehand or afterward. If someone stayed overnight, they were given a key to the house so they did not have to depend on our schedules.

Our open-door-policy stuck with me for the rest of my life. It was enchanting and permanently unlocked doors inside my own mind. I learned to treasure friends beyond measure, and from then on, always enjoyed making time for guests, no matter my circumstances.

After a year of inspiring each other, our farmhouse community broke apart. My friends were moving on, buying their own houses, heading towards new private and professional adventures. I searched and quickly found another housing community to move into. Even though it wasn't bad, I couldn't shake the feeling of having stepped back through the closet from a colorful *Narnia* into a grey reality.

During my remaining four years at the Academy, I moved ten times. But no matter where I moved, I never again found as deep a connection with my housemates as I had in that very first year of being an independent adult. I was tremendously lucky to have had the privilege of experiencing a true community – even if only for a short, very precious time.

I rode an emotional roller coaster from the very beginning of my art studies at the Academy. Art is impossible without reflection and self-awareness. With every art project, with every group critique session discussing our work, I would discover more about myself. Much of what I discovered made me uncomfortable.

I undeniably still tended to avoid conflict whenever possible. I seemed to be incapable of clearly voicing my needs and desires. I didn't say "no" when I should and I still dealt with any sort of confrontation as I would a blazing furnace: circling it warily at a comfortable distance.

Seeking solace and strength, I would go for long walks, which would inevitably bring me to the remnants of Zurich's medieval moat. The

Schanzengraben stretched the length of the entire old city and all the way to the lake. Romantic walkways followed the dark green water. Lower than street level, the eerily quiet sanctuary was only a step away from the metropolis' vivid heartbeat of clubs, theaters, bars, and shops.

I would sit on one of the many benches that were spaced along the moat in regular intervals. Mesmerized by the rich smell of algae and the sunlight transforming the water in the old moat into a sea of jade, I would practice complex battles of wit inside my mind. After only one hour in my sanctuary, I would feel confident to hold my own during next day's discussions at the Academy. But as soon as I opened my mouth to respond to the critical questions of my peers, all I would be able to do was clear my throat and say, "Yes".

The other students mocked me because I smiled often, nodded my head like a bobble-head doll and labeled everything as "fantastic". Being aware of the fine line between enthusiasm and liking everything indiscriminately, I felt foolish and frustrated, sometimes even disgusted with myself. I wanted to be a person of honor, not someone unable to stand up for herself.

As soon as I felt safe, alone with my own thoughts at the Schanzengraben or amongst friends and family, I *did* have strong opinions. I often even verged on being arrogant about them. But with fellow students and strangers, I kept falling into the same pattern of smiling brightly and circling issues diplomatically. Would I ever learn?

My sexuality was another grave concern of mine. Since Heinrich, I had thrown myself into multiple one-night stands with males and females alike. This should have aided me in discovering more about myself. It didn't. Whether my men and women were handsome or plain, intriguing or boring, gentle or harsh made no difference. I never enjoyed having sex with any of them. I never felt anything except the urge to scream with exasperation, or – only slightly more diplomatically – ask what time it was.

I was getting tired of baggy sweaters, but covering up still seemed to be the best option. I hated everything about my physical self – my breasts in particular. Alone, I would stare at my body. I would touch it. But it remained stubbornly sullen and unresponsive.

Apart from the obvious discomfort and bloodbath, my period was an additional monthly reminder of my gender being a complex mystery still in need of solving. I began to wonder whether I was simply a very screwed up individual. I was depressed and, for the second time in my life, contemplated suicide often. Perhaps I had simply been born on the wrong planet? Perhaps I would do better to retreat into nothingness until a better world or body materialized in front of my drifting, shapeless self?

Feeling lost led to impulsive actions. I was incapable of managing Dad's monthly allowance. If I saw something I felt would help transform me more into whoever I was, I would need to have it immediately – even if it cost a thousand dollars. Leather jackets, especially heavy black ones with a dense, ferocious smell made me feel safe and tough. I ended up borrowing money from acquaintances without knowing if I would ever be able to pay them back. Some months I barely survived.

Eventually, I tried getting a student loan from the German government. I needed signatures from both my parents for the application. Dad signed immediately but Hildegard panicked. She imagined everything from hidden paragraphs in which I was selling my body or soul, to the State hunting her down in the future, to demand their money back. Her adamant refusal to sign anything made it impossible for me to acquire any extra funds.

Thankfully, it was legal for me as a foreigner in Switzerland to work during my semester breaks. I found work in a movie theater and worked seven days a week, each week, during every semester break.

During the semester, I was able to make money modeling nude for art classes. As strange as it may seem given my discomfort with my body, I did not mind being completely exposed in front of a big group of people who stared at every detail of my physique for hours at a time. While modeling, I would feel detached from my body. Also, their gazes weren't sexual but rather neutral, with a focus on the canvas rather than me, the actual person who was sitting in front of them stark naked. Looking at the sculptures, drawings and paintings after each session was a mind-altering experience. Every single art student depicted me differently. They interpreted what they saw, and made it their own. I was no longer a female body. I was hundreds of different shapes, lines, curves, shadow, and light.

The first year at the Academy was designed to be an introduction. Students were exposed to all forms of visual art, anything from technical drawing to painting, and multimedia installations. We learned as many techniques as possible, exploring our strengths and weaknesses. One lesson I took away from this intensive initiation was how much it helps to learn as much as possible about our chosen artistic field. It enables us to slowly develop our own language and character. We look at established techniques and decide for ourselves what to incorporate into our work and what to rebel against.

Over the course of my basic year, I lost my heart to black and white photography. It was still the dark ages – literally: many hours were spent in the darkroom developing film and prints. I loved prowling through Zurich's surrounding landscapes with my Nikon FM2. So much more than just a camera, it was a natural extension of my eyes and hand.

After deciding on a photography major, I had to go through a tough application process all over again since the Academy did not just advance us automatically to the next educational level.

As I had done before, I focused my entire being on the task at hand. I spent months in the darkroom, battling the perfect grey scale until the early morning hours. After the perpetual darkness and red lights, the sunrises greeting me outside after a long night's work took on a magic quality. I wondered if the first known painters in Lascaux had felt the same, after creating their cave paintings. Had they labored for hours by the light of a small flame, immersed in a dream-like state? Had they almost forgotten about the lively brilliance of colors and sunshine, only to be reborn into the world after finishing their intricate works of art?

Three hundred of us dreamt of becoming photographers and applied for the "Fotoklasse" that year. Only ten of us were chosen. Bursting with glowing pride and happiness, I found myself amongst them. Another exciting – and daunting – four years of study lay ahead of me.

Our professors were one of a kind. They ranged from compassionate coaches to eccentric maniacs. From day one, I ran into a wall. This wall had a name: Andreas Gerber, a well-known German art photographer from the Eighties. I was still smiling and talking my way diplomatically out of almost every conflict that arose. Andreas would have none of it. He would look at me, smile his enigmatic smile, and say, "These tactics won't work with me. If you want to get anywhere in life, there is only one way to go – straight ahead. No short cuts, no evasive action."

The man was my nemesis and my salvation. As much as I longed to avoid verbal conflict of any kind, I never backed away from a challenge per se. I welcomed it. Challenge incited growth. So when it came to choosing a mentor, I picked Andreas precisely because I knew he would be the firm wall I would crash my head against time and again.

During his mentor meetings, it was never my work we analyzed, but rather my personality since it was reflected in the choice of every subject or perspective. I would say, "Well, I don't know. It is art. It is what it is."

Andreas wouldn't let me get away with it and immediately retort, "You and I both know that's a load of crap. You can do better than that. Why do you think you chose that particular time of day and angle for the shot?'

Sometimes the uncomfortable people in our lives inspire our greatest learning curves. My personal and artistic battle with Andreas became an obsession. No encounter was without mental pain. No discussion ended without conflict. Yet I couldn't get enough. I felt myself mature under his scrutiny, and as much as I hated him for it, I was glad for it. He provoked me to dig deeper, to not accept things as given, and ultimately, to grow as a human being.

Using simple examples, he explained the absence of coincidence in art. "Imagine, you walk into a room with two chairs, one occupied, one unoccupied. Which one do you choose to photograph? What influences your choice? As a photographer, everything you capture on film reveals a tiny piece of the puzzle that is you."

Consequently, even more than Andreas, art became my salvation. Photography became the tool I had needed to discover myself. First, I focused on landscapes, allowing my melancholy, doubts, and inner demons to materialize in my haunting depictions of hills and forests in the early evening light.

But whatever I showed Andreas, it wasn't strong enough, good enough, or personal enough. He showed me his own projects. They were rough and very personal photographs, oozing an almost primal sexuality. My mentor looked at me with his most direct gaze and said, "Do you understand yet? Be hard on yourself, painfully honest and clear, or you will never find your answers."

He shocked me and confronted me over and over again because he cared. Behind this confused young woman with hardly a concept of who she was, he knew, hid a unique individual with powerful artistic potential. He seemed to sense my emotional turmoil like a shark following the scent of blood. And for him, transforming turmoil into art was as natural and logical as breathing.

In the break between my first and second year at Photography College, I joined a summer workshop in Prague, offered by Czech photographers.

A classmate, Francesca, came along for the adventure in her orange Volkswagen camper bus. During that month, living in our cheerful, rolling home, we discovered the Czech Republic through the eyes of our Czech mentors.

I soon discovered that their mentality was much like my own, tending towards introspection and melancholy. The Czech artists created a mystical photographic universe in which all their subjects seemed to be suspended in perpetual twilight. Their sensitivity fascinated me.

It had been an exhausting year at the Academy. Only now did I fully comprehend how exhausted I had become under Andreas' constant scrutiny. He believed in destroying his students so as to find their core and build them up again from the rubble. As much as I appreciated his good intentions, not being attacked for a while rested my soul.

At the end of the summer, touched and inspired by four weeks of intense collaboration, I felt myself rising from the ashes. A group exhibition of our work in a small gallery in the ancient city of Prague marked the end of this memorable workshop. As Francesca and I headed home in our joyful mobile home, we looked forward to our next year of school.

Buoyed by my Czech experiences, I worked harder than ever in my second year. Besides doing the projects dictated by Andreas, I began to explore my vision more thoroughly by working on my own projects at the same time.

Visiting international artists often came to teach us workshops. They would stop in their tracks, with intrigued expressions on their faces, whenever they saw some of my extracurricular activities in the darkroom. Many of them talked with me privately, encouraging me to show what I was doing, maybe even find a publisher. But I was too young and unsettled, too intimidated by the world and its possibilities to tackle such an ambitious endeavor.

During my fourth semester, Andreas sent me on a quest to explore my photojournalistic capabilities. With the crooked smile he used whenever he meant to tickle one of my weaknesses, he said, "Do some research and choose a refugee camp. Spend time with the people there and tell the photographic story of their flight from injustice. Some of them might even have faced certain death if they had stayed on. Try to express that urgency, that intensity, in your pictures."

I was intrigued and determined to excel at this exercise. After some searching, I found a refugee camp harboring Albanian intellectuals. It was located in a run-down apartment building at the edge of town. Even so, racists found their way there quite frequently. Anonymous protesters would throw bricks through already shattered windows, or the refugees would wake up in the morning to find racist slogans spray-painted onto their walls. The Albanian families did their best to protect their children and survive the undignified treatment until the Swiss government legally accepted them. This would enable them to move to a regular apartment, stay long-term and acquire a work permit. Until then, they all suffered through the agony of uncertainty. Sitting at home day and night, afraid to fall asleep, staring at their walls, they tried hard to keep a low profile and not be overcome by fear and desperation.

The more I learned about them, the more mortified I felt at having to photograph them. I spent days amongst the families, listening to their stories, admiring their courage and resilience. We talked far into the night, amongst the armada of cockroaches that had long ago taken over the dilapidated building. The Albanian intellectuals told me about their past. They recounted their meaningful lives as college professors, poets, and philosophers, which had inevitably caused them to be seen as a political threat in their home country.

As the weeks went past, Andreas kept asking me about my photographic progress. There was none. I never photographed. Talking to the refugees, I felt like a traitor who had come professing peace with the full intention of using the loaded gun in his pocket. The camera, hidden in my backpack under the table, seemed to emanate heat. Surely, at some point the shameful apparatus would ignite.

One day before my final deadline, I couldn't put photographing off any longer. Terrified of invading the refugee's privacy, I made my way to Schanzengraben with a bottle of Baileys. Talking to myself, soothed by the peaceful, green stream and a procession of quacking ducks, I downed the entire bottle. Then around 1 p.m., I took a bus to the refugee camp and photographed all day.

Still drunk, I rushed to the Academy darkroom in the late evening and developed the photos. I hoped to get at least a handful of presentable prints out of my foggy journalistic endeavor. When I finally opened the developing canister to examine the negatives, I stared at roll after roll of empty film.

It dawned on me then. I had been so drunk I had forgotten to remove the lens cap. The refugees had either not noticed or exhibited extreme self-restraint in watching my comical attempts at being a photojournalist. They must have collapsed with laughter after I left. I consoled myself with the thought of at least having brought some humor into their unsettled lives.

Andreas was appalled by my unprofessionalism. I was ashamed to have failed but it dawned on me that my heart beat to a different rhythm. As a photojournalist, an emotional distance to the events unfolding in front of our eyes is imperative in order to be able to stay close to the action and deliver. But I didn't know the first thing about emotional distance.

From that day onward, I knew I would never become a photojournalist. To me, the photographic story would always become irrelevant in the face of a struggling individual.

Mid-way through our course of study, we had to pass examinations – again. It was the Academy's way of separating the wheat from the chaff. At first I almost became the chaff. I failed the exams. I had never seen Andreas so enraged.

He pulled me to the side and said in a dangerously quiet voice, " You are a non-committal coward. I need you to stop pussyfooting around and take a stand, artistically as well as personally. I am dead-tired of you hiding behind a wall of friendliness."

I dry-swallowed, hurt but knowing full well he was right.

He continued, "You know, I have seen so many students who just don't have what it takes. No matter how hard they work, they never create anything of substance. But you, you have it all: the intensity, the talent, and the potential. I *hate* to see you waste it all by not focusing and being too afraid to stand up to your demons. So this is it: are you finally willing to stand up for who you are? If yes, I will give you another chance. We will grant you one additional year, at the end of which you'll have to repeat the exams. You can tell me your decision after the weekend." With that, he stalked off.

I spent the entire weekend sitting at Schanzengraben, torturing myself with self-hatred, doubt, hurt pride, and a good measure of anger. On Monday, ashamed, still angry, but understanding his tough-love support, I found Andreas in the hallway on the way to his office. I stopped him and said, "Thank you for offering me a second chance. I'll be happy to accept."

He kept walking, clapped me on the back as he passed and said, "Of course. I knew you would."

The next year, I insisted on keeping Andreas as my mentor. I loved and hated everything about him. Andreas possessed a dangerous mixture of intelligence, intuition and impulse. I knew he had counted on driving me into a rage so he could succeed in pushing me far out of my comfort zone into a state of open creation.

It worked. I was on fire. Finally shaken awake, I focused with total intensity. My camera and I were inseparable. I reinvented the grey scale in the darkroom and teased a perfect brilliance out of my negatives onto the finished print. Sometimes I dedicated many hours on one print alone, striving for perfection.

I began to defend my vision and got so obsessive about my artwork that I locked myself into the school dark rooms at night and worked until the early morning hours.

Another classmate of mine, Ellie, often joined me during my nightly excesses. Since we were supposed to vacate the premises at midnight, we had to stay alert and watch out for security guards. Normally, we would turn off all lights and jump into the maintenance closet as soon as we heard someone coming. Some nights though, we would get too absorbed in our work and forget to watch our backs. All of a sudden, the door to the darkroom would be ripped open and a flashlight beam would blind us, at the same time destroying the prints we had not yet transferred into the fixative bath. Ellie and I didn't so much regret getting caught as we regretted having to leave the premises before we were able to finish our work for the night. We became oddly proud of our collection of disciplinary warnings.

Soon, my second round of exams loomed on the horizon. I dug deep for a slam-dunk, and pulled a special photo project out of my subconscious. I worked for weeks like a person possessed as I travelled back into my childhood. I physically visited all the places where I had found moments of peace – crawling through bushes, under balconies, into the darkest corners of our cellar, under my blanket, into my Steinway hideaway, and through remote corners of our local forest where I used to build caves. I photographed close to the ground, in an attempt to capture a child's perspective. I tried to figuratively immerse myself in foliage, to yank my viewers into secluded corners within my mind. There, they would feel the raw power of my vulnerability, my despair, and my dreams of being a romantic hero. The photographs were complemented with uncensored written accounts of my childhood fantasies. In them I almost died, was hunted, bound and tortured. But in the end, no matter how dark and brutal any of these fantasies had been, I had always prevailed.

On the day of the exams, Andreas and his fellow professors went through my portfolio. They fully expected me to fail again. I had consulted them less after flunking the first time, and many of my extra hours had gone unnoticed.

At first, they spent about an hour, evaluating the portfolio I had submitted. Then the door opened and Andreas waved me into a classroom in which my work was spread out over the tables. As I walked towards them, the professors looked at me in open astonishment. Andreas's eyes sparkled as he looked at me with an odd mixture of excitement, pride, and deadly seriousness. For the first time I could see respect in his eyes. Nodding gravely, he said: "This is only the beginning."

9

Northern Mediterranean Sea

I advanced into the final stages of my photography major. In only two more years, I would graduate with a Bachelor of Fine Arts. My course of study was divided into a two-step program of Basic and Main Studies. The Basic Studies – in my case three instead of two years – were meant to be a rite of passage. Those who showed enough prowess in both a technical and a psychological sense were allowed to continue with Main Studies.

Having proved myself, I was now trusted to work mostly unsupervised. I would still agree on projects with my mentor, but only had to meet with him once a month to discuss any progress or decline.

By this time, I lived with one of my classmates in an old house in the outskirts of Zurich. His name was Truong. After failing my first set of exams a year earlier, I had been transferred into his class. We had been best friends ever since.

Truong had escaped from Vietnam with his parents when he was just a child. He had grown up first in France, then in Switzerland. The hardships my friend had endured had molded him into an incredibly thoughtful young man. We enjoyed talking late into the night, pondering philosophical questions or watching horror movies.

Divided by two, our rent was negligible since our house was scheduled for demolition. There was no warm water and no shower. Our toilet was in a tiny shack in the secluded garden.

When we first moved in, we discovered a chimney, but no open fireplace or heater. Freezing half to death at the onset of winter, we decided to illegally punch a big hole into our chimney wall. We stuck a rusty metal pipe into the rugged hole. The other end of the pipe, we connected to an old wood stove we had found in the garbage. A local farmer gave us enough wood to last the winter and we were set. Fire hazard or not, we welcomed the unregulated heat from our little stove.

In the toilet shack, we learned to do our business with lightening speed. Oh God, it was cold. I would run out, dump what I had, and run back inside. After a few months, I set new shitting-time records. Toilet visits in the middle of the night were a special agony.

In the mornings, we would boil hot water, then attempt to shower over the kitchen sink. Mice watched through holes in the ceiling, rats through holes in the floor and, believe it or not, cows stuck their heads through the window and joined the party.

Sometimes Truong and I were so low on money, our whole month of cooking was limited to spaghetti and rice, seasoned alternately with olive oil or just salt and pepper. So we got resourceful and found the local Hare Krishna temple. The monks there gave out free food in exchange for listening to their chanting during lunch. My stomach would grumble audibly in expectation of nourishment as I tried to look interested to respect our hosts. In all honesty, my sole focus rested on the plentiful buffet.

The Academy expected us to visit galleries regularly. We did. Famished Truong and I could be found at every exhibition opening, appreciating the artwork – and the free tasty nibbles and champagne, too. We worked the floor, engaged in conversations, and nodded appreciatively, all the while grabbing as many appetizers as we could.

Another source of food were high-end malls. All sorts of tidbits were up for grabs to entice rich customers to open their wallets and walk home carrying bags stuffed with pricey meat, cheese, as well as assorted rare delicacies. Truong and I sampled, nodding while pretending to assess the quality as though we were connoisseurs, and left without spending a cent.

One afternoon, I had just given in to my impulse to buy yet another unnecessary and pricey leather jacket. I had gone hungry for days and my monthly subsidy from my dad wasn't due into my bank account for another few days. While stumbling moodily towards the Academy, I noticed a pedestrian in front of me dropping a half-eaten sandwich onto the sidewalk. Instinct kicked in as if I was a survivor after an apocalypse who had raided city after city unsuccessfully before finally coming upon an edible scrap of food. I swooped onto the precious half-sandwich. Five people had already stepped on it but all my reason had vanished. I stuffed it into my mouth.

I was deeply ashamed by this personal low. Truong was far more in control of his actions but had scarcer funds. His parents were poor and couldn't help him as much as they would have liked to. Yet even he hadn't stooped to my level. Clearly I needed to get a grip on my compulsive shopping habits, or eat garbage for years to come.

My Vietnamese friend was a highly intriguing young artist who managed to combine intellectual and sensitive depth. Our working styles were polar opposites. Truong was a thinker. He intellectualized and analyzed for weeks in the initial stages of his projects. Then he went systematically to work, creating his masterpieces. Conversely, my work thrived on feelings and impulse. Ideas would topple all over themselves in my mind. I started burning through piles of material, shooting hundreds of photographs, comparing, evaluating, and developing my projects on the go, through trial and error, following gut instinct.

After years of exploring every aspect of landscape photography, I started experimenting with self-portraits. I didn't feel photogenic – quite the contrary. My body felt raw, bordering on surreal. I tried to capture my physical sense of misshapen roughness in my photographs.

Andreas became very supportive of my work. The confrontational aspect of my images and the increasingly brutal honesty they reflected intrigued him. "You are touching on something important here," he said. "Keep going! Your self-portraits aren't pretty and they're not easy to look at. That's what gives them a very unique quality."

Motivated by my mentor's support, I gave it all I had and worked without pause. I explored my body on camera. My lens travelled along the ambivalent landscape of my body, explored my folds of fat, my curves and angles. I masturbated and captured moments of orgasm. My photographic obsession with the alienness of my body wasn't providing the answers I sought. Yet, without being aware at the time, each picture I took and contemplated brought me closer to at least part of the answer of who I truly was.

For a while, Andreas and I were able to discuss progress in his mentor meetings. He told me, "I am proud of you. I am finally seeing evidence of the raw artistic potential I had known existed in you from the beginning."

Under his tutelage, I exhibited my work a few times in Academy exhibitions. When two famous New York photographers visited and offered extensive workshops, both expressed their belief that there was brilliance in my work.

For a short while, Andreas and I grew so close, we attempted to merge our artistic efforts. During sessions in his studio, we sought to combine his extrovertedly sexual artwork with my introvertedly sexual artwork to create a nude photo series. Unfortunately, there was no spark and no emotional connection. We both couldn't find inspiration during our encounters. I was too deeply involved in myself as a subject, photographically as well as personally, to be able to connect with another human being on the intimate level required by such intense artistic collaboration.

Between twenty and twenty-one years of age, I felt like a marathon runner who, after hours of dogged determination, still doesn't find himself any closer to the finish line. I had run my race to exhaustion and wasn't sure how much longer my legs would carry me. Daily, the Academy had stripped me to the bone. I had exposed my heart and soul to tease out the answers I still sought so desperately. Yet I had no answers. Who was I? Why could I not find peace in my own body? Why was I plagued with melancholy and self-hatred?

It was precisely during this time that my dad became very active amongst the Rumanian refugees in our town and made a friend named Timotei.

Unaware of my increasingly fragile state, Dad chose this critical time in my life to jump out of the proverbial closet. He longed for me to become the person he could talk to about his homosexuality, a non-judgmental person who would accept him the way he was. I appreciated his measure of trust, as well as his decision to finally be honest with me. At the same time, however, I felt the ground beneath my feet shaking. As if a volcano was going to erupt, fissures seemed to open up all around me, threatening to swallow me whole. It took all my self-control to not run away screaming in terror.

My terror had nothing to do with homophobia. It originated from an entirely different source: certain aspects of his uncensored confiding in me were very hard to face. They were linked to my childhood and changed my life as I knew it. As I nodded and smiled and did my best to be an empathetic listener, the waves crashing onto the shores of my mind almost threatened to drown me.

Dad had not been going to saunas for a regular steamy experience because he was a health nut. Rather, he had gone to saunas catering exclusively to a gay clientele, to find relief in other men's arms. He had not been enjoying tranquility and reading a book out in the paddleboat on the Swabian Ocean during our summer family holidays. While Hildegard and I had stayed behind on the beach, he had been paddling in search of other men who made themselves available for sexual encounters in the tall reed grass surrounding the placid lake. Meanwhile, I had sat at the waterfront, uncomfortable in my mom's presence, hoping for my dad's swift return and working hard to lose myself in positive thoughts. But often, he didn't come back for hours.

Walter had not been Dad's hiking buddy, but his first boyfriend. Step-by-step, he had introduced Dad to the surprisingly abundant opportunities within the gay community of conservative Southern Germany.

Walter's previously inexplicable jealous reactions towards me suddenly made sense. My dad bringing me along to their romantic weekend getaways couldn't have thrilled Walter. We had always booked two rooms. One for them and one for me, but it must have been odd to have sex with a married man whose clueless daughter is sleeping in the adjacent room. Walter had never had a family and children of his own. He was still a child himself. Like Heinrich, he had never left his mother and couldn't possibly comprehend that even though my dad was gay at heart, he loved his daughter very much and wanted her to be a part of his life.

Over the years, I had kept in contact with Hildegard. She had found herself a small apartment on the other side of town. We saw each other once or twice a year. In between we kept in touch over the phone. Our encounters always reminded me of two wary armies during a cease-fire. We were always ready to dive into the trenches to avoid being hit by sniper fire. Carrying Dad's secrets added to my uneasiness. To this day, I am not sure if Hildegard had ever sensed her former husband's sexual orientation. She had been extremely prudish and hardly wanted a sexual relationship in the first place. So it is entirely likely she never noticed his disinterest.

Dad himself pondered his sexuality and for a long time didn't quite know where he belonged. There were gay men throughout Germany, of course, but a naïve country boy of his generation would not have been exposed to them. Also, in my dad's day, there were no talk shows, no magazines at every street corner talking openly about homosexuality.

When we don't conform to the prescribed norm, sometimes all we are sure of at first is that we feel "different". Unless we can compare our situation to accounts of others with similar experiences, we may spend years not entirely understanding who we are. We continue to try and follow the social norm. We will feel uncomfortable in our skin, almost able to pinpoint where the difference lies, but falling short.

Much later in Dad's life, when he started seeing homosexuality discussed in the media, some of his ambiguous feelings towards men became clear. By the time Dad finally had his epiphany he was already married. From then on, he had even hoped for a medicine to "cure" him of being gay.

Dad's relationship with his first boyfriend had ended about a year after his divorce from Hildegard. Afterwards, he had walked on the wild side – visiting highway rest areas, parks, and other public spaces where homosexual trysts took place on a daily basis. This overdue "coming of age" phase had lasted a few years, and was abruptly slowed down by a couple of modern-day Nazis carrying baseball bats. Dad had been lucky. He had gotten away with a black eye and a shock, broken glasses and bruises. It could have been a lot worse.

Scared, he had kept to the saunas after that. Several romances had followed. Then, Dad had met Timotei and the other men of the Rumanian refugee community. Now almost fifty, Dad was experiencing a love for Timotei reminiscent of a teenager's first infatuation. I was glad to see him so rejuvenated.

After his confessions, we sat for a few minutes in silence. Like a criminal waiting for the judge's verdict, he looked down and waited while I tried to get my emotional bearings. As hard as it was for me to cope with the sheer number of lies I had been told over the years, I forgave my dad almost instantly. Fissures were still opening up all around me, but at the same time, I found myself smiling. After his failed marriage, my dad's retreat from all human contact outside of work had worried me. I was flooded with immeasurable relief at the thought of him having spent time with other people. He had even been in love twice, with Walter and now with Timotei – and he had had a sex life to boot.

As we kept talking, the lines between father and daughter blurred. It occurred to me that Dad still needed my guidance much more than I needed his. Maybe he always would.

For a while I had to take care of the adults in my family yet again. Oma was no fool. Dad had never told her his true sexual orientation, but seeing

Timotei strutting naked through her son's apartment spoke for itself. Her son had turned out to be not quite the calm, conservative pillar of society she had believed him to be. Oma disapproved, often exclaiming, "Aiaiaiaiaiaiai!" during my weekend visits from the Academy. I didn't try to change her mind, and we didn't talk about it. But I felt her anguish and showed her as much love as I could.

We would spend afternoons in her living room while she worked on dresses she had promised her friends. To the soothing rhythm of her Singer sewing machine clattering as loud as ever, we would talk about our lives. I didn't like carrot puree anymore, but couldn't convince Oma of that fact. So she would make it for us in the evenings. We would sit at her dining room table, looking out at the moon and stars, spooning orange puree into our mouths.

With the selflessness and strength of a wise and withered superwoman, Oma rose above her misgivings. Her love and loyalty towards her son got the upper hand. She loved Dad and began making an effort to include his boyfriend into our family.

Dad, meanwhile, seized every opportunity to tell me about his sex life. He related the most intimate details of his encounters, and often seemed puzzled by the depth and breadth of his desires. Once more, I soothed and gave advice, all the while wishing I could do the same concerning my own life.

While my entire being was already stretched to its limit, we finalized a decision we had been pondering for a while: I would marry the refugee Timotei, thus helping him avoid deportation and separation from my dad. Focusing on this plan helped me to forget my own troubles for a while. I threw myself into the bureaucratic battles necessary for our wedding. Once more, I hoped that by doing good I could restore some semblance of balance to my life.

Then Dad received the *Abstammungsurkunde* (parenthood certificate) I would need to present at the registrar's office.

Consequently, he divulged the long-kept secret of my adoption.

And, for a while, all balance was lost.

Shortly after my dad's second revelation, our class went on a weeklong photography trip to Genoa. I was more depressed than ever before, Eeyore's rain cloud covering almost the entire hemisphere.

I had promptly sought out the authorities and had been granted access to the meager file on my birth parents. Sitting on the bus to Genoa, I could still clearly see my birth dad's address in my mind's eye: Taranto, Italy. Somehow, traveling to Italy with the Academy worsened my emotional state. I was half Italian and would be in the same country as my biological father for the first time. The closer we got to our destination at the Northern Mediterranean Sea, the more I felt myself slipping away. Like an unconscious apnea diver, the depths seemed to claim me, their long tentacles pulling me deep into the abyss.

During the entire week in Genoa, I found myself avoiding all contact with my lecturers and fellow students. Instead, I wandered aimlessly through town, trying to control the mounting emotional pain.

One afternoon, I found myself in the legendary cemetery of Staglieno. An entire mountainside had been converted into a graveyard, surrounded by scented gardens. Hundreds of terraces held intimate gravesites bearing beautifully decorated tombs, romantic statues, and photographs of the deceased. The complete silence amidst bustling city life was exactly what I needed.

Halfway up the mountainside, I spotted a woman standing at the edge of one of the cemetery's terraces. She was of medium height, her physique so compact it reminded me of a tree trunk. She had short brown hair and wore clothes that looked like robes. Her gaze was riveted on a point or thought in the distance. I recognized her as a fellow student from Zurich. Her name was Sienna. We had never talked much. Sienna was one year ahead of me in her studies and always kept to herself.

I was unsure what to do. Sienna obviously enjoyed the solitude and special atmosphere of the large cemetery as much as I did. But I thought it impolite not to acknowledge her presence. So I approached cautiously, not wanting to startle her. I said, "Hello" and she nodded. Her eyes were a gentle blue I had never noticed before. We fell into an uncomfortable silence, at a loss of what to say. Neither of us wanted to leave the peaceful surroundings though, so we gradually engaged in conversation. Sienna pulled a Swiss chocolate bar from her bag and asked, "Do you want some?" Of course I did.

Sienna and I stood on the cemetery terrace for hours. The bright Mediterranean sun, the clear blue sky, the thought of loved ones resting peacefully all around us, and the deliciously sweet chocolate all added to the magic of the moment. We talked about our problems, about feeling lost, and about our personal histories. We were astonished how comfortable we felt with each other, how easily we understood each other's feelings and trusted each other. By the end of the day, we had become close friends.

After almost thirty years, we both still remember the old-fashioned packaging of the chocolate. A brilliant-white daisy featured prominently, floating on a light blue background. We remember the sweet, nutty taste of our shared chocolate bar, the stickiness, and the crunchy sensation as our molars crushed the hazelnuts. We remember how happy we felt, and we marvel how friendships can be made in the unlikeliest of places. We had passed each other in the Academy hallways for years, never expecting to have anything in common. It took an afternoon eating chocolate amongst the dead for us to discover a friendship that would last a lifetime.

After this notable afternoon, we both nevertheless preferred to keep following our own separate paths for the remainder of our Italian week. I kept wandering the streets. Most evenings, while my fellow students were partying, I would find myself on a small, rocky beach close to our hotel. I would sit there each night, listening to the waves, inhaling the powerful salty scent of the Northern Mediterranean Sea, wondering if I was not only depressed but also seriously disturbed. Was everyone's life this insane, or had I made mine this way? Was my deep unhappiness my own doing or was this simply life? Was this all there was? Was this as good as it would ever get?

Even as I spiraled further into gloominess, I welcomed the proximity of the ocean. I felt at home looking out at the black waves and feeling the salty mist all over my body. Here, at the ocean, was where I needed to be. The sea magnified my emotions and it also reminded me of my love for life. Emotion battled with reason and, while I realized that I wanted to live, I couldn't deny the pain of feeling homeless in family and body as much as in country. Where did I belong? What would happen if I simply surrendered to despair and walked out into the liquid darkness?

On one of those nights on the beach, towards the end of our week, the voices in my head got too loud. I couldn't listen to them, couldn't analyze them anymore. I needed to feel something real, something tangible and painful, to anchor myself in reality. So I picked up a jagged rock and systematically and very slowly moved it up and down from my wrist to my elbow. I applied more and more pressure, letting the sharp edges first break the skin, then go deeper and deeper, for hours, while I listened to the waves pounding against the steady rocks beneath me.

When I later returned to the hotel, blood streaming from my arm, skin and flesh open to the gentle Mediterranean breeze, I met two of my lecturers at the hotel entrance: Andreas and Lars. Whereas my mentor Andreas had kept challenging me, Lars had become a trusted friend. He had a gentle soul and always helped me through technical problems with the utmost patience. Both men ran towards me the moment they laid eyes on me.

"What on Earth happened to you? Are you alright?"

Feeling a bit lightheaded, I nodded.

"I am fine. Just might need a bandage. I tripped while climbing over some boulders on the beach and fell on sharp barnacles." The lie slipped from my lips as easily as a flying fish leaps from the ocean.

Lars led me gently towards the first aid kit at reception. By then, my arm pulsated with pain and felt hot to the touch. Yet I felt better than I had in months. With each heartbeat, blood and tension were leaving my body in equal measure.

10

River Limmat

I would stare at the healing wounds on my arm and eventually marvel at the scars. They spelled a reminder: "Beware of the abyss."

After Genoa, I knew hurting myself was not a solution. No matter how much tension might have left my body through those wounds that night, inflicting physical pain on myself was not a sufficient answer to my emotional distress. Quite the contrary – it was a treacherous road to an undesired destination I preferred not to travel.

The aftermath of multiple family revelations lingered. Yet, in stark contrast to the gloomy Italy trip, my next semester began with an uplifting project. I had made acquaintances at Zurich's drama school and asked if I would be allowed to document an entire production, from creation through to opening night.

The cast and crew of the school's latest artistic endeavor welcomed me with open arms. It was the beginning of three magical months. I attended all rehearsals to Coline Serreau's *Lapin Lapin*. I photographed every day at the theater, as well as following the artists to makeup sessions and wardrobe fittings.

Initially, the inexperienced cast and crew felt self-conscious about my prowling around backstage with camera in hand. But after only a few weeks, they had all but forgotten about me. I began blending into the background like just another piece of production scenery. This was when I started to take incredible pictures. My camera recorded not only the concrete details, but the emotional growth of both the young artists and the play.

The soul of theater enchanted me. Here was a group of people, in complete collaboration, creating an emotional journey for an audience that would soon bear witness to the result of months of hard work.

I was charmed by how close the artists became in the process. They were completely comfortable – with their own as well as with each other's bodies. I had never before witnessed so much tactile interaction between people. At times, tears flowed and emotions flared high. No one was ashamed. No one held back. It was all part of the creative process. I took hundreds of pictures, longing to possess their level of comfort with themselves.

On opening night, cast and crew surprised me during the final bow and invited me to come on stage with them. As is the custom in Switzerland, each of us was handed a red rose. I beamed with happiness and couldn't have been prouder to share the stage with this fabulous group of aspiring artists.

My emotional struggles re-surfaced as soon as my enchanting backstage life came to an end. For the rest of the semester, I felt increasingly empty. I didn't know where to point my camera, or myself for that matter. I became stuck in a psychological spiral of depression, which started to suffocate my creativity. My weekly mentor meetings with Andreas at the Academy documented a steady decline.

The Academy darkrooms were on the top floor of our building, facing the river Limmat. Whenever I found myself stuck with emotional or technical difficulties, I would stick my head out the window, breathe deeply and gaze upon the beautiful green-blue hues of the shallow water. It took only a few minutes, to feel more relaxed and focused. Being close to water calmed my soul as it always had.

On particularly bad days, when I felt myself close to tumbling into the abyss, I would spend hours sitting on the riverbank instead of working on my projects. Like a scuba diver hanging onto a strong mooring line in raging currents, the Limmat became my lifeline.

A footbridge led across the river from the Academy grounds to a youth center. An old mansion had been converted into a bustling hub of creativity. The multicolored haven looked as if it had sprung from the page of a comic book and was covered in graffiti. Just under the bridge, the Limmat thundered over a small dam.

Every so often, during summer, I would literally catapult myself out of darkness. Fully clothed, I would climb over the bridge railing and jump into the deep river water below the dam. I would rise from the depths of the riverbed and my depression at the same time, breaking the surface with a joyous gasp. Enveloped by the refreshing liquid, I would surrender to the gentle flow and float several hundred meters downstream. There I would exit from one of many ladders along the riverbank, like a dripping wet poodle drying off in the blazing summer sun. Sometimes, I skipped classes in favor of staying close to the river Limmat, thus prolonging the good energy and peace it gave me.

During my next semester break, I worked non-stop at the movie theater again. I appreciated the change in routine. Intense bursts of activity would leave no time to brood over my existence. But each long workday would also bring extensive periods of downtime. To use these involuntary breaks constructively, I had gotten into the habit of always keeping a stash of books under the kiosk counter.

On this particular semester break, I decided to dedicate my reading adventures to society's fringe groups. I bought and borrowed as many books as I could on cults, homosexuality, gender identity, sadomasochism and other rarely-discussed elements of human existence. It was a slow summer when it came to movies, with a rather mediocre selection of new releases, so I was looking at seven workweeks with probably up to five hours of reading time a day. I dove into my books.

About mid-summer, on a day like any other, I stumbled upon a book that finally answered the many identity-related questions I had struggled with since those long-forgotten summers on Sylt when I was a little four-year old girl-become-boy, roaming the streets with my buddies.

As a child, I had instinctively known who I was but hadn't been able to articulate that awareness. Over the years, the hormonal changes of my body, as well as the gender stereotypes reinforced all around me, had clouded my judgment and confused me. Longing to fit in, I had lost myself in stages as my gender identity became more and more obscured. It was as if I had been clutching my useless passport in hand while stranded in an increasingly isolated and ruined airport building. Windows had been boarded up. The electricity had failed step-by-step, leaving me in deepening darkness. But I had never stopped searching for exits, even while dodging the debris falling onto me from crumbling ceilings.

As I was slouched over in a chair at my popcorn sales station that day, reading a collection of short stories with the corny title, 'Knives in the

Belly', I suddenly glimpsed a ray of light through one of the boarded-up windows of my prison of confusion. Mid-way through the first story, I knew this book with a dime-store novel title was about my life.

As I read on, each story affected me more deeply and led me back to the little boy who had loved being himself on a North Sea beach. The re-awakening struck like a lightening bolt. An invisible hurricane raged behind the counter at my popcorn stand. My customers were blissfully unaware. I talked, smiled, and sold treats as usual, all the time thinking, "Oh... My... God!"

Every story was the personal account of a man or woman who had found themselves in a wrongly-gendered body and had at some point understood the deeper source of their unhappiness. They had then courageously taken steps to grow into their own skin. This meant having to change the body they had been born with so it could finally match the person inside.

Reading about their desperation and their experiences, I found myself recognizing many elements from my own life. Like a starving refugee, I was hungry for more. I dumped all accumulated summer reading material and came back to the movie theater with a whole new stack of books entirely on transgender people – which was, I discovered, what people who were stuck in the wrong body were called.

Learning more about these people became an obsession. By the end of summer, I had researched and read every scrap of documentation I could lay my eyes on. It all made bewildering sense. Stunned, I knew I had finally found the mirror that reflected me back to myself. One major riddle had been answered.

This was where the movie was supposed to end with a walk into the sunset. Life is not a movie, however. Instead, my story now began in all seriousness. I now had to figure out what to do with my newfound enlightenment, and take action.

Pondering the best course, I understood it all came down to two simple choices: I could stay within the uncomfortable familiarity of what I had and resign myself to being unhappy in the wrong body for the rest of my life, or I could risk everything I had and everything I knew. Maybe in the process of doing so, I would at least be able to solve one problem in a life that had consisted of a complex web of daily problems.

Maybe, just maybe, being physically more myself would make me happier. The more I thought about it, I knew there was really only one choice: I had to forge ahead. Continuing with things as they were was tantamount to slow-motion suicide.

As my last year at the Academy started, my inner turmoil forced me to set priorities. Like an army of squirrels on cocaine, a multitude of thoughts were racing up and down the branches of my mind. I couldn't concentrate on my studies anymore.

My mentor and I sat down for a serious powwow. I explained my situation. Andreas was one of the first I confided in. He was also the first of many who told me he wasn't surprised and had always known.

Andreas presented my case to the other lecturers. They conferred, and decided to keep me enrolled for the year. This would give me one gap year, with the option to return once I had a better grip on my life. I already knew I wouldn't be back. Nevertheless, I was happy to accept their offer because staying enrolled would enable me to keep my student visa and go on working at the movie theater during all official school breaks.

During the first two weeks without a regular schedule to ground me, I became a complete recluse. I needed time and space to clear my head. Thankfully, Truong was rarely seen at our shared apartment during this time. He spent the majority of his days and nights in the Academy darkrooms.

I stayed in our dilapidated home for two weeks, barricading myself inside, longing to be completely hidden from the world. I sat in our living room, alternately staring at the ceiling or watching countless movies. This allowed my thoughts do what they needed to do – roam freely to the point of dizziness.

I didn't want to run into anybody, not even our neighbors. So, to avoid having to walk the few meters to our toilet shack in the garden, I climbed up onto our counter. There I squatted and did my business into the kitchen sink.

On day fourteen, I finally reemerged. The solitude had helped clear my head. I felt more composed than I had in years.

One of my most liberating insights about life with Hildegard had been that whatever she suffered was not my fault. Now again, understanding that being transgender was not my fault brought immense relief. My research showed that a small percentage of people had suffered the same fate for as long as history could remember. I had not brought this upon myself. I had not failed. I had not done anything wrong. Trans people like me, who had been assigned a sex at birth they later couldn't identify with, could be found all over the world. I had simply been dealt a very screwed up deck of cards.

Overall, I was elated. It is hard to describe the relief of finally understanding who I was. Imagine yourself roaming bright yellow beaches as a child. Some years later you are abducted by invisible forces and find yourself imprisoned in a dark basement. Losing your freedom gradually eats away your soul. You remember the vibrant colors of the wide-open plains and seas. You recall the happiness. And you wonder: will I ever feel that again? Then, when you least expect it, you are given a key to the door. You open it with trembling hands and slowly crawl towards the light. Your eyes are still too sensitive from the prolonged darkness, but your heart opens wide with renewed hope. You know, given time, you will regain your strength and be able to see the entire world. And it will be more vibrant than ever before.

Nevertheless, I was as scared as I was exhilarated. All my fact-finding had revealed some harsh truths. The transition process would be lengthy. The transformation would never be complete because science and medicine were not yet advanced enough. The semi-metamorphosis would leave me sterile, never able to father my own child. Any penis I had would either be a malfunctioning sausage, patched together from thighbones and skin, or non-existent. I would have horrendous scars. The hormone therapy could cause gross side effects such as severe muscle atrophy. Some transgender people died way before their time. Many felt never complete. Other recorded cases showed that trans people often suffered from severe depression, some taking their lives only a few years after their successful transformation. There were no guarantees.

It didn't matter how gruesome a picture the gender specialists painted. I accepted the risks and consequences. No matter how scared I was, there was only one possible way to go, and that was forward.

Apart from preparing myself for the physical complications, I also braced myself to face losing all my friends and acquaintances. There was no way of knowing how they would react. I feared they would all start screaming, arms windmilling wildly, and run out of the room, never to be seen again.

Hoping to find a vote of confidence and support from people who had already overcome all the obstacles I still had in front of me, I visited a self-help group in Freiburg. I longed for someone to put his hands on my shoulders like some kind of transgender Santa Clause and tell me in a cheerful voice, "Ho ho ho! Don't worry kid, it's only half as bad as it looks. You'll be fine. We are all very happy about the choices we have made."

Instead, most individuals I met in that group seemed to be drowning in an ocean of self-pity. They felt doomed, broken and forever incomplete. Others seemed to take their unusual situation as an excuse to celebrate being an exotic outcast. Many reduced their entire identity to being trans. They ceased to be personalities, ceased to define themselves by any other means. Once they had been diagnosed, everything they had done in life or would do in the future became linked to their being transgender. Their exotic status in society became an excuse, a crutch, and a curse to everything they were.

People, be they transgendered, heterosexual, or homosexual, are too hung up on classifying gender. We all seem to need to put everything in its proper place, into a little box with a sealed lid, neatly labeled for all eternity. Yet it's not that simple.

Listening to other people who had been born trapped in a wrongly-gendered body, I realized it was even more important for them than for the regular citizen to emphasize their "real" gender as strongly as possible. I had never seen females who wore more makeup and garish clothing, or had bigger boobs. Almost without exception, transgender women looked like a party-version of *Cruella de Vil*. And I had never seen men try so hard to fulfill the cliché of being a man as some transgender men did. They wore military boots, or looked like they had worked in their lumberjack clothing for days on end while cutting down an entire mountain forest. Many of them looked ready to wrestle a Yeti if he happened to pass by. Needless to say, none of them were actual lumberjacks.

I myself had fallen prey to stereotype some years earlier by adopting a swagger and hiding my curves beneath voluminous North Sea sweaters. Now, talking with other transgender people, I learned more about who I had become since then.

I had no intention of becoming a stereotypical male. Rather, why not become my own species? I was going to simply be myself, whatever that might mean. I was not going to be a victim, but would be who I was born to be. I would not think of the years I had lost, for nothing is ever lost. I didn't want to have regrets or doubts.

In essence, it was important to me to be perceived as a man. It felt like the true foundation of my personality, as well as part of my true soul. Continuing on as a female-bodied person would never be an option. Contrary to most of the trans people I met in Freiburg however, I valued my years spent in a female body. Life had been hard, had even seemed close to unlivable at times, but it had been *my* life. The body I found myself in had shaped this life inevitably. It had influenced my perceptions, my actions, and my reactions to the world around me. Furthermore, it had strongly influenced how others perceived me and reacted to me.

All things considered, I hadn't turned out too badly so far. Yes, I was impulsive, worried too much about everything, and said "yes" too often, but I was also sensitive, compassionate, caring, soft-spoken, and possessed integrity and courage.

Even though I deeply empathized with other trans people, I never went back to them for help.

Now that I was sensitized to the subject, suddenly news reports and TV interviews with transgender people seemed to be everywhere. Mostly these individuals were portrayed to the general public as colorful butterflies whose entire lives could only be lived on the fringe. Butterflies were captivating creatures, yet I envisioned a quiet, fulfilled life for myself – a life without boundaries.

Listening to the interviews, I felt that the public, as well as many trans people themselves seemed to assume that once their metamorphosis was complete, all their problems would disappear. I had no such illusions. Being transgender was just one problem I was facing. Granted, it was one of my more exotic ones, but I still had to continue to battle on all other fronts of life, just like everyone else. My life wasn't more difficult or easier because of my newfound clarity. I had simply uncovered another layer.

The very first step on my gender alignment journey was to seek out a German university clinic with a good reputation amongst transgendered people. I found a renowned institution and met with a professor of endocrinology.

We had a long consultation after which he prescribed regular injections of the male hormone testosterone. According to German law in the Nineties, I had to take these injections for at least a year before I was allowed to have any gender-adjusting surgeries. During this year, I would also have to get two independent psychiatric evaluations.

Thankfully, the endocrinologist soothed all my financial worries. It seemed I was far luckier than trans people in other countries. Since the beginning of the Nineties, German health insurances were required by law to cover all gender reassignment related costs, be they due to hormone therapy, psychiatric evaluations or surgeries. I left the university hospital that day relieved and hopeful, my first testosterone prescription safely tucked away in my wallet. The next day, my doctor in Zurich administered the first injection.

In general, the physical changes induced by the testosterone treatment were profound. After a few months of hormone therapy, I caused serious confusion during day-to-day human encounters. My features and body shape were still primarily feminine. My breasts were as massive as ever. At the same time, I was growing hair all over my body and the timbre of my voice had dropped significantly.

I was undergoing a second adolescence. Scientific research on transgender individuals during the last decades had shown my body would need a total of seven years to catch up with all the hormonal changes and reach its final state. I felt good instead of daunted, rather like a little boy waiting for the *Polar Express*. I was ready for the big journey.

As part of the "new" me, I wanted to find the perfect name. It needed to fit my personality like well-worn mukluks on lucky feet – enfolding me perfectly, completing me and protecting me from the coldness of the world. After months of diligent research, I found just the one. It sounded right, it felt right, and had the right meaning. It was the name that would encompass my entire existence.

My full new name was going to be Liam Kieran Klenk. Liam derives from William, which means: "the one with the strong will who is wearing a helmet." I could see parallels to my own existence in this historical meaning. I had always had a strong will. I never wore a helmet but, whenever I felt the armies of solitude and despair closing in, I would turn to body armor of a different kind: a heavy leather jacket. Kieran means "the little dark one", which literally described me, since I was going to be a short man at only five feet six inches, and I did have dark brown hair.

Even though it was still the early days – I'd had only four months of hormone therapy – it was time to announce to the people in my life what had been happening. I couldn't pretend forever that my voice sounded deeper because of a cold, and I didn't want to shave off the rapidly growing amount of body hair. It was time to jump into the bottomless ocean and reveal myself.

In the months following my decision to come out, my faith in humanity was restored many times over. Almost all reactions to my revelations were entirely, and sometimes surprisingly, positive. Many of my friends and acquaintances simply smiled a knowing smile when I told them, and confessed they had always taken me for either a hardcore butch or a transgender person. My behavior seemed to have given me away for years. People had known who I was, long before I myself had re-awakened to my identity.

Some reactions towards my disclosure about my real gender and my new name were outright comical. My team at the movie theater consisted of an elderly, conservative Swiss projectionist, as well as elderly Swiss ladies, stout-looking workers from Serbia, and other unique characters. One evening, I asked them all to gather in our small office because I had an important announcement to make. I was sure they would be outraged. I was sweating buckets and my heart raced.

In short, I told them I was actually a man and was going to change my body accordingly. Forthwith, my name would be Liam. Erich, the projectionist, just emitted a deep, rumbling "Hmmm?!" The elderly ladies exclaimed, "You will be such a handsome young man!" and the Serbians unanimously stated, "You are part of our gang. We'll always have your back". I was dumbfounded. Half an hour later, Erich passed by my popcorn stand. He stared at me very seriously and after a lengthy pause grumbled, "Couldn't you have picked an easier name? How am I supposed to remember an odd one like Liam?" He stared at me for a moment longer, then turned abruptly, and walked away with a big grin on his face.

Only three days later, my company informed me of my appointment with the tailor who would change my work uniform into pants, blazer, and tie as soon as possible. I was in heaven.

While visiting Dad one weekend, I told him my story. I explained how desperate I had been all these years, and assured him I had no doubt of a gender change being the only viable option. My dad is a very sensitive, thoughtful man. He listened to me trying to describe my feelings and thoughts patiently for hours. Then he said, "You know, I am of course a bit shocked but it all makes a lot of sense. Already when you were a little kid at the North Sea, I couldn't help but wonder about your true gender identity."

The next day, I had to return to my Swiss home. Dad gave me a parting gift. He asked me to wait and open the little gift-wrapped box on the train back to Zurich. When I did, I found my very first razor and a bottle of Davidoff *Cool Water* aftershave. At that time, I still had no beard to speak of. My heart almost burst. My dad's loving gesture was the equivalent of receiving a Lifetime Achievement Award at the Oscars. Thankfully the train was empty. Alone in my compartment, I couldn't stop crying and marveling at the beautiful souls surrounding me.

As much as I hated bureaucracy, after six months of hormone therapy, it was time to tackle the formal elements of my transition. Overall, it looked to be a long and painstaking process. Thankfully, I discovered reference material on the legal procedures and potential problems. I officially registered my "case" with the German authorities.

As first order of business, they referred me to two psychiatrists who specialized in gender disorders. I questioned the necessity of consulting two psychiatrists.

"It is for your own protection," said the official.

"How is that?" I asked, confused. "I don't understand. I just want to adjust this wrong body as soon as possible."

"Over the past ten years, there have been several cases where patients misdiagnosed themselves. They believed themselves to be transgender when in fact they were schizophrenic. Their gender reassignment surgeries were approved and quickly executed. Only then did these patients realize their mistake. They had actually been in the correct body to start with. Now their bodies had been altered to reflect someone they were not. It exacerbated their schizophrenia. In some cases, it led to suicide. Before we approve any further action, we want to be absolutely positive that you are, in fact, a transgender man."

Resigning myself to the stringent guidelines, I nodded, thanked the man, and left the office with a big, impatient sigh.

I wasn't schizophrenic. Of that I was reasonably sure. But a schizophrenic would be convinced of his sanity, wouldn't he? I decided to trust the authorities' wisdom.

One of my assigned psychiatrists resided in Stuttgart, the other in Ulm. The psychiatrist in Ulm was a professor who had specialized in cases like mine for decades. He was receptive, kind, insightful, and nonjudgmental. We had a few encouraging sessions together, after which he gave me the green light to go ahead with reassignment surgeries in six months' time.

The Stuttgart psychiatrist, on the other hand, made me furious. How he had ended up becoming one of the specialists for gender issues was beyond me. He oozed contempt and sneered at everything I said. I was accused of all sorts of Freudian afflictions. At one point, I began wondering in all earnestness whether I were trapped in a staggering nightmare and needed to pinch myself.

"Considering your close relationship to your gay father," he said, "I strongly suspect the only reason for your wanting to change your body is a desire to have intercourse with him."

I felt as if a Klingon warship had just materialized out of its cloak and blindsided me. Outwardly, I stayed calm and argued my case. Inwardly, I wanted to set my phaser to disintegrate and shoot the psychiatrist's condescending head off. Surprisingly, he conceded in the end and gave me the go-ahead as well.

The people in my life remained amazingly supportive. Everyone got used to calling me Liam as well as using the pronoun "he" instead of "she".

The only one struggling was Hildegard. When I first broke the news, she had reacted hysterically.

"Oh my God, what are we going to do? How can this be happening to us? How are the people in town going to react? How can I ever survive the shame?"

After a while, she calmed down and turned to evasive action. She clearly seemed to believe doggedly avoiding the issue would revert me back to "normal." Then she resigned herself to her fate and made an effort. She kept trying, but it was hard for her to get her head around the complexity of having raised someone like me. During our phone conversations she referred to me as "son", "daughter", "he", "she", "Stefanie", and "Liam" interchangeably. She still uses all these terms to this day.

Uniting my body with my soul meant breaking the heart of the one person who had always been there for me – my oma. As the hormones took an ever-firmer hold, I tried explaining to her who I was. Unfortunately, she was becoming progressively more senile. Oma sadly asked for me. Countless times, she would ask Dad, "Why does Stefanie never come home to visit us anymore?"

Every time I visited, I would cook her favorite rice pudding. We would sit together at her small dining room table, holding hands and gazing together out the window at the night sky. Sometimes, say when there was a full moon, Oma would happily point and exclaim, "Look! The moon has come to say hello. Isn't this magical?" It was. But, while my eyes followed her outstretched arm, she would try to hide my, to her palate, unsuccessful attempt at making rice pudding. She would spit the gelatinous mass quickly into her napkin and throw it under the table. I noticed each time this happened, but would always pretend I hadn't. Immediately after she shuffled to another room, I would quickly grab a rag and bucket and clean up the mess. On other occasions, I would search for her dentures. Due to her ever-increasing senility, they would end up in the oddest places – inside flowerpots, in the oven, or under her bed.

During her clearer moments, Oma would look at me and I would hope to see a small spark of recognition in her searching eyes. Most times, though, her eyes would seek out Dad with a confused, heart-breaking expression on her beautiful, deeply-lined face that spoke of such a long, well-lived life.

"Konrad," Oma would ask, "who is this nice young man who is taking such good care of me?"

To this day, it breaks my heart if I let myself think too much about Oma's last years. I hope on some deeper level she understood I was always right by her side. She meant the world to me.

As the end of the mandatory year of hormone therapy slowly crept closer, I needed to make vital decisions.

One of the things to be thoroughly pondered was the penis question. In the Nineties, a surgically-created penis was an imperfect solution. It was possible to have a member created from thighbones and skin transplants, but those who chose this option needed to have multiple corrective surgeries over the years, never quite reaching a satisfying result. The best doctors could do at the time was a numb, very ugly, sausage-like contraption.

I decided against it. A penis doesn't make a man. I'd rather have genital sensation then a bulge in my pants. When I confided this to my psychiatrist in Ulm, he smiled.

"I am very happy to hear this. If I hadn't already been confident of your sanity then this clear-headed decision would have removed any lingering doubts. You are going to be just fine."

The remainder of my initial year of hormone therapy passed quickly. The testosterone did its job. A beard started growing, and I started using the aftershave Dad had given me. My new voice finally sounded good to my own ears. I remained very clear on who I was and what needed to be done. Reassignment surgeries would soon be scheduled. The *Polar Express* had so far ambled along at an idle pace. Soon, it was going to whisk me away like a Japanese bullet train.

All the while, I had to get used to everyday male routines. Shaving, for example, was not one of my favorite elements of being a man, and neither was wearing ties. It was a small price to pay, however, considering how close I was to matching the packaging with its contents.

Finally, in autumn of 1995, the sluggish locomotive went into high gear. In two major sweeps, the last physical obstacles were cleared away.

The doctor at the hospital warned me of complications before both the ovary- and the breast-removal surgeries.

"Mr. Klenk, I need you to be aware that most patients suffer from multiple complications for months. Please sign here."

I signed the liability agreement with a smile. So certain was I of doing the right thing. I knew with every fiber of my being that there would be no complications. For the first time in my life, I was feeling whole. My metamorphosis would not be complete without major surgeries, and so, how could they be anything other than a positive event? My Apollo 11 had landed. Like Neil Armstrong, all I had to do now to complete my mission was take a big step.

My ovaries were removed in a first sweep. The usual recuperation time of two weeks condensed itself to only three days in my case. My body surged with positive energy. The surgeon was speechless.

A few weeks later, in the second sweep, I said a very happy goodbye to my two immense breasts. I woke up in the foggy realm of an anesthesia hangover. Even so, the very first thing I did was struggle to sit up a bit and hazard a glance towards my toes. I could actually see them! The two

Himalayan peaks that had obstructed my view for most of my life were gone. I was free! From now on, I would be able to run, drop my slouch and walk upright, as well as jump up and down, swim, and fly unencumbered. My body would not betray me anymore.

Lying in my hospital bed, I remembered the warnings of both psychiatrists. "Brace yourself and expect the worst after your surgeries, Mr. Klenk. Waking up to your body being radically altered, combined with the post-surgery pain, can be quite a lot to handle."

Yet all I felt was relief and happiness. My *Polar Express* had accelerated to blast-off speed and indeed seemed to have brought me to the moon. I felt weightless. Step by step, the walls of my life-long prison began to crumble.

During both short stays in hospital, my friends amazed me with their frequent visits and heartfelt gifts. Amongst them was Sienna, my closest friend since our first encounter at the Genoa cemetery, as were several workmates from the movie theater who had become trusted friends. I received flowers, poems, a pink stuffed animal pig and, most importantly, an overwhelming amount of love and support. The people in my life genuinely cared. I was truly fortunate.

My immediate family worried but chose to keep their distance for both medical events. Hildegard still struggled with the mere concept of me being a man, while Dad was afraid he wouldn't be able to bear the emotional shock of seeing me in a hospital. My birth mom, Sandra, and I had kept loosely in touch. I had explained over time that I, her returned daughter, was instead a returned son. She had reacted surprisingly calmly to this revelation, but we were too estranged for her to make a hospital visit.

My second and last stay at the hospital was over as quickly as the first. Instead of mountains, I now had angry red scars and little brown saucers where my nipples used to be. I was so happy. Anything was better than what had been there before.

It still took a few years to lose the rest of my physical femininity. My body lost its curves in stages. Body hair continued to sprout, my Adam's apple grew more pronounced and my muscles, stronger. My genitalia became slightly bigger, as well as much more sensitive to stimuli. Surprisingly, the continuing hormone therapy also caused my clitoris to grow into a miniature penis that stayed hidden between the folds of my enlarged labia. I found myself grinning, happy to have the world's smallest penis.

As for the lingering psychological femininity, the successful surgeries had strengthened my resolve even further to embrace the person I had started out being. I would integrate my female side into the male adult I was becoming. I was Liam, and something inside my soul knew with absolute certainty he was who I had been all my life. More than ever, I was confident to not let my life be controlled by clichés and abstract societal constructs. I had just escaped one prison and saw no reason to voluntarily admit myself to the next one. I knew I was a man – not by anyone else's standards but by my own.

Immediately after my second surgery, I was reminded of life still happening outside the small universe of my existence. My oma fell and broke her hip. I dropped all pills and infusions and rushed back to Germany to see her. As soon as I arrived, I took her in my arms, ignoring her confused, who-is-this-young-man look. I spent many hours sitting by her bedside.

Outwardly, Oma looked like a tiny stick figure on her narrow bed, yet she still emitted a strong aura of love and positivity. We were both battered yet strong souls, who would never give up easily.

Oma stroked her belly and, with a brave but confused smile said, "I am in so much pain but somehow feeling my warm hands on my stomach makes everything better. It is as if I am singing my body to sleep."

All too soon, I had to return to my life in Zurich. I was content working at the movie theater whenever I could, and had no intentions of returning to my life as a photography student. However, I delayed informing the Academy of my intentions. Before dropping my student status, I needed to figure out how to remain in town.

Zurich had grown to be a safe haven in which I felt I could be myself and begin anew. At this stage of my life, what I needed most of all was a true home to ensure balance and mental health. I wasn't prepared to give up my precious circle of friends or my many favorite sanctuaries along the picturesque lake and rivers in the charming Swiss metropolis. The uncertainty about my status as a foreigner in a non-EU country loomed on the horizon. Would I be allowed to stay in Switzerland? I was afraid but wouldn't go down without a fight.

Adding to my mounting worries, the bureaucratic side of my gender change was far from complete. Even though I looked like a man now, my passport still boldly declared me as female. At least the German authorities had agreed to officially change my name months earlier.

During these tumultuous times, I existed as *Miss* William Kieran Klenk. The name Liam had been refused by the authorities as not gender-specific enough. I could think of countless, very manly, Irish and Scottish nationals who would strongly disagree. There was nothing I could do, however, so William became the official me, while everyone called me "Liam." Whenever I had to produce my passport, most people kept perfectly neutral expressions and didn't bat an eyelid at my being Miss William. As such, the status quo I was temporarily forced into was amusing as much as it was exasperating.

To adhere to German regulations concerning transgender people, I was required to live another year in my "new" gender identity. Afterwards, I would have to reconvene with my two psychiatrists for a final evaluation. They would deduce if I was living well enough under my new circumstances. To keep making this path as hard and long-winded as possible, I would then be required to submit the two psychiatric follow-ups to my local court. Then, finally, I would have to speak to the appointed district judge to get his official approval concerning my gender.

As always – the laws in Germany being clear and unbendable – there was no option but to comply. "Grin and bear it" was my motto. "Don't worry about what you cannot change" was another one. I was well aware that what I needed most for now was to concentrate simply on living day-to-day. I would cross the bureaucratic bridges once I got to them.

11

Greifensee

I had been busy with my transition. Keeping in touch with my birth mom had become a very low priority. One day, she called with fantastic news: her youngest daughter, my half-sister, was coming home.

Sandra had weathered all the psychological storms of divorcing her abusive husband. She was finally considered stable enough to be allowed to take care of her youngest child again. Petra was taken from foster care and delivered back into the arms of her mother. Sandra must have felt even happier than when she had held her for the first time. Finally, she had at least her youngest daughter back under her own roof.

Soon after being reunited with her mother, and shortly after my surgeries, I met my sister Petra for the first time. She was fourteen at the time – fourteen years younger than me. She was the little sister I had always dreamed of. We instantly felt like family. It was an unforgettable moment. One minute of staring at each other as just-introduced strangers turned into a lifetime of being connected.

Sandra and I had edged carefully closer towards each other. Now, with Petra thrown into the mix, our fragile bond became threatened. Since my sister's arrival I felt far more motivated to visit. Petra and I laughed together. My shy little sister looked up to me and asked many questions. I could feel the tension with Sandra mounting with each visit. My birth mother began regarding me with jealous suspicion.

Then, one fateful afternoon, my sister and I were discussing marijuana and the inevitability of stumbling into it in schoolyards or other places where kids congregated.

"Liam, what should I do?" Petra asked me. "Mom keeps saying I can't ever smoke a joint, but it is almost impossible. Everyone is smoking them. All my friends are offering them to me. They are laughing at me, because I keep saying no and they think I am a wimp."

"Well, first of all," I said, "just because you don't do what everyone else does, doesn't make you a wimp. If your friends don't understand that, then maybe they are not the right friends. On the other hand, there is no harm in trying to smoke a joint at some point. It just shouldn't become a habit. You have to be very careful if you ever try one to see it as a one-off or two-off experience at the most."

Of all the conversations Sandra could have overheard, this was the worst.

"Are you out of your mind?" an outraged Sandra confronted me only minutes later. "How can you advertise drugs like that? In the future, you won't talk to your little sister unless I am in the room with you."

I overreacted and screamed obscenities at my biological mom, then rushed out of her house.

Days later, still overreacting, I wrote her a heated letter.

"You know what?" the letter concluded, "Forget it. I already have one crazy mom and dad who are often too selfish and afraid to be of much help. I don't need another unstable parent."

I had suffered under Hildegard's neuroses. I had dealt with Dad's helplessness as well as his tendency to run away from pain by escaping, just as he had during our holidays at the Swabian Ocean when, instead of facing Hildegard, he had run into the arms of other men. He had left me with her on the beach for hours, even though he knew we struggled to get along.

Unfortunately, I had now truly reached the point of the proverbial pot boiling over. Actually, it wasn't just boiling over. A tsunami was raging under the rattling lid. I could take no more from my parents, be they biological or adoptive ones.

Sandra and I never talked again. I tried contacting my sister a few times, but failed. I had found a mother, found a sister, found my gender identity, then lost my mother and my sister, all in the space of only a few months. Life was so volatile, so fragile.

For a while, depression threatened to overwhelm me once more. This time, I was having none of it and decided to battle the early onsets with vigorous, rather idyllic, exercise.

The small town outside Zurich in which I had lived with Truong was located right next to a romantic lake, called Greifensee. I had moved to Zurich after leaving the Academy, but still enjoyed the odd trip to the small body of water. Frustrated, angry, and helpless concerning my muddled family situation, I now embarked on frequent nightly expeditions around the lake.

Greifensee was a beauty. Contrary to Lake Zurich, there were no houses on the lakeshore. With its many weeping willows and dense vegetation, Greifensee transported me into a mystical landscape far from civilization. I could breathe here and would walk for hours without meeting a single person.

Hiking once around the entire lake would take roughly three hours. Like a hamster on steroids, I circled Greifensee for weeks after my altercation with Sandra. I would take the train from Zurich almost every night. When I arrived at the lakeside, the water surface and outlying hills would be shrouded in dense fog. Around 8.p.m., I would start following the small footpath, right next to the gently lapping waves, hiking into the night, soaking up the moonlight and gazing up at the stars. I would ponder the tendrils of fog, wondering if they were the long arms of alien beings. Would they take me by the hand and lead me out into the obscure waters of the lake? Inhaling deeply with every step, I would savor the strong aroma of algae and reed grass. It was nature's perfume at its best and most invigorating. As the hours went by, the beauty of the water world and its surrounding forests would heal me.

Physically exhausted but mentally restored by my nightly endeavor, I would manage to catch the last train back to Zurich. Once arrived in my room, I would fall into a deep, contented sleep.

Ten years later, I found my sister again – through Facebook of all places. She had undergone a metamorphosis of her own. The shy, introverted fourteen-year old girl I had known had transformed into a beautiful, sensitive, self-confident young lady.

At first, Petra was very careful. I offered to give her my time and stay loosely in touch through Facebook. She would be able to follow my social movements and have a chance to decide slowly, from a distance, if I was a psychopath she preferred to stay away from, or rather a unique individual, a brother, whom she would love to welcome back into her life.

Petra did eventually, very carefully, an inch at a time, open the door for me. I was proud of her. I still am, and always will be. We are both survivors. Though much younger, I sometimes feel my sister is the more mature sibling. She is calm and thoughtfully structures her life, whereas I am often impulsive and very emotional.

Over the years, I often wondered what had become of my birth mom. I never heard from her again. At first, I felt anger towards her for not forgiving my angry outburst. I shook my head at my impulsiveness. After a while, I forgave both her and myself. We had made a mountain out of a molehill.

In the midst of my gender change procedures, I had been absorbed by the enormity of what I was facing. Usually a compassionate human being with boundless energy to be there for others, I had needed to focus my spiritedness on myself in order to make it through the challenges stretching into the distance before me. On top of that, Hildegard was still Hildegard and Dad was still Dad. Stirred up by the revelation of my adoption, I couldn't have helped but painfully analyze and reevaluate our entire relationship. Even more psychological stress had been added due to my pseudo-marriage with Timotei.

Sandra on the other hand, had experienced nothing but trouble ever since she and I had been admitted into the halfway house for prostitutes in 1970. My biological father and her parents had abandoned her. Then she had married a monster. She had been threatened and beaten by him and had lost another two children – even if only temporarily, in the case of Petra.

By the time she had opened her door and led me into her home, my birth mom had just barely survived her own battles. Only weeks before we had met she had been released from a recovery center for alcoholics as well as from a psychiatric care facility.

When Petra had been returned to her at last, my birth mom had held on to her little girl with a fierce tenacity, afraid of any further harm coming to her, reluctant to share her, and terrified of losing her again.

Considering our circumstances, we were both in no state to build up a mother-child relationship from scratch when we met. We were two strangers in the midst of maybe the biggest crisis of our lives, desperately holding on to what we had left: Sandra to her one remaining child and me, to my individuality and independence.

After a while, I accepted losing my birth mom yet again. I felt respect for her and understood the importance of her stubbornness. It was precisely this rigidity that had helped her survive events that would have shattered other people's lives beyond repair. Inheriting her bull-headed inner strength was without a doubt what had enabled me to wiggle my little body into this world weeks before my due date in April of 1971. It is also part of what has kept me alive ever since – sane and reasonably happy.

12

Lake Zurich

The otherworldly fog and rippling waves of my Greifensee excursions had helped me to let go and move on. For a while, day-to-day life in Zurich continued, blissfully uneventful.

I rejoiced in my now almost-male body. Quite frankly, like a marathon runner at the finish line, I was relieved and happy to have come as far as I had. I was glad to be alive. Thankfully, my life was far from over. My adjusted body granted me a level of freedom I had never before experienced. A new life was only just beginning.

I worked at the movie theater whenever possible. Donning my work uniform – a dark blue tailored suit and tie – never lost its appeal. I could have been James Bond, manly and glamorous. In my abundant free time, I met friends, read books, and enjoyed the idyllic lakeside of Lake Zurich as often as possible.

My closest friends had become even closer friends since I had come out to them about my gender identity. They stood by me, and most importantly, understood that despite my radically-altered body, I was still the person they had always known: Liam, a fairly regular someone who in everyday life was happy sitting on his couch or in the park while philosophizing, daydreaming, and reading books.

Since early childhood, there had been more than enough excitement in my life without my having to create any more of it. Thus, I wasn't an adrenaline junkie. I loved slow sports and greatly preferred walking to running. I loved thoughtful, slow, and intimate moments with friends. Evenings at the lakeshore with a glass of wine, or a few beers in a cozy bar were always preferable to the party life in loud clubs.

In 1996, I turned twenty-five. An important era of healing began. With my friends I spent many summer hours at Lake Zurich, pondering life while sipping wine from paper cups.

Instead of lounging at the lakeside, Sienna and I preferred going on long walks, observing swans, ducks, and humans alike. We spent many hours strolling along Zurich's lakes and rivers and took turns in lifting each other up on a bad day. The sunlight would reflect and sparkle so brightly on Lake Zurich's surface, its water might as well have been coated with millions of Swarovski crystals.

Zurich was fabulous all year around but especially so during summer. Our entire town would vibrate with liveliness and creativity. The old townhouses right next to the picture-book lake looked so heavenly, I often wanted to pinch myself.

Whenever I needed to recharge my batteries, I would seek nature and solitude. During the early hours of the day, the lakeside was deserted. The soft morning sun gently caressed the waves. I would sit on the grass as dew sparkled all around me. Sipping a caramel macchiato, I would gaze out over the water towards the Swiss Alps beckoning on the horizon.

Many summer events, especially the movie-related ones, made me feel as if I was savoring one delicious appetizer after another. A very unique movie festival was held every June inside Zurich's main train station. The cathedral-like hall was breathtaking, open on all sides to the outdoors, with enough space for two thousand spectators and an eleven-hundred square-foot screen. During this event, I would usually take a few days off and throw myself into one movie marathon after another.

Another favorite was the open air movie festival at Lake Zurich in July. During the day, the colossal screen would rest flat just above the surface of the lake. At sunset, a medley of classic movie soundtracks ranging from *Blues Brothers* to *Out of Africa* would alert us the movie was about to begin. The screen would rise majestically on silent, hydraulic poles. A warm orange light reminiscent of ancient glowing gaslights would eerily illuminate its reflective surface.

Usually, all two thousand seats would be sold out each night for an entire month, no matter how rainy the evening would turn out to be.

Sienna and I once watched the premiere of *The Perfect Storm* during a fierce thunderstorm. We wrapped up in garbage bags and huddled closer, freezing our butts off but strangely excited by the special effects nature had decided to lend to the raging storm on screen.

August would bring the annual street parade, with one million people joining in a celebration of life while dancing in the streets to loudly pounding techno music. I never cared much for techno – except for on this one day. People whose paths would never cross on a regular day would end up joyously dancing the afternoon away together. Grandmothers would wave their walking sticks rhythmically above their heads, swinging their hips next to half-naked teenagers who sported neon-colored boobs, swinging in plain sight.

The residents living along the parade route would wave from their windows and refresh the wildly dancing crowd by filling bucket after bucket with water and pouring it onto their grateful heads. A roar of joy would rise up each time a shower of water found its targets.

By September, Zurich would usually slow down a little. Each Indian summer would be celebrated with a theater festival at the lakeside. Underneath hundreds of lanterns, street performers would enchant their audiences. Theater groups from all over the world would perform on small wooden stages built for the occasion. Sienna and I would spend many evenings in this rejuvenating, creative atmosphere. We would lounge on the meadow, a cool microbrew in hand and listen to the contagious laughter of clapping audiences all around us.

Zurich was a true home. It was invigorating and relaxing at the same time. I enjoyed the warm glow of the historical city, the joyful cultural experiences, the politeness of its populace, and the romantic presence of water throughout town.

My home is wherever my heart is, wherever my people are. There have been many places fitting this description along the way, but Zurich is special. It still holds a large group of irreplaceable friends. During every visit, while walking through the compact little metropolis, I feel myself relaxing as if a master massage therapist is kneading every inch of my body, and offering me a relaxing glass of Port on top of it. Zurich fits like an old, comfortable shoe I can slip into with ease, releasing the audible sigh of a world traveler come home. Part of me will always belong there, in that charming, open-minded lakeside oasis where I chose to undergo a metamorphosis beyond my wildest dreams.

After five years at my Swiss refuge, I felt better than ever. I joyously embraced the old and new challenges awaiting me. My outlook had subtly changed. I knew myself better now and began to grasp what my sensitivity meant. It was a sign of strength. Growing self-confidence followed comprehension.

One morning, fate led me to share a park bench with a therapist. During our chat, I couldn't resist pondering why I had had to deal with so much adversity.

The middle-aged, elegantly-dressed therapist and I had known each other for only an hour of animated conversation, but she smiled and answered, "Isn't it obvious? Because you can. You have amazing strength and courage within you. Your eyes sparkle with it. Life will keep pushing. And you'll instinctively take on as much as you can handle. In your case, that amounts to a lot."

Never quite having approached my predicaments from such a positive angle, I shook my head in wonder and said, "Thank you for your vote of confidence. I've really enjoyed talking with you."

"The pleasure is entirely mine." She said. "It's been a while since I've had such an inspiring talk with someone over morning coffee."

My surprising encounter with the lady at the lakeside reminded me of unfinished business. An urgent issue had crept ever closer: the gap year granted me by the Academy was coming to an end.

Technically, I would have to leave Switzerland as soon as my student visa was revoked – which would be in only one more month. I didn't know where to go. Zurich, its many bodies of water and my circle of friends were my refuge and inspiration. I needed to keep growing in this city in which I had found myself, before I was ready to move on.

Going back to the Academy was not an option. I couldn't simply continue on the path to becoming a photographer. Too much had happened for me. My experiences had shown life to be a minefield of horrendous surprises. As a result, I over-analyzed everything, always attempting to anticipate the next bomb before it would hit. The analytical nature of photography drove me insane. All of a sudden everything became a symbol or metaphor. I didn't have sufficient mental barriers to filter all these visual signs. Using my senses as a photographer pushed me too far into the abyss, turning me into a sleepless bundle of nerves in the process.

Additionally, photography didn't allow me to get emotionally close enough to my subjects. As a photographer, I needed to be the eternal objective observer, with the camera lens firmly separating me from the world. I didn't want to hide behind a lens anymore. I wanted to be directly involved, and be there for others. What I most craved was to absorb it all, experiencing first-hand whatever life wanted to show me. I needed to belong.

Still wondering if, for the sake of keeping my home, I should return to my studies after all, one memorable occasion cemented my decision. A friend hired me for two days and nights to help with the load-in and load-out for Zurich's biggest fashion ball of the year. We carried the heavy lighting and sound equipment into the old castle where the ball was to be held. There we installed everything. Then we remained for troubleshooting purposes. Backstage during the ball, I struggled to stay awake. After a dozen Red Bulls, my stomach protested with painful cramps. The night seemed to last forever, yet I felt intensely alive.

At some point I noticed photographers in the crowd. I knew most of them and surprised myself by feeling sorry for them. Whereas they were observing, I was living the event, feeling the intensity of what happened with every fiber of my exhausted body and soul.

In the early morning hours of the next day, we dismantled everything. We loaded the equipment back into the truck then proceeded to unload back at the warehouse. When we were done my friend offered to drive me home. It had been forty hours since the initial load-in. I had never been so tired before in my life. Arriving at my front door, I waved a grateful goodbye. My tired eyes could barely focus on the keyhole. Nevertheless, I somehow managed to drag myself to bed, keeled over and slept, oblivious to the world and fully-dressed, for over twenty hours.

The vivid fashion ball experience left no doubt in my mind: there *was* no going back. It was time to officially leave the Academy. Sad to say goodbye, but fortified in my decision, I met with Andreas. For the first time, he didn't discuss and second-guess me. He simply nodded and wished me all the best. Minutes later, we shook hands and I left, never to return.

My student visa's expiration date crept ever closer. I dreaded the thought of having to go back to where I grew up. In the hope of finding a previously undiscovered loophole that would allow me to remain in paradise, I researched relentlessly.

During my semester breaks, I had learned all aspects of movie theater work. I was proud to be able to pitch in wherever needed, whether in the projectionist's booth, the reservations call center, the ticket office, the concession stand, or directly in the theater as an usher. I longed simply to be able to continue in a profession I loved.

Then, only one month before being expelled from Switzerland, in early 1997, I confided in Salvatore, a work colleague at the movie theater. He had joined our team a few months prior. He was gay, had a tender heart and boundless sensitivity. He was also in constant angst about the world and suffered from depression. Above all, Salvatore was a loyal and non-judgmental friend.

When I told him how much I needed to stay in Zurich, history repeated itself, only this time I stood on the other side of the fence. Salvatore instantly nodded, "I will marry you. You don't need to pay me anything. There are no conditions. We are friends and I want to help." I was very skeptical at first, knowing only too well nothing was ever that simple. Memories of the confines of my last marriage rose to the surface. It had felt suffocating. I had promised myself to never again be tied to a virtual stranger.

My passport still listed me as "female", but I was mere inches from the legal deadline of being able to start the process of changing my gender identity to "male" in all official papers. One incredible downside of a marriage to Salvatore at this point was that I would be saddled with the incorrect identity for another five years. It was 1997. We were still ten years away from the first same-sex marriage in Switzerland.

As the weeks went by, I pondered my situation. I would have to take a giant leap of faith into my second quasi-marriage. The thought of being legally bound again scared me. At the same time, I would have to put up with being Mrs. William for a while longer. This prospect was as daunting as a root canal, but so was the prospect of having to leave my life in Zurich.

Out of options, I summoned my courage, took a very deep breath, and accepted his "proposal" with a long, heart-felt bear hug. As my fears of losing my home evaporated, relief flooded me like a wave of iridescent butterflies. Salvatore and I would have to live together for at least five years. We laughed about that. Even before his surprising offer, we had planned to soon share a place together. Within days we found a cozy three-bedroom apartment, only minutes away from Lake Zurich.

After only a few months of braving bureaucratic hurdles, Salvatore and I took the plunge in the spring of 1997. Our wedding can only be described as an odd yet charming little event. All of our closest friends were present, making it a festive, intimate group of a dozen people. Everyone was dressed in joyful colors. My Serbian friends from the movie theater had brought a big jug of very strong, homemade Slivovitz, their traditional plum brandy. Lars, one of my lecturers from the Academy and a close friend, joined in the occasion. Being a seasoned, white-haired gentleman, he lent a very sincere paternal presence to our colorful entourage.

Our main problem at the wedding was my physical transformation, which had gone far enough at this point to make me look very masculine. One of my friends who worked as a make-up artist spent the better half of that morning transforming me back into a woman. We couldn't help but chuckle at the irony of our actions, and topped it all off with a very ugly red dress and grandmotherly clip-on earrings scored at a local thrift store. I ended up looking like a cross between a hobo version of *The Flash* and a mother from the Fifties.

Our city hall wedding ceremony was a total success. We rushed out of the historical building, half-drunk from Slivovitz, and celebrated the curious proceedings with rum-spiked coffee and cake at a picturesque riverside café. Apart from us, only very serious senior citizens seemed to frequent the establishment. As we loudly clapped each other on the shoulders, hugged and laughed, we were given stares ranging from annoyed to very amused.

In our shared apartment, Salvatore and I sank onto our comfortable couch with a glass of champagne. We decided on the movie *Green Card* with Gerard Depardieu as appropriate evening entertainment.

13

River Sihl

The impossible had become possible: Zurich would remain my much needed home for the time being. Having climbed the equivalent of K2 while wearing grotesque red drag, I was now allowed to stay at my lakeside sanctuary. Being married to a Swiss national, I was automatically granted a work permit. Full of new hope, I visited Sergio, the head of our human resources department at the movie theater company.

"Would you guys be interested in having me on full-time as an usher, instead of just helping out part-time?"

"Give me a couple of days," Sergio answered. "I'll have a talk with upper management."

A few days later, Sergio walked into the entrance hall of Cinema Metropol just as I was locking up.

"Hey Liam, do you have time for a chat over a glass of wine?"

Of course I did. We talked about my plans and our shared passion for the world of movies.

"We have all been very satisfied with your performance over the last three years, Liam. We appreciate your sincerity and strong work ethic, and we see a lot of potential."

We sipped some more wine, then he cut to the chase.

"Rather than working as an usher, would you be interested in taking on the position of team coordinator at Cinema ABC?"

I was dumbstruck.

"You would be in charge of fourteen ushers and kiosk staff. You would coordinate basic maintenance, staff scheduling, and manage kiosk merchandise. And you would be in charge of daily and monthly bookkeeping."

My mind reeled. ABC was being renovated as we spoke. It was much bigger than Metropol, the movie theater I was used to. After renovations, ABC would feature four screens with two thousand seats in total. It would cater mainly to a young audience, featuring the latest in action, adventure, and comedy flicks. I felt immensely honored and a bit overwhelmed by the implications of Sergio's offer. Goose bumps rose on my arms. My heart welcomed the challenge.

"Thanks so much!" I said with a big, happy grin. "That would be fabulous. I accept. I'll work my heart out for you."

"I know," Sergio said with a warm smile.

Celebrating the moment, we ordered another bottle of wine. I floated home that night.

My life at Cinema ABC began in late spring of 1997. More than any previous endeavor, it was my springboard into the world. Going from student to full-time employee for the first time in my life was a momentous occasion. I was being trusted with facilitating the daily business of a small multiplex as well as ensuring the wellbeing of over a dozen employees. These shoes seemed way too big but I had every intention of growing into them.

Initially, I had no idea how to organize my work. True to my nature, I passionately prioritized *everything*. During my two years at ABC, my team and I kept the multiplex theater in pristine shape. However, I drove my employees and fellow managers up the walls. Proud of the chance I had been given, I pushed myself harder than anyone else, running a high-speed marathon without ever slowing down. I was always the first to arrive and the last to leave. I kept my ushers and kiosk staff on a strict schedule. We operated, served, cleaned, and maintained all day without pause.

The only breather I allowed myself each day was a half hour break at the River Sihl. The refreshing waterway was only minutes away from my workplace. Limmat and Schanzengraben were rather narrow and deep. The Sihl, on the other hand, was a wide, shallow river. Though it lacked dense foliage on its banks, to me it felt like the Amazon of Zurich. It flowed proudly, flanked by houses that had weathered the centuries.

Each day, during my precious moments of downtime, I would grab a snack and run from the theater to a small meadow only ten minutes away and seemingly forgotten in the middle of town. The Sihl streamed right through this green oasis, rippling gently over stones and around big boulders that had been spray painted a bright red by local graffiti artists.

If the weather allowed it, I would take off my shoes and first sit in the grass, feeling the soft blades between my toes and on the soles of my feet. Each tiny blade seemed to connect with hundreds of pressure points. I felt instantly calmed and revived all at the same time. Sometimes I would roll up the pant legs of my expensive, custom-made uniform and wade far out into the river. It felt good to have my toes tickled by tiny river fish while rounded stones massaged the soles of my feet. Only one hundred fifty feet to each side, the meadow gave way to city streets. Passengers of passing trams would look out at me and I would wonder if they wished they could join me.

I rarely had the luxury of taking more than a thirty-minute break. After ten minutes of absorbing as much of nature's power as I could, I would run the ten minutes back to work, stuffing my sandwich down as I went, and feeling charged with more positive energy than I would ever need.

Years later, I met Marina, one of my former employees, over a cup of coffee.

"I hated working with you," she confessed. "You were always running ahead and never sat down. Like a wind-up toy with its own undying power source, you never stopped. This made us all feel bad the second we sat down for a break, even if it should have felt completely natural to rest for a few minutes between customer onslaughts."

Activity bursts at ABC could be brutal. Swiss movie theaters take a ten-minute break midway through the movie. Alternating constantly between ravenous pre-movie-crowds and animated break-customers, we couldn't keep ahead of our popcorn production and merchandise orders. On good sales days, I would sprint back and forth between the scalding hot popcorn machine, the concession stand, the storage room, and the phone to order more fresh merchandise. Depending on the popularity of the latest Hollywood production, we could have up to eight hundred impatient teenagers invading our sales stations before and during every movie.

The theater I had worked in during my time as a student had had only one screen and three screenings a day. Now I was dealing with four screens and up to twenty screenings a day. Full-time staff was hard to come by. I mostly worked with inexperienced students and being under-staffed was par for the course. Juggling everything, I could easily accumulate five hundred overtime hours within four months.

On an extremely tough opening day, Elsbeth, a fellow manager, shook her head in amazement and said, "You know, I kept watching you dealing with wave after wave of customers today, waiting for you to pass out. I am amazed you never did."

Most days, I ran on pure passion and loved every minute of it. It was as if I had been chained behind a wall for years, and now I had somehow broken the chains as well as the wall, and was surging on an endless high.

In addition to all my responsibilities as coordinator in ABC, I volunteered for any special events that were happening in one of the other five theaters belonging to our company. I spent entire nights with other volunteers helping with renovations, such as ripping out hundreds of old seats and installing new ones. I knew every nut and screw in most of our theaters around town because I had helped tighten most of them. After long construction nights, my workmates and I would treasure an early breakfast of spaghetti marinara covered in parmesan at The Spaghetti Factory.

At one point, the two craziest nighttime volunteers and I spent three full nights renovating the offices at Cinema Metropol. After two nights, we were hacking and sputtering. Our lungs and all of our pores were saturated with plaster dust. Instead of turning to proper safety gear, we started smoking – anything to distract from the sickly, dusty taste in our mouths. The cigarettes made us feel dizzy and sophisticated. The smoke tasted disgusting in a completely new way but at least inhaling burning tobacco obscured the fine dust covering our taste buds. I sneezed and cried plaster dust for weeks afterward. As a "bonus", I left this particular job with a bad smoking habit, inhaling thirty Camel Filters a day for the next seven years.

Cinema Corso was the biggest movie theater our company operated in Zurich. Every two months, Corso featured red carpet events. I helped during as many of them as I could physically survive. Proving my worth, my resilience, and my competence – to myself more than to anyone else – had become a question of honor. On the other hand, coming face-to-face with my Hollywood heroes, whose tales reminded me so often that it was possible to be larger than life, became an addiction. To a big movie lover like me, it was heaven to be asked to carry Hollywood director Kathryn

Bigelow's oversized fur coat – even though the woman was impossibly tall and her coat weighed more than an old-fashioned diving bell.

Eventually, the responsibility of operating our follow spot during special events was handed to me. I was over the moon and couldn't think of anything better than to work with legends like Phil Collins, Harrison Ford, Oliver Stone, Luc Besson, and Roland Emmerich during rehearsals.

Salvatore still worked at Cinema Metropol where we had first met. With all the overtime I did, our paths rarely crossed. Nevertheless, we enjoyed short moments of being home at the same time. We watched movies together and talked about the world. As always, Salvatore was in deep angst about the state of our planet. I was worried about him, and knew he cared deeply about me as well. We continued to support each other like brothers.

Then unfortunately, Sergio promoted Salvatore. I warned Sergio but he chose to interpret my comments as rivalry. To an extent I *was* jealous, but I was far more concerned about Salvatore's wellbeing than my ego. Sergio had no knowledge of the extent of Salvatore's depression. I was afraid the huge amount of added responsibility would push my friend over the edge.

Suddenly, Salvatore was responsible for ushers and kiosk employees in six movie theaters across town. His work hours doubled, and he went from being one of the gang to being the guy on top whom nobody liked. Every day, he fell another few steps behind. I was torn between protecting Salvatore, his sanity and integrity, while at the same time protecting my staff from his incompetence.

After six months of struggling bravely in his new role, Salvatore's depression got the better of him. The walls of his room in our apartment turned an oily black from the number of joints he consumed. I left him in the morning sitting at breakfast only to come back at night and find breakfast had never ended. He would still be sitting on the same chair, newspaper in hand, eating what had to be the fortieth piece of bread with butter and jam.

Salvatore had to give up on work, and lost most of his self-esteem in the process. He was consumed by his ups and downs. After some bureaucratic tap dancing, he managed to secure a disability pension from the Swiss authorities.

We still had four years to go in our marriage before I would be given a permanent residence permit. But I wasn't sure how much longer I would be able to live with my quasi-husband under the same roof. At times his fragile mental state became almost too much for me. Every day, I would pause for a moment before unlocking the door to our apartment, not sure what I would find.

I was struggling with insecurities of my own as well as ongoing family problems. Despite each of us battling our own demons, however, Salvatore and I held on and continued to be there for each other.

During this turbulent first year of working full-time, I experienced a short love affair with a flight attendant from Singapore. He bought popcorn at my concession stand, batted his eyelashes as if his life depended on it and asked me out to dinner. For just a few months, we dated. Al was adorable and caring. He would have moved to the remotest corner of the world for me. I, on the other hand, had become a consummate workaholic who didn't know how to fit anyone into my schedule anymore.

During this frantic era in my life, I disrespected many of my closest friends. They had stuck by me and I repaid them by being constantly late if they needed me. Often, I didn't even bother showing up. To their everlasting credit, none of my friends ever gave up on me. My Zurich family remains an important part of my life to this day.

Al worked Singapore-Zurich once a week. Upon arrival, he would run straight to Cinema ABC, flowers in hand. I would wave, say "I'll be in touch later," and turn my back on him. I behaved like a spoiled, overbooked super model. On top of that, having sex with Al had triggered a monumental insight: my romantic interest had shifted entirely to women. I was at a loss of how to explain this to my boyfriend.

Before breaking up with Heinrich, I had been interested in men only. Following our relationship, and throughout my transition, I had fantasized about everything and everybody. Then, ever since my gender reassignment surgeries, my sex life had been limited to masturbation. For a while, I had been content with my own fingers or other handy objects, like pens, sticks, dildos, or vibrators. I needed time to inhabit my "new" body comfortably and hadn't thought about things like sexual orientation for months. Now, considering my complete lack of physical reaction to Al's outstanding handsomeness, it seemed he had arrived a few years too late.

My lover, and many bouquets of flowers, kept appearing at the theater. I politely maintained the ruse of being unavailable. He was such a caring, good-hearted soul and I was terrified of hurting him. In the end, my silence hurt him more than honest words ever would. My gorgeous flight attendant disappeared into the skies, never to be seen again.

On New Year's Eve of 1997, my shift at ABC went until 1 a.m. I was exhausted from a fifteen-hour work day and barely conscious as I stumbled through the streets of Zurich, evading people who were still toasting each other into the New Year.

Cinema ABC was located in the center of town. Finding a taxi proved to be impossible and all public transport had stopped for the night. I resigned myself to a long walk home.

After a while, I got out of the thickest throng of people. The streets started to thin out. Like stepping out of a blizzard, the sudden silence was eerie and began to lull my exhausted body to sleep. I paused for a moment at a bus stop, willing myself to *not* sit down. I would have been dead to the world in a heartbeat. While I was debating whether to sleep right there on the bench after all, a large silver Mercedes pulled up and the window rolled down.

"Hi, do you need a ride? Hop in," offered an elderly gentleman.

I had never hitchhiked before but figured this was as good a time as any to give it a try. I longed to get home and disappear under my blankets.

The man agreed to drive me home. Relieved and too deeply lost in the fog of sleepiness to be worried, I gave him directions and we made polite conversation. Ten minutes later, we were parked in front of my house and still talking. He came from the same area in southern Germany and many years earlier had worked in a movie theater as well. Laughing at his anecdotes, some of my tiredness disappeared. He was a charming man.

After a while, his right hand meandered from the driver's side onto my thigh. Ever slow on the uptake in the flirting department, it finally dawned on me: he was trying to pick me up.

"Thank you, I'm flattered. But I am not gay and not interested," I said as light heartedly as possible.

Inwardly, I berated myself for having pushed myself to the limit that day. What had I been thinking, staying two hours longer than everyone else on New Year's Eve to do inventory on our concession stock? I had never even thought about how I would get home. Annoyed with myself,

I was conscious of the old man's fingers being only two inches away from discovering my lack of penis.

Thankfully, he removed his hand just in time. Then, after a few more minutes, we parted ways amiably.

"Would you mind giving me your address?" he asked. "I really enjoyed our conversation. Maybe we can meet again sometime?"

Sighing inwardly at my ever-present politeness, I said "yes".

Approximately two months later, Salvatore and I received a letter from the Zurich homicide department. They wanted to see both of us on official business. I called, yet was told nothing.

"Sir, I cannot divulge any information on the phone," I was told harshly. "You and your wife are both obligated to appear at the homicide department at the requested time."

I swallowed hard and neglected to mention to the officer that he was, in fact, talking to Mrs. William.

At the end of February that year, a very nervous and mystified married couple made their way into town to confront the homicide detectives. We were not just nervous about being questioned by the police. We were far more concerned about the fact that we had been summoned as husband and wife. How would the police officers react when Mrs. William was quite obviously a man? To my surprise, they checked our passports and then gracefully overlooked this unusual fact, never once even blinking at the sight of me.

It turned out I was the main person of interest in their investigation, but if a suspect was married, Swiss procedure dictated the spouse be interrogated as well. Poor Salvatore. In the midst of his major depression, he had to deal with stern-faced detectives. It was not the way I wanted to repay his unwavering loyalty and friendship.

As I was led into the interrogation room, I was nervous and relaxed at the same time. As controversial as my history might have been thus far, I didn't remember any homicides being in the mix. I saw Salvatore being led into an adjacent room. His hands were shaking uncontrollably. My heart went out to him.

It wasn't like in the movies. There wasn't a good cop-bad cop scenario. I faced only one detective who bluntly informed me that the elderly gentleman I had amiably chatted with at New Year's Eve had been shot. It turned out this had come to pass only ten days after we had parted ways on my doorstep.

"Can you explain why your fingerprints were all over the interior of the crashed Mercedes, as well as a handwritten note with your address in the glove compartment?" the detective asked.

Like a deer suddenly caught in the headlights, I timidly recounted my New Year's Eve adventure.

In the next room, poor, clueless Salvatore was let go very quickly. I was interrogated a bit longer, and once more found my experience to be entirely different from what I had seen in the movies. In silver-screen interrogations, everyone answered questions readily, even months after the fact. But when I was asked to provide an alibi for the particular time the elderly gentleman had been shot six weeks earlier, I drew a complete blank.

"I'm not sure," I stammered. "It could have been a workday… but I have no memory of when breaks were that day… My schedule changes constantly…"

The dour detective gave me a long look and a suspicious "Hmmmm." He then asked, "Do you own a blue baseball cap?"

"No." I answered truthfully, painfully aware that even a perpetrator with a microscopically small IQ would have answered such an obvious question in the negative as well. Still, after three hours, I was grudgingly let go.

Months later, I received a polite letter from the homicide department, stating the murderer had been found and my name had been expunged from the records. The elderly gentleman had picked up young men on a regular basis. On the fateful night of his murder, he had unknowingly opened his front-seat passenger door for a right-wing extremist hitchhiker who hated homosexuals.

I didn't cry when I read the short report included in the letter. I felt sad, yes, but rather composed. I hoped, it had been worth it and the elderly gentleman had at least been able to live a very fulfilled life before the murderer's bullet found him. Switzerland is a highly civilized country. It is also the world's oldest democracy. It was sobering to see that even here, in a world of regulations, reason, and compromise, anything could happen. We could still be killed simply because we invited someone into our car who didn't share our way of life.

If anything, I drew strength from this realization. Nothing and nowhere was safe or predictable. Even more reason to be bold, true to my heart and make the most of every precious moment.

Thinking of how close I had come to be arrested for a capital crime, however, I also understood that working myself to death wasn't necessarily the best way to seize the day. Becoming a murder suspect as a direct result of being unable to resist making overtime was a wakeup call.

What exactly was I trying to prove? Why the need to work longer and harder than anyone else? Was I succumbing to male stereotypes after all, trying to fit the image of an overworked provider, tough and efficient? In part, yes. I was on a mission to prove my masculinity.

But it was more than that. I was testing the waters, too, exploring the depths of my capabilities. I was overcompensating for years of not being able to go all in. My life had been too fragmented to focus on anything for a long period of time. Now, like a poker player who had always watched from the sidelines, I was eager to get in the game at last. And I was determined to make it count.

Still, there was another aspect as to why I gave my simple work as coordinator, usher, and concession stand salesperson all I had: I loved every minute of it. Like many, I often pondered life, which unlike the movies undoubtedly had few happy endings. The service we provided was invaluable. The movies gave people hope, a sense of community, and a few hours of untainted happiness. As soon as they sat down in front of the silver screen, they were given a reprieve. When the curtain opened and the theater lights dimmed to a barely perceptible glow, moviegoers forgot everything. For just a little while they stopped pushing, let go, and, under the veil of darkness, were safe to become themselves.

I had been an avid cineaste all my life and knew only too well how profoundly two hours of film can infuse us with strength and a sense of destiny. Each time I sat in the dark as a paying guest, or stood in the aisle as an usher, my world expanded. As soon as the movie titles appeared on screen I would feel magic embracing me. It was as if the dimming lights transported me into a dark forest. Remembering the child I once was, I would begin to listen to the tale being told and the voices of the actors on screen would become the narrators of ancient fairy tales. In my mind's eye, I would see elders imparting their wisdoms with frail yet commanding voices.

The flickering screen would become reminiscent of an orange and yellow campfire. As the story unfolded, I would dream of being the hero rising from the flames, as he no doubt would in the end. I would look around me into the faces and hearts of those listening as intently as I did, and enjoy the experience even more because, even though we all came from different backgrounds, we were mesmerized and transported into another realm together. Sinking ever more into the comfort of the surrounding darkness, I would feel the blazing fire's heat, almost too warm to sit too close, but comfortable nonetheless. I would smell the sweet scent of wood smoke and burning pine needles. And I would be profoundly happy.

I couldn't get enough and pitched in as an usher whenever I could. Many nights, I would have to wait inside the theater at the end of the movie. Standing close to the exits, I would get ready to open the doors as soon as the lights dimmed back up. While I waited, watching the hundreds of faces riveted to the screen enchanted me.

I remember the opening weekend of *Forrest Gump* in Cinema Corso. At each showing, eight hundred completely unrelated people would be united by their emotions as the story concluded. They looked up at the screen, tears streaming down their faces. As soon as the house lights came on, our customers landed back on planet Earth and hid their tears in embarrassment. For one small moment though, I had seen into their very souls. The knowledge that we dealt in magic and moved people's hearts sustained me for years.

Then one day, magic met magic.

As a beginning photography student in 1992, I had documented the rehearsals of Switzerland's famous Circus Knie in Zurich. That year, Knie had collaborated with a Canadian show unknown at the time to European audiences. I had marveled at their poetry of motion, their colorful costumes and seductive use of lighting and special effects. Unknowingly, I had witnessed Cirque du Soleil's entrance on the European scene. And I had instantly fallen in love with their boisterous, creative genius.

When the, now world-famous, Cirque du Soleil toured through Zurich with Alegría six years later, they approached our company. Cirque needed a movie theater for a special team event. As they arrived one rainy afternoon, filling our foyer with laughter and dozens of different languages, we brought them to the privacy of our smallest theater. There, the entire cast and crew of Alegría began to watch a documentary about themselves on the silver screen.

Our General Manager asked me to stay around and be available, should they need anything from us. He didn't need to tell me twice. Never did I see a more colorful and internationally diverse group of people. I loved the atmosphere of the unrestrained laughter, the many hugs and kisses and the obviously very close relationship these people shared. They felt like a big, charmingly chaotic family.

While my ushers kept a watchful eye on bored circus children who invaded every corner of our theater like a horde of climbing chimps, I stayed inside the theater for the duration of the screening. The documentary cast a soft light on the vivid faces all around me. As I watched the cast and crew of Alegría watching themselves, and as I listened to their easy banter, I found myself crying uncontrollably. Happiness flooded my heart. I loved being amongst them and wished I could pause time, or hit rewind over and over again.

Slowly, my many working hours were beginning to take their toll. And yet I became hyperactive, almost frantic, as I continued to gain momentum. At night, I curled up under my blanket while my brain tried to process the day's array of different experiences. This led to many sleepless nights. If I managed to sleep, I would have nightmares in which I battled exotic movie theater emergencies. Essentially, I was working non-stop.

More than ever, I tried to find at least half an hour each day to dash off to the Sihl. My soul seemed to breathe through my toes as soon as I reached the river and took off my shoes. It grew progressively lighter with each tickling blade of grass and refreshing drop of water. Even the cold and long Swiss winter could not diminish the river's effects. I would bundle up in a thick coat and sit as close to the wide stream as possible, breathing the scent of life – an irresistible cocktail of river water, algae, cold grass, wet stones, fallen leaves, and rich, dark soil.

I needed this badly because work was slowly becoming more complicated. The concession stand cash register fluctuated from day to day. It was normal. All the kiosk staff and ushers pitched in during movie breaks, so there were many hands in the till. On top of that, the pace was manic. No one expected the register to come out perfectly even. Except me. It became a question of honor for me to get the register as close to even as possible. I wanted my concession stand to be the best in the company.

Most days our losses were negligible. But sometimes the amounts varied from ten Francs to as much as one hundred. My perfectionism got the better of me as I started to put money into the cash register out of my own pocket to make up for whatever was missing. Some months, I invested up to three hundred Francs of my personal money.

Slowly, unknown parties within my team realized what I was doing and started taking advantage. People began stealing, knowing full well I would replace whatever was missing. Soon they became so bold that even someone as trusting as I was had to rule out coincidence.

I was two years into my time at ABC when, all of a sudden, an entire envelope of banknotes disappeared. I turned around for a second, and one thousand Francs were gone. Half an hour later, one of my employees came back from break wearing new designer shoes way too pricey for a student salary. But I couldn't prove a thing.

The amounts were now beyond a scope I could cover on my salary. So I swallowed my pride and confided in my superiors. They shook their heads. Suspicion hung in the room as noxious as acid rain, turning the vibrantly sprawling tree of my enthusiasm into a lifeless skeleton. Sergio regarded me with sad eyes.

"Liam, you need to understand. You are telling us you put money into the cash register on a regular basis. And that it has been going on for almost six months. Of course, this makes us wonder if maybe you took money *out* as well."

The General Manager as well as Sergio agreed under the circumstances, it would be best to transfer me to another venue. I was transferred immediately and became team coordinator at Cinema Metropol where I had worked before as a student. Contrary to ABC where I dealt mostly with inexperienced part-time students, Metropol had a solid, long-standing team. As much as I was happy to be reunited with them, I felt like a failure. My pride was hurt and most of all, being mistrusted after all the boundless energy I had invested felt like falling into a field of poison ivy because I had gazed too intently into the sun.

Looking back with more maturity and less of my characteristic explosive impulsiveness, I realize moving me out of the picture was the wisest course of action at the time. My ambition and enthusiasm had been like gas-filled balloons tied to a heavy cart. With rising enthusiasm, the balloons had grown bigger until finally the cart – my world – had been lifted from the safety of the ground and carried out into space. I had learned a valuable lesson: my willingness to go the extra mile could become my downfall.

Thefts continued after I was gone at Cinema ABC, thankfully confirming my innocence. A new coordinator came in with fresh eyes and was quickly able to pick out the bad seeds.

My transfer was a blessing in disguise. For the first time in years, I had time to breathe. Even the River Sihl was just around the corner. I now sat at the opposite bank and could luxuriate in breaks of up to an hour.

Working with my old team was like coming home. The few new members of staff were delightful to work with as well. The audience in Cinema Metropol was more mature. We experienced less daily vandalism and hysteria. I relaxed and delegated far more work to those around me than I had in the previous two years.

One young woman on our team, Naomi, radiated positive energy like a small sun. Her smile lit up the room. She was supporting herself while working full-time during a four-year-apprenticeship in the travel industry. Naomi didn't need prompting. She was the most reliable employee I ever had, independent, honest and polite at all times.

Naomi loved movies as much as I did. We soon became inseparable at work. We developed a strong bond, but our friendship was never motivated by sexual interest. We simply appreciated each other and learned to trust each other explicitly, personally as much as professionally. To this day, Naomi remains one of my most trusted friends.

Finding myself with time to relax made me wonder about new horizons. Maybe I didn't want to grow old in a movie theater after all. Were there more interesting professions I could strive for? I enjoyed organizing and administration. I enjoyed having responsibility. It had been six years since I had started as a part-time usher at Cinema Metropol. The movies had taken me on an unforgettable journey. But I decided my lucky seventh year would be my last.

Still working full time, I asked to have my weekend moved to Fridays and Saturdays, so I could attend a local Business College. I planned to finish what I had started before breaking off my studies to work at the *Phaenomena* ten years earlier: I was going to get a Business Diploma in my free time. Once I had it, I would jump into the unknown once more.

I was so absorbed by my life at the movie theater that my gender identity wasn't on my mind very often. Having scars seemed as normal to me as having two ears, and the empty space between my legs as natural as not having two noses.

But still, I needed to work on my self-confidence. Truth be told, I couldn't bring myself to take my shirt off in public. I cared far too much about other people's opinions, and Swiss people had an awful habit of openly staring at anything out of the ordinary. I would imagine everyone scrutinizing the scars from my breast removal surgery and bristle at the thought. The beaches at the lakeside were packed during summer. I didn't fancy being the one anchovy in the can getting singled out, unable to slide by in oily anonymity.

It wasn't a major problem though. In my heart of hearts I knew staring people could be found the world over. Like with so many other things, I would simply need to take it in stride and give myself time to overcome any lingering inhibitions.

For a while, family issues worried me far more than sunbathing my imperfect upper body. Since 1997, Dad and I's relationship seemed to gradually deteriorate.

Over the years, no matter how busy I got, I never stopped visiting my parents. Sometimes, I was touchy and grumpy, slowly working on overcoming delayed anger, and struggling with forgiveness. Other times we clashed or misunderstood each other. No matter how I felt about them, however, I would always make time and show up for short visits.

Nonetheless, Dad seemed to tense up more and more. I wondered why. Was it related to my body becoming more male? Did he not understand my being transgender after all? Was he too selfishly absorbed by his many sexual adventures? Or, had I begun to look too much like the young men he craved for? Did this make him uncomfortable? Or was I reading too much into it? Was I simply working too much and he was upset with me not spending enough time with him? My relationship with Hildegard had always been turbulent. But this uncertainty with Dad sent me reeling.

One visiting weekend, I had had enough of Dad's behavior and confronted him directly.

"What on Earth is going on? You're becoming ever more distant towards me."

As emotional as he was, Dad struggled to find the right words. After hours of evasive small talk concerning the stock market and German history, he finally came out with it.

"I am so worried about you. I keep thinking, what if your sex change was a major mistake and now you will be unhappy and damaged for the rest of your life? I am terrified to ask you how you are. What if you say you're horribly unhappy? I just don't know if I could cope with it. I need you to be happy."

Deeply touched and somewhat taken by surprise, I said, "But Dad, I'm happier than ever. I'm fine. I'm finally able to be myself. No matter what else happens in my life, I'll be able to manage."

He tried to give me a reassuring smile, but I could still see the worry and doubt in his eyes.

In time, he would realize that I truly was fine. I was on the regular roller coaster of life, just like everyone else. For now at least, our open conversation had served in relaxing us both to the point where we could be our old teddy bear selves again. We went back to hugging each other as much and as often as we could.

14

Oma's Bathtub

Every time I visited Dad, I spent a lot of time with Oma. She was becoming ever more senile, sometimes giving me suspicious looks when she thought me to be one of her son's many lovers. Mostly I would sit with her, watching horrible Eurovision Song Contests on TV at full volume. Oma had grown quite deaf over the years.

At first, I tried patiently to somehow get her to realize she was actually talking with the same beloved grandchild, that I was the same person though my gender appeared different. But she would keep asking, "Where is Stefanie? Why doesn't she come visit us anymore?" My thoughts would spiral downwards into depths of sadness as vast as the Mariana Trench. But I would keep smiling and return to easy conversation to keep Oma company and at least try to give her a few happy hours. Meanwhile, my heart felt crushed to the point of breaking.

Each visit, I kept trying to explain. One day, I looked deeply into Oma's eyes while I went over the same information for the umpteenth time and saw a maelstrom of battling emotions. They ranged from mild confusion and bewilderment, to agony and fear.

Trying to convince her of something her mind couldn't possibly comprehend anymore only exacerbated the pain of her condition. Trying to explain my presence reminded her of my absence, keeping the wound open and festering, instead of letting it heal as best as it could. What Oma needed most of all was peace of mind. That's what I wanted to give to her. So I stopped explaining.

She didn't mind the nice young man sitting with her. Quite the contrary, she enjoyed my company and chatted with me about her memories and favorite TV shows. Often, she surprised me by sharing very personal details of her married life, such as when her second husband, my Dad's father, had come home too drunk to find the keyhole on their front door. Annoyed by his drunkenness, she had fetched a bucket of ice-cold water and poured it out of a second floor window onto his head, sobering him up instantly. I smiled and laughed with her, hoping it would convey how much she meant to me.

I was like a shipwrecked sailor who is surrounded by water but cannot drink. Oma was right there, in front of me. But I didn't need her kindness or her stories. Only the pure and matchless love of a grandma and her grandchild could slake my thirst. I needed to be able to hold her in my arms, to see her sparkling eyes ignite with happiness and recognition and the unconditional love she had always felt for me. But this could not happen.

We used to bake cookies together. I would end up eating so much of Oma's mouthwatering cookie dough, she would have to make a second batch. First she would chase me good-naturedly from her kitchen. Then, when the cookies finally came out of the oven, she would eat only one and insist I take all the rest.

In the early Eighties, when acid-washed jeans were all the rage, I had labored for days, ruining a perfectly new pair of jeans. I had left them out in the rain, rubbed them with rocks, and ripped holes into them at the knees and several other places. Satisfied with my result, I had put them in the washing machine and looked forward to wearing them. The next day, I found my jeans dry and folded – and unrecognizable, almost perfectly restored. Oma had treated them with a special washing solution. She had so painstakingly and subtly mended all the holes that they were hardly visible.

I ran to her, brandishing the jeans like a CSI presenting evidence at a court hearing.

"Oma, what have you done?"

"Ay-ay-ay-ay-ay-ay-ay-ay! Stefanie, you can't wear them the way they were. It's not proper."

"Oma, I need those jeans the way they were. Everyone's wearing them like this now. You know I have enough trouble with the other kids as it is. Maybe they'll accept me a little better if I at least wear the coolest jeans in school."

Oma didn't argue the stupidity of my desperate teenage logic. She only sighed, uttered another softly repressed "ay-ay-ay-ay" and got out her scissors. For the rest of the afternoon, Oma and I ripped my pants back apart. Then she helped me stain them strategically with bleach and other aggressive chemicals. The end result was far more sophisticated than what I had accomplished.

Even though I understood about the relentless passage of time, it was shattering to imagine Oma and I would never be able to share moments like this again. And what was happening inside her mind? Did any of the memories of our shared time together remain in her consciousness, or had she lost me in there, too?

In 1998, Oma broke her hip a second time. This time around, her body deteriorated too much. She was weak and hardly able to sit up in bed. Somehow her senility was adversely affected as well, and worsened considerably over a matter of days. Now she didn't even recognize Dad anymore. Instead she kept lovingly calling him "Karl" – her late husband's name.

During one of her rare moments of clarity, she begged Dad to take her home from the hospital. He complied and spent eleven months taking care of her as much as he could in his off hours while continuing to work full time.

Oma had a hospital bed at home. She had Dad's care in the mornings and evenings as well as the help of a professional caretaker during the day. Witnessing her steady but painfully slow decline was one of the most heartbreaking experiences Dad and I ever shared.

On my visiting weekends, Dad and I would go next door together. The ugly hospital bed with its pragmatically white-painted metal frame sat in the center of Oma's cozy living room like an intimidating, robotic preying mantis. Oma looked smaller than ever in the clutches of this monstrosity. Machines surrounded the bed, monitoring her vitals and keeping her alive.

Amazingly, Oma's eyes still sparkled. She almost always greeted us with a sweet smile. Dad and I would stay a while, smiling back bravely and talking with her. We would bring her water, or prop her up in bed so we could gently spoon some potato soup into her mouth.

Each weekend, Dad would bathe his mother in her bathtub. I didn't visit every weekend, and since Oma wasn't quite sure who I was, I couldn't easily be in the bathroom with them. But Oma's bathtub still became one of the more important bodies of water in my life journey.

Dad would fill the tub with water of a balmy temperature and add some enlivening bath salts for good measure. Oma's favorite scent was chamomile. Thick clouds of the soothing fragrance would waft through the entire apartment preceding each of Oma's bath times. After everything was prepared just perfectly, Dad would come back to help Oma out of her nightgown. In only her underpants and worn bra, she looked incredibly haggard. Dad would then pick her up and carry her the short way from her living room into the bathroom. The way he held her would make it obvious that she had diminished to the weight of a feather.

Closing the door halfway, Dad would then proceed to tenderly remove his mom's undergarments. I would follow, transfixed, somehow needing to see with my own eyes. But I would remain at a distance, outside the bathroom door, just out of Oma's view, to respect her privacy.

Her entire skeleton was clearly visible. Her soft, leathery skin, which I had adored so much and spent years snuggling against, hung from her frame. I had always enjoyed the warm energy emanating from her skin. Now it seemed lifeless and brittle like paper from an ancient manuscript.

With utter gentleness, Dad would lower his mom slowly into the pre-prepared bathwater. She was so weak, he would need to stay with her to make sure she wouldn't slip under the water accidentally, unable to surface alone.

Once immersed in the warm bathwater, resting against Dad's strong arms, Oma's transformation would be astonishing. A grateful smile would begin animating her entire countenance. I could see her letting go of all mental anguish and physical pain. Her eyes would sparkle as if she was back to being the strong, vivid character she had always been. Sometimes even her mind would regain some of its lucidity. Thankfully, during these bathing sessions her mind would only re-surface partly – just enough for her to enjoy her surroundings but not enough to feel sorrow in the face of her decline. She would laugh and have full conversations with her son, calling him "Konrad" once more. After a while, she would float peacefully, closing her eyes, soaking up warmth and reassurance in equal measure.

I would keep watching, tears in my eyes, happy to see my oma restored to at least a portion of her former self. Seeing her smile so genuinely was a wondrous experience. For just a short spell, Oma's bathtub brought her happiness and restored her back into our lives.

Overall however, her physical state was declining ever more swiftly. Nature was cruel. Oma's doctor ascribed her the strong, healthy heart of an eighteen year-old, a powerful drum, pounding steadily. Yet, bit-by-bit, the rest of her body stopped dancing to the beat. Towards the end, she couldn't sit, talk, or even swallow on her own. Her bodily functions were shutting down one by one, yet her heart kept its mighty rhythm.

The most dreadful moments were when, for just an instant, my oma would fully surface from her state of blissfully senile cluelessness. Her eyes would clear up, and the full extent of her helplessness would split through her like an axe. Tears would well up in her eyes as her heart broke into a million pieces.

Oma had always been there for me. She had reassured me, had given me comfort, energy, and an abundance of laughter and smiles, lighting up my life like brightly glowing candles on dark winter nights. In her moments of anguish, I wished I could do the same for her.

At the end, so little was left of Oma, her body looked scarily reminiscent to the bodies of concentration camp survivors I had seen in documentaries. The hospital bed seemed to have expanded to the dimensions of a small, forbidding spaceship. Oma's pale, shrunken face looked up at us, seemingly floating on her pillow like a bodiless ghost. The duvet was completely flat, not betraying even a hint of the shriveled body underneath. A machine extracted saliva from Oma's mouth every few minutes so she wouldn't suffocate on the accumulating liquid.

Throughout her hard life, Oma had been a pillar of strength. Now Dad and I wished with all our hearts she weren't so unbelievably strong.

I was in Zurich on December 26, 1998, busy with the usual holiday season craziness at the movie theater. We were constantly sold out and people were happily spending their Christmas bonuses like there was no tomorrow.

Dad called me during my dinner break. I was sitting in my favorite Italian restaurant eating Gnocchi alla Sorrentina covered with a generous pile of Parmesan. Dad was crying, and soon so was I. Dad and Oma's doctor had made a merciful decision. They had kept her on a saline drip like before, but no more calories were added to the liquid. About a week later, at the age of eighty-nine, she had fallen asleep for the last time.

Oma was dead and I found myself having trouble processing that I would never see her loving smile again. It seemed impossible.

I was devastated, stricken by the fact that I had never been able to say goodbye to the woman who had in effect raised me. She had saved me over and over again and had, against all odds, instilled a deep love of life in me. With eternal positivity and tirelessness, she had been the first one to make sure I never lost my trusting nature. Above all, she had inspired me to never stop believing in the good within others as well as within myself.

I dropped everything and took the next train home. The funeral was held two days later. All of our relatives were there along with all of Oma's remaining friends.

It was a sunny winter day. Temperatures were freezing. We looked like an Inuit tribe, huddled up in our thick winter coats and paraphernalia. The pastor had prepared a beautiful, lengthy speech. We all exercised patience, wiggling our toes inside our winter boots to keep them from freezing off. I stood with the children in one corner, contemplating the coffin and how unreal Oma had looked inside of it before the lid was closed.

The pastor concluded his heartfelt speech with the traditional expression "earth to earth, ashes to ashes, dust to dust". While quoting these final words, he picked up a small, pre-prepared shovelful of earth to cast onto my oma's coffin. At the completion of his elegant movement, nothing happened. All eyes went to the shovel. The little mound of earth had firmly frozen onto the metal during his nearly thirty-minute-long speech. Adult mouths started to twitch, then the children started giggling, and finally I lost it and started laughing uncontrollably.

Oma had always had a good sense of humor and would have appreciated this final, comically-awkward gesture in her name. I imagined both her and God watching with twinkling eyes.

15

Two Lakes

By 1999, I was a handsome twenty-eight year old man. I was also a passionate workaholic. With my boundless positive energy, I continued to inspire those around me as much as I exasperated them.

I still sped through life and work like a Duracell bunny on crack. There was just so much to see and experience. Now that I was moving more freely in a body reflecting more of my true self, I wanted to go everywhere, meet everyone, and enjoy my freedom.

I already felt comfortable and liberated while engaging in slow or static activities like swimming, walking and going to the movies, but I dreamed of skydiving, skateboarding, surfing, and other risky activities, things I was still too inhibited to try. Here my subconscious stepped in while I was asleep. In my dreams, I would soar through the skies, race through familiar streets on a skateboard, and plummet down steep hills without a trace of fear in my heart. I often awoke feeling dazed and happy.

The life of my helpful friend and husband Salvatore, on the other hand, seemed to be spiraling ever deeper into the abyss. His disability pension enabled him to keep having breakfast all day long. He would stare into space, pondering the futility of life. A big music lover, his choice of music reflected his gradually darkening moods.

Winter had always managed to brighten his spirits in previous years. Salvatore was passionate about Christmas trees. He would seize the moment as early as possible and start decorating up to a dozen pine trees every early November. He would spread them like a magical forest throughout our entire apartment.

That year, I came home on Christmas Day, after a grueling fifteen-hour workday at Cinema Metropol. When I opened our front door, all I saw was destruction. The pine trees had crashed to the floor. Shards of broken Christmas tree ornaments covered our carpets. On second glance, my heart twisted. Drops of a thick, dark, red fluid covered much of the debris. A strange metallic smell hung in the air.

I found Salvatore in his room. Here, the stench of puke dominated. My friend was covered in blood and completely unresponsive. His face rested in a big puddle of what looked like half-digested pizza. Against all better judgment, I decided to shake him awake instead of calling Emergency Services immediately. Salvatore was in a daze, but conscious enough to beg me not to call an ambulance.

"Liam, please, I know how bad this looks, but if you call them, they'll notify my psychiatrist. A suicide attempt will get me admitted to a closed psychiatric ward. I don't want to end up there. Please, don't call?"

I nodded. Of course I would protect him and respect his wishes. We were close friends. And I had never forgotten how he had saved me years earlier. So I sat next to him all night while he slept, checking his pulse every now and then, making sure he didn't quietly slip away on me.

The next morning, Salvatore awoke surprisingly refreshed. After cleaning up most of the debris and bodily fluids together, we sat down for another extended breakfast. I didn't ask any questions. When my friend was ready, he explained, "Sitting alone in my room all day yesterday, I just couldn't see the point to any of this anymore. Christmas is always the worst time for me. You were at work and I felt so useless and lonely. I know my depression is a real problem, and it's great to get the disability pension… but I am only thirty-four years old, Liam. What am I going to do? Listen to music and smoke joints for the rest of my life? That's going to be one hell of a long and desperate existence. So I figured, why not end it all at Christmas. Might as well."

Salvatore had celebrated with his favorite pizza first. For dessert, he had swallowed fifty sleeping pills and helped himself to a few bottles of wine. Instead of blissfully drifting away into nothingness as he had hoped, he had gotten violently ill. He had then toppled over multiple times, crashed into Christmas trees, and cut himself on ornament shards. Finally, he had collapsed on his mattress unable to move. Still bleeding and throwing up, he had fallen asleep, coming to for only an instant when I shook him awake. He had re-submerged into a deep, dreamless sleep from which he had just awakened unscathed.

Salvatore looked at me, bracing himself for whatever I would have to say. Instead of giving him a big speech, I told him the simple truth.

"I'm so happy you are still here with me."

Still, it was time to take a step back. Salvatore and I had taken care of each other for three years. Over the years, I had felt an increasing helplessness in the face of his worsening clinical depression. I wasn't his psychiatrist. I needed more space to take care of myself. Business College was almost done. I would need to find a new challenge professionally. At the end of the day, my home needed to be a sanctuary where I could relax and recharge my Duracells for the next day.

I found a studio apartment, not far away from where Salvatore and I lived. It was hard for him to see me go, yet we lived close enough to easily reach out whenever we needed each other.

With more time to relax at home, I found the energy to start looking for a new profession. In an effort to combine my creative talents with my newly-acquired business knowledge, I followed a friend's recommendation and started looking for Desktop Publishing jobs in banks and consulting companies.

Soon, I was invited to an interview at a major bank in Zurich. My interviewer was a very well-dressed, middle-aged lady who seemed interested in hiring me as part of her creative team. As the offer got more tangible, I was inevitably forced to explain that my papers and social security number belonged to a female Klenk – and why. Following my disclosure, I received a polite letter, stating, "We are sorry to inform you that we have shortlisted other more qualified applicants for the position."

Most days, my being transgender wasn't an issue. It wasn't the first thing I thought about after waking up. The more time passed since my operations, the more often I went without thinking of my gender identity, sometimes for weeks at a time. Friends rarely asked me about it anymore. Amongst many roses in an Italian rose garden, I was just one more species. My friends and I were all from the same exquisite genus, yet at the same time, we valued each other's individuality.

My unique situation only became tricky when encountering strangers. They all had watched countless talk shows on TV, shows that loved to introduce only very exotic trans people in order to push their ratings. As a result, most people who didn't know me often assumed too much and came to conclusions having nothing to do with my personality but everything to do with the talk show they had just seen the previous day.

Over the years, I honed my people skills and became very careful about when and how much I would divulge about my gender history. Meeting potential new friends, I would wait until we knew each other well enough, before mentioning anything about my past.

This was not an option in business or immigration-related encounters, however. Because of my marriage to Salvatore, I had needed to postpone applying for a passport reflecting my true gender. Thus, I was still listed as female. Whenever official paperwork was required, I had to face coming out to complete strangers. It was becoming harder and harder for me to deal with these vulnerable moments of losing all privacy. As free as I now felt in my every day life, dealing with the authorities never failed to bring me down to Earth. In only a matter of hours, I would feel like a wild dolphin suddenly getting captured and transferred to an aquarium pool. I felt the walls closing in. I longed to at last be unconditionally free and shed the last remaining bonds tying me to the gender identity I had physically transcended four years prior.

Once a year, I visited the Zurich immigration offices to renew my work permit. Each year, I would approach the counter giving the lady a wide smile, producing my application papers and passport. Each year, a new lady would smile back politely and tell me, "It's so nice of you to run this errand for your wife, but she really needs to come see us in person."

I couldn't help but be amused as well as frustrated. With yet another smile, I would then patiently explain.

"I'm sorry, I don't mean to confuse you. But this passport is in fact mine. I had a gender change a few years back and I'm now physically a man. Unfortunately though, my official papers haven't been changed to "male" yet and I'm also still the wife of Mr. Eschbach."

Without fail, the lady at the immigration counter would react politely and professionally and simply say, "Oh, I see. In this case, can I have your application papers, please?"

Still, by the time I left the premises, my smile would be frozen in place, my face muscles hurting as much as my pride.

My search for new professional horizons continued. While Salvatore and I were still married, I would simply need to accept the inevitability of awkward moments and push through. After another month of scouting for a new professional challenge, I was suddenly faced with two open-minded employers at the same time.

One of the potential employers was a graphic design office. They were a small, young team, taking on diverse, creative contracts. They weren't bothered by my very limited graphic design knowledge or my history. The owners were open about liking my personality and offered to engage me straight away.

At the same time, I had an interview at the renowned consulting firm McKinsey & Company. They had an opening in their internal Visual Aids team whose task it was to produce PowerPoint presentations and multimedia content for their consultants. This potential employer sounded infinitely duller than the charming graphic design crew I had just met. Yet I couldn't help being attracted to what was, for me, very atypical: a well-structured environment.

I spent an entire day at McKinsey being screened by all members of five separate Visual Aids teams, as well as having multiple interviews with human resources representatives. Everything was very professional, well-organized, and respectful, and the atmosphere was surprisingly upbeat.

Regula, the head of human resources at McKinsey was an energetic redhead. Towards the end of my interview day, she said, "It's been an intense day for you, I'm sure. You'll be happy to hear that so far I've heard nothing but positive feedback. We're very interested in offering you a position."

"Here we go again", I thought. I took a deep breath, and responded, "That's wonderful. I've had a very good impression of everyone as well. In this case though, I need to tell you something I haven't mentioned yet because it's very personal. I am transgender, and even though I'm sitting before you as a man, all my official papers still list me as female. I want to be up front rather than having McKinsey & Company find out about my uncommon situation through registering my passport and social security number with the relevant authorities."

Regula greeted my comments with an open smile and not a shred of irritation. She thanked me and said, "Thank you very much for your honesty but the information you just gave me isn't really relevant for me. I trust my instincts and they tell me you will be an excellent fit for our company."

I was stunned and amazed by her openness. What mattered to her were my work ethic, my skills and personality.

I was highly interested in both potential positions and pondered my decision for a few days. In the end, I surprised myself by – for the first time in my life – deciding on more security and less creativity. I happily agreed to start work at McKinsey & Company in two months' time.

It was late February of 2000. I was busy counting the concession stand stock at Cinema Metropol one early evening when my phone rang. Dad was on the other end of the line, his words tumbling out like a waterfall. I was barely able to understand him. All I heard was "storm." He seemed terrified. I still harbored anger towards both my adoptive parents. I was trying to slowly let it all go and move on, but so far my emotions concerning the events of my childhood were still too overwhelming. Nevertheless, I loved my dad. Hearing the terror in his voice, I stopped asking questions and said, "Hang in there, Dad. I'll come over straight away. I'll be with you tomorrow morning."

"But all public transport has been suspended due to the storm." he said, still at the edge of panic.

"Don't worry Dad. I'll be there. I'll find a way."

I immediately called Sergio, and explained, "I am sorry, but I need to leave work immediately. My dad's caught in a bad storm in Germany and needs my help. I need to somehow get over there as soon as possible."

"No problem. I'll send a replacement from Cinema Corso right away." Then Sergio caught me by surprise. "You can borrow my car. Just hang on for an hour."

Stunned, all I could think of to say was, "Ok," and I hung up.

Precisely an hour later, Sergio arrived in front of Cinema Metropol in a beautiful, red VW Golf. Swallowing hard, I said, "I'm a bit worried. I'll be driving through severe snowstorms. What if I damage your car?"

Sergio held out his keys. "It's only a car. Just make sure *you* come back in one piece."

I had never owned a car. My skills were rusty at best. To avoid overly tempting fate, I decided not to drive through a snowstorm in complete darkness. I waited until the early morning hours and started on an odyssey through a storm front that hadn't lost any of its force during the night. The snowflakes were thick. With the storm blowing them towards me almost horizontally, visibility was reduced to thirty feet, if that. My hands hurt from white-knuckling the steering wheel. My eyes hurt from staring out at the white wilderness. When I finally arrived four hours later, I ached all over and felt as if I had been run over by several buses at once.

Thankfully, the storm had abated. My dad's neighborhood was a picture of destruction. Sections of roofs littered the streets. Trees had been uprooted everywhere, falling onto parked cars. Neighbors were coming out of their houses, looking slightly dazed and inspecting the extensive property damage. I hurried upstairs to my dad's penthouse, worried as to what I would find.

Konrad practically fell into my arms with relief. Upon entering his apartment, it became clear why he had been so terrified. Part of his roof had been ripped off. His penthouse garden lay in ruin, most of it covered with debris from surrounding buildings. Surrounded by chaos, I was eerily reminded of the nightmares that had plagued me during my childhood. Only the alien ships and firestorms were missing to complete the picture.

I spent two days with my dad, cleaning up and catching up. Repair crews started work immediately. Radio broadcasts confirmed what we already knew. The storm had punched its way through Germany at one hundred and twenty miles per hour. Nature's forces being quite gentle in Central Europe on a regular day, this was as close as we would ever get to a full-blown hurricane.

Practically overnight, Dad decided to sell his penthouse and move to Lake Constance, the Swabian Ocean, where we had spent many of our family vacations during my childhood.

The place he loved the most at the lake was only forty-five minutes away from my home in Zurich. In record time, Dad managed to sell most of the possessions he had accumulated while residing at the same location for thirty-five years. He found a small ground floor apartment in a four-hundred-year-old village house, adjacent to the lake and surrounded by green hills, and flowers.

Living close to each other helped our relationship. I drove the short distance to his nostalgic new home every second weekend. We would go for long walks together, gazing out at Lake Constance stretching all the way to the horizon. As a child, I had hated coming here. Now as an adult, I was able to appreciate the peaceful atmosphere radiating from the ocean-like body of water. I would breathe deeply and enjoy the moment.

Dad in turn visited Zurich often. This gave us the chance to enjoy the beautiful town together, and have beers at the lakeside while contemplating our lives. We both loved Lake Zurich with all our hearts. In tune with the romantic atmosphere generated by the historical surroundings and blissfully blue lake, we made lots of headway and talked more openly than we had since my childhood.

At the same time, Zurich offered my sexually-frustrated dad the chance to frequent gay establishments in the Swiss metropolis, searching for pleasure and hoping for love. He would have never come to Zurich on his own. My presence there gave him the courage he needed to overcome his insecurities and finally branch out.

16

Columbia River

Towards the end of my era at the movies, time seemed to accelerate faster than *Secretariat* at the Belmont Stakes. My last day of work came all too soon. The entire team sat in the foyer of Cinema Metropol, toasting each other and devouring tasty nibbles I had ordered at the local delicatessen.

These ten people from Switzerland and Serbia had been a loyal family. In the very beginning of my transition, when I was risking it all, they had shown me a depth of generosity and compassion I would never forget. Even Erich had learned how to say my name. Over the years, my teammates had continued to awe me with their open-mindedness, never once doubting my actions or my identity.

I was leaving them *mit einem lachenden und einem weinenden Auge* as we say in German – with one eye laughing and the other, crying. The movie theater had given me passion and fulfillment, but my inner nomad was happily looking forward to sailing towards new horizons.

Fortunately, growing into my new role at McKinsey proved to be a good experience from day one. The daily content I dealt with in Visual Aids wasn't stimulating. I wasn't passionately engaged, as I had been in my magical movie world. However, the five small Visual Aids teams were refreshing to work with.

Visual Aids consisted of around twenty people. Their backgrounds were colorful – an aspiring veterinarian, two whale researchers, theater actors, an opera singer, a DJ, visual artists, and versatile survivors like myself. We rarely developed relationships outside work, but genuinely looked out for each other at the office. Since we had no direct client contact, we were able to come to work as colorful and casual as we pleased. We worked in shifts, which suited me very much.

"For the sake of professionalism, please keep your gender change confidential, even within your team." the human resources manager Regula had asked me.

Her request didn't bother me. I felt she simply wanted to separate work from personal: my very intimate history was not necessarily anyone's business but my own. I kept my word. Since office work never included having to take my shirt or pants off, none of my workmates were ever the wiser.

I looked forward to going to the office every morning and have never worked in a more professional environment since. McKinsey picked their people well. Employees treated each other with respect and friendly politeness. Everyone worked very hard, yet kept calm at all times. We were well taken care of, with amazing benefits, delicious food, all-you-can-eat fruit and sandwiches, and countless other perks. Staff evaluations were done every six months. We felt appreciated and taken seriously. Management was fantastic, competent and motivating. I treasured this new environment of reliability, structure and peacefulness after the much more ardent, yet much less professional, work environment at the movie theater.

Life at my little studio apartment was superb as well. I enjoyed the company of my books and movies, relieved to not have to take care of anyone else but myself for a change. I cooked in my tiny kitchen corner and enjoyed glimpses of rare Swiss sunshine on a small terrace I had managed to turn into a veritable green wilderness.

Within a few months, I became aware of my next-door neighbor's cats. Every so often they would wander into my domain. A little while later, I also became aware of Natasha, my next-door neighbor herself. She was a petite, curvaceous blonde, sexy and self-confident. With true male obliviousness, it dawned on me much too late that she had a crush on me and had used her cats to get my attention.

I hadn't had a relationship with anyone in years. I felt comfortable with my own company, yet I was also lonely. It felt good to have someone smile at me adoringly, someone who actually craved spending time with me. Slowly, I began to reciprocate, even though I knew from the beginning that I wasn't in love with her.

I couldn't resist being wanted. Natasha flirted heavily with me and let me know how much intellectual men turned her on. I was flattered and we started spending more time together. At almost thirty years of age, I was still utterly hopeless in the relationship department and inexperienced in bed. I had only had that long relationship with Heinrich, my short affair with Al – the flight attendant from Singapore, as well as a string of unsuccessful one-night stands. Since my gender reassignment surgeries five years earlier, only Al had seen my naked body.

Even if I didn't feel the stirrings of passion, why not finally deal with my cluelessness and go with the flow? But taking off my clothes in front of Natasha terrified me more than anything else. Concerning sexual relations, I felt like a patient who surfaces from an extended coma but has no recollection of how to use his muscles. How would I have sex with her? How would she react to a man with ugly scars on his chest and no penis? One evening, I summoned all my courage and explained myself to Natasha. I admitted to my fears and physical incompleteness.

Once again, I was surprised and amazed by the beauty of human hearts. Against all my expectations, Natasha wasn't rattled. We sat on my couch. She took me in her arms and made it clear she was in love with me exactly the way I was.

In exchange for my forthrightness, Natasha shared some of her history as well. She had spent some years in the US, working illegally as an exotic dancer and prostitute. In the end, the police had caught her. Officers had suddenly and roughly escorted her to the airport and put her on a plane. An angry red stamp in her passport made it clear: future entry into the US would be denied. Natasha had been back in Switzerland for only a few months when she moved in next door. She worked at a call center to make ends meet. It never occurred to me to judge her based on her past, just as she had not judged me on mine.

I was deeply touched – but not in love. Throughout our relationship, I lacked patience and kindness. Some moments were as exasperating as they were humorous. During one rainy weekend, we spent an entire day under fluffy covers. We were right in the middle of awkward sex and I was moments away from orgasm, when Natasha received text messages on both of her mobile phones. Imagine my surprise when she sat up, pulled the phones out from under the pillow and, still straddling me, started texting her friends back. I had landed on planet Nokia.

Often, Natasha had no idea what I was on about. She wasn't stupid, but lived solely in the moment and had never read a book in her life. I, on the other hand, had spent my entire life reading and absorbing random knowledge and was becoming more and more of an amateur philosopher. One day I shared an inspiring Winston Churchill quote with her. Natasha beamed and said, "Ah, brilliant. I have always loved that American writer."

Natasha did have her strengths. One of her most amazing qualities was a fierce loyalty. One evening in our short relationship will stay with me forever. I had organized tickets for the movie premiere of *Gladiator* at my old haunt Cinema Metropol. A little bit into the movie, four drunken teenagers behind us became progressively louder. After a while, my irritation got the better of me. I turned around.

"Can you please be quiet?" I asked them politely. "I would love to actually be able to hear what is happening on screen."

Four pairs of eyes glared back at me. Surprisingly, the little gang didn't make a sound for the rest of the movie. However, I could feel their stares burning into the back of my neck like probing tractor beams from a hostile space ship. But with quiet restored, I soon forgot about them and we re-immersed ourselves in the story unfolding on screen.

Once the movie was over, we waited until the credits had rolled and most of the five hundred guests had left the theater before heading to my car parked right outside one of the main emergency exits. While getting in, Natasha and I talked animatedly about the heroic tale we had just enjoyed. All around us, other premiere guests were still engaged in conversation on the sidewalk, slowly getting ready to disperse in search of their evening's next entertainment.

I was about to put the key in the ignition when the door on the driver's side was yanked open. I was jerked out of the car to face one of the drunken teenagers who had been seated behind us. The smartest thing I could think of to say was, "Oh, it's you." I had no idea what to do. The bald-shaved, compact little street fighter had obviously seen way too many Hollywood gangster flics. He was glaring at me like Robert De Niro in *Taxi Driver* as he rolled up his sleeves. It didn't help his mood any when his cliché attitude made me laugh out loud.

I had never been in a physical fight with anyone and didn't know the first thing about hitting someone. As I began to try and talk some sense into the guy, I realized I was wasting my breath. It didn't matter who I was. He loved fighting and would have taken any opportunity to do it. By speaking up, I had appointed myself his target of the night.

I felt some strange male pride. Suddenly, some ancient caveman within me wanted nothing more than to impress my lady. As my opponent rushed towards me for the attack, I somehow managed to grab him and get him into a chokehold. While we struggled and shuffled, a little conversation with myself played out inside my head.

"Be careful Liam, don't hurt him too much." I inwardly shook my head and answered this unlikely thought with, "What's wrong with you, moron? Worry about yourself not about the guy who attacked you in the first place."

But I couldn't help it. The thing that terrified me the most was hurting him.

I hung on to the guy like a clumsy orangutan, and he seemed to lose some of his initial enthusiasm. It seemed I had a chance to swiftly end this farce. Then Natasha screamed a warning. Too late, I saw the other three guys coming up behind me, just before I got hit over the head with a wooden plank.

As I went down, everything went black for a moment. With returning consciousness, I realized I wasn't going to make it back up. My mind went back to my encounter in the horse corral with Mr. Bojangles – but there was no fence to roll under this time. I was down for the count with four pairs of boots kicking me.

Pain exploded over every inch of my body. I wished I could be like *Gladiator*, and simply jump up, larger than life, oblivious to pain. I would beat the crap out of these little cowards. But my body didn't cooperate in acting out this brave scenario. As I felt myself fade, I wondered if a movie was worth getting seriously injured for.

All of a sudden, a siren seemed to go off. But it was Natasha, screaming like a banshee. Resurfacing to full consciousness, I was stunned to see her take her high heels off and run at the guys. She was so small and lithe. I was worried the brutes would seriously hurt her. It was the first time someone physically fought for me with no concern for her own safety. My head was spinning and blood ran into my eyes. As much as I wanted to do my part, I couldn't coordinate my limbs to get up.

Natasha turned out to be perfectly capable on her own. She was the equivalent of an angrily buzzing wasp. She was everywhere at once, too fast for them to grab, and wildly annoying since she kept trying to stab them in the eye with her high-heeled shoes.

Meanwhile the gang did their best to continue inflicting as much pain as possible – kicking me in the head, ribs, and (non-existent) balls. The attack seemed to go on for hours. In reality, it can't have been much more than a few minutes. Eventually the little street gang realized Natasha was making too much noise. They gave up and disappeared as fast as they had come.

Natasha hurried to my side. I looked around at hundreds of premiere guests still standing within a short distance of us. They were all quietly watching. No one had lent assistance. Couldn't someone have used their cell phone to call the police, at least? I was far angrier with them then with my assailants.

As I struggled to get to my feet, a cyclist drove by and came to an abrupt, concerned halt.

"Are you ok?" he asked, ready to help.

I stared at him, blood dripping from my nose, my ears swelling to the size of a baby elephant's. I couldn't help myself. My anger boiled over.

"Do I look 'ok' to you?" I snapped.

My aggressive reaction surprised him. He shrugged, and was gone in an instant. Anger still rising within me, I felt an overpowering urge to get away from the gawking, disgustingly apathetic crowd as swiftly as possible.

Ignoring Natasha's concerned protests, I slid behind the wheel of my car and we drove off. My head was pounding and everything in my vision seemed slightly askew. Blood was still flowing from my nose and several cuts. Within minutes, my trusty old ride looked like the restaurant in *Kill Bill*, after *The Bride* had cleaned house with her sword. We stopped at a pharmacy for bandages and a large supply of painkillers. Natasha spent the rest of the evening cleaning all my cuts and bruises. She was simply amazing.

In movies, people fight for extended periods of time until they start to seem a bit shaken. They get pounded into the ground and still walk away with perfectly coiffed hair and no serious injuries. I discovered how different real-life fighting was, first hand. The beating I had experienced was most likely not even severe. Still, I hurt all over and I had been taken out of action in the blink of an eye.

Being attacked like that showed me how fragile the human body really is. Paradoxically, I had been lucky the three rogues had come up from behind and hit me over the head. Being a boring opponent who wasn't able to defend himself, I had presented no challenge for them. Still, I had a concussion, elephant ears, a pounding head, swollen-shut eyes and bruises to show for the involuntary experience. Thankfully, the doctor confirmed the next day how lucky I had been. I had sustained no serious injuries.

Far more unsettling was the psychological damage I suffered. For a while afterward, my heart pounded like a kettledrum whenever I saw someone even remotely resembling the guy who had pulled me out of my car. I was nervous and jumpy when walking through town on my own. It took months before I could leisurely stroll through the streets again without a care in the world.

I couldn't help but wonder what would have happened had they realized I was transgender. The way they had craved violence, would my being different have given them the excuse they needed to beat me to death? I shuddered at the thought.

Our brush with violence drew Natasha and I closer for a while. Only a few months later, we gave up on the relationship. We had touched each other's lives and earned each other's respect. But with me lacking deeper feelings for her, our break-up was inevitable.

I was strangely unfazed and happy to be alone again. Maybe a solitary existence was my destiny? I settled back into a smooth balance, utterly content with the freedom of single life.

Because I needed a break from emotional intensity, the structured work environment at McKinsey was bliss. But after the first twelve months, I started feeling restless.

I hadn't yet realized how essential passion was for my survival, how much I needed to belong, heart and soul. Over the years, work had become a substitute for the family I never had. The nature of my work at McKinsey however, didn't inspire me to invest myself fully.

Part of my restlessness was due to the testosterone injections still re-shaping my body. My mind grew in stride. It worked in high gear day and night, producing thoughts, ideas, worries, and boundless overthinking. Going through a second puberty, my responses to the world around me were often highly emotional.

Sometimes this affected my work relationships. One of my teammates at McKinsey, Julia, had become a good friend. Caught up in my late blooming process, I was too intense and became clingy. Julia retreated. I alienated a lot of people during these years, Julia being only one of them.

The truth was, I was still a novice when it came to maintaining relationships of any kind. Living and interacting frequently with people had only become a genuine pleasure since my move to Switzerland.

Additionally to having about twenty years of catching up to do, I was slowly readjusting and learning to rein in my temper. I had always had one, but the male hormones had given it a boost. Clumsy, like an adolescent bull in a crowded ballroom, I was in the process of discovering the intricacies of the dance, frequently planting my testosterone-fueled hooves on sensitive toes. Only my closest friends understood. They knew me well enough to be able to take my exaggerations and impatience with a grain of salt.

On September 11, 2001, I was scheduled for the late shift. I spent my morning lounging lazily on the couch. Sunshine flooded through the windows. The phone rang. "Are you watching TV?" It was one of my work mates from the morning shift. "If not, turn on the news right away!"

I tuned in just in time to witness the first tower of the World Trade Center beginning to crumble. Ask anyone about their whereabouts during the hours of the terrorist attacks on 9/11. Everyone remembers exactly what they were doing when a safe haven of civilization literally collapsed before their very eyes. Unbeknownst to me, 9/11 would prove to be a personal watershed.

I was still in touch with my arts mentor Mrs. Moorcroft in the State of Washington. We contacted each other about the horrific events in New York. I mentioned how ambivalent European reactions were. Empathy collided with long-harbored anger. Mrs. Moorcroft was intrigued and asked me if I could write reports documenting my findings. I agreed and wrote honestly about the reactions I witnessed around me, ranging from solidarity to hate, from people celebrating that the US had finally gotten what it deserved to people being devastated by grief, and all shades of grey in between these unsettling polarizations.

Mo read my reports to her Advanced Arts class every morning. My long-time mentor and her students were amazed. American news reports reflected only exaggerated patriotism, bravado, and plans of retaliation. Anything not pro-American was censored.

The Advanced Arts crowd was fascinated with catching a glimpse of the rest of the world, uncensored. Some of Mo's students asked her for my email address because they were hungry for more. Eventually only one of Mo's students got in touch with me.

Her name was Alana. We became key pals. She was eighteen and I was almost thirty, yet she was an equal spirit in every way, with an inquisitive mind and a good soul.

At first our conversations focused solely on the aftermath of 9/11. Gradually the conversation shifted, incorporating anything from our private lives to global and philosophical questions.

As the months passed, I caught myself checking my email more and more often. Eventually, we were writing each other several times a day. Due to the time change between Switzerland and the US West Coast, most of Alana's emails arrived while I was sleeping, so I got into the habit of getting up in the middle of the night.

After about five months, all I could think about was Alana. I would circle my laptop all day and night like a hungry puppy, hoping for another scrap to fall my way. We had never seen each other, never heard each other's voice, yet I was falling very much in love. In a way, it was the best love of all. I didn't care what she looked like. I had had the privilege of seeing her soul before I saw her body. And I loved what I saw.

The more we shared, the more I felt the need to let Alana know about my gender identity. I sensed she was considering a possible future for us as much as I did. If we ever wanted to be more than friends, I needed her to have full knowledge of what she was getting herself into before she made any decisions.

Consequently, I wrote a long email, recounting the story of my life thus far. As I wrote, I was shivering from top to bottom like a mountain climber caught in a crevice shouting for help, hoping with all his heart the person he calls out to will find the courage within herself to rappel down to fetch him. After many sleepless hours of biting my nails down to the quick, Alana *did* respond to my call with compassion and curiosity. She was clearly intrigued, instead of repulsed by me.

I was a spectacularly awkward flirt – even via email. Sleeplessness became a constant affliction. I knew I needed to step up even more and be forthright about what an impact Alana had on my life. I must have deleted hundreds of unfinished emails in an attempt to find the right words. Four weeks later, I finally mentioned, "My thoughts are always with you," I confessed, "I adore you. I am falling more in love with you every single day."

Once more, I didn't sleep that night and was checking my email every thirty seconds. I scolded myself for acting like an adolescent idiot, but I couldn't stop – refresh… refresh… refresh…

Finally at 5 a.m., Alana answered. She was careful to not lean too far over the edge but let me know she was interested to lean out farther, gradually, to see if she might fall into my arms. "Thank you so much for your kind words, Liam. I too feel something very special between us. Let's continue slowly and see where it leads."

I was delighted. My romantic heart was beating loud and strong.

We got into a comfortable rhythm of emailing twice a day. After putting into words what we both had felt, our conversations changed and became more personal. We still had no idea what the other looked like. I couldn't stop thinking about this fantastic female on the other side of the planet.

I must have driven my workmates crazy. I needed to process the intensity of my feelings by talking about them. Everyone was supportive. Inwardly, I am sure some of them were shaking their heads at the fool who had an online relationship with someone he had never met in person.

For me, it was perfect. We explored each other's souls and fell for each other's hearts. I was able to express myself without any fear of failure in the physical department. I was like an eagle learning to fly by being given miles of open space, making it possible for him to find the right momentum, the perfect surge. Then, when he felt truly ready, he could lift off into infinity. It was incredible. My heart was almost bursting with happiness. For the first time in my adult life, I was afraid to get on an airplane, afraid to cross the street. I was deeply afraid of losing what I had found and wanted to keep feeling the strong wind underneath my wings forever. At thirty years of age, I was the ultimate love-struck teenager, allowing my passion to carry me away.

After around seven months of getting closer at a distance, we finally agreed to send each other a picture. Imagine our pleasant surprise when we both discovered we were falling in love with someone who met our aesthetic tastes as well. Alana was Korean, adopted by a family from the US when she was five months old, just like I had been by my German family. She looked adorable in her photograph. Slowly we started making each other paintings and other creative presents and mailing them across the world.

When the time came for our first phone conversation, I was very nervous. I feared we might destroy the magic. I envisioned her having one of these squeaky American cheerleader voices I had heard many times in the movies. The hairs on the back of my neck stood up and quivered as I imagined Alana squeaking, "I love you" at me like Kermit on helium. What a blissful experience when she picked up the phone and I was greeted by a beautiful, resonant voice. Her voice had a soulful timbre and poured into me like a strong, full-bodied red wine. I couldn't stop listening to her.

We continued emailing each other twice a day, yet from that moment on, a good third of my monthly wages went into phone bills. Most of my nights were spent talking with Alana. For me this was an incredible experience since usually I was a self-professed phone grouch for whom one minute of conversation was already too long. Alana and I had three to five-hour-long conversations. Our longest had lasted eight hours.

True love was comically proven during one of our phone calls. Alana had stepped into cat vomit when picking up the phone and chose to simply leave it on her foot for five hours so our chat would not need to be interrupted. She finally said the words: "I love you."

I was enchanted and thought of instructing my friends to lay cat vomit booby traps for their future girlfriends to find out if they were truly enamored with them.

All the while, my work at McKinsey fluctuated between periods of frantic activity and days with nothing coming across our desks at all. There was a silent agreement we all honored: during periods of downtime we could do whatever we wanted, yet as soon as work came in, we had to drop everything and focus solely on the job at hand. While on a project, we worked non-stop until it was completed. It was fantastic to not be micromanaged, to be trusted and treated as a competent adult.

I was lucky to have met Alana during my time at McKinsey. My boss, Marjorie smiled at my teenage passion. She was very supportive and made it clear if I needed time off during periods of downtime, I was more than welcome to take it.

Inevitably, Alana and I did begin to think about meeting in person. We were one year into our online relationship and ready to step into the unknown. I offered to be the one to travel. I looked forward to visiting my former American home.

Alana had informed her family about me. Mitchell and Eleanor, father and mother, were divorced. Alana lived with her mom. Eleanor was a nurse. Her compassion for everyone around her was easily comparable to Mother Teresa. She was also fiercely loyal to her daughter, encouraging her to follow her heart at all times. Mitchell was a control freak. His child had to live exactly the life he deemed appropriate. Alana was a strong-willed artist but, of course, gaining her father's approval, which was so much harder to achieve than her mother's, became a fundamental goal in her life.

Mitchell lost it as soon as he heard about me. He was appalled at his daughter for having a relationship with a man who was twelve years her senior and even worse, a man she had never met in person. Mitchell's argument was understandable. His methods to get rid of me weren't.

Alana was a senior, dreaming of going to Art College. Mitchell threatened to freeze his daughter's funds. He told all of Alana's relatives she was with an older man who was an abuser and rapist. He repeatedly told Alana how disappointed he was in her. Mitchell's campaigning became comical when he warned his daughter, "You should be careful. Everyone coming from that dark African country is infected with AIDS." He was obviously confusing Switzerland with Swaziland.

Despite Mitchell's efforts – or perhaps because of them – Alana was falling deeper in love with me. I provided her with a solid outlet for rebellion, which she needed in order to break free of him.

At this initial stage, Alana was enchanted by my romantic, passionate indignation towards her father. In a sense, I opened her eyes to the world. Alana in turn opened my eyes to what love could truly be. We felt like *Romeo and Juliet*.

I trailed far behind Alana in relationship experience and was in way over my head. Even though I was thirty at the time, I had mostly experienced family life and romantic love at its most dysfunctional. All I had to go on was my overflowing heart that had never been swept away like this before, as well as a deep longing for love and belonging.

I did not know how to control my passion, did not understand how much of a burden I put on the shoulders of a loved one by needing too much as well as giving bottomless attention and love. I also did not understand that I could not ask a woman to give up her family for the man she loved. I never asked her directly, but by openly raging against her father Mitchell, I put Alana in an impossible position from the start: torn between the man she loved and the other man she so desperately wanted to make proud of her.

Eleanor was the polar opposite of her ex-husband. She was supportive of her daughter's infatuation and invited me for a visit. She did not directly invite me into her home since a complete stranger staying under the same roof as her much younger daughter was deemed very inappropriate. But she offered a small camper instead, borrowed from friends. It would be parked in front of their house as a separate home for me during my stay.

As excited as Alana and I were with my impending visit, we also understood it could mean the end of our romantic, virtual relationship. We both felt prepared to take the risk.

As Mitchell's threats became more frequent, Alana and I comforted each other. His actions drove us ever closer together. We truly became star-crossed lovers who were prepared to cross whole worlds – be they real or imagined – to be together, if necessary.

Mitchel insisted I meet him upon arrival before allowing me to see his daughter. In an effort to show good faith, I agreed. The closer my travel date beckoned, the more anxious I became.

Until now, distance had been a good defense against Mitchell. He had only been able to use verbal aggression and disrespect in his attempts to break his daughter and me apart. There was no knowing what he would do during a personal meeting.

My own dad stood by me during this difficult time. I gave him all relevant contact information, openly admitting how panicked I felt. It was one of the moments of my life when my adoptive father showed me the amazing parent he truly was. He was simply there for me. He was the safety net I could let myself fall into, should all else fail.

I reserved two weeks vacation for this incredible adventure. Should things go south, I would travel along the Pacific Northwest coast for a while and let myself be healed by the enigmatic strength of what I knew to be one of the most beautiful coastlines in the world.

Alana and I were bursting with anticipation. If all went well, who knew what would happen? At the same time, we tried to keep a sane perspective.

It would be a leap into the unknown as well as a revisiting of the first true family home I had ever experienced. I had no illusions about my very religious host family. After finding out about my transition, they had cut off all contact. Reconnecting with them would be impossible. Instead, I greatly looked forward to revisiting my favorite places. I longed to feel the beautiful desert all around me once again. The shores of the Columbia River had been my first home away from home. It had awakened the nomad in me.

The time of departure to Richland, Washington arrived. It was December 2002. Dad wished me luck. We hugged for a long time in Zurich airport and I was on my way. My heart pounded the entire twenty hours it took to fly from Zurich to Atlanta and then onwards to Portland. Around midnight, I picked up my rental car at Portland airport and made my way along the Columbia River.

I loved the five-hour drive. There was nothing like driving through this breathtaking landscape. To keep myself awake, I opened the windows wide and cranked *Alanis Morissette* and *Air* up to full volume. As music pounded from the speakers, my elated heart was ready to shoot off towards the stars.

The sunrise greeting me beyond Walla Walla was spectacular. It felt overwhelmingly like coming home. Eleven years earlier, I had left a bigger part of my heart behind than I realized.

The closer I got to Richland, the harder my heart thundered in my chest. I was prepared for my encounter with Mitchell to be anything from disgusting to violent. He had asked to meet at 10 a.m.

I arrived at the roadhouse diner he had suggested and settled down at a table. I was famished, exhausted from my nearly thirty hours of traveling, and annoyed with myself for having agreed to this senseless encounter.

Mitchell walked in. he was a short man with a thinning hairline, tightly compressed lips, and a calculating, hostile stare. Determined to be the better man in this peculiar exchange, I invited him to my table, offered a polite "good morning" and a friendly smile.

Mitchell sat down stiffly. We made idle small talk for half an hour, circling each other like heavyweight boxers, expecting a fatal blow from their opponent at any moment. I attempted to express, how much I valued and respected his daughter, how I understood that our relationship must seem surreal to anyone other than Alana and me. Then Mitchell's lips thinned to a barely visible line.

"What would you say if I told you that I have every intention to go through with freezing all of Alana's funds unless you stop your relationship with her?"

I was outraged. Trying to stay calm, my lips quivering with the effort of restraining myself from jumping at his throat, I looked him in the eye.

"I'd say you are a bastard."

Mitchell's and my encounter had taken exactly the turn I had expected it to take all along. Mitchell walked out, head held high. I stayed behind, feeling sick to my stomach by his barely-concealed hatred and blatant attempt at emotional blackmail.

Immediately following the unfortunate moment, I tried to get a grip on myself, swallowed hard, and focused on what was to come. In only three hours, I would meet Alana for the first time. The butterflies in my stomach won out. I could barely hear myself speaking to the waitress my heart was beating so loud.

Years later, whenever I passed a roadhouse diner of the same chain, bile would come up and I wouldn't be able to bring myself to enter, even if it meant starving or having to take a dump in a parking lot instead.

I drove towards the high school I had attended eleven years ago, parked in the school parking lot and listened to more *Alanis Morissette*. Finally, school was out and hundreds of high school students streamed towards their cars. I stood at the corner of a building, looking out for my magical lady. When the stream of people had slowed to a trickle, I saw her. Even from far away, I already knew it had to be Alana. Her eyes found mine, too, and she bee-lined towards me. She was a head shorter than me. I could easily imagine us embracing, our bodies melding together perfectly.

Time stood still. One of those rare magic moments ensued, the kind when everything ceased to exist, except perfection. Like heaven on earth everything aligned: past, present and future became one. So did hopes, dreams and reality. Our eyes met and seemed to read each other's innermost thoughts. Distance and worry faded and were replaced by the momentous realization that we had indeed managed to find a soul mate across continents and through glass fiber cables. Our eyes remained locked. We both felt the spark we had hoped for all along. We embraced gently. Contrary to my nature, I didn't say a word. We just stood there, holding on to each other for the longest time, falling into each other, marveling at the beauty of life. Feeling Alana's heartbeat beating in sync with mine, I felt complete.

As we drove towards her home, we kept looking at each other, making sure we hadn't met a mirage that would dissolve at any moment. We both had an innocent, childlike wonder in our eyes. At the door to Alana's house, Eleanor and Snowflake, the family cat, greeted us.

The following two weeks count as some of the most entrancing days of my life. The promised small camper became my hideaway for the duration. I loved the small space, consisting of a tiny kitchen nook and queen-sized bed. I loved waking up in the early morning, making myself a coffee and smoking a cigarette on the trailer steps, all the while looking up at Alana's window and dreaming about a life together. My late mornings were spent walking along the Columbia River as the past, present, and future streamed together in my thoughts. As the river flowed past, the golden desert colors lent the blue of the majestic river a dark, iridescent quality.

After school finished for the day, Alana would come home quickly. We wisely kept our distance from Mitchell. For now, we wanted to treasure our time and rejoice. We spent unforgettable afternoons and evenings together. Even sharing mundane activities like boiling water and watching TV felt like we had just discovered Atlantis.

Alana and I met with Mrs. Moorcroft, our enigmatic Advanced Arts mentor. Mo hadn't changed in the eleven years since I had last seen her. Time evaporated as my slow-witted mind stumbled over Mo's fine sense of humor and my eyes tried to seek out the mysterious eyebrows still hidden under the dense bangs of her towering hair. Mo was elated by our blooming love. For her, passion was priceless, a gift from the heavens to be savored.

Eleanor and Snowflake adopted me unconditionally. Soon I had white hair all over me as Snowflake followed me like a shadow. Eleanor became my true mom. She was a beautifully energetic, positive woman who felt her purpose in life was to live for her children.

Following her divorce from Mitchell, she made ends meet by working as a nurse in small clinics and community hospitals. Eleanor was tiny and round, with a wobbly wattle under her chin and a smile that could melt polar ice caps. She was always rushing somewhere or other on an errand for her loved ones. As her little legs pumped, her wattle would wobble with increasing speed, giving her the appearance of an over-caffeinated hamster. Eleanor was chaotic, forever carrying a huge handbag seemingly holding all essentials for human survival. She would have given her life for Alana without a thought. And she treated her eighteen-year old daughter as a fellow adult. In turn, Alana who was an introverted, respectful young woman, did not take advantage of her selfless mom.

I experienced an odd paradox. All of my life, I had looked for a home, longed for a family. Now, with Eleanor endeavoring to integrate me seamlessly into the fold, I realized for the first time in my life that part of me treasured being a nomad, treasured being self-reliant without having to balance a huge family. Still, the family life Eleanor so generously shared with me turned on lights in darkened corners of my soul. Witnessing her actions, I understood the true meaning of family. Eleanor even treated her despicable ex-husband with love and respect. I never heard her utter a negative word about him, no matter how intrusive or abusive he became. Eleanor taught me about unconditional loyalty and love.

Richland – the unassuming, ugly desert town sporting little more than nuclear reactors and wineries – seemed to be the place destined to teach me about family. My host family had delivered the first lesson eleven years earlier. Now Eleanor's genuine, caring approach to everyone around her reinforced what I had started to grasp back then. Family was forever. No argument was too big. Nothing was the end of anything. We were meant to forgive, meant to embrace the family before us exactly as they were. Hurting each other was as much a part of life and love as lifting each other up. The important thing was to keep on moving and to laugh in the face of adversity – a positive, boisterous, beaming laugh, bright enough to light the way for ourselves, as well as for those we carry in our hearts.

Eleanor saw her daughter happier than ever. She trusted me. Alana, who usually trusted no one, opened up to me like a beautiful orchid that had been dormant for years, waiting to finally emerge when the climate was perfect.

We had agreed not to become sexually involved right away. Alana's room was like a cozy cave, filled with colorful lights, mementos, and the chaos of a brilliant mind creating her own visual universe. In this enchanting haven, we kissed and talked, and realized we couldn't remember why we were waiting. The inevitable began to happen.

Looking into Alana's loving eyes, I forgot many of my fears and inhibitions. I was a bit afraid of what she might say upon seeing me naked. Trembling, I surrendered to the moment. She explored me from head to toe with her lips then worked her way up to my head again. Her eyes, alive and sparkling, met mine. Smiling at me, her voice breaking with emotion, she said, "You are so handsome."

The beauty of a moment of pure happiness lies precisely in the fact that we can't hold on to it. We grasp it for just an instant. It burns itself into our hearts, creating strength and longing for years to come. I was floating, butterflies maddeningly tickling, swarming through my entire body and soul. For just a second, I was nowhere else except in the present. Then I closed my eyes and counted to three, hoping I could save at least a small imprint of my emotional, physical, and visual experience for eternity.

The little camper became our romantic love nest. We couldn't stop touching each other. Eleanor and Snowflake both smiled. I remembered people talking about their first great love and how they never forgot it. Already, I understood what they meant. The cloud Alana and I were floating on was such a perfectly creamy pink. Like the softest cotton candy you just couldn't resist taking a nibble of. Its taste would always linger, no matter how delicious whatever followed might turn out to be. Everything we did appeared to somehow both last forever and yet never be enough.

After two weeks, the moment we had dreaded arrived. It was time to say goodbye. We vowed to keep writing and talking on the phone as much as we could and I promised to be back as soon as I was able to get away again.

Years after I had come across my farmhouse family in Switzerland, I had found a true home again, this time on the other side of the world, in the arms of Alana, surrounded by Eleanor and Snowflake. I was dizzy with happiness. Everything felt vibrant to the point of being almost painful. If I had known how to yodel, I swear I would have yodeled for all to hear – and I mean the entire cosmos: planets, the universe, infinity, and whatever comes after that.

My heart was heavy with sadness at having to leave. But I was high on a complete overdose of endorphins. Alana and I cried and hugged, then hugged and cried some more. Finally, I was on my way towards Portland International airport. The desert and the Columbia River looked more dazzling than ever before.

Back in Switzerland and back at work, I drove people crazier than ever. I couldn't stop talking about Alana. I immediately looked for the next opportunity to fly halfway around the world and see her again. I informed my buddies every day, whether they cared or not, how many days it would be until our next encounter. I alternated between levitating and bouncing around like a rubber ball.

17

River Neckar

Aside from romantic bliss, more serious business had to be taken care of. Salvatore and I came to the end of our marriage. Having been married for six years ensured I would be free to remain in Switzerland on my own.

Bureaucratic procedure had me stumped. The officials looked at me and then at my papers. Looking at the person standing before them with a three-day growth of beard and a decidedly masculine physique, they didn't seem to question the discrepancy with my 'female' documents. Since every official we encountered was similarly unfazed, our divorce procedure was blessedly unproblematic. Mr. Salvatore and Mrs. William showed up at the Zurich courthouse a few weeks later, and no one batted an eyelid. I was divorced again, and would finally be able to officially change my gender in my passport.

I braced myself to cross the bureaucratic bridges I had anticipated and dreaded for years. Having to wait for many years to officially carry a 'male' passport had taken its toll on me. For almost a decade, I had been forced to live and travel as Mrs. William Klenk. Even though people usually reacted well or not at all, I was tense and felt trapped. Like an escaped prisoner, I kept looking over my shoulder, expecting the worst at all times. I yearned to officially receive this validation of my true identity. What if I died and was put to rest as a woman? The thought was appalling.

Motivated by being so close to my goal, I contacted the German authorities and sent a formal application to my district court. The district judge, Judge Schaefer, responded promptly to my letter, ordering me to get two psychiatric follow-up evaluations from the same psychiatrists who had been assigned to my case years earlier.

Irrespective of this process, my Mrs. William Klenk's German passport was due for renewal. I went to my dad's village and dropped off my papers. Thankfully, the ladies at the office didn't ask any gender-related questions. I didn't bring them up, either. The gossiping village folk had me worried, for Dad's sake. The small municipality he resided in had a population of only two thousand inhabitants. As a recent member of the community, the conservative villagers were scrutinizing my dad as it was. No need for them to know about his daughter-turned-son at this point in time. I awaited my new passport, increasingly worried about the village officials figuring it out and spreading the word faster than a virus.

Weeks later, they informed me my new papers had arrived. When they handed me my passport, I was dumbstruck to find the document stated me as *Mr.* William Klenk. My gender identity hadn't been officially approved yet so I knew it wasn't possible for the authorities to already be declaring me as male. It was an amazing stroke of luck and I just couldn't give it up. I simply said, "Thank you" and walked out the door.

Double-checking my copy of the forms it dawned on me: the lady who had processed my application must have automatically ticked 'male' before sending it on. Dad had always talked about his son in the village. They hadn't noticed that my expired passport stated me as being 'female'.

I was relieved, excited, and fascinated to learn how, in a country like Germany, which is built on a pyramid of bureaucracy infiltrating every moment of our lives, it is actually possible to outsmart the system. With millions of authorities throughout the country, it seemed sometimes one hand literally didn't know what the other was doing. In the extensive paper trail, information could get lost or changed.

Good news for me. I decided to keep my 'male' passport and not alert our small village authority to their mistake. After all, it was only the letter 'M' embedded in a code comprised of a string of letters and numbers on the passport's main page declaring me as 'male'. Strictly speaking, I was now in possession of an illegal document, even if it reflected my true identity.

Thinking of being able to travel as Mr. William Klenk brought a big, happy smile to my face. I would have to be careful though. My Swiss foreign resident papers were still 'female'. In situations where I would have to produce my German passport alongside the Swiss papers, I would simply have to hope the Swiss authorities wouldn't look too closely. As for the German authorities I would soon have to deal with concerning the actual legal change of my passport, I would have to perform a tightrope act, hoping they would be too focused on paperwork to notice it had already been changed accidentally.

I dreaded seeing my psychiatrists again. Having postponed the bureaucratic side of my gender change was going to make the process with them more difficult. The change of gender in passports generally takes place one year after the reassignment. Since trans people usually couldn't wait to jump through all bureaucratic hoops and be done with it, the professionals would wonder what took me so long. Defending my delay by explaining that I had needed to stay a woman officially so I could marry someone in order to obtain a Swiss work permit would not go over well.

It had all gotten complicated. The situation could easily get interpreted as me not really knowing who I was and what I wanted, thus indicating psychological instability. I would need to convince them of a good reason why I had waited so inexplicably long. What could I say? What was a logical argument? Would they believe me if I told them I had wanted to be absolutely 100% certain? Would they believe I had decided to give it a few extra years to see how I was faring in my developing 'new' body before taking the final step in officially becoming Mr. William Klenk?

I was glad to have the evaluation with my psychiatrist in Ulm first. He was supportive once again, very pleased at my overall appearance and state of mind. The professor didn't really question me. We had an amiable conversation for several hours.

"Mr. Klenk, there was no need to question you. I can see the young man sitting in front of me, and am very happy for you. My paperwork is going to reflect just that." As parting advice, the professor mentioned, "Be very careful when you see my colleague in Stuttgart. He is well known for deriving a perverted satisfaction from thwarting the hopeful steps taken by individuals such as yourself. Additionally, your court hearing with Judge Schaefer might prove to be difficult. Go well prepared. He is renowned for being ancient and conservative. I am sure he hasn't handled many cases like yours. He might not fully understand the complex nature of what he is dealing with."

I thanked the professor for his well-meant warning. I would indeed be very careful.

More than anything, I was determined. I had waited too long for my freedom. I was not going to let anyone get in my way. It was 2004. Since my gender reassignment surgeries nine years earlier, I had lived as a man. Better yet, I never even thought anymore about how I came across as a man. I was well beyond concerning myself with how a cisgendered man would behave and rather followed my own emotional compass. I loved myself the way I was, incomplete body and all, without regrets.

With a heavy but resolute heart, I headed to Stuttgart to face the demon. The hour I spent with that man was a waste of my time and a dreadful experience I could have done without. Even walking through the door, I was already second-guessed by the hostile psychiatrist who, by virtue of his Hippocratic oath, should have felt compelled to be supportive of my situation. My stride and handshake hadn't been manly enough for his taste. Throughout our interview he continued to scrutinize, humiliate, and disrespect me in a distasteful manner.

His conduct could easily be called negligent or criminal. Leaving a transgender person unable to officially complete his transition makes this individual more vulnerable than ever to depression or suicide, or mortal danger from others. People who found themselves in the wrong body have been beaten to death throughout history, when exposed to the wrong crowd. Even in our more enlightened times, society in general has a long way to go. The possibilities of dangerous encounters are still a very real part of a trans person's every day life.

I grudgingly held on and kept being polite to the unsympathetic 'professional'. I was well aware of needing two positive evaluations for Judge Schaefer. I couldn't afford to aggravate one of my evaluators, no matter how offensive his actions might be.

Leaving in an angry haze, I longed for a punching bag to kick at for a few hours until all anger left my exhausted body. For a while, I seriously played with the thought of exposing the Stuttgart psychiatrist to the media. He was abusing his position and dishonoring his profession. Desperate human beings came to him seeking help, and he did his very best to destroy them.

But I realized I wasn't strong enough yet to stand in the spotlight. For now, I needed the peace and quiet of an anonymous existence in order to find a lasting balance. I thought of all my trans peers who lived their lives exposed to the curious, often cruel public eye and shuddered. This particularly bad excuse of a doctor wasn't worth losing my private life as well as my peace of mind over.

The evaluation forms arriving from Stuttgart a few weeks later were aimed to destroy me as a person. According to the psychiatrist's evaluation, I was a confused individual who still seemed too feminine. I was screwed. I held two evaluations in my hand – one very favorable, one damning. Copies had already been sent to Judge Schaefer.

My court hearing would be scheduled for a month after he received both evaluations. I was at a loss how to help myself, getting more anxious by the day, debating with myself, pep-talking my weary reflection in the mirror. I tried to convince myself it really didn't matter what was stated in my passport. In my heart, however, I knew it mattered all too much. If I ever wanted to work abroad, or undertake a multitude of other endeavors as simple as applying for my next job, I would always be at a disadvantage. I would never be completely free. This outlook was quite simply not an option.

The fateful day arrived. I got to the courthouse one hour too early, surprised to see that it was a beautiful *Gruenderzeit* mansion, overlooking a bend in the River Neckar. Thankful for an aquatic haven in such close proximity to the lion's den, I walked towards the water. The stream was strong here, the water shooting over boulders as well as accelerating between them, creating powerful rapids. The air was fresh and saturated with spray. I sat down on a bench overlooking the white water and sucked in breath after breath of the naturally purified air, in an attempt to calm myself.

At first, my heart's pace outmatched the powerfully surging river. Breathing deeply and rhythmically like a student in a birthing class, I slowly managed to push away some of the apprehension concerning the imminent meeting with Judge Schaefer. I touched wood, knocked on my own head, and sent all sorts of mantras to the universe.

Finally, I couldn't delay getting up from my comfortable seat any longer. I stood and took one last, long look at the Neckar, praying for the rapids to carry all obstacles away from me. One more deep breath of air, saturated with millions of minuscule water droplets, and I was as ready as I was ever going to be. I steeled myself. All my determination and powers of persuasion were going to go with me into that courtroom.

I walked towards the courthouse's main doors, then made my way to the room I had been assigned. It was located on the second floor of the gorgeous building. I knocked and only seconds later heard a strict, clearly enunciated, "Come in."

Opening the door and stepping into a surprisingly small chamber, I realized my hearing would be with the judge alone. He sat behind a wide mahogany desk, in an expensive suit rather than a judge's robe. He was about sixty years old, perfectly groomed, with a strict yet pleasant demeanor. His still full head of hair was pure white, giving him an almost royal appearance.

This judge seemed nice enough, definitely close to retirement age, proper and traditional, but not outright hostile. My fingers were crossed in my pockets as I was sending even more mantras to all entities known to mankind.

Judge Schaefer didn't beat around the bush.

"With one positive and one negative evaluation, the final verdict is entirely up to my final assessment of your person. Please proceed to present your case."

I laid out my case for him.

"I have always been the man you now see sitting in front of you," I said in closing. "I don't mean to sound melodramatic, but essentially, not allowing me to officially live as who I am will be tantamount to killing me."

After my lengthy discourse, Judge Schaefer took a long look at me. I could see the kindness in his eyes, yet I could see indecision as well.

"How can I ignore the findings of an expert in his field?" he asked himself as much as me, gravely serious. "Two experts disagreeing with each other leave me in an impossible position."

With another deep sigh, Judge Schaefer let me know his final verdict would be communicated to me via official mail in about a week.

"Do you have anything else you want to add before taking your leave?"

I thought for a long moment then said, "Judge Schaefer, please try and simply trust your eyes. I've been sitting in front of you for a good hour. This is who I am. The best you can do is forget about any paperwork and simply look at the man sitting in front of you, asking you to be officially recognized as who he is."

Judge Schaefer gave me a solemn look. "I will take all you have presented under consideration."

We took another long look at each other. There was nothing left to say. Finally, I got up and we shook hands. I gently closed the chamber door behind me.

Bureaucracy can be exhausting at the best of times. This time my entire existence was on the line. Everyone around me was supportive, cheering me on. Dad was too worried about me to get very involved. He retreated to a safe emotional distance. My sensitive dad couldn't bear the thought of what might happen if my request were denied. Alana and I still emailed every day and spent many meaningful, encouraging hours on the phone together. I held on to all the many people and things that were good in my life.

Precisely one week after my encounter with Judge Schaefer an official letter was delivered to my doorstep. I took a very deep breath and opened the envelope. What I saw turned my knees to jelly. Feeling light headed, I abruptly sat down on my couch.

Judge Schaefer had decided in my favor.

After all these years of struggle, I was finally free!

According to proper procedure, I would have to apply for a new passport immediately. I grinned to myself, knowing I needed to do nothing of the sort. It wasn't necessary. My illegal 'male' passport had just become legal.

I breathed freely, released of all worries, if only for that moment, as I pondered my odyssey. How fortunate I had been to meet an amazing person at almost every point along the way. Many of them had taught me valuable life lessons, or had simply left me speechless with their love, generosity, and kindness. Even here, in the depths of German bureaucracy, I had been blessed to meet Judge Schaefer, who had proven to be a compassionate man. He had decided to face the unknown with kindness instead of hostility. The old judge had trusted his own eyes and instincts over the words of a misguided psychiatrist.

18

Southern Mediterranean Sea

The existence of Mr. William Kieran Klenk was finally a matter of public record. This made it possible for me to begin the painstaking process of sending letters to any relevant organization, school, or company I had ever been a part of. Any previously-issued document considered relevant in the future needed to be revised to reflect my 'new' gender. The mountain of paperwork I had accumulated during the course of my life was astonishing. Apart from my passport and birth certificate, I had diplomas from every school I had ever attended, drivers licenses, bank cards, letters of reference, and the like.

Many organizations and people were helpful, others not so much. Some needed continuous prodding, others I had to threaten with the press before getting anywhere. I spent so many hours diplomatically talking on the phone or winding my way through dusty, yellowed offices that the phrase "out of the frying pan and into the fire" did cross my mind more than once. Finally, with the arrival of each amended official paper, the load lightened. My step grew more confident. My entire posture straightened. Awkward encounters with all kinds of authorities would soon be a thing of the past.

Jumping through one hoop after another like an overworked circus animal never reaching the end of his act, I was glad to have Alana. Her presence in my life gave me abundant hope and strength. At the same time, it helped that my working life at McKinsey continued to be smooth, with no trace of drama.

My teammates and I worked hard and inspired each other with our creative endeavors as well as our diverse opinions on pretty much everything. My generous salary enabled me to enjoy previously impossible luxuries. I had upgraded to a bigger flat. For the first time in my life, I had an entire two-bedroom apartment to myself.

To celebrate life and mark my newfound personal freedom, I asked a workmate from McKinsey to transform my living space. René and I had become good friends. He spent most of his nights roaming the city of Zurich, using his spray cans to transform areas of depressingly-grey urban desert into lands of rebellious color. I gave René Robert Frost's *The Road Not Taken*, and entrusted the rest to his imagination.

I had come across this poem for the first time when I was fifteen. It became one of my mantras. I believed then, as I do now, in the road not taken. I believe in seizing the moment and exploring life. I believe in listening to our heart and following its advice. No matter how hard and perilous an unpaved track might turn out to be at times, I wouldn't want to miss any of the experiences I was fortunate to have because I "took the road less traveled by."

My friend created an intriguing graffiti, transforming the walls of my entire home into a brightly colored wonderland. Rolling hills, larger-than-life sheep, purple sunsets, blood-red fields, and an overarchingly wild dreamscape covered all the walls leading to my living room. René's visual story culminated in a mural on the living room wall. It depicted a light blue monster perched on a rock in the foreground, happily gazing out at us from an orange-crimson sunset vista. The little blue fellow and I had something in common: we were both ready to jump out into the unknown beckoning beyond the wall.

I counted down the days until my next hop over the Atlantic to see Alana. My entire body would tingle with anticipation. People around me would keep smiling good-naturedly and shake their heads over my ongoing, obsessive love affair.

I felt invigorated and experienced a rush of creativity. Since being a teenager, I hadn't drawn, painted or written so much. Now poems and short stories materialized on paper, while elaborate paintings emerged on canvas. Having no intentions of publishing or selling anything, I stacked it all in the corners of my new apartment. My soul overflowed – as well as my living quarters.

Alana and I still wrote each other long and loving emails every day. To help overcome the void between visits, we bridged time and space by crafting presents for each other, sending them on their way to the other side of the planet. Our creativity knew no boundaries. Once, Alana presented me with tiny glass cubes in which she had built little scenes of our life together. She also drew comic strips of our adventures. I wrote poems for her. With each of my physical letters, I sent drawings and paintings, illustrating how much I loved her.

Although my days were already filled to the brim, I was so inspired by love and life that I decided to tackle my bucket list on top of everything else. Scuba diving had been my dream for many years but life had had a way of getting in the way of fulfilling it. Being thirty-one years old, I realized the right moment would never come unless I took it.

Between two major projects at work, I used one week of downtime to travel to the Southern Mediterranean Sea, to Malta. My old friend Pippin, whom I had shared shoes with many years ago in the Lichtenstein Mountains as a fourteen-year old environmentalist, welcomed me with open arms. We hadn't seen each other since before my transition but we had always stayed in touch. During the first year of my hormone therapy, Pippin had surprised me by painting an amazing gift card. It depicted two, well-toned male figures holding on to opposite ends of a thick rope. Underneath it, he had simply written, "I care". Pippin and I had always connected on a spiritual level. What mattered was the heart, the character of the person in front of us. Gender was a second thought at best, if ever a thought at all.

Pippin's home became my base of operations for a week of oceanic experience. Malta is a very small island state, yet Pippin lived as far away as you could get from the beach in any direction. Reaching the dive center every morning was an odyssey in itself. I was either picked up by a barely capable driver from the diving school, or rode on bumpy local buses for over an hour to get there.

It was the end of the season. The days were stormy and the diving instructors were bored. Dreamers like me were the only ones crazy enough to still venture out for scuba diving during that time of year.

As much as I loved water and felt its healing influence in my life, I still barely managed to survive the first days of my Mediterranean adventure. I could barely swim and only passed the six-hundred-and-fifty-foot swim test by cheating my way through it. Whenever I came to the shallow section of the tiny hotel pool, I stood up, pretending to swim onwards with graceful breaststrokes.

Looking back, with my now abundant scuba diving experience, I am positive my instructor was aware of every single time I cheated. She took pity on her last, spastic, student of the season. But even though I had spent half of my time standing rather than swimming, I still finished my test puffing like an old locomotive.

The first confined-water session underneath the rough autumn waves of the Southern Mediterranean Sea continued in a similar fashion. I wasn't afraid but had trouble grasping the exercises my teacher demonstrated. Instead of the usual hour, we spent *four* hours in the cold lagoon water. I froze, and swallowed half the sea. The next day, I ran a high fever and was completely congested.

I spent the day at Pippin's home and repeatedly tried to flush my sinuses. Half of my day was spent in the bathroom snorting saltwater and spraying it back out like a baby elephant. The next day, I still had a fever and felt like a wobbly sea cucumber, but at least I was able to equalize my ears and sinuses, and descend to exercise depth. I had dedicated this week to learning scuba; I was *not* going to fly home in five days time without having a scuba diving certification in my pocket.

Luckily, it was a one-on-one course. Some exercises took me so long to grasp, the preternaturally patient instructor would smile at me, gently teasing, "You know, I'd love to get out of the water at some point this year." I stubbornly persisted and accomplished each objective. As soon as I reached Pippin's home, I would resume snorting as much salt water as I could, to battle the mucus collecting in my sinuses. The local pharmacist shook his head at the amount of cold and fever medicine I bought from him. In the evenings, I would collapse onto the mattress in Pippin's guest bedroom, coughing my way through the night.

My sinuses were not the only things in Malta battling with congestion. My instructor and I got stuck in lengthy traffic jams many times during the course of the week. Once, as we tried to overtake the line, we managed to drive our truck into a ditch, losing half a day of underwater time.

The underwater world presented unique challenges as well. I nearly planted my butt onto a poisonous scorpion fish that week. Jellyfish stung me. Strong ocean currents threw me around like a shirt in a washing machine. Add a nasty ear infection to the list. The pain from my ears radiated into my skull, making it hard for me to focus on my instructor's words of wisdom.

Somehow, we made it to the last course day. Despite all struggles and pain, I looked forward to my final open-water dives. The waves were high and the water, turbid. Several dive centers had chartered a boat together for their open-water students. Due to choppy seas, we barely made it into Comino's Blue Lagoon.

On board with us was an eighty-year old lady. She was an experienced diver who came along for the fun. She seemed incredibly fragile and could barely walk. When we got to the dive site, she simply let herself fall overboard while the boat crew dropped her gear into the water. On the water surface, she slipped into her buoyancy-compensating device, inflating it and floating comfortably while adjusting her diving equipment. A minute later, she descended with our group. Underwater, she transformed into an agile mermaid who could easily teach all of us a bag full of tricks. I felt inspired by her and hoped to one day be able to be just as graceful, no matter my limitations.

Dark clouds began to form on the horizon during our break on the boat, in between the two dives. A storm was on its way but we all wanted to brave the elements for a second dive nonetheless. I deeply enjoyed both dives, even if my movements still closely resembled those of a drowning poodle.

When we surfaced after the second dive of the day, the storm had picked up. The waves threatened to throw our boat against the cliffs. Under the circumstances, it was too dangerous for us to climb back on board. The boat crew threw us a rope instead, and asked us to hold on. They would drag us out of the narrow lagoon into the open ocean. Once free of the looming cliffs, we would be able to give the ladder a second try.

We were instructed to keep our regulators in our mouths during the entire maneuver. Being a scuba diving rookie, I didn't know it was better to turn away from the waves and face backwards. I faced the boat. The waves crashed into my face, causing the regulator to free-flow continuously. I was choking on too much air, as well as water, since I couldn't help but spit out my regulator a few times. I was unable to catch my breath. Sheer stubborn willpower helped me not to panic. Our small dive boat was thrown around violently as we all held on to the rope for dear life. When we finally reached the open sea and the waves became less violent, it was an acrobatic accomplishment to make it back on board without breaking our necks nonetheless.

Thankfully, even our elderly dive buddy made it safely back up the haphazardly swinging aluminium ladder. We resigned ourselves to a very bumpy ride back. While all of us turned green and threw up over the side, our diving grandma made me smile. She reminded me of Leonardo DiCaprio in *Titanic*. Throughout our journey, she sat in the bow, facing seaward, her wide smile without a doubt communicating a happy "I am the queen of the world!"

We had almost reached the pier when our captain realized the waves were too rough at this location to moor the boat. We needed to head to a pier on the other side of the island, which would be more protected from the strong winds. After an additional half hour of synchronized puking, we stumbled onto the alternate pier. Our land transportation, with all our towels and dry clothing, was conveniently parked at the pier we had left behind. Cold and wet, we waited another hour on wobbly legs before the trucks arrived to bring us to shelter.

I left Malta exhausted to the bone at the end of the following day. It had been a horrific week. Despite, or maybe because of all the adversity, I was hooked. I could still feel the refreshing spray, and wave after wave of the Mediterranean Sea in every fiber of my battered body. I loved being underwater, as well as being on the ocean, with all my heart. I was ready for more.

After my turbulent Maltese adventures, being back in the regulated tranquility of our office building was like a vacation. As my work mates and I dove into our next projects together, I felt a lingering taste of the mighty Southern Mediterranean Sea in my mouth. It was so tangible, I lived off of it for months.

Vibrating with the energy of the ocean and eager to dive further into unknown territory, I decided to tackle another item on my bucket list right away. Since childhood, I had wanted a tattoo. I always understood, however, the need for patience, the need to wait until it was clear which specific design would resonate well with my personality. Over the years, I had researched indigenous tattoos of cultures around the world. The more I searched, the more I became intrigued by Polynesian designs in particular.

Steven, another one of my co-workers, was slowly transforming his body into a work of art. He went to regular sessions at the studio of a well-known Swiss artist who specialized in Japanese tattoos. His pale northern European skin glowed with a body suit of vivid, colorful images, depicting tigers, koi, lotus flowers, and dragons. He offered to ask his tattoo artist if he had any well-known peers in the Swiss tattooing community who specialized in Polynesian skin art. A few days later, he gave me the address of a studio in Lucerne, a picturesque town only one hour by train from Zurich. The artist, Katarina, was booked solid for months in advance but agreed nevertheless to see me for a consultation.

Alana wasn't thrilled with me using my skin as a canvas, and neither were my parents. But I was determined. It was my body. They would just have to get used to my blossoming skin.

I met Katarina at her studio in Lucerne. Her shop was located on the ground floor of an old building. It was a small, open space, roughly the size of a one-bedroom apartment. Coming through the door, I was greeted by a cloud of incense, paired with whiffs of coffee and disinfectant. The walls were covered in artwork. Indigenous paintings and intricately carved figurines from Mexico and Polynesia captured my imagination and transported me to these faraway lands.

Two comfortable couches, a coffee machine, and a coffee table were on one side, the professional tattooing corner on the other. Everything felt well-looked-after, friendly and inviting.

Katarina herself was a small woman with deep dimples on her cheeks. Her smile was genuinely welcoming and curious. Her brown eyes sparkled with energy while at the same time holding a deep sadness. I was intrigued by her and immediately knew I wanted no one else to tattoo me.

While preparing some coffee for us, Katarina told me how she had come to be a tattoo artist. "I was a graphic designer. While sitting on the toilet, I always flipped through tattoo magazines. Most designs in these magazines were awful. Then, one day, it hit me. I could do much better than that. So I found a tattoo master who agreed to teach me the tricks of the trade."

Some years later, Katarina was the only authority on Polynesian tattoos in Central Europe. Her reputation eventually reached all the way over to the Maori tribes in New Zealand. Maori *Tatau-ing* was strictly in male hands and an important part of indigenous New Zealand culture. Katarina became the first woman to be respected by the Maori warriors as a fellow artist.

I explained the scope of my project to her. "I want to have a traditional Polynesian tattoo, covering chest, shoulders, and thighs."

She nodded, "What designs were you thinking of specifically?"

"Honestly," I said, "I was thinking we'd work together on that. You know much better what fits my physique and what makes sense. How about you design step-by-step, and we look at it before every session and finalize it together?"

We looked at the sizeable scars across my chest. Katarina asked gently, yet directly, "Do you want those tattoos so you can hide your scars?"

I had given the subject much thought over the years, and was able to answer with a clear "no." I knew it would be wrong to use a work of art to cover my bodily imperfections.

"I want my tattoos to be a celebration of my body and life experiences. I don't care much about the individual meaning of each design element. But I love the tradition in Polynesian society to mark every major life experience with a *Tatau*." I added with a twinkle in my eye, "Since I've accumulated quite a bit of experience, there is a lot of catching up to do on the tattoo side of things."

Relieved by my answer, Katarina laughed.

"I'm intrigued, and would love to work on a really big piece again. You'd be surprised, but chances to be truly creative come along very rarely in my business. Most people just want, 'I love Mom' or a small tattoo, following the latest fashion. I'll make time for you. It'll be my pleasure!"

I couldn't believe it and hugged her impulsively. "Thanks so much. I can't wait to get started!"

The skin art adventure I had dreamed about for almost twenty years was about to become a reality.

I went to tattooing once a month. As agreed, Katarina would introduce me to the next part of her design before we started each session. I never needed to disagree with her. Her creations were beyond reproach and precisely what I wanted. In order to avoid scarring, not too much could be done at once. Like a puzzle, we completed the mesmerizing skin art one little patch at a time.

Whenever I arrived, Katarina would say a quick "hello" and immediately stare at my skin. Sometimes, after this rather comical visual inspection, she would ascertain, "Liam, you are too stressed. You'll bleed like a stuck pig if I tattoo you today." Her prognosis was always correct, even if sometimes I had been unaware of being stressed. Since then, I take a moment every now and then to stare at my arms, trying to find a difference between emotional states, manifesting itself physically. How

Katarina could see my personal situation just by inspecting my skin is still a mystery to me.

Over the years, my tattoos became amazing works of art. Katarina and I became each other's confidante. During our many hours together in the tattoo parlor, we also shared our sentiments on life in general, and our personal stories. Every so often, we would relate fateful developments in our lives, both feeling as if we had been thrown into a pond and life kept dunking us in rapid succession, leaving us barely enough time to catch our breaths before submerging us yet again. While the needle whirred away in an almost hypnotizing rhythm, we would comfort each other about the relentless passage of time and the inevitability of pain.

Halfway along our elaborate skin art project, Katarina confided in me, "I have a rare eye condition that twists the way I perceive angles. I've never told anyone. I am too afraid people will lose faith in my abilities and stop coming to my parlor." Judging by the perfect artwork unfolding on my shoulders, she had overcome this natural obstacle admirably. I knew a thing or two about conquering seemingly impossible odds. We became closer than ever before.

The diversity of individuals at the tattoo studio was a journey in itself. I was grateful for every hour at the parlor. Each time I was there, I learned more about not judging a book by its cover. Guys looking like *The Incredible Hulk* would scare the crap out of me but turn out to be gentle giants. Some of them would even faint on the bench. Some men whose entire bodies were covered in the most frightening adornments and who seemed to sport a perpetual hostile stare would open up to me – once I dared approach them. Over several sessions, they would tell me their entire life stories, and none of their tales contained anything particularly shocking.

At times, the pain of the tattooing process was too much for me to bear. When we tattooed my back, I got too impatient and asked Katarina to finish that particular piece all at once. She tattooed for five hours, the pain becoming more excruciating with every passing hour. The pain during the session, however, was nothing compared to the pain after. My back felt like it was on fire. I could barely concentrate on weaving through pedestrian traffic on the way from Katarina's studio to the train station. Feeling very clever, I bought myself a package of Camel Filters and started to smoke one after another. I hoped the strong tobacco would send me into a numbed stupor, as it sometimes did. But I only succeeded in developing a pounding headache and puking my guts out on top of the ever-stronger pain still radiating from my newly tattooed back.

Nevertheless, all in all, tackling my large-scale tattoo with Katarina was an invaluable experience. Just like a traditional Polynesian *Tatau*, each prick of the needle acknowledged steps in maturity, moments and events in my young life.

After three intensive years in the tattoo parlor, both Katarina and I were satisfied her skin art was truly reflecting my personal odyssey thus far. We didn't want to overdo it, but rather left large parts of my body free of adornment to emphasize the flowing shapes beautifully accentuating my anatomy. After our very last session in Lucerne, I said a sad goodbye to Katarina's tattoo shop, a world that had broadened my horizons in so many ways.

All the while, my job at McKinsey kept enabling me to take long stretches of leave to visit Alana. I would travel to Portland every two months, rent a car at the airport and fall in love with the road trip along the Columbia River all over again. I usually arrived at Alana's home at sunrise. There is nothing better then falling into the loving arms of your favorite person at 5 a.m. after a two-month absence.

The camper had long since disappeared. Eleanor and Snowflake had accepted me as part of their family. As conservative as their outlook had been when I had first started getting tattooed, both Eleanor and Alana came to love the intricate designs Katarina was embedding in my skin. Ripley, a stray cat they had rescued, seemed not to share their enthusiasm. Each time I visited, the defiant little street fighter would rip my arms and shoulders to shreds. Thankfully, my tattoos were never affected.

Alana's father kept waging his war against his daughter's relationship. Yet, despite Mitchell's persistent hostility and scheming against Alana and I, our first year of being physically together was incredibly romantic. We couldn't keep our hands off each other, couldn't stop listening to each other. Alana always thought up surprises for me. My birthday that year became an unforgettable barbecue in Eleanor's backyard, illuminated by hundreds of candles and lanterns. The small garden space felt like our own universe, glowing warm with heart and promise.

Thankfully there is no such thing as a perfect romance – or a perfect anything for that matter. Immersed in a veil of continuous light, we would easily forget to appreciate the beauty of our existence. The Milky Way would be right above us but we would be unaware. Only with darkness claiming us every once in a while, will we be able to see the starlight and be reminded of the stars' dazzling beauty.

One source of discontent between Alana and me was my considerable smoking habit. Alana's granddad had died of lung cancer years before. She felt traumatized about losing him in such a horrible manner and begged me to stop risking the same gruesome death. She wouldn't let it go. I knew she was right, yet couldn't bring myself to give in.

After a while, I asked her to stop pressuring me. Alana's pleading made me smoke more rather than less.

"I'm sorry, but in order to truly stop, I need to arrive at the right moment on my own terms. I can't do it for you. If I do, it will only mean that, as soon as we experience any trouble, I'll be back to inhaling smoke like my life depends on it. To stop for good, I need to stop for myself."

Alana didn't like it, but she bit her tongue and tried her best to support me in silence.

For months she and I never mentioned smoking again. I didn't want to announce I had stopped, only to bounce back and have to admit defeat. I rebounded several times before I eventually managed to wean myself off those obstinate little smoke sticks for good. Even then, I waited another few months to be sure this time I would stay on course. When I felt I'd truly quit, I announced my success proudly to a very surprised, relieved, and equally proud Alana.

Another of our grievances was traveling. Alana was very opposed to straying far from her home. Her introverted heart felt quickly overwhelmed by meeting strangers or venturing too far out of her comfort zone. I, on the other hand, became addicted to traveling after having escaped the prison of my female body and passport. I wanted to learn as much as I could about everything and connect with people along the way.

At the end of one of my visits in Washington State, I managed to lure Alana into a mini-road trip along the Washington and Oregon coast. We found a romantic hotel room in Cannon Beach featuring a fireplace and a clear view of the beautifully rough Pacific Ocean. Enormous sea gulls sat on our balcony watching us through large picture-glass windows while we had passionate sex for hours. In the mornings, we enjoyed pancakes. The dense, half-inch-thick flapjacks were literally swimming in maple syrup and topped with fresh blueberries.

As her initial misgivings evaporated, Alana began to enjoy every moment of our short Pacific Coast exploits. One especially amusing moment occurred when she raced towards me on the beach, surprising me by jumping forward. As she propelled her whole body towards me, she of course expected me to catch her in my arms, but my reaction time was comically slow. I stood staring at her rapidly approaching form, arms hanging limp at my sides. I recognized the ancient, gendered script an instant too late. Alana seemed suspended in mid-air for an instant before painfully crashing into me, then succumbing to gravity and falling onto her bum, ripping the only pair of jeans she had packed for the trip. We couldn't stop laughing about my clumsy failure at enfolding her romantically into my strong, manly arms.

On the third and last day of our adventure, Alana and I made our way from Cannon Beach to Portland. We reached the outskirts of Portland around 2 a.m. Our hearts were heavy with the impending separation. We gazed at each other, smiled and knew what we both craved. Finding some sparse undergrowth to cover our car, we parked under it, and transferred our longing bodies into the back seat.

Neither of us had had sex in a car before. It was an incredibly uncomfortable experience. Seat belts and other paraphernalia were digging into our backs. Our clumsy limbs got entangled in seatbelts and around each other. Nevertheless, we were enjoying the experience.

Just then, a very strong searchlight completely illuminated the interior of our car, including our stark naked selves. The windows had steamed up, so we couldn't see outside at first. Hunched low on the backset, we carefully wiped a small portion of fog from the window. A short distance away lurked a police cruiser. One of the police officers was holding a searchlight out of his open passenger-side window. Alana and I giggled and hastily put on our underwear. The policemen came over with their guns drawn, ordering us out of the car. Thankfully, my boxer shorts were hiding my nonexistent penis. They instantly realized they had simply caught an innocent romantic couple. Both policemen couldn't help but be amused. We were sent on our way with a mild warning, "Please be on your way and keep future sexual activity contained within your own four walls. It's illegal to be indecent in public."

We heeded their advice, got quickly dressed and, still giggling, drove on. For the rest of the way to Portland, we were caught in a mix of emotions ranging from adrenalin-spiked excitement, to happiness, to deepening sadness the closer we got to town. When we arrived at our destination, we went for Chinese noodles in Portland's Chinatown. Afterwards, I saw Alana off at the Greyhound station, sending her homeward-bound, to Richland. We hugged, kissed, and cried a lot.

I headed back to Portland airport and Europe. Our crazy love was bittersweet. Everything felt dramatically vivid. We had only spent a few days traveling, yet they had been as full as three years might have been under other circumstances, bringing an abundance of light. We parted more in love than ever before.

As time went on, the long distance relationship naturally started to take its toll on us. I realized we needed to think of long-term solutions. Maybe there was a possibility of Alana coming to Europe or me moving to the US? One thing was clear to me: passion alone could only take us so far.

Alana paid the price of being a sensitive artist. Her amazing depth of feeling made possible works of art way beyond her years. Unfortunately, that same depth also contributed to her struggling with the emotional mountain ranges of every day life. Alana struggled to get in touch with her own feelings. She often felt upset without being able to pinpoint the source of her heavy emotional burden. We both became increasingly affected by being so far apart. I remained obsessed, feeling more strongly about her every day. Alana on the other hand tended to protect herself by retreating emotionally, becoming unreadable and very distant.

At one point, midway into our second year together, Alana became increasingly depressed about being caught between Mitchell and myself. He had started to call her almost every day, leaning into her.

"You need to stop this insanity. I don't recognize my girl anymore. You are becoming corrupted, being with this old, abusive foreigner. I am ashamed of you. You should know better."

Alana felt lost and became inconsolable during our phone conversations. I wished I could reach out physically, hold her in my arms for just a moment. She needed the real me, not a virtual substitute. Nothing I could do from halfway across the planet would make a tangible difference in Alana's everyday struggles.

A crazy plan formed in my mind. When I told my teammates about it, they unanimously agreed.

"You're crazy, Liam, but definitely go for it. Don't worry about the current projects or us. We've got your back."

I thanked them and asked our manager Marjorie for two days off. Since I had anticipated and cleared up her major concern – the wellbeing of the team – she readily agreed.

The next day, a Thursday, I managed to get seats on flights bound for New York and onwards to Portland. Once in New York, because I had only hand luggage, US immigration found me highly suspicious. Immigration officers questioned me for three hours before it finally dawned on them that I was truly no threat to their country. They set me free with a smile and a shake of their heads at my love-struck passion. With a final wave, I leapt through the interrogation room door and ran for the gate. Luckily, my layover had been long enough. As I ran, I could hear repeated loudspeaker announcements.

"Last call, William Klenk."

I made it onto my connecting flight just seconds before they closed the door.

I arrived in Portland at 11 p.m. By then, I had already been traveling for twenty-two hours. The five-hour drive along the Columbia River to Walla Walla passed in a daze. I was running on pure adrenaline and love during this last leg of my journey.

At 5 a.m., I rang Eleanor and Alana's doorbell. Eleanor didn't get up. I had informed her beforehand to ignore any ringing in the early morning. So it took a few minutes before anyone besides Snowflake the cat stirred.

When the door finally opened, the expression of pure wonder and love in Alana's eyes made the entire trip worthwhile. Her eyes were sparkling with an unearthly quality of surprise and happiness. I've not seen it on anyone else since. I took her in my arms. After a while of just holding on to each other on the living room couch, we went upstairs to Alana's room. We didn't let go of each other. Arms wrapped around each other, we cuddled on her bed and fell asleep.

When we awoke a few hours later, we were still clinging to each other. We didn't talk. I just held her and looked into her eyes. After a late breakfast, we held each other once more for a long time. It was already time for me to go. The sole purpose of my trip had been to surprise Alana out of her funk, to hold her tight for just a few hours and make up for all those times we had only been able to hug and kiss virtually. We kissed and cried like we always did. Then, after several cups of strong coffee, I was ready for the long drive back through the picturesque wilderness of Washington State to Portland.

With a profound feeling of happiness, I fell deeply asleep on the airplane soon after take off in Portland. An annoyed passenger shook me awake upon arrival in New York; I had apparently snored my way across the North American continent. I stumbled from gate to gate, then fell straight back asleep for the remainder of my connecting flight to Zurich. Both flights barely registered in my consciousness.

In the second year of being together, we agreed Alana would come visit me in Switzerland during the summer. It would be a long break for her before heading off to college.

Alana had been offered several scholarships to art schools across the country. She had decided on studying at the Art Institute of Chicago for a four-year bachelor's degree in Fine Arts. We were both excited about her move to the Windy City.

Eleanor was as enthusiastic and supportive as ever, prepared to spend her very last dime on her daughter's happiness. True to his morose, mistrusting nature, Mitchell was against everything, and her going away to school was no exception. I was immensely proud of Alana for standing up to him. After many fights and relentless attempts to control his daughter with emotional blackmail, he gave up and grudgingly agreed to support her future studies in Chicago.

But now, Mitchell was once again up in arms, this time over Alana's trip to see me in Switzerland. Realizing his approach of categorically being hostile towards me had an adverse effect he unearthed his "AIDS infestation" theories and argued for the health of his daughter. As when we first met, I didn't have the heart to enlighten him about his mix-up in countries as well as continents. In Mitchell's conservative mind, everything beyond Richland was a danger zone threatening Alana's safety in many different ways. After ugly shouting matches between father and daughter, he insisted on at least renting an oversized military-grade satellite phone for Alana. The contraption filled up a quarter of her suitcase and looked like something CIA operatives usually used to infiltrate hostile territory.

I was just glad Alana was going to come. The simple fact that she was ready to endure over twenty hours of flights and stopovers to be together was testimony that, so far, neither the distance nor Mitchell's nagging had gotten the better of us. Our love remained strong. I couldn't contain my happiness and again drove everyone around me crazy by bouncing up and down like a boisterous puppy.

Alana experienced her share of culture shock during her four weeks in Zurich. Except for our road trip along the Pacific Northwest coastline, she had never been outside the small, protected universe of Richland and its surrounding desert. With only the best intentions and in an innocent attempt to show my country girl a tranquil, romantic oasis in the center of Zurich, I took her to Platzspitz Park on her very first day.

We had only just entered the park when a bizarre sight took our breath away. In the midst of pedestrians, green meadows, and office workers eating their lunches, a young man was leaning on a beautiful old maple tree, sitting down, with his pants tangled around his knees. A woman was lying on her belly with her head in his lap, giving him a very enthusiastic blowjob. Meanwhile, the couple's toy poodle whizzed around them happily in circles, barking its little head off. I had never seen anything like that before in Zurich, but Alana was shocked, wondering if she had landed in a country of perverts and lunatics.

Many elements of Swiss cultural life that seemed perfectly normal to me were offensive to Alana. The romantic little old town featured small strip clubs, some of which served coffee during the day. Old men would sit amiably together outdoors in the sunshine, sipping their coffees, whilst looking at pictures of naked dancers displayed in the nightclub shop windows behind them. Women would sunbathe topless on the meadows surrounding Lake Zurich, mirroring the accompanying artwork – statues of naked muses – along the shoreline. Children would play naked in fountains throughout town. Experiencing Alana's shocked reactions, it struck me ever more clearly: even though we were both raised in Western cultures, the differences between the North American and Mid-European mentalities were tremendous.

We struggled with these differences. Alana's introverted nature made it hard for her to cope with so many unknowns, so much diversity. She was young and had just escaped the vacuum-sealed world of her conservative childhood. I was pushing too hard, expecting her to outgrow a lifetime of fatherly and cultural restrictions in a matter of months.

Alana on the other hand never pushed me. She would patiently listen to me rant about her culture as I tried to readjust to the American lifestyle.

No matter how often I visited her, life in the US felt too polarized for me. People exasperated me. They seemed to lead a life of extremes, believing in the battle of good and evil with the tenacity of a psychotic first-grader who wants to believe in Santa Claus and is willing to kill for it. I saw an existence ruled by dogma and artificiality. The daily paranoia, prejudice, prudishness, doormen, ID checks, and an overwhelming police presence made me feel more than uncomfortable.

It was hard to admit at the time, but I was just as swamped by all my new impressions of her side of the planet as Alana was by hers of mine. I had loved my stay in the US in 1990. Now, a bit over a decade later, I felt lost in the "land of the free" and missed the true freedom of mind I experienced in Switzerland.

Most encounters I experienced in Alana's world seemed shallow and meaningless to me. Her friends would shake my hand once, when we met. After this initial personal contact, they would barely acknowledge my presence. I felt threatened by how little Alana's contemporaries seemed to care for each other.

Would we ever be able to find a happy medium? So many chasms seemed to open up, threatening to separate us eventually. Was our love strong enough to bridge our many differences in culture and personality? I sensed Alana was reluctant to ever leave the United States – and felt increasingly trapped. Would I be able to live with her in Chicago? I couldn't tell. I was also increasingly unsure if I even wanted to consider that option.

During her month in Europe, we visited my family in Germany. Dad was as supportive as ever. If he had any worries, he kept them to himself.

Alana and I went to my hometown, where I introduced her to Hildegard. The experience was painful to say the least. Even though we met outdoors in a beautiful park, I was tempted to look for windows – anything to keep from suffocating. Hildegard's paranoia made the air we were breathing feel as thick as liquid mercury. Navigating our conversation was like hacking through an impenetrable, venomous jungle. My adoptive mom stared at Alana with open hostility and asked one abrasive question after another. I could see her mind working overtime, coming up with countless scenarios of how my too-young American girlfriend was taking advantage of me. After only a day with Hildegard, Alana and I fled back to Switzerland. We both felt relieved and breathed deeply, inhaling the soft, flowery scent of the Zurich summer air.

For the sake of our relationship, Alana tried very hard to overcome her inertia. I was too energetic and impatient. I was fully aware of my shortcomings, but found I had a hard time controlling my impulsive nature. Consumed by my passion and oblivious to Alana's much more moderate pace, I often dragged her from A to B to C to D, and on through the entire alphabet. Slightly puzzled by her disinterest, I kept pushing harder, trying to sweep her along with my enthusiasm. We loved each other very deeply, so both of us kept trying to grow and understand each other as best as we could. Alana's greenness concerning committed intimate relationships met my even greater inexperience. We were a classic case of the blind leading the blind.

Remarkably enough, as emotionally handicapped as we were, we didn't crash. In the grand scheme of things, we still found more than enough stars in the dark to light our way, only stumbling every now and then.

We were enchanted, almost more in love with being in love than we were with each other. We experienced many excellent moments together. The warm summer nights caressed us like velvet. Under a sea of stars, we went to concerts in medieval courtyards. Back in my colorful home, we read stories to each other, decorated each other's breakfast plates with loving words written in chocolate powder, and spent whole days in bed delighted by each other's slightest touch.

After our summer together, Alana returned to the States and plunged into the adventure of her first semester in Chicago. Soon, she would face a battle on four fronts all at once: with Mitchell, her college life, her tendency for depression, and with me – her intense, slightly over-dominant boyfriend.

19

Kuredu Lagoon

Remembering my turbulent scuba diving experiences in Malta, I longed to brave the oceans again. I wanted to motivate Alana to join me.

"How about you and I travel together to the West Coast again? During one of your next semester breaks we could explore the Pacific Ocean a little further towards California. They have kelp forests there. We could swim with seals."

Alana responded with her usual reticence towards travel. As for any ocean-going activities, she got seasick just swimming in Lake Zurich, with its hardly noticeable swell generated by passing rowboats.

In part, Alana's reserve was due to not having any funds of her own. She didn't want to take advantage of me, a sentiment I greatly appreciated. As much as I tried to understand though, I felt let down. I never cared much about money and would have gladly paid for both of us.

My mind was spinning with ideas and the barely-contained urge to explore the world. I was an orca in a small pool, probing all corners, longing to break free and roam ocean after ocean. I would have greatly preferred to do so with my mate, but it seemed I needed to resign myself to go it, or rather swim it, alone.

I pored over travel magazines for weeks. If I was going to book for myself only, I might as well make it count and start my ocean excursions with a bang. So in another dip between work projects, I booked a trip to the northern Maldives. My destination, Kuredu Island, was a three-star resort with a huge dive center.

I will never forget my first arrival in the Maldives. The Male airport was so small, we had to walk across the runway to get from the airplane to the tiny immigration hall. The equatorial light was impossibly warm and bright. The gentle wind carried a delicious salty smell devoid of exhaust fumes or other irritating distractions. The ocean presented a dazzling array of blues in thousands of different hues, ranging from a brilliant dark indigo to a dreamy turquoise. I fell in love instantly. To this day, I haven't seen anything more profoundly beautiful.

An old Twin Otter seaplane transported me to the Lhaviyani Atoll, way up north in the chain of twelve-hundred tiny islands. The view from above was gorgeous. The azure seas were even more striking from this elevated perspective. The pilots were flying our plane barefoot. There was no door separating the few passengers from the flight crew. We had a perfect vantage point from which to observe everything going on inside the plane as well as around it. Our seaplane was making one hell of a racket but I refused to wear the earplugs I had been given. I wanted to feel it all. Uncensored. Uncut. I felt intensely alive, happy, and filled with excitement.

The island of Kuredu was yet another level of magic. Gone was the bustling activity of the airport island. Even though this holiday resort island counted as one of the biggest, with its one-mile length and nine-hundred-eighty-foot width, all was eerily quiet. The salty ocean scent was the only perfume. Blue sky and the unearthly, iridescent blues of the Indian Ocean were the dominating colors.

A lone heron stalked ahead of me, oblivious to my arrival. Walking slowly along the jetty, I could *feel* the abundant ocean wildlife already. I saw moray eels and countless juvenile reef fish seeking shelter in the shallow lagoon surrounding this unparalleled sandy patch of paradise. As juvenile predators joined into the fray, little triangular fins broke the surface and could be seen circling the many small schools of fish huddling close to shore.

For two long weeks, this was going to be my sanctuary. The sand under my feet was white and almost as fine-grained as flour. Sand was everywhere, even in the restaurants and bars, so I felt like a little boy at Christmas when I was able to lock shoes and socks away for the duration of my stay.

I practically ran to the dive center to sign up for an orientation dive.

From the moment I hit the water, I found out how much my scuba diving style was still reminiscent of a drowning poodle. My buoyancy was non-existent. I used my arms and legs like windmills. The more I wanted to avoid crashing into corals, the more I flapped my arms around, hence destroying more ocean life than if I had crashed.

An experienced scuba diver fine-tunes and stabilizes his position in the water with his lung volume. He uses his lungs much like a hot air balloon. If he wants to sink he exhales more deeply than he inhales. To rise slowly, he then inhales more deeply than he exhales. If done right, it is a beautiful, calm and controlled process.

I, on the other hand, still didn't quite comprehend how to use my lungs to be neutrally buoyant underwater. There was nothing pretty about what I was doing. To be able to stay submerged, I wore too much weight and had to constantly inflate my buoyancy compensating device to its fullest. Otherwise, I might have plummeted into the depths like a block of concrete. To resurface, I alternated inflating and deflating my buoyancy control device like a backpack-cum-elevator, all the while flapping and kicking like an angry toddler to slow my ascent. I loved every minute of being underwater, but neither the other divers nor the local wildlife enjoyed my presence. Something needed to be done.

After a lengthy consultation at the dive center, I signed up to take an Advanced Open Water Diver course from an adventurous, charismatic French diving instructor. After only two days of training with her in the shallow lagoon as well as on Kuredu's house reef, my frantic paddling turned into effortless hovering. I delighted in the feeling of using my lungs as buoyancy devices, filling or emptying them of air one little breath at a time, to control my position underwater. It was awesome. For the very first time, I felt beautiful and elegant.

With my clumsiness gone, water became my ally. Amidst the turquoise depths of the Indian Ocean, I gracefully floated, somersaulted, vaulted, stopped, and turned at my leisure. I was weightless and graceful in body – yet even more important, I was weightless and graceful in soul as well. This was the true sanctuary I had always searched and hoped for.

In addition to the Indian Ocean wrapping its strong, tender arms around me, I was blown away by the underwater life. Now that my uncoordinated struggles didn't scare them into flight anymore, most reef inhabitants ignored my presence entirely. During every dive, hundreds of brightly-colored, graceful creatures went about their daily routines without so much as a glance towards the little guy hovering peacefully in front of them with a tank on his back. My first encounters with fully grown sharks took my breath away. Amazingly, while immersed in the Big Blue, I wasn't scared of anything – respectful yes, but not fearful. I felt at home.

One morning, towards the end of my stay, I went snorkeling along the island's house reef. I had bought an underwater housing for my camera and hoped to get some good practice shots from above. As I was floating along, a Green Sea Turtle surfaced less than a meter in front of me. I was beside myself with excitement and forgot all about being subtle. Instead I created splashes worthy of a breaching whale and scared the poor creature away while trying to capture this amazing moment with my camera. The turtle quickly took a big breath then paddled back down to the reef as fast as she could, away from the clumsy lunatic. It took a moment to compose myself on the surface. I was out of breath, sputtering and coughing. In all the excitement, I had inhaled quite a bit of seawater through my snorkel.

The Green Sea Turtle had been five feet in length. Her big head had popped up right in front of my eyes, her gentle eyes staring into mine. A realization hit me: in so frantically trying to capture the moment in a photograph, I had lost the chance to live it. I could have experienced one of the most wondrous moments of my life, but I had missed it because I had instantly been consumed by wanting to hold onto it.

Disappointed with myself, I looked down, scanning the reef with my eyes until I could make out the turtle far below me, resting on the bottom at around sixty-five feet of depth. I knew Green Sea Turtles could hold their breath for up to five hours but my mind was made up. I would wait right here until she surfaced again for another precious breath of air. And this time, I would savor the moment.

After about one and a half hours, my stubborn patience was rewarded. The Green Sea Turtle rose slowly to the surface. I floated, staying completely still so as not to scare her away once more. Her head softly broke the surface only fifteen feet away from me. She took a deep breath, which sounded almost like a reverse sigh.

The gorgeous animal stayed floating comfortably on the calm water surface of the lagoon. Meanwhile, I let myself drift carefully closer. She was beautiful, a creature of the ages, perfect since the beginning of time. I closed my eyes to paint the image in my memory. When I opened them again the unearthly turtle lady was right next to me, still enjoying her rest on the gentle turquoise waves.

The long five minutes during which she stayed with me etched themselves forever into my heart. The turtle's large eyes held a tranquility and innocence I had never before encountered. With an unwavering gaze, she seemed to see straight into my soul.

Her colors were myriads of green. Her scales reminded me of autumn leaves. Did I see a net of barely visible, fragile veins, or did my enraptured mind imagine them? What if they were nerve endings, letting her feel plankton and every droplet of the sea that touched her? Feeling everything, she would literally become one with the seas embracing her.

Small barnacles held on to her carapace. I envied them and wished I could trade places for a little while. Could there be a better place to be than perched on the strong back of a sea turtle?

She took one last, long breath and descended leisurely towards her underwater domicile. I swam back to shore in a dreamlike state, happy, and almost delirious. I promised myself to never take a camera into the water again. The ocean was my true home. Now that I'd found it, I intended to consciously absorb every precious second I spent embraced by it.

Two of the best weeks of my life ended much too quickly. Reality struck as soon as shoes and socks enclosed my feet again. As the sun rose on my final day in paradise, I walked down the jetty to the seaplane and found myself a window seat.

We took off along the reef line. My eyes were riveted onto the heavenly lagoon encircling Kuredu. I had never been up so early and discovered shades of turquoise even more striking then any I had seen before.

I couldn't believe I was leaving. A dam inside my longing soul broke and I found myself crying. Gazing out of the small seaplane window like a man about to go blind, I drank in the last glimpses of Kuredu Island and its surrounding waters for as long as I possibly could.

Just as we lifted off the surface, I saw a school of dolphins breaching the water not far from us. They jumped high, spinning in the air, their playful silhouettes outlined in stark contrast to the rising sun. After this unexpected spectacle of nature, my tears flowed even more freely. I sobbed my way almost all the way back to Male International Airport. The poor little child seated next to me on the seaplane looked terrified by my emotion, while his mom held on to him with a forlorn expression of her own.

20

Puget Sound

During my entire time in Kuredu, I had hardly thought of Alana. In our obsessive love affair, that was a first for me. Were we maybe not as made for each other as I thought? I quickly pushed the whispers of doubt back into the furthest recesses of my mind. Alana was the lady of my dreams. I had fantasies of marrying her. But the thought of always having to explore the world on my own, of not being able to share the profound experiences of being on the road with my partner, made me feel miserable.

Returning from my island paradise was intensely anti-climactic. My work mates greeted me with amused smiles. I now had two obsessions I couldn't stop talking about – Alana *and* scuba diving.

Thanks to my work schedule, I was able to keep visiting my lady every two months. Like a deep-sea diver, eagerly counting down the hours until he can leave the recompression chamber and reenter the world, I kept a calendar on the wall behind my desk, counting down the days to each trip over the Atlantic.

In Chicago, it became increasingly hard for Alana and I to find moments of privacy. Even though her dormitory was located conveniently in Chicago's bustling city center, it was far from perfect for a couple longing for intimate moments. Alana shared her room with another female student. Their room was just big enough to fit a kitchen counter and two beds.

The roommate, Stacy, understood our predicament and tried to be discrete. Each night, during my visits, she would use earplugs and turn her back to us. This was good enough for me. Like a hobo who had managed to score a bottle of the finest single malt whiskey after a long period of abstaining, I would drink in the sight of Alana. Even fully clothed, she would look more beautiful and desirable than ever before, leaving me almost unable to contain myself. Alana, on the other hand, would be stiff as a board and barely allow me to touch her. To give us at least a semblance of privacy, I would pull the blanket all the way over our ears, bundling us up like two Inuit in a whiteout. I would then try to take Alana into my arms and begin to caress her nipples, or any part of her body. Without fail, she would react annoyed and slap my hand away, leaving me tense, with a burning ache in my stomach.

Only during the rare event of Stacy managing to stay away for a few hours, did Alana relax a little. We would cautiously touch each other like shy strangers on a first date. But even then, Alana would freeze at any sound in the busy dormitory hallway. Snowbanks of frustration began piling up between us.

Continuously sounding sirens, horns and a disjointed symphony of braking and accelerating cars eight floors down didn't help to ease my irritation. Chicago felt incredibly large and uncomfortable to me. Being a nature boy at heart, I felt overwhelmed by the big city. A smell of burnt rubber lingered in the air, making me long for a breath of crisp, fresh air. Climate changes were extreme, from sweltering hot and almost tropically humid in the summer, to extremely cold and dry in the winter.

For one of my visits, Alana had researched city hotels and booked us a room for two nights in one of the Windy City's cheaper establishments. The walk from Alana's room along bustling city streets seemed to take forever. My grumpy, jet-lagged brain wondered what we were doing. When we arrived at our hotel, I wasn't very impressed with the ugly concrete facility greeting us. We picked up our keys and headed upstairs to find our weekend love nest.

When we opened the door, I fell into a dark abyss of disillusionment. Our room was a concrete box of about a hundred square feet, illuminated by a single light bulb hanging from a wire. The walls had been left raw concrete. Not even kitschy pictures hung on the walls to soften the blow. The ceiling was very high. About seven feet up was a small window with bars. A queen-sized bed, a very cheap wardrobe, and a basic toilet and sink completed the interior.

I loved Alana so much, my world turned into *Lothlórien*, the enchanted land of the elves, whenever we were together. I wanted to touch her, kiss her and cherish her. So, of course, there was nothing better than having a room to ourselves again. Looking at our surroundings, however, I was filled with desperation. The hotel room looked exactly like a prison cell. Everything about it felt wrong. As usual, not able to control my impulses very well, my facial expression spoke volumes. I made it worse by saying what I felt out loud.

"This room is horrible."

Alana broke into tears and was inconsolable for hours. She had looked forward to surprising me with booking the room for us, so we could spend a romantic weekend together. She had searched for weeks to find a balance between price and location she would be able to manage. It was important to her to pay for our accommodation since her being a student often prevented her from helping with our long distance costs, be they hotels, flights, or simply phone bills. She had saved money and been happy to contribute to our relationship.

I had ruined it all. I felt terrible and wished I could take back both my physical and verbal reaction. Hers was such a beautiful, loving gesture. I berated myself to stop being an idiot. Having our own room should have been all that mattered, but somehow, I just couldn't shake feeling glum in these soulless surroundings.

"Alana, I am so very sorry. Please try and forget all I just said," I begged her. "The room is just fine. Really. Being together is all that matters." I soothed her and held her in my arms, repeating over and over again, "Please forgive me. I am so sorry about my thoughtless reaction."

Our tears were flowing freely and Alana's wracking sobs felt as if her heart might burst from the intensity of her sorrow. What had I done? Fear of loss made me hold her tight, trying to let the soft but steady pressure of my warm body convey how deeply I loved her. We lay in each other's arms, both exhausted from crying, clutching each other under the blankets, never letting go until the next morning.

The rest of our weekend passed without further incident. We were painfully aware of having only a few days together. The memories we created now would be what we would carry in our hearts until our next reunion. We fiercely held on to each other, love and tension going hand-in-hand.

It was one of the main problems we experienced with our long distance relationship. Life went on relentlessly and didn't wait for us to catch up. In the beginning of our passionate love affair, no duration in between visits had been too long. Each time we saw each other, we had been able to pick up exactly where we had left off. In our second year, we started needing to re-connect, to find each other again. The first few days would be fraught with irritability and misunderstandings. We would hurt each other more each time we reunited. I would wish for a device to stop time so we could hover on our own cloud, cushioning us from everything for as long as was necessary to resynchronize our heartbeats and separate worlds. As it was, however, our bodies and minds would remember the depth of our love and passion in seemingly slow-motion-real-time. Only when the time came for one of us to leave, would we be at the point of our souls being reunited once again.

We attempted to strike a balance by buying plane tickets to Switzerland for Alana whenever possible. She never got more comfortable with traveling, but bravely fought through her nausea and travel anxiety. On her semester breaks, Alana alternated between visiting her family in Richland and visiting me in Switzerland. Mitchell still ranted against us whenever he managed to get a hold of his daughter, but he seemed to at least have finally learned that Switzerland was not in Africa.

Meanwhile, I dreamed of exotic destinations – and Africa was amongst them.

I had worked at McKinsey for over three years. The powerful company provided me with comfort and structure. Whereas I had at first enjoyed my peaceful existence and generous paycheck, I now found myself longing for more. As practical as a high income was – especially considering an existence that involved commuting between Zurich and Chicago – having money had never meant much to me in and of itself. Producing PowerPoint presentations and internal print media was as pleasant as ever, yet the philosopher in me was missing essential elements. I didn't feel enough passion, didn't see any deeper meaning to what we were doing in our cozy offices. I had the safest, most structured, best paid, most comfortable profession of my entire working life – yet I felt far from fulfilled.

Living in Switzerland's financial capital of Zurich was as high a standard of living as I could ever achieve, yet I was starting to feel paralyzed. Everything was insured: life, health, dental, house and home, travel and retirement. I was thirty years old and could see a painfully straight, predictable road leading all the way to the horizon. I saw a beautiful, comfortable, safe and prosperous path, with very few surprises and risks along the way. I was in the proverbial gilded cage, and it scared me more than anything. As the glittering bars closed in on me, it became increasingly harder to breathe. I knew I needed to break out. Not immediately, but in time to stop my adventurous spirit from becoming cryogenically frozen in this world of "perfection".

But where would I go? Considering Alana's and my relationship, it seemed we had come to a standoff. I still loved Zurich. It was as close to home as I had ever gotten. And I loved Alana but couldn't see myself moving to Chicago for her, even though I craved significant changes in my life. Would she ever consider moving for me? For the moment, I could only hope so.

I started to ponder adjustments in my Swiss microcosmos. Maybe I could change my career path so I wouldn't have to leave my Zurich family just yet? Could I discover something fabulous and meaningful in this country of excessive structure, neatness and materialism?

After a few weeks of randomly leafing through newspaper advertisements, I discovered an interesting opportunity amidst hundreds of office positions very similar to my own. Zurich's zoo was looking for an animal handler. My romantic heart felt immediately intrigued. I assembled an application. To make up for my lack of prior zoo experience, I artfully adorned my folder with photographs I had taken of animal life over the years.

Amazingly, the photos must have hit a nerve. I was invited for an interview. I was as afraid as the unknown excited me. Yet knowing that my chances of being offered a position at the zoo were slim to none had a relaxing effect on me. Maybe it was exactly this laid-back curiosity that made me appear far more self-confident than I had seemed in previous job interviews.

Imagine my surprise when the head of personnel was very interested in hiring me. According to him, the zoo team was greatly impressed by my enthusiasm and wouldn't mind giving me a chance. If I agreed to come and work with the animal handler team for one day, and manage to not get eaten by a wild beast in the process, I'd be considered part of the gang. I buzzed with excitement and agreed to make myself available for one day the following weekend.

When the big day came, I was paralyzed with fear. My alarm clock went off at 4 a.m. From the second I woke up, all I could think about was how to talk my way out of my day at the zoo without sounding like a complete idiot. The head of personnel as well as the whole zoo team had taken a giant leap of faith by giving someone with no relevant experience a shot at the animal handler position. I felt horrible betraying their trust, yet I couldn't get out of my bed. My limbs seemed to have been replaced by tree trunks during the night. I was rooted to the mattress.

At the time, I couldn't pinpoint the origin of my anxiety attack. Some years later, I understood the cause of my paralyzing fear more clearly. It was the very rough-seeming, all-male animal handler team.

I knew I would have passed. The zoo would have hired me. But then what? So far I had always worked either amongst sensitive artists or in teams with a majority of women.

I had been scared of a potentially threatening new world of roughhousing masculinity, scared of finding myself in over my head. I had feared becoming stuck in a team of Swiss hillbillies, who upon discovering my gender history might end up beating the male impostor to death, or feeding him to the lions. The thoughts of sharing a locker room with these seemingly tough fellows, of facing the banter of men amongst themselves and the possibility of testosterone-driven homophobia – these had all terrified me. In short, entering a world of pure maleness had intimidated me beyond all rationality. What if I couldn't handle it?

I knew I still had a lot to learn about the social behavior of men amongst each other. The stereotypes of men my mind conjured up were not quite representations of the real world. Most likely, I harbored the same kind of prejudice and irrational angst towards them that some cisgendered people feel towards people like me.

In the end, I was anxious enough to let a lifelong dream pass me by. My longing to work with animals dated all the way back to my precious childhood afternoons with my best buddy Markus, leafing through animal books and dreaming of a future in wildlife conservation together.

I didn't get up that morning, and later emailed a feeble excuse about how I had suddenly fallen very ill. The zoo never got in touch with me again. I didn't overcome my fear enough to follow-up with them either, as I should have. Instead I gave up, tucked my tail between my legs and ran away from a chance at a profession that could possibly have made me happy for the rest of my life.

Clearly not enough time had passed for me to feel entirely confident when it came to male socialization. By the winter of 2003, seven years after my gender reassignment surgery, I felt happy in my skin, but overall was still more comfortable socializing and talking with women. Most men felt alien to me.

I loved having meaningful conversations about feelings, as I always had. Honest conversations, deeply rooted in personal experiences of everyday life, pleased me the most. But posturing seemed to be an essential part of male interaction. In the company of men, I found myself lost and bored out of my mind, a tourist on a barren planet. In my mind I would keep looking over my shoulder for my spaceship, so I could fly back out to either greener or more turquoise pastures. Surely there had to be more depth to most of these men, but on the surface it was all cliché – strength, power, sports, beer and boobs.

Of course, there was nothing wrong with any of that. But it was not my world. I wanted something different. My gender history gave me a unique insight into stereotypes. And even though I was in essence a male soul, my experiences trapped in a female body had shaped me and molded me into an inquisitive, analyzing personality, standing between the worlds. To me, life was a rainbow. There was no need to ever reach the end of it. Each and every one of us represented a glow of intense and unique color, far too interesting to be marred by clichés.

As a result, I was mostly drawn to artists and scholars and felt more comfortable amongst sensitive men. Over time, I would slowly filter out which male-isms of our society I wanted to incorporate into my life and which ones I could do without. The road less traveled – and preferably uncategorized – beckoned.

After the zoo episode, I forgave myself and pushed all disappointment aside. I vowed to keep searching for a more adventurous, meaningful existence beyond office cubicles.

Thankfully, my brush with the world of zoo animals had re-awakened my wish to work in wildlife conservation. Being thirty-two already, I was not sure how much I could still achieve. But I felt compelled to seek a profession that would bring me closer to animals. Eventually, this might lead me to become the protector of nature I had already been as a teenager, when I had led my group into the forests to safe frogs and birds.

Relaxing on my couch, I regained my balance and dove into biology literature with a passion. Books had often been my salvation. They had opened my eyes, warmed my heart, and given me shelter when life became too complex to bear.

Setback aside, my longing for change had only grown. The nomad within me was straining at the bit, hungry for new horizons. My new plan was to take a more subtle approach and give myself ample time to let go of the world I knew. The safe bubble I had created for myself in my Swiss home had served the important purpose of grounding me when I had needed stability more than anything. Now I would slowly sneak up on leaving my haven. After all, no matter how comfortable my Swiss bed might be made, no matter how deeply I snuggled into those soft down covers, I was highly aware that eventually, it would be time to get up and explore.

By taking a correspondence course with a British university, I planned to prepare for entering a broader world. In the spring of 2004, I reduced work at McKinsey to eighty percent and threw myself into my studies for a diploma in Natural Sciences.

I found studying more enjoyable as an adult than ever before. I liked distance education. There was no pressure to perform at the same speed as others. Even math made sense suddenly, when I was able to work on calculations at my own pace. I discovered my dyscalculia wasn't as dramatic as I had been led to believe by my high school teachers. In the safety of my home, I finally understood: math was simply another language, required for scientific communication.

The Internet provided a platform for meaningful scientific as well as personal discussions. Students and mentors from around the world were connected through chat rooms and Skype. Friendships developed.

Elliot was taking the same courses as I and lived in Basel. We met first online, then in person. We would get together once a month on a Saturday. We came up with a routine, and followed it religiously: first, lunch at a delicious Australian restaurant, then, a caramel macchiato at Starbucks, followed by hours of roaming around Zurich's largest English book store.

Elliot had Asperger's Syndrome, a very highly-functioning variant of autism. His personality was intriguing and I greatly appreciated his honesty and brilliant mind. He openly admitted to not feeling any emotional attachment to me, but he enjoyed our discussions. I was surprised when he said, "I really appreciate your intellect." Mostly, Elliot preferred his own company and his books. He had a tendency to get impatient with people who couldn't follow his thought processes. I had never before considered the extent of my own intelligence and was astonished he found me smart enough to interact with.

Our program required us to attend a laboratory week at Edinburgh University. It was the one time when hundreds of us long-distance nerds suddenly came face-to-face with each other. Students of all ages were present. Some were in their twenties, others in their eighties.

Elliot and I traveled together to Edinburgh. We teamed up. When it came to working through mathematical equations, he was way ahead of me. He could solve a problem in less than ten seconds while it took me an hour to think my way through it. I deeply respected him letting me come to my own conclusions. He would keep himself busy with other equations until I was ready to move on to the next problem.

Living on the big university campus for one week was an invigorating experience. Elliot and I greedily absorbed as much knowledge as we could and attended every lecture. During breaks, we sipped a hot Scottish beverage barely recognizable as coffee. The campus was home to a large community of rabbits. As we looked out the cafeteria windows, the fluffy creatures even sat on top of bushes, eying us curiously or joyfully bounded around in circles.

I loved to wander through the great halls, inhaling deeply. I could taste the dusty, slightly moldy smell of thousands of books. Roaming the school, Elliot and I would open the large, double doors dividing the hallways into smaller partitions. We noticed that there was no rhyme or reason to how the doors opened. Some opened towards us, some away from us. The architect must have had a quirky sense of humor.

On the first day, Elliot and I kept trying to predict which way the next set of doors would open. We ended up mostly guessing wrong, running our heads into the ancient wooden wings. On the second day, I noticed that, on the doors swinging inwards, the hinges pointed towards us. On doors swinging outwards, the hinges were not visible. I tested my theory and did not crash into any more doors. Elliot was amazed. As he had done for me, I respected his need to find out for himself. Two days later, he understood the principle. It seemed my intelligence was rooted in practical and visual stimuli, whereas Elliot thrived on the abstract.

While my studies progressed, Alana and I faced increasing difficulties. We were in the third year of our long-distance relationship. My studies helped divert my thoughts from my obsessive craving for Alana as her life at the Art Institute of Chicago picked up speed. We still wrote each other daily, yet we shared fewer details. As a direct consequence, our lives began to grow in separate directions and we misunderstood each other more often. Worst of all, we lost our sense of humor. We slowly grew unable to understand each other's jokes. Like two continental plates, we had softly connected and rubbed against each other for a while. Now the tremors of our individual worlds caused us to slowly but inescapably drift away from each other.

Each time I pondered our love, I would panic at the thought of losing Alana and the family I had gained through our relationship. With her, for the first time, all loneliness had been lifted from my soul. Now, the more we struggled, the more I could feel loneliness creeping back into my life. It felt worse than ever before, because now I knew what I had been missing.

I didn't know what to do. My passion for Alana had me trapped in a spiral threatening to spin out of control. The more she pulled away from me in a desperate attempt to find room to breathe, the more obsessive I became.

Eleanor proved to be a loving mom who tried to give me plenty of useful advice. She warned me about the effects of smothering another person with love and obsession. My closest friends attempted to guide me through the worsening relationship crisis as well, persistently whispering in my ear to back off and give Alana more space.

But I was the proverbial slobbering bulldog and Alana, the bone I couldn't drop. I couldn't, I wouldn't listen to anyone. All of my life, I had survived by trying harder when things didn't work out. My inexperience with close human bonds made it impossible for me to understand how threatening and suffocating this strategy could be in an intimate relationship.

During Alana's early summer visit to Switzerland in 2004, I started pushing her to do an exchange year with an art school in Lucerne. She hesitated, but indulged me and was invited to present her portfolio to the school. As I knew they would, the faculty loved her work and immediately invited her to stay.

Alana was undecided and obviously afraid, giving me countless signals to give her time and let her make the decision on her own. I ignored all of those signals and kept urging her on. I strongly believed that geographical distance was the cause of our problems. Also, most of our time together had been spent in Alana's culture. Living in Lucerne would give her a chance to explore the European culture that had shaped me. I hoped she would understand me better if we lived together in my world for a while. Perhaps this would enable us to rekindle the magic between us.

It had been easy for me to leave the home I grew up in. So I selfishly forgot to stop and think about who Alana was and how different her family situation was to mine. Alana had Eleanor and preferred living her life in the safety of what was familiar. For her, just the relatively minor move from Richland to Chicago had been like a change of universe. She wasn't an adventurer. In order to be happy and feel safe, she needed continuity.

After Alana's two-week visit, I was alone in Switzerland once more. This time, we had felt irritated and confused during most of our time together. Our world was slowly but surely tilting out of balance.

I plunged even more vigorously into my studies and my elaborate plans for a career in marine biology. At the same time, I researched possibilities of studying in the United States. If Mohammed wouldn't come to the mountain, maybe the mountain could go to Mohammed. It was still inconceivable to me to live in a metropolis as densely populated as Chicago, but maybe I could find a place more suited to my personality.

Just a few weeks later, during one of my next visits to the US, Alana and I visited Eleanor together. She had moved to Seattle after her daughter left home. Our first few days together were spent exploring the Puget Sound area. We took ferry after ferry. The air was chilly, even though it was the middle of summer. Water temperatures barely reached sixty degrees Fahrenheit. The water was a deep, dark cerulean blue. Sitting on one of the many rocky beaches of Orca's Island, I inhaled as much of the salty scent as I could. My heart confirmed what my eyes saw: this area suited me. It felt good, like a possible home.

Buoyed by my discovery, I took some time for myself during my visit with Alana. It was a first in our relationship. Dreaming about becoming a deep sea explorer and having the underwater realm of Puget Sound as my lecture hall, I went to talk with several professors at the University of Washington. Going back to studying full-time would eat up all my savings, but the Biological Oceanography program at the University of Washington sounded breathtaking. They even had their own research vessel to explore black smokers at the bottom of the sea. Puget Sound sounded ever more attractive.

One marine biology professor invited me to attend several lectures on plankton and fish behavior. I was overjoyed and not the least bit bored, even though I hardly grasped a word of what was being taught.

The next day, a professor of Oceanography took me on a tour of the research ship Thomas G. Thompson. Seeing the laboratory on board and watching students preparing for their next field trip made me want to rip my return ticket into microscopically small bits. I wanted to stay with them right then and there.

The professors valued my enthusiasm. We agreed their institution would be a good place for me to pursue my dreams. Becoming a marine biologist seemed to be within touching distance. Fuelled by my usual intensity and my German perfectionism, I spent the following weeks systematically organizing my budget and all necessary paperwork to embark on this grand scientific adventure. I could almost hear the rough winds above Puget Sound calling out to me.

Over the years, I had amassed books, memorabilia, and furniture. Looking at all of it, my mentor Andreas's wisdom still resounded loudly in my mind: "Always keep a very low standard of living. What you own, owns you. Freedom comes from owning very little. Go out there, and make the world your playground."

While beginning to shed a small portion of my possessions and becoming increasingly restless, I was profoundly inspired by two of my workmates. The graffiti artist, René, and his girlfriend, Ulla, dreamed of flying from Africa to Switzerland. After months of careful considerations and preparation, they set out for Johannesburg in early 2004. During their first month in South Africa, they both took flying lessons for ultra-light aircraft. Using all their savings, the amazing couple then bought their own ultra-light plane and took to the skies, northward bound.

The airborne couple sent pictures and updated us regularly. While I greedily absorbed every detail of their endeavor, I felt a pang in my heart. René and Ulla were living their dream – together. How I wished to be able to do the same.

But for the moment it seemed, all I could do was content myself with witnessing the experience of my friends. I had a front-row seat to the adventure, since René's brother, Martin, worked in our office. He would contact African airports for his brother, trying to communicate with the officials as best he could each time his brother needed a landing permit. With a mix of English, French, and German, Martin would manage to get through to them all and pave the way for René.

Through Martin, we saw and felt the happiness and struggle experienced by our brave friends in more detail. We learned about René almost dying of yellow fever, then coming down with malaria immediately after.

But Ulla and René persevered. They encountered dangerous situations in several countries. Sometimes they were held at gunpoint. More than once, they were saved by the Swiss flag on their tail wings, which was mistaken by local rebels to be the symbol for the Red Cross. Nature itself also presented a challenge for their tiny plane, which was no match for strong winds and storms.

After three months, René and Ulla reached Ethiopia. They stopped in a local village they had contacted before leaving Switzerland and presented a cheque with donations to the village elders. A few weeks later, just as I returned from my short trip to Puget Sound, they reached Sudan, where they found themselves too broke to continue.

Martin tried everything from his chair in our office, but neither bank transfer nor Western Union seemed a viable option. Desperate for cash to continue their journey, René and Ulla happened upon an influential, Sudanese politician who was delighted by their tale. He generously invited them into his home, sharing food and warm water. Our friends felt like they had arrived in heaven. A few days later, the politician presented them with a wonderful gift – enough cash to take to the skies again.

In their fifth month of traveling, the young couple were denied entry to Egypt. Almost out of fuel, René and Ulla had no choice but to risk being shot down. Upon landing at Alexandria International airport, armed guards awaited them.

Egypt was experiencing a period of civil unrest at the time. The officials were mostly annoyed with the young travelers. They did not want two foreigners shot down in Egyptian air space. An international scandal would not help their cause while being on the brink of civil war.

Wanting to get rid of the Swiss nationals as soon as possible, the airport authority helped René and Ulla prepare their tiny plane for their riskiest undertaking yet – crossing the Mediterranean Sea to Cyprus. The back of their cabin was outfitted with an extra fuel tank. Water and other provisions were crammed into the rest of the space. When it was time to leave, the plane was so heavy it needed to accelerate the entire length of the runway to lift off.

Our friends were scared. They would have to fly more than ten hours to reach Cyprus. After a while, René saw nothing but blue. He became disoriented and couldn't tell for sure where the sky ended and the sea began. To compensate for lacking instrumentation, he hung a pocketknife from the plane's ceiling to help him keep the plane in a horizontal position as he steadily advanced into the seemingly endless blue. As the hours progressed, the fuel gage again began reading dangerously low. When they finally saw Cyprus appear in front of them, René breathed deeply, as though he were Columbus relieved to see land at last.

In late summer of 2004, after six months of incredible adventures, René and Ulla asked for permission to land in Switzerland. After all they had been through – braving insurmountable odds, being helped by countless strangers, finding support everywhere they turned – their home country denied them access. No matter how intensely Martin discussed matters with officials over the phone, they remained adamant: an ultra-light airplane registered in Johannesburg would not be allowed to land anywhere on Swiss soil.

René and Ulla decided to touch down on a meadow in Germany instead, mere feet away from the Swiss border. All of their friends and workmates showed up in force to welcome them on this memorable summer day. McKinsey even gave us the morning off. As it came closer, René and Ulla's tiny airplane was just a pinprick in the clear blue sky. They taxied to a stop right in front of us and happily jumped out of their plane, marveling at the large group of people holding banners, balloons and flowers. René and Ulla both looked haggard and weak. The journey had taken its toll. We partied on the meadow, with champagne corks flying in all directions, many of us unable to hold back tears of happiness.

With their aircraft right in front of me, I was even more inspired by my friends' courage. How could an entire continent be crossed in something so small? It seemed impossible.

Only a few days later, René and Ulla returned to work at McKinsey. We talked for many days, our office walls disappearing as we relived the African journey with them – pushing through Saharan winds, seeing a rolling landscape change beneath us, from iridescent greens to glowing browns to yellows the farther north we traveled. Both of them admitted it had been unbelievably hard at times. Both thought it highly likely they never would have left Switzerland in the first place, had they known how taxing their journey would be. Yet, neither of them regretted one minute of their experiences. While the six-month journey had exhausted their bodies, it had greatly strengthened their spirits. Our friends were filled with hope and resolve. They were determined to continue living life to the fullest and go after their dreams.

They had been changed forever. And so had I. Supporting them from a distance, thinking of them for months, and simply listening to their story gave me courage.

That same summer, I was invited to the birthday party of another of my work mates. Amidst drinking colleagues, I met a gentleman in a red sweater. He was the retired father of the birthday girl and had just turned seventy years old. Being a true Swiss mountain boy, he had never left his home country – until he reached retirement, that is.

Not long after his last day at work, when he was sixty-five, he had informed his family he would go on a trip. The adventurous senior had packed a small backpack and taken a plane to Sydney. Speaking not a single word of English, he had followed a group of teenage backpackers to a hostel.

An idea had formed in his mind. A few days later, he had asked them if they wanted to buy an old car together and drive through Australia for a few months. He had been a mechanic his entire life. In exchange for their helping him get around, he would make sure their car survived the trip. They all ended up exploring Australia together for many months, in a rusty old van, having the time of their lives.

During our short conversation, my friend's charming father had me in awe with his tale. Raising his wine glass to me and offering a bright smile, my new acquaintance disappeared into the birthday crowd.

He has remained with me ever since. Whenever I catch myself being scared to face the unknown, I remember this friendly and positive old man in his bright red sweater, and off I go, happily plunging ahead towards new horizons. Sometimes all it takes is to meet someone for a brief moment, and they end up inspiring us for a whole lifetime.

2004 had been a pivotal year. I had crossed paths with amazing characters who seemed to be destined to convince me once and for all to not accept boundaries. Since then, I always become intrigued whenever people tell me something cannot be done. And I look for ways to prove them wrong. Ours is a beautiful existence. Nothing is impossible.

21

Pacific Ocean

As I dreamt of becoming a marine biologist, my thoughts often went back to Puget Sound. I could easily picture myself, piloting a submersible to explore the dark underwater realm of the Cascadia subduction zone in the future.

For now, unfortunately, my mind explored a dark realm of a different nature. During our visit to Seattle, I had looked over Alana's shoulder and she had unknowingly given me a glimpse of her email password.

Plagued by worries about our relationship, I inevitably found myself playing with the thought of using it. I struggled for weeks and kicked myself over and over again, each time I came close to invading her privacy. In the end, I lost the battle I was waging within. Thousands of miles away, from the safety of my Swiss desktop, I started peeking into Alana's inbox every day. I knew very well what I was doing was wrong, but was so desperate in my longing for her, I couldn't help myself. I opened most of her private correspondence.

Including the twelve months we had spent emailing each other before our fateful first rendezvous on Alana's continent, we were nearing the end of our third year together. I was consumed by fear of loss, while at the same time realizing my unhealthy behavior wasn't helping the situation. Like a true addict, I despised my actions yet couldn't control myself. Every day I struggled, lost, and ended up yet again invading the privacy and potentially damaging the trust of an amazing woman I loved with all my heart.

For many weeks, I felt ashamed as well as relieved, since I never stumbled upon anything of interest. Until one night, in the fall of 2004.

I opened an email from Eleanor to Alana. It read like the follow-up to a recent phone call between mother and daughter. What I could gather from Eleanor's imparted wisdom was the worst kind of realization: Alana must have confessed to her mom she had been with another man.

My universe shattered into a million pieces.

I had always believed heartache was just a metaphor. That day, it became all too real. My heart felt close to exploding inside my chest. I felt as if all life was being crushed out of me in a medieval torture device. I could barely breathe. My vision blurred with pain and tears.

Alana's daily emails made matters worse. As always she ended with, "I love you very much." I needed to confront her about her betrayal without divulging how I had betrayed her trust for months by reading her private emails. The sadness and irony of the situation didn't strike me.

I was in shock and could barely focus my thoughts enough to dial Alana's number. When I finally reached her on the phone, I did my utmost to sound relaxed and happy.

After chatting a while, I casually mentioned, "I don't know what it is exactly, but I am having an odd feeling about us." I gathered all my courage. "Alana, are you seeing someone else?"

True to her primarily honest nature, she answered, "Yes."

I willed myself to stay calm. "Do you love him?"

"I am not sure."

"Will you keep seeing him?" I asked almost in a whisper.

The love of my life answered my question with a very quiet and sad, "Yes."

It felt as if I was falling from a mountaintop, plummeting towards the ground, anticipating crashing and dying upon impact at any moment. Reading about her affair in Eleanor's email, I had still held hope it would all magically go away – just a faux pas. I envisioned Alana having an epiphany followed by the realization she couldn't possibly live without me. Clearly I had seen way too many Hollywood movies.

Alana did write me several emails in the ensuing days. She also tried reaching me over the phone. I felt she was as heartbroken as I was, and needed to connect.

I didn't respond. I couldn't. For the first time in my life, I had been rendered more than speechless. I couldn't think. I didn't trust myself to make a sound, afraid of what might come out if I did. The depth of my feelings scared me. Madness seemed to lurk just around the corner. My entire body felt paralyzed. I simply sat on my couch, staring at the brightly graffitied wall across from me.

When I finally got back in touch after about a week, Alana said, "It's over between us."

She had obviously come to a clear decision and her sad, yet stern tone of voice left no doubt: it was final.

For years to come, I would keep asking myself the same questions.

What would have happened had I awakened from my stupor and responded to her attempts to get in touch with me? What if I had been forgiving and had talked with her about her infidelity? What if I had asked her why, instead of judging her actions immediately? What if I had simply tried to listen to her for once? Instead, I had been enveloped in an emotional fog, making it impossible for me to come to any rational decisions. I had been reduced to bare emotional instinct and raw pain.

I was an emotional wreck. Trying to come to terms with the sudden separation while going to work and continuing my studies became a superhuman effort. I tried to figure out what to do.

Once, on a vacation as a teenager, I was stuck on a fishing boat during heavy seas, sick as a dog. After trying to find my equilibrium for a while, I realized the only way to overcome my seasickness was to climb all the way to the top of the boat where the motion of the waves could be felt most violently. For the rest of the turbulent journey, I stood on the roof of the boat, screaming into the wind, hanging onto the mast for dear life. My seasickness vanished and I felt intensely alive – happy, even. For years after that incident, whenever life shook me to the core, I would remember to face the storm. I would climb higher, hold on for dear life, and scream into the wind with all the passion contained in my longing heart.

I realized it was again time to take drastic action.

Despite the finality of her decision, Alana and I kept emailing. Then, one day, I called her.

"Please don't break up with me from a distance. Can you honor the amazing love we shared by making one last trip to Switzerland so we can say goodbye in person?" My heart was in my mouth as I awaited her response.

Experiencing some final, private moments with Alana was not going to restore my happiness. I knew it was going to make both of us feel miserable. Nevertheless, I felt the irrational need to dive more deeply into the pain, so as to overcome it and, hopefully, understand it.

Even as the words left my mouth, I was fully aware of asking my ex-girlfriend for an enormous favor. I fully expected her response to be: "Are you nuts? I am staying on my own continent, you psycho. Get over it! Bye-bye!"

Incredibly, Alana gave in to my begging and said, "Ok, I will come over one last time. I can stay for two weeks. I'll be there in one month." She must have loved me far more deeply than I was able to comprehend at the time.

I spent the weeks leading up to Alana's visit crafting a final present for her. My heart was beating faster with every passing week and creativity helped focus my mind. Like a heartbroken teenager, I designed a goodbye scrapbook, swearing my everlasting love to the woman of my dreams, celebrating our best moments together, and hoping through my book they would become immortal.

When Alana finally arrived, our time together was as painful as I had expected it to be. Passion had often saved my life, yet it proved just as often to be a formidable Achilles heel. Our last days together were an unbelievable emotional nightmare for both of us.

Like any man who has been betrayed, I wondered about the guy who had come between us. More than anything, I wanted to quiz Alana and find out as much as possible about him. Who was he? What did he do? Was he good-looking? Charming? Was he a *Chippendale* kind of guy, or *Dirk Diggler*? I restrained myself and didn't ask her any of these questions.

At least I knew losing Alana didn't have anything to do with my being clumsy in bed or not having a penis. She had never cared about my physical incompleteness. But she had needed space and had given me countless signals to back off just a little. Instead of letting go, I had plunged ahead with even more intensity. Had she finally seen no other way but to break free? Had being trapped between her father and me finally gotten too much for her? Had I become a burden once she had managed to establish herself in Chicago? It could have been a multitude of factors and even as my mind rotated like a high-speed kaleidoscope, I knew I needed to stop torturing myself.

But then, during our last week together, Alana did let me know her lover's name, as well as part of her reason for leaving me.

"His name is Jack, Liam. He works as a room boy at the Best Western in Richland and is your complete opposite. You're so organized and have to plan everything. I don't want to live like that anymore. Jack is fun and wild. He plays the guitar like *Bryan Adams*, drinks a lot, and doesn't care how often we see each other. We simply enjoy the moment."

Her words stung me like a *Portuguese man'o war*. I had longed for answers. Now, as poison seemed to paralyze my entire body, I wished I hadn't gotten any.

I didn't send Alana away early, nor did she ask to leave before her scheduled departure date. We endured. I begged and cried.

When we went to bed, I would ask her, "Can I please rest my cheek on your hand for a while?"

Humiliating myself over and over again, I was incapable of controlling the flood of emotions to save my last scraps of dignity. I must have hit the top of the masochistic scale when Alana made a final request.

"Can you do me a favor Liam? I've got a problem. Jack infected me with chlamydia. Can you help me find some treatment for it?"

I agreed. Ever the helpful ex-boyfriend, I went to a pharmacy with the woman I still loved with every fiber of my being and bought her the medication she urgently needed.

Like a bullet train going off the rails, our two last weeks together finalized our relationship at warp speed, leaving no trace of doubt. The overwhelming experience broke our hearts, yet cut short the process of grasping it was truly over, which under regular circumstances might have taken me months.

On our final day together, I accompanied Alana to the airport. I could barely walk, feeling more helpless and hopeless than ever before in my life. We hugged each other one last time and said goodbye. As Alana walked through the security checkpoint, stepping onto an escalator, then vanishing from my sight, my heart constricted to its very limits. It is impossible for me to describe the pain I felt. A thousand daggers couldn't hurt as much as watching her go. I couldn't see, couldn't move, couldn't fill my lungs with the air they so desperately needed. Tears streamed from my eyes. Moaning like a wounded animal, I wobbled on unsteady legs and had to hold on to one of the barriers dividing non-travelers like me from the lucky ones bound for the skies.

I must have been rooted to the spot for ages, hoping against hope that maybe, just in this one special case, life would turn out to be like in the movies. Alana would enter the airplane. She would take a seat, suddenly realizing she couldn't live without me. She would jump up and, breaking every airport regulation, run back up the escalator right into my longing arms. Of course, the last scrap of sanity I had left told me I was hoping against hope. It was irrevocably over. I was alone once more, homeless again, belonging to no one but myself.

Somehow, I managed to stop staring towards the escalator and go home. I found myself in my living room with no recollection of how I had gotten there. I called my friend Sienna who had been a gentle yet solid presence in my life ever since we had connected years ago while eating chocolate in the old Genoa graveyard. Sienna came to my aid and stayed with me for two days. I hadn't had sleepovers since kindergarten. Her presence soothed me. We talked and watched movies while Sienna literally held my hand and stayed at my side, making sure I didn't fall into an abyss too deep to climb back out of.

Naomi, my old friend from Cinema Metropol, was another invaluable presence during my time of need. Over the years, we had gotten into the habit of meeting for a latte macchiato once a month. When Naomi felt me being closer to breaking than I had ever been before, she made sure to chat daily with me online, as well as quadrupling our latte macchiato outings, whether I wanted them, or not.

I was blessed with the best friends you could wish for. Nevertheless, I struggled to function. The last semester of my natural sciences diploma was coming to an end. I had several semester papers due in just a few weeks time. At McKinsey, our team juggled several projects at once, which required our full attention. I was a dead weight. Thankfully, my teammates were as understanding as ever, and carried me on their shoulders.

As I pushed on with my daily responsibilities, I realized I was barely able to string two sensible sentences together – and I wasn't getting better. The entire world seemed to consist of pain. It was time to climb even higher on that mast. I had to stop running, and face the storm raging inside of me. Instinctively I knew the only thing saving me would be to approach the waves at manic speed. They could either destroy me, or more likely – I hoped – shake me out of the spiral of despair I was trapped in.

Two weeks after Alana's departure, I explained to my team and my boss Marjorie, "Guys, I'm really sorry. But under the current circumstances, I'm unable to fulfill my duties. I'm a mess. Can I please have two weeks off, to sort myself out? Afterwards I'm sure, I'll finally be able to do my part again and not be a burden anymore. I promise."

As always, everyone at McKinsey was incredibly supportive.

My instincts told me to return to where it all began and take a self-therapeutic tour-de-force through memory lane. It was time to embark on a road trip of transcendence. I was still in touch with Alana's mom, and came up with a plan bordering on insanity.

Two days after consulting with Marjorie and my teammates, I was on a flight to London. While waiting for my connecting flight to Atlanta, my grief overflowed like a pot of violently boiling water. All around me were a ridiculous number of kissing couples. On top of that, overcrowded Heathrow airport treated its travelers to an unending barrage of love songs blaring from loudspeakers overhead. *Un-break My Heart* by Toni Braxton was the final straw leading me to break down in tears amidst thousands of happy travelers. Thankfully, the romantic musical onslaught ended as soon as I boarded the plane. My eyes were swollen from too much crying. I spent the entire flight to Atlanta in a daze.

At US Immigration, I was escorted into the airport police station. Apparently, a red flag had popped up when my name was entered into the system. I was barely holding it together as it was. Two hours of waiting and interrogations did not help make me feel any more composed. Thankfully, the tough interrogators soon realized they were dealing with a very unthreatening, sniveling mess.

"Our apologies, sir. A dangerous fugitive with the name 'William Klenk' is listed in our FBI database. No photograph is attached to the file. We had to make sure. Travel safely."

A very harmless me went stumbling along his teary way, feeling acutely vulnerable, thankful for my passport reflecting my male gender. Having to explain to the imposing police officers why my appearance didn't match the gender identity of my identification papers could have pushed me over the edge.

I was grateful when the seemingly endless, five-hour layover in Atlanta came to an end. Immediately after boarding my flight to Seattle, I fell into a comatose sleep, waking up only as we touched down at our final destination.

Eleanor welcomed me at arrivals. Seeing my surrogate mom made me happy and immeasurably sad at the same time. Absurdly, as Eleanor and I hugged tightly, the first fond memory popping into my head was of Alana and I cooking penis-shaped pasta for Eleanor's birthday two years earlier, followed by a colorful dessert of penis gummies.

Eleanor took a few days off to take care of me. She invited me into her new home unconditionally, offering shelter and understanding. Just recently, she had moved into a spacious house with her sister and brother-in-law. They were both very impartial and welcoming as well.

Eleanor and I discussed the immediate future as well as my intentions concerning my studies. My plans to come to Seattle within the next year were still in full swing. Losing the first, and maybe only true love of my life made it seem even more important to not lose my opportunities for growth as well. Like a bouncy safety net to a falling trapeze artist, studying marine biology seemed more attractive than ever.

Eleanor generously offered to help me lower my budget when the time came. "You are very welcome to set up camp in an old trailer we've parked in our garden."

The idea sounded fantastic to my adventurous soul. I had always dreamt of living in an old trailer, and had greatly enjoyed Alana's and my first two weeks together in our love-nest-on-wheels.

Eleanor tried to cheer me up by taking me sightseeing. We went to Pike Place Market together. The intense colors and scents of the old public market usually brought tears of joy to my eyes. Now my overwhelming melancholy covered everything like an opaque veil.

Soon I felt restless and ready to move on. After all, seeing Eleanor was only meant to be the starting shot to a grand state of Washington/ Oregon remembrance tour. Ever the worried mom, Eleanor tried to keep me from continuing my travels. She was understandably scared I might end up doing something incredibly stupid while traversing the wilderness of the Pacific Northwest. But I needed to go on and be on my own. I felt an irresistible urge to revisit all places that had held deeper meaning for Alana and me.

On the third day of my visit, Eleanor and I hugged each other goodbye. I headed along the Pacific coast towards Oregon and Cannon Beach. Immersing myself in wild nature has always helped me to find balance. As I drove along lonely winding roads, I listened to Peter Gabriel and Alanis Morisette and stopped at all the landmarks I had visited with Alana. I called Eleanor every evening to let her know I was still alive and kicking.

Shortly before arriving in Cannon Beach, I was deeply immersed in my thoughts, cruising along a lonely stretch of road when a police cruiser suddenly pulled up beside me. The officer signaled for me to pull over. For the life of me, I couldn't think of what I had done wrong. While my body had been driving, my mind had been floating among fluffy, nostalgic clouds. Following the officers order, I rolled to a stop at the side of the road. I must have still seemed lost in space when the officer looked at me. This prompted him to check my person as well as my rental car thoroughly for evidence of drug use. Finding nothing, he clearly wasn't sure what to make of me. He finally let me go with a warning.

"Sir, the speed at which you were crawling along can obstruct traffic and endanger the lives of others. Speed up!"

Amused, I nodded and drove away along the completely deserted scenic route at a swift speed that seemed to satisfy him.

Cannon Beach was as picturesque as I remembered it. The hotel Alana and I had stayed in didn't have the same room available. I took the only room up for grabs with full ocean view, and prepared to stare at iconic Haystack Rock for a few days while writing my term papers.

Memories of Alana and I spending our perfect lovers-getaway weekend to the sound of screeching seagulls threatened to overwhelm me. But my daily check-in with Eleanor gave me reason to resurface from the fog of reminiscing and get my bearings. Experiencing the rough Pacific Ocean again also helped to ground me, not to mention my imminent term paper deadlines.

There was no time to waste. I decided to stay three days and nights at the Hallmark Resort.

On the first day, I enjoyed short walks along the beach, savoring the salty ocean spray with all my senses, and listening for the distinct sounds of humpback whales expelling spouts of breath through their blowholes. Monolithic Haystack Rock outside the hotel window, and the crackling fireplace indoors, gave me the peace of mind I needed.

On the second day, I managed to forge ahead with my schoolwork. The university had asked us to write a final paper on how biological and chemical forces aid in shaping the geology of our planet. I had brought my laptop and an entire folder of research material with me. Systematically incorporating all my findings, I wrote day and night. Forty hours later, my finished semester papers were on their way to Milton Keynes in England, arriving in my mentor's inbox not a moment too soon. Had grief left me with enough capacity to finish my diploma successfully? I could only hope.

It was my last night in Cannon Beach. At midnight, exhausted from writing non-stop, I nevertheless decided to savor the crisp Pacific Ocean air one last time and went for a walk on the beach. While gazing up at the stars, I fell and tore my jeans just as Alana had done years earlier.

"This must be a sign," I thought.

An hour later, wearing a new pair of jeans, I gave the old ones a ritualistic sea burial. As the heavy surf proceeded to drag the garment further and further out into the unknown, I hoped the Pacific Ocean would be able to mend what had been ripped apart.

The next morning, I followed the Oregon coastline back towards the Columbia River. I was going to drive along the unrivaled Columbia valley towards Walla Walla one last time. My love for this historical route, taken by Lewis and Clarke long before my time, was undiminished.

As soon as one leaves the lush wilderness of the Columbia River and turns northward bound on the highway, the surrounding landscape changes to flat expanses of barren desert and irrigated fields. But even the dry parts of the Columbia Basin countryside held a charm I closely associated with some of the best years of my life.

The closer I got to Richland, the more my heart constricted. With each passing minute, I reveled in nostalgia. The more tumbleweed blew past me, the closer I got to where it all began.

My beloved art teacher, Mrs. Moorcroft, my mentor and inspiration, offered to give me shelter. Mo was a logical piece of the puzzle. She had nurtured the talent, which eventually led me to move to Zurich and discover myself. Years later, she had pushed Alana to create artwork almost otherworldly, coming from the hands of a teenager. Mo had helped Alana apply for scholarships, those reserved only for the very best. Mo had believed in us both and had also been supportive of our passion for each other.

But before reconnecting with the teacher who had had by far the most influence on my life, I wanted to pay homage to all the sites still reverberating with the power of my lost love.

Was I taking the confrontational healing process a tad bit too far? I needed to tread carefully. Knowing where Jack, Alana's new boyfriend worked didn't help. I was conscious of a certain – for me unusual – level of aggressive impulse. It seemed the male hormone testosterone had taken a firmer hold of my body and mind than I had previously realized. I felt empowered, like a cowboy on steroids. Half of my ride towards Richland had been spent talking myself out of confronting the chlamydia-riddled bastard and bashing his head in with a tire iron – and a baseball bat, and a tree trunk as well, for good measure.

I drove past the diner where Mitchell and I had clashed so infamously on the day Alana and I finally met in the flesh. I continued to my old high school where I had picked her up and swept her into my arms for the first time. I drove to Eleanor and Alana's old house, parking in front of their old home for hours, staring at the large trees covering the garden in which we had spent so many romantic moments.

Finally, I arrived at the river and found our favorite bench, overlooking the Columbia River as it majestically meandered through the dry desert landscape. I seemed to have used up all my tears, yet the heaviness in my heart manifested itself throughout my entire being. I felt as if I might plummet through the Earth's crust and into its violent molten core, should I fail to keep a grip.

The worn-out, dark-green park bench at the river held so many memories of Alana and me conspiring and trusting each other. I couldn't bring myself to sit alone on it, but rather stood and stared for many hours, watching young couples enjoy the afternoon sunshine together. At that moment, it was impossible for me to believe life could ever make sense again. Melancholy, nostalgia and a dark gloominess were taking over my soul. My grief threatened to weaken me to a point where I'd be rooted to this very spot in Richland Park forever. I couldn't help but constantly batter myself with asking what I had done wrong.

Years later, I understood that, even though I had been far from the perfect boyfriend, apart from being very inexperienced for my years and hungry for true love, I had done nothing wrong. Neither had Alana. Sometimes relationships develop in a way beyond our control. Getting hurt, hurting others, heartbreak, losing and letting go are all part of what it means to be alive.

In the evening, when I finally managed to tear myself away, I headed to Mrs. Moorcroft's magical abode. My former teacher welcomed me with open arms. Her husband had died years earlier. She still lived in the house they had shared for decades. The entire space was a haven of creativity emanating irresistible warmth. Artwork and little trinkets were everywhere, in every available space. Many vintage toys were even hanging from the ceiling. Two playful Siamese cats roamed this jungle of color and snugness. Mo herself was a pillar of positivity and encouragement. She held regular barbecues for former art students in her expansive garden, forever staying a loving mentor in the lives of hundreds of protégés.

Mo was one of the few people who had always fully understood the extent and value of my passionate nature. Over the years, Mo had enthusiastically embraced every change in my life, offering sarcastic comments, sharp humor, and unwavering support.

My two self-therapeutic weeks of coming to terms with what I had lost were coming to an end. Already the next day after lunch, I would have to tackle a fourteen-hour drive to San Francisco airport. I had planned this on purpose, needing to end the journey with a physically exhausting, long drive to cleanse my tortured mind.

But that was tomorrow. For now, it was evening and Mo and I were relaxing in her cozy living room, drinking glass after glass of delicious, dark red wine while she listened to the ramblings of my broken heart, offering comfort and a very strong shoulder to lean on.

I longed to finally ask her about her mysterious, hidden eyebrows. At the same time, there was comfort in not knowing.

We philosophized way into the early morning hours. At last, Mo led me to her guest bedroom and gently closed the door behind her.

I could see it now, sparkling shyly at the outer edges of my consciousness: hope.

As the comfortable pillows and blanket enveloped me, I could hear something rustling under my arm. Mo had left a quote on the bed for me, words to take on the road with me, and never forget: "How lucky I am to have known someone who meant so much to me that saying goodbye was so damn awful." Thankful tears soaking into the fluffy pillow, I finally passed out from exhaustion.

Late the next morning, Mo and I enjoyed oceans of hot coffee together. I should have left around noon to make my schedule. But I only managed to extricate myself from our delightful conversation around 2 p.m. After a long, heartfelt hug, I was on my way. My flight from San Francisco airport was due to depart at 9 a.m., leaving me with seventeen hours to reach the airport in time. The roughly nine hundred miles should take me a maximum of fourteen hours.

Usually I would find small, romantic roads off the beaten path. This time around, I took major highways for optimum speed. Rolling down the almost empty highways, I stuck my head out the window at 80mph and released my pain. I screamed into the wind at the top of my lungs for hours, until my vocal chords felt completely raw. Purging grief in this manner felt frightful and amazingly liberating all at once.

Speeding towards the Oregon-California border, I made a tactical mistake costing me several hours. As I passed the last gas station in Oregon, I figured I'd fill up at the first one in California. I had miscalculated the vast distances of Northern California. The sun had set and many hours of complete darkness followed. With each hour, the needle of my gas indicator dropped further into the red. The few settlements I passed on my way all had tiny gas stations that seemed to have closed down many years earlier.

I was starting to panic slightly, and decided to leave the main highway to find another settlement as quickly as possible. More darkness followed. The stars were eerily bright, yet I was in no state to enjoy this romantic element of my journey. The indicator dropped all the way to "empty". I was running on fumes. To use up the remaining drops of fuel as slowly as possible, I slowed down to a crawl. As the car sputtered over the crest of a hill, I finally saw lights on the horizon. I kept rolling along in slow motion, horrified at the thought of having to hike for hours along deserted highways to finally reach the distant lights.

After another thirty minutes, I made it into town on the remainder of my car's fumes. At the exact moment a gas station came into view, the engine sputtered, coughed, and died. I gracefully rolled the last few feet to the gas pump. It was close to 1 a.m. I hadn't had a break since leaving Mo's haven at 2 p.m., eleven hours earlier. Driving through the pitch-black countryside had left me exhausted.

For the moment, I was high on adrenaline from barely escaping being stranded in the middle of the Northern Californian wilderness without a cell phone. I filled the tanks to overflowing – the car's with fuel and mine with coffee – and continued towards the highway and San Francisco.

At 3 a.m., after thirteen hours of continuous driving, determination and coffee weren't able to take me any further. I kept falling asleep on the wheel for seconds at a time, and decided to stop at a parking lot for a power nap.

I set my alarm clock for a thirty-minute break and closed my eyes. When I opened them again, it was 5 a.m. – two hours later! An instant adrenalin rush helped shake me fully awake. My alarm clock was still blaring, yet I had slept through it soundly for one and a half hours. I instantly rushed off towards the highway. San Francisco was at least another hour away. As I got closer, the highway expanded – from one lane to two, to finally six lanes going in each direction. I needed to drive to the other side of town, while morning rush hour grew exponentially congested with each passing minute.

Finally, at 8:30 a.m., I arrived at the check-in counter of San Francisco International Airport. The lady gave me a kind smile and shook her head. "I am sorry sir, but the gate is closing this minute. Today's flight will have to leave without you."

Thankfully, changing my ticket to the next morning didn't present any problems.

I called Eleanor to let her know I was safe, even though I was stuck in San Francisco. Eleanor offered to help. She went online, and booked me into a cozy hotel room at San Francisco airport. Thanks to her, I had the luxury of stumbling onto an express shuttle and collapsing on an impossibly large king-sized bed a short five minutes later.

The involuntary delay proved to be a lucky draw. I stayed in my hotel room, letting my thoughts take off and land with each airplane I was able to spot from the room's large floor-to-ceiling windows. This enabled me to ease my mind and begin processing the wild emotional roller coaster ride I had taken over the last fourteen days.

Irrevocably, through reliving countless loving milestones, I had come to understand that I had experienced far more than only loss. Rather, I had been lucky to experience true love and had gained so much in the process. My relationship with Alana and my friendship with her mother Eleanor had given me an insight into family and love. For the duration of our years together, I had been allowed the privilege to be loved for exactly who I was. I was immeasurably richer than ever before.

I still felt like the survivor of an extinction event, yet knew my shock therapy had worked, accelerating the grieving process. At least I would be able to function again in every day life.

The next morning, I left the United States, hoping to return in only a few months time to begin my studies of marine biology.

Back in Switzerland, reunited with my workmates at McKinsey, I did what I had promised to them and to myself – I functioned and did my part. Nevertheless, alone again, I still struggled to find meaning in life. The tiny sparkle of hope I had felt with Mo seemed to have disappeared. I dragged myself through each day, like a little boy on a never-ending hike with his parents, slogging along while the question "are we there yet?" repeated itself over and over again in my tired soul. Every little step needed some internal pep-talking and almost more energy than I could muster.

Longing to regain my balance rather sooner than later, I decided to take action and seek professional help voluntarily for the first time in my life. Functioning just wasn't going to be enough on its own. I went through the White Pages in search of an English-speaking psychologist.

Ever since my Richland exchange year, English had become the language I wrote and read, thought and felt in. Because of its openness to change and its continuous growth, English felt more natural to me. Even though I still used German in everyday life, English had long ago become my mother tongue of choice.

Apart from language considerations, I still shuddered at the thought of my traumatic experiences with the Stuttgart psychiatrist. To get as far away from an involuntary déjà vu as possible, I opted for entrusting my emotional life to a young, female therapist.

For six months, I went to see her once a week. The unconventional Swedish therapist I had found helped me to understand more about grief and anger, my fears, and my occasional bouts of low self-esteem. When I described the road-trip I had just put myself through, my therapist surprised me by enthusiastically applauding me.

"Incredible. Did you know this is in fact a recognized therapeutic strategy for helping patients overcome intense grief and other traumatizing life events? It is the emotional equivalent of rebooting your system. Well done."

Our long, weekly talks helped me to overcome my loss, albeit very slowly. I rediscovered joy one small step at a time. Being alone again was hardest in unexpected moments. I would catch myself in the supermarket vegetable section, staring into space and remembering the joy of going shopping together. Sitting on benches at the Zurich lakeside, I wondered if I would ever be able to enjoy a romantic sunset again on my own.

As time went on, the pain subsided. I learned to laugh again and surprised myself by going hours at a time without once thinking about the black hole of Alana's departure.

The young therapist was uniquely qualified to help me understand more about living in a not-quite-conventional body as well. True, I had found a balance and was happier by far than I had been before my gender transition. But no matter how much I wanted to be just one of the guys, I wasn't. My body hadn't undergone a complete change. Alignment was a more accurate description. I had done the best I could under the circumstances, yet at times I did repine some things, such as having to get testosterone injections every twenty days, not being able to pee in public like other men, and not being able to father children of my own.

Moments of sorrow were few and far between though. More bothersome on a daily basis were the reactions of strangers. If I divulged my trans identity, their entire evaluation of me as a person would then be based on this one fact. Whatever I did, they would attribute my actions and reactions to having been born in the wrong body. If I was depressed, having a bad day, tired, or didn't have an appetite, people would seem to nod and say to themselves, "Oh, of course, it must be tough for him, considering what he went through." It exasperated me to have my entire life and personality reduced in such a manner.

My therapist immediately understood what I was talking about. She had been born with a malformed right hand. She helped me by sharing impressions of her own life, making me realize that my situation was far less special than I had assumed. Many people had reduced her to being handicapped. Similar to my experiences, when she wasn't energetic or extroverted enough, people assumed it must be related to her missing hand.

My therapy sessions often became inspiring for both of us. Contrary to people's assumptions, we both simply lived, and dealt with ups and downs like everyone else. Of course there were exceptions, but most days, missing a hand or a penis had no impact on how we led our lives. In essence, neither of us felt handicapped, even though our so-called handicap had helped mold us into the personalities we were. We honored the life we had been given and were determined to make the most of it.

Up until then, I had been too shy to remove my shirt in public. Talking about my inhibitions made me realize how unnecessary they were. Almost everyone had scars. So what? Seizing sunny afternoons at the lakeside, I started to take my shirt off more and more frequently.

My teammates had been nothing short of amazing in their support of my recovery. I reciprocated their patience of the past months by investing all my energy in our projects.

In November of 2004, the Open University informed me, "Congratulations Mr. Klenk, you have passed all requirements for your course of study. We will be sending you your diploma shortly."

I couldn't believe it. Even though swiftly written at the Hallmark Resort under duress, my final paper had been sufficient. I had managed to finish my diploma in Natural Sciences.

Sitting down with relief and savoring my success, I could almost hear the Pacific surf and wanted to pack my bags immediately. But I would need to prepare for six more months before being financially ready for my move to Seattle. Only then would I become a full-time student and begin to explore the world's oceans, following in the footsteps of Jacques Cousteau. For the moment, the future seemed a bright ultramarine blue.

Then Christmas 2004 arrived to remind me of my loneliness. Without warning, I was hit by a massive depression. More often than not, my mind was crafting elaborate suicide scenarios.

Spending Christmas with Dad was out of the question. I couldn't face meeting anyone from my adoptive family so soon after losing the chosen family I had found in Alana and Eleanor. My therapy sessions had once more reawakened many things forgotten – good memories as well as bad. I felt renewed anger towards Dad and needed some time to lay my childhood memories to rest once and for all. Dad had always had a soft heart. He had been human. He loved me very much. I needed to forgive him for not being the perfect superhero I had always wanted him to be. I was too depressed however, and that bridge needed to be built on another day.

I decided to celebrate Christmas alone, in the powerful but gentle arms of my beloved ocean. I would treat myself to a scuba diving vacation in Khao Lak, Thailand. Either I would have an amazing time, or manage to somehow slip into the depths and never return. Scenes from Luc Besson's movie *The Big Blue* hovered at the forefront of my mind. Life was most definitely better down there, in the deep…

Eleanor and I had remained good friends. While talking on the phone, with continents and oceans separating us, she was still able to see right through me. And she was having none of it.

"I'm *not* letting you spend Christmas all alone on a lonely godforsaken island in the middle of nowhere. Who knows what'll happen or what you'll end up doing to yourself? You shouldn't be alone over the holiday season. Your emotions are still too raw, Liam. Why don't you come spend the holidays with us in Seattle? It'll just be my sister, her family and I. They're good people, fun to be around. Alana won't celebrate with us this year. It's Mitchell's turn to have her for Christmas. So the coast is clear."

I wasn't convinced and kept dreaming of disappearing into the Big Blue. Eleanor wouldn't let it go and kept calling me. Come to think of it, I had always enjoyed Christmas with my surrogate families in the US. I loved kitschy Christmas decorations, eggnog, chocolate chip cookies, fast food and movies on the couch.

My flight to Thailand was supposed to leave on 22nd of December 2004. On the 21st of December, I made a last minute decision to cancel my trip to Khao Lak and booked a flight to the US instead. The 22nd of December saw me flying over the Atlantic, on my way to New York with a connecting flight to Seattle.

Christmas in her home was everything Eleanor had promised it would be. Her sister's whole family was visiting. Seeing my surrogate mom inevitably brought up memories of Alana. For the most part however, I delighted in being part of her sister's fun-loving family circle. We stuffed ourselves with pizza, watched countless movies together, and kept the fireplace going for days. I found myself smiling and thoughts of suicide flashed through my mind far less frequently.

On 26th of December, we were all lounging lazily on the big family couch when news from the tsunami in Asia reached us through CNN.

As we watched the heartbreaking live footage, I couldn't help but think of myself. Apart from the shock of seeing one of the biggest tragedies of our time, I realized Eleanor had just saved my life. It was her persistent urging that had led me to make an impulsive decision to change my plans, to choose my surrogate family over potentially finding romantic ways of killing myself in Thailand.

From the safety of a Seattle couch, I now learned that death would have found me on the idyllic island of Khao Lak, even if I hadn't been seeking it. The tropical paradise had been devastated. The Beach Front Resort in which I had booked a beautiful sea-view room had been completely destroyed. In fact, reports stated my planned holiday destination had been within the area worst hit by the natural disaster.

Eleanor and I sat next to each other with tears in our eyes. Both lost in our own thoughts, we continued watching live news coverage for hours. I found no words to express what I felt. I was grateful to be alive. What had I done to deserve the armada of guardian angels that must have come to my rescue?

22

Lake Lucerne

After the charmingly dysfunctional family atmosphere in Seattle, it was hard to come back to my safe, yet lonely, Swiss existence. 2005 was my fourteenth year in Zurich. It was as close to being home as any location had ever felt to me. More importantly, I was fortunate to still have my faithful and invaluable group of friends and acquaintances.

Nevertheless, the bars of my beautiful gilded cage crept increasingly closer as I grew ever hungrier for new challenges. One undeniable element of my cravings was the urge to finally fully enjoy the freedom of having united my soul with my body. I had visions of bounding around the beach, enjoying the little pleasures I had been denied for so long, finally making the most of inhabiting a body that showed the world the man I truly was. It was time to run in the wind – wearing just my boxer shorts.

Certain elements of male life would remain forever unattainable. I was still coming to terms with my inability to father my own children. I imagined myself melting at my little ones' slightest smiles, and longed to have a chance to be that softhearted dad. The only way that would happen would be through adoption. Maybe one day, I would adopt children and do my best to give them a happy home.

Another challenge was flirting. Flirting could swiftly lead to petting, which I couldn't help feeling worried about. My mind conjured comically fearful visions of women screaming in panic as soon as I dropped my boxer shorts, running off in only their panties.

I also still couldn't pee without squatting. This meant I always had to use the privacy of a toilet booth, to avoid attracting attention.

Other male-isms remained alien to me as well. I would never think it wrong or unmanly to openly show my sensitivity and compassion or even cry in public. I would never be afraid to admit I was wrong, never whistle or wink at women, never go binge drinking in pubs, never talk trash about women's boobs or asses, nor do a host of common things other men seemed to do as naturally as breathing. Every so often, I would listen to my fellow men and cringe in embarrassment.

I would be a hybrid for the rest of my life. I couldn't erase having grown up in a female body. And I didn't want to. Having grown up in a girl's body was a gift of grand proportions and had influenced all aspects of my behavior. Most days, I was happy making the most of my own unique species. Liamus Erectus, creature of thought and dreams, compassion and passion, love and tears and joy – creature of imperfection, confusion, thick-headedness, endless battles with inner demons, and the incessant search for a home within myself as well as a home in the world.

Even though I easily managed to talk anyone's ears off, I seemed to be an introvert by nature. I had always been too much of a thoughtful loner to enjoy partying and club atmospheres. I was incapable of recharging my batteries by throwing myself into a crowd. Instead, I needed solitude and tranquility to regain my strength and energy.

Thankfully, my predisposition matched my limitations. Partying hard, leading to possibly getting arrested anywhere in the world, was a scary prospect. Many of my friends adventurously enjoyed the night life, complete with frequent scuffles. I couldn't take the risk of getting picked up or frisked by the police. Worst-case scenario? I would end up in a holding cell with a bunch of little Hitlers. Or, in some countries, I could simply disappear once found out as a freak-sans-penis. The local unenlightened police force as well as their contingent of thugs could easily feel threatened by what I represented. I had every chance of getting raped, tortured or even beaten to death. Over the years, this understanding inevitably led me to always try to keep a low profile. I invested my full energy and courage into elaborate life pursuits rather than in random acts of rebellion while partying with my peers.

I faced the constant danger of finding myself in potentially life-threatening situations. More traveling drove that point home. It's a dramatic thing to say, I know. But imagine ending up in a small-town holding cell somewhere in the rural United States, or many other corners of the world where people still feel threatened to the point of violence by what they cannot comprehend?

Despite this fact, my charming nature, open-mindedness, integrity, exceptional people skills, and formidable instincts had protected me over the years. If I sensed danger, I retreated quietly and rarely encountered violent conflict of any kind.

I respected people and their opinions and never expected them to understand my somewhat unique history. I never advertised it either. We all have our load to carry. No one escapes the toughness of life.

No one needed me to drop my entire life history in his or her lap just because I was a little different from the norm. If we dig more deeply, everyone has intimate problems or desires. Most people deviate in some way or other from what society considers normal. It can be anything, from protruding ears to epilepsy, homosexuality, Asperger's, depression, sadomasochistic proclivities, or any other manifestations of our human existence. If someone asked me about myself directly, however, I was always happy to open up and share my thoughts. Whenever I told them about my being transgender, I would make it clear that I didn't take their acceptance for granted. I would say, "I completely understand if what I am telling you is maybe hard to understand. It's just as hard for me to explain. I'm not even sure I'd be able to empathize with someone like me if I hadn't been born in the wrong body myself. I won't be angry if you'd rather keep your distance in the future. It's ok."

No one ever wanted to keep their distance. Due to my respect for everyone's freedom of mind, people reciprocated by accepting me entirely. They appreciated me, and took me at face value. Even the most macho of men, who would usually comment on my gentleness and think me odd at first sight, would gradually come to appreciate me for my honest, compassionate personality.

Despite numerous and undeniable limitations, there were so many simple pleasures and adventures for me to enjoy, which would have previously been far out of reach. My self-confidence had grown. Despite my sizeable scars, I learned to enjoy taking my shirt off whenever sunshine or sparkling blue ocean water beckoned. I was able to walk among my peers, able to live my life as the clumsy little man I was. Most importantly, I was able to smile at my reflection in the mirror most mornings, feeling a profound happiness at being alive.

2005 marked my last year of being sheltered in a well-structured, thoroughly professional work environment. My work experiences had revealed two kinds of jobs: either the work was highly stimulating and passion-inducing, which translated into enormous stress levels and complicated work relationships, or it offered a highly professional and positive atmosphere with fantastic teamwork, but was rather dull and had no direct impact on my personal life.

Being in the latter group, my years at McKinsey were never unhappy. Quite the contrary. Working at the highly-structured international consulting company taught me the true meaning of professionalism and collaboration. It was an amazing experience that made it hard to quietly accept mediocre working conditions elsewhere. Yet, despite all obvious advantages, the character of our daily work at McKinsey lacked verve. My years at the consulting company were characterized by a moderate tranquility. Like a roller coaster ride for toddlers, the carts rolled stoically on even tracks, firmly anchored to the ground. I missed the inclines, loop-de-loops, and heart-twisting drops of a more engaging profession.

I *did* experience some rather awful double-dips whenever memories of Alana overwhelmed me. By never answering any of my emails after our break-up, she showed me the biggest kindness of all. It enabled me to eventually, over the course of eight years, get over my loss and let go. In 2005, however, my emotions were still raw, every corner of Zurich holding memories loaded with happiness and pain. This was the best incentive to finally leave my self-made nest. I needed a fresh start.

A tsunami had killed thousands, yet had spared me. Having been a distant observer to a horrendous force of nature made it clear: I needed to snap out of feeling sorry for myself. Eleanor's intervention had given me a second chance at life. It was time to stop being miserable. I needed to embrace the pain of losing Alana, transcend my emotional difficulties once more, and enjoy this one beautiful life of mine.

Three additional and unrelated experiences helped me to regain my balance. I found much-needed escape by reading the time-consuming *Dark Tower* series by Stephen King; my therapist encouraged me to follow my heart and told me repeatedly how much she admired the beautiful person I was (and I can't deny that it felt immeasurably good to hear such praise); and last but not least, my upcoming life as a marine biology student provided daily doses of hope and happiness.

Researching my future profession on the Internet, I discovered a lot of scuba diving experience proved very helpful for marine biologists, enabling them to conduct their own fieldwork. Having thrown myself fully into daily work at McKinsey, I had accumulated oceans of overtime in the process. Now I started considering using this off-time constructively to refine my underwater skills. Would I be able to go as far as to fulfill my dream of becoming a divemaster?

If this was ever to become a reality, I needed to spend some time underwater in Switzerland. Though shivering at the mere thought of it, I decided to obtain my Rescue Diver certification in the cold, muddy waters of Lake Zurich, as well as accumulate more logged dives.

My first dive in the chilly mountain lakes with a Swiss dive center made me question my plan.

Against my protests, they insisted on a twenty-pound weight belt for the slim, inexperienced diver that was me. Even in much denser seawater, I had, at last count, only needed two pounds when wearing a full wetsuit. I yielded to the loudly proclaiming men of greater experience. As I deflated my buoyancy-compensating device on the lake's surface, I found myself plummeting into the depths, making a speedy decent of sixty-five feet in only two seconds. Gladly, I had always been much tougher than I look. My eardrums should have blown. Instead, the only thing that blew was my temper. I aborted the dive, yelling at my Swiss guides as soon as we reached the surface. I could have been gravely injured, and made sure to never dive with these so-called professionals ever again.

Round two of my Swiss diving experiences involved a small dive center located downtown. To get a feel for the level of professionalism in this outfit, I visited their dive shop and asked countless questions about diving in general, and about their equipment. The owner was the only instructor of the dive shop. He seemed knowledgeable and easy going. So I signed up for a first aid course with him, which I passed without incident.

Feeling relatively confident under the tutelage of this seasoned Swiss veteran of freshwater diving, I took heart and signed up for a rescue course in Lake Zurich. To save money on rentals, I bought random pieces of second-hand gear from a number of different shops around town.

The first classroom session went well. So did day one of the rescue course at the lake. But my instructor's behavior towards me seemed to have shifted inexplicably. Uncomfortable silences and tension lingered between us. Over the next few sessions, he stonewalled me and postured like a schoolyard bully. I kept forging ahead despite my increasing discomfort. The other students would be taught theory sessions I would only hear about *after* our dives. Briefings would be done without me, leaving me struggling to fulfill the daily requirements of the course.

When it came to the training task of finding a missing diver in the shape of a lovingly decorated plastic bottle, the other students mysteriously arrived ahead of me. Since the briefings had already been done, the grumpy instructor delivered a hasty synopsis for my benefit. Heavy mudslides had disturbed nearby mountainsides just the day before, heavily affecting visibility in the lake. It was down to almost zero. Underwater, I literally couldn't see my hand in front of my face. The numbers on the dive computer strapped to my wrist were undecipherable. Floating particles saturated the water. Diving in my morning coffee would have yielded better results.

The objective of the day was to find the poor lost plastic bottle within ten minutes by using search patterns of our choice. Any longer than ten, and the missing plastic-bottle/missing-diver would have irreparable brain damage and our mission would be deemed a failure.

I felt nervous about the minimal information I had received. Determined to give it my best shot, I plunged in nevertheless, all the while puzzling over the strange behavior of our instructor. Everyone else seemed to be very satisfied with him and the course, leaving me wondering if maybe I was being paranoid. What I did not realize was that everyone else had been given in-depth instruction on how to safely navigate in zero visibility.

Within minutes in the diluted mud, I managed to get separated from my dive buddy. Since I couldn't make out my dive computer's screen, much less anything displayed on it, I felt increasingly disoriented. One major rule of scuba diving is to never dive alone. After one minute of searching for your buddy, best practice dictates returning to the surface to reunite and regroup.

I tried to surface, yet my ears told me I was in fact descending rather than ascending. Hovering on the edge of reason, just moments away from the red fog of panic, I tried to correct my mistake. As I turned around, I managed to entangle myself in kelp, losing my regulator and swallowing muddy water in the process. Sheer willpower kept me from giving in to the now growing panic clouding the remnants of my good sense. Screaming at myself to get a grip, I came to a full stop and managed to retrieve my regulator. I forced myself to wiggle out of the equipment that had been strapped to my back, so I could cut away the obstinate green mass holding me in its potentially deadly embrace. As I was taught during my Maltese open-water course, I held my equipment in front of me with one hand, so as to be able to continue breathing through my regulator. With my other hand, I dug in and ripped away clumps of kelp.

The incident seemed to last hours. It couldn't have taken more than a minute though. At last, I wiggled back into my equipment. Luckily, I bumped into my buddy on my way to the surface. Annoyed, he pointed to his watch, and shook his head. He had no way of knowing how close to drowning I had come. Both seething with anger, we grudgingly descended together once more and managed to retrieve our lost plastic bottle/diver through sheer dumb luck, after five minutes of searching.

I was still furious when we surfaced, and shaking from the aftereffects of the biggest adrenaline rush of my life. The instructor seemed oddly disappointed that I had braved the moment. Clearly, he had wanted me to fail.

The next day, I went to the dive shop and confronted the man who had almost gotten me killed.

"Oh, I really enjoyed sabotaging your efforts," he openly admitted. "I wanted to teach you a lesson about loyalty, because you didn't buy your equipment from my shop."

I was dumbfounded. My life had been on the line because I had failed to buy my regulator, fins and wetsuit in this irresponsible fool's shop?

I barely restrained myself from jumping over the counter and kicking him in the balls. I didn't know how to respond. So I simply said, "I want my money back. And a referral form for the elements of the rescue course I have already completed so I don't have to repeat the whole course again."

"You should've read the small print," he grinned. "It says very clearly that the money is non-refundable if the student chooses to discontinue the course. But sure, I'll write you a referral form. Oh, and by the way, don't even think of complaining to PADI. The other three students in the class were good friends of mine. They'll gladly vouch for me and discredit anything you might have to say."

I did the only thing I could do. I watched the instructor sign the document and left without another word.

I grudgingly lost this round. I swallowed my anger, strengthened my resolve, and went on to round three – which I decided would consist solely of getting more dive experiences under my belt. Further pursuing the matter was useless, and I was done with taking courses in Switzerland. My rescue course would be completed upon arrival at the tropical destination where I planned to tackle my divemaster education.

I was also done with diving in Lake Zurich. As much as I had come to love this body of water, I now preferred looking at it from a distance. Researching lakes in Switzerland, I discovered Lake Lucerne to be even colder, around sixty degrees Fahrenheit in summer. But apparently its sediment consists entirely of large rocks and pebbles. Its water is crystal clear, all the way to the bottom.

It was a one-hour drive to get there, but I figured, why not? Even though I didn't want to continue with the rescue course in any Swiss waters, I still needed to get more dive experience under my belt before tackling both rescue and divemaster course.

I drove to Lucerne and visited shop after shop. I needed to find a dive center, run by people who weren't clinically insane, whom I could join for scuba excursions. Third time was the charm. Ben, one of the instructors of Lucerne's Eagle Ray Dive Center, became my dive buddy. We agreed to meet once a week for a dive in Lake Lucerne for the rest of the summer.

The fourth-largest lake in Switzerland has an odd shape, with bends and arms reaching from the town of Lucerne all the way into the mountains.

Ben and I would meet every Saturday afternoon at 1.p.m. sharp. I would drive up to our meeting point at the lakeshore in my old Volkswagen, trunk filled with diving paraphernalia, mind filled with dread about the near-freezing lake. The landscape only thirty minutes outside Lucerne was stunning. I would park my car in a daze and step out onto the beautiful lakeshore, framed by picturesque forests and mountains. It felt as if I was stepping into a glossy postcard. I almost had to pinch myself every time I arrived.

Nevertheless, the emotional roller coaster I went through on each of those diving Saturdays was hilarious. Packing my equipment at home, I would find myself happily anticipating the dive experience. As I arrived at the lake, I would proceed to cram myself into layer-upon-layer of neoprene, while freezing my butt off and fighting with the unyielding material. I would ask myself, "Why on Earth am I subjecting myself to such a high level of discomfort, *voluntarily?*"

Once enveloped in layers of gear and loaded down with equipment, and sweating rivers inside the zipped-up neoprene, I would find relief in the bewitching waters of the cold lake water and feel happy again, as happy as a little duckling. I would then proceed to enjoy each dive immensely – until we hit the thermocline. There, temperatures would drop from sixty-eight to forty degrees Fahrenheit in an instant. Each and every time, this would feel as if someone had driven his fist into my diaphragm, leaving me breathless. This would last a good fifteen minutes as we made our way underneath the thermocline, making me wonder all over again if I had nothing better to do with my time.

Once I got over the cold, however, I would be fascinated by a clear visibility often reaching as far as a hundred and thirty feet. Carps and trout would be swimming all around us. Sometimes we would see majestic pike hovering amidst gently flowing lake grass. Some of them would be up to four feet in length. I was enthralled and for a short while forgot all about being cold. Growing fatigue and trembling limbs would remind me soon enough, and Ben and I would signal each other to begin a slow ascent. As soon as we reached the warmer layer of water above the thermocline, I would start enjoying the underwater experience once more.

Arriving back at the surface, all good feelings would evaporate immediately. We would peel off all the layers of neoprene, then shiver uncontrollably until we managed to burrow under layers of dry towels and sweaters. Finally, we would gulp down cup after cup of hot chocolate. Then, back home, I would immediately forget all the negatives and eagerly await the next week's submersion in Lake Lucerne's icy water. I was like a child puking his corn dogs over the side of the rails one minute, and begging to go again the next.

23

Lhaviyani Atoll

A few months and twenty dives later, it was time to embark on a month of tropical adventure. My boss Marjorie signed off on four weeks of overtime compensation. My heart led me back to the island of Kuredu, the place where I had truly fallen for the deep blue sea. I couldn't wait to get back to the Maldives and rediscover the countless magnificent shades of turquoise and blue.

On my first visit a year earlier, I had left Kuredu in tears as I watched dolphins play on the horizon. Coming back now, the time in between visits simply vanished like sand rushing through the holes of a sieve as soon as I stepped onto the seaplane in the Maldivian capital of Male. It felt like coming home. One hour later, after landing, I was back on Kuredu Island – not just an island, but a whole other universe. I wanted never to leave again.

I buried my shoes in the closet like before, happy to be barefoot for an entire month this time. My toes wiggled gladly, making little sand angels in the infinitely fine, white sand. The soles of my feet still remembered the velvet-like sensations from the year before. I walked the beaches around the entire island, reclaiming my one-mile by nine-hundred-eighty-foot territory in less than one hour.

The wide ocean expanse, ranging from turquoise to a deep blue at the horizon, put a spring in my step. The wind rustled peacefully through palm leaves. The overpowering stench of civilization was gone completely, replaced by a pure, heavenly fragrance, perfuming the air with a subtle scent of salty equatorial freshness. My lungs and heart opened up like a blooming rose in spring. I felt free.

On the way back to my room I stopped at the dive center to touch base with the instructors. I was assigned a mentor for the month, who presented me with a busy schedule of theory, in-water training, and scuba diving.

But first, I would need to tackle the remainder of my Rescue Diver course. I teamed up with two other students. Our instructor was a towering Welsh man with a beautiful sense of humor. He delighted in surprising us and challenging our improvisation skills. He had obviously recruited half the dive center to help with his course. Panicking and drowning instructors popped up everywhere we went in the Lhaviyani Atoll. Even underwater, our guides suddenly dropped their equipment, lost their fins or unexpectedly stopped moving and lay suspended in the deep blue. We started to get paranoid. If someone as much as coughed, I would race instantly to his aid, staring into wide-open eyes framed by the diver's scuba mask. I would invariably detect a twinkle in those eyes, followed by a big grin as the diver lunged at me, faking a panic attack.

The difference in professionalism between these and my Swiss experiences was profound. Most importantly, here scuba diving was treated as serious *and* fun at the same time. Throughout my experiences in Lake Zurich, divers as well as instructors had been deathly serious about everything, waging quasi-religious wars about the right equipment and the best dive practices. Instead of appreciating the magic of the element they were immersing themselves in, they had been concerned with being right. I treasured the relaxed atmosphere on Kuredu Island. The dive center was under South African-German management, run very professionally, yet with a good sense of humor and with an undeniable passion for the ocean.

After two days of rest, I met my assigned divemaster mentor, Friedrich, for the first time to start going through the comprehensive theory. I was on the threshold between recreational and professional diver. Becoming a divemaster meant that from this point onwards, I would hold more responsibility when hovering amidst other divers.

My first week of divemaster training was divided between classroom work and increasing my level of experience through diving at multiple locations throughout the Lhaviyani Atoll. There wasn't any time to rest or throw myself into the island's tourist scene. Frankly, I didn't care. I had never been much of a regular tourist. I preferred to avoid the bars in favor of being active during the day, studying, and exposing myself to new challenges.

Being on the dive boats and in the dive center every day brought me closer to the instructor team on the island. The more I mingled, the more I wondered what it might be like to live and work with these adventurers on a tiny speck of sand in the middle of the Indian Ocean.

Week two and three were packed with more dives, theory discussions, exams, and water skill exercises. They pushed me to my limit. Thankfully, I had come well prepared. I no longer swam like a drowning poodle. In the months leading up to my long stay on Kuredu, I had taken swimming lessons at a local indoor pool in Zurich. I was still one of the slowest swimmers you could possibly imagine, but at least I now swam without sputtering and swallowing gallons of water. Unfortunately, part of the divemaster examinations was swimming a long distance within a certain time. I managed it on pure willpower with just seconds to spare. Being an ungraceful creature on the water surface, I delighted in being an elegant sea creature. I seemed to shed all awkwardness as soon as I was fully immersed.

By week three, my mind was engaged in a constant internal battle. A little Poseidon sat on my right shoulder persistently pushing towards me becoming a full-time scuba instructor in the Lhaviyani Atoll, while a little Jacques Cousteau sat on my left shoulder, debating that my spot at Seattle University, all the effort, planning, and dreaming I had invested into starting an education in Marine Biology, couldn't just be dropped for bumbling along coral reefs.

Being thirty-four already, postponing my Marine Biology studies could mean the dream of becoming an ocean scientist might never become a reality. Research assistants older than thirty-five were practically unheard of. On the other hand, here I was, on Kuredu Island, feeling more tempted with every passing day to forget all about the science and marry the sea instead.

I asked myself what I would regret more at this point: not completing my marine biology studies in Seattle, or not submerging myself in the Indian Ocean and a diving instructor career? Poseidon whispered enthusiastically about how amazing it would be to mingle with moray eels, reef fish, sharks, and manta rays on a daily basis. Jacques Cousteau reminded me of future fantastic research trips to black smokers on the bottom of the Pacific Ocean.

I decided to toss a coin, assigning heads to Seattle and tails to Kuredu. First toss brought up heads. So did several consecutive tosses. Had the bloody coin somehow miraculously grown two heads within the last thirty seconds? I kept tossing the coin. Each toss made it clearer how much I wanted to see tails for validation that Kuredu was the right choice to make at this unexpected crossroads in my life. By not showing me the answer I longed to see, my coin toss very successfully revealed the path I wanted to pursue at that moment. Looking out over the turquoise waters of the Lhaviyani Atoll, I knew the decision had already been made. At some point, during my last days on the island, I would have to take decisive action.

After a particularly busy course day, I collapsed in the armchair of one of the island bars for a short break before returning to the dive center for a night boat dive. I ordered a beer and relished the short period of delicious laziness, savoring the taste of a Corona in the sweltering afternoon heat. An hour later, I was back at the dive center packing my gear to go on the boat. One of the diving instructors approached me with a serious expression on his face.

"You should pass this one up, Liam," he told me. "I saw you in the bar with a beer. You shouldn't dive after drinking. This is, of course, only a suggestion. The decision is up to you."

I knew he was right. Frustrated with myself for having been so thoughtless, I sadly removed my gear from the trolley and watched the other divers leave towards the jetty. I celebrated my stupidity with a few more Coronas in the same cozy armchair.

The intense month passed far too quickly. Only a few days later, after successful completion of my divemaster certification, I had four precious days left to take my courage in hand and approach the Kuredu dive center manager about a job before I had to leave this magical speck of sand.

Rube was a South African giant who bore an unsettling likeness to the *Hulk*, only with tan skin instead of green. His muscles nearly burst out of his skin and he oozed testosterone. His dark eyebrows were inquisitively curved. Despite him being perfectly polite all through my stay, I couldn't help but feel slightly intimidated by his dominant presence. But how could I leave the island without asking what could be one of the most important questions of my life?

Stumbling and stuttering, I approached Rube in front of the dive center. Once I managed to get my tongue working properly, I seized the moment.

"Might it be possible, some time soon… I mean, would you consider… well, are you interested, to maybe hire me?"

Rube stood before me, muscled arms crossed in front of his massive chest. His eyebrows arched even higher than usual, making me feel more apprehensive and nervous than I already was. In his deep-throated South African rumbling voice, Rube gave his reply.

"I was wondering if you would ever get around to asking. It's about time! I've already asked all the instructors if they would be comfortable with you working here, and everyone agreed they'd love to have you on the team."

It was one of those rare moments that left me at a loss for words. I simply stared at him for a long while, absorbing his unexpected response.

Not asking for the job opportunity had been out of the question. I would have wondered "what if" for the rest of my life and would have never forgiven myself for leaving the question unanswered. But I had never dreamed Rube would consider actually hiring me. I thought I would just tick that box "done" and move on to my marine biology studies in Seattle without doubt or regret.

Rube patiently waited for my response, a smile playing on his lips. He obviously enjoyed my astonishment. His eyebrows arched so high, they almost leapt off his forehead. I realized there was really only one answer I could give. I had to take the plunge, quite literally, and see where this sudden window would lead.

Stuttering possibly worse than before, unable to contain my excitement, I told Rube, "Yes, I am honored, wow, yes! Absolutely, I would love to come work with you guys."

"We need to plan this well to get you into the diving team as soon as possible. You don't have enough experience just yet," Rube said. "How about we take you on as a snorkel guide for the first six months? During those months, you'll be able to scuba dive often and gain more experience. You'll slowly get to know all fifty dive sites scattered throughout the Lhaviyani Atoll. If all goes well, we'll let you do your instructor course here on Kuredu. After that, you can immediately start working as a diving instructor and dive guide."

I bubbled with enthusiasm and agreed to his sensible-sounding plan. "When do you need me to start work?"

Eyebrows arching ever higher, he answered, "I'll need you in four weeks' time at the latest. We have a snorkel guide vacancy we need to fill as soon as possible."

I was shocked by the short time frame but by now also quivering with excitement, positively thriving on it. I knew McKinsey required employees to give three months notice, yet in my current state of rising happiness, I was sure I would find a way to sort things out back in Switzerland. Living on a Maldivian island was a rare opportunity. I needed to embrace it without hesitation.

Rube had had several negative experiences with people agreeing to come to Kuredu, then never being heard from again.

"How do I know, you'll be back in a month?" he asked, arms still crossed, eyebrows almost taking flight.

Valid question. I thought for a moment, then replied with a big grin, "Because I will leave all my luggage here, and take only my wallet back to Switzerland."

His eyebrows lost their arch, two soldiers finally at ease. He laughed, and we shook hands.

During the night, it dawned on me what working on Kuredu would mean: I was going to push my limits once again. I was going to accomplish a feat that, considering my history of being hidden beneath tent-like North Sea sweaters, was comparable to breaking the sound barrier or landing on the moon. I was going to work and live in an environment where not sweaters or shirts but swim shorts and skin were regular attire. For the first time in my life, I would be sharing my scars with the world on a daily basis.

I would need to explain my special circumstances to both Rube and the owner of the dive center, Magnus, before I started working for them. I felt it was only fair to give them a heads up. After all, they might be faced with questions from tourists who, seeing the obvious scars across my chest, might wonder if two sharks had attacked their dive instructor simultaneously.

On a more serious note, I could have a medical emergency at some point, making it necessary for Magnus and Rube to protect me. In a fundamentalist Muslim country like the Maldives, I might find myself in need of their years of local experience in managing sensitive situations. I couldn't think of what precisely to say, but sensed being forthright and giving them the option to back out gracefully was the best course of action, as it had always been.

I went to speak with Rube and Magnus the next morning.

"Thanks for trusting us," they both simply said. "We're very happy to soon have you on our team."

We shook hands once more.

Again, life had taught me not to assume how people will react based on their history, upbringing, or anything else for that matter. Magnus was a free-spirited Swedish liberal, yet Rube had served many years with the South African army. He had grown up in a country riddled with prejudice. Both Rube and Magnus quietly put their faith in me. As long as my history did not affect my work, or my integrity, they didn't see a problem. Both men acknowledged the person standing in front of them, his heart and actions. It was all that mattered. I felt very fortunate and couldn't wait to become part of their unique dive center family. We did agree to keep my information confidential. Who knew what might happen if too many Maldivian nationals knew about my trans identity? Most likely we were worrying too much, but since the fragile existence of Magnus and Rube's business was involved as much as my person, there was no reason to invite unnecessary trouble. Besides, why risk attracting attention with information irrelevant to daily island life?

My last evening as a tourist on Kuredu was spent celebrating with my soon-to-be teammates.

The young Swedish instructor who had confronted me on the night I had thoughtlessly wanted to go scuba diving after enjoying a beer shook my hand.

"You made the responsible choice during that crucial moment before the night dive. It's made all the difference, and has shown the team you are trustworthy and reliable. Welcome to the family!"

I felt humbled and honored by his compliment. Better yet, it assured I would be working with a professional group of people who cared passionately about their daily responsibilities as guides and instructors. As much as everyone liked to laugh and party, they knew people's lives rested in their hands every single day.

The evening with the Kuredu team remains unmatched in my experience. We enjoyed take-away pizza and beer under the stars, everyone openly showing their support and excitement about the new addition to their team.

I had already put my suitcase in Rube's care and was scheduled to leave the island in the early morning hours. In only four weeks, I would be back as a member of staff, embarking on an adventure of completely new proportions. I felt intensely alive. For the first time in many months, pain and grief were pushed into the furthest recesses of my rapidly beating heart. My life had perspective. The future felt bright and turquoise blue.

The next morning, the entire dive center team surprised me by gathering at Kuredu jetty to wave goodbye at the dreadfully early time of 6 a.m. This time, as I watched the sunrise through small seaplane windows, I had tears of happiness in my eyes. I again sobbed quietly for the entire hour back to Male airport, amazed and grateful at the unexpected twists and turns our lives can take if we just find the inner strength to seize the moment.

Traveling back with only my wallet provoked many comical encounters with airport security and immigration officers. The authorities didn't know what to make of me. My self-confidence had grown and I was in the best mood of my life. As a result, I was more amused than annoyed by the proceedings. After many interrogations in Male and Zurich airport, I finally arrived at my apartment, exhausted yet quivering with excitement for what was to come.

The following four weeks can only be characterized as manic.

Breaking the news to my astoundingly supportive boss at McKinsey was first on the agenda. After all she had done for me, after her unwavering support, I knew leaving with only one-month's notice was a lot to ask. But Marjorie was supportive once again, delighted by my plans to venture into an Indian Ocean adventure.

She signed all necessary documents officially ending my employment with McKinsey as of September 2005. A few days later, Marjorie handed me one of the best letters of reference I have ever read.

"It's been very hard for me to sign your letter of resignation," she admitted with tears in her eyes.

Saying goodbye to my McKinsey family proved to be harder than I had expected. I was ready to move on, yet the upstanding Visual Aids team had made all the difference over the years. Working in their midst had given me the peace of mind I had needed to recuperate from the craziness of the previous years. My teammates' unwavering professionalism had grounded me and given me shelter.

Four weeks can prove to be shorter than you'd ever imagine when there is so much to do. Parents needed to be pacified and paperwork taken care of, in Switzerland as well as in Germany and the Maldives. I had to withdraw from the University of Washington in Seattle and inform them my plans had taken an unexpected turn. On top of all that, I had to find a new tenant for my apartment. Luckily I found someone who offered to buy the contents of my entire household as well. Last but not least, I needed to spend time with the treasured friends who had supported me during my fourteen, often tumultuous, years in Zurich.

On the day of my departure, I was beyond exhaustion. I had met people for breakfast, brunch, lunch, and dinner almost every day for the last two weeks in Switzerland. I touched base one last time with everyone, letting my friends know I cared and would be there for them no matter how far away my journey might take me.

Everyone was supportive. They were happy to see someone they cared about embark on an adventure only few would ever experience. In a sense, they would accompany me. From a safe distance, they would be able to witness an adventure that, for diverse personal reasons, they felt they could not attempt themselves. I felt like a beloved child, leaving his parents' home for the first time to venture out into the great unknown. Happiness and sadness walked side-by-side in a tight embrace. My head and heart were bursting with thoughts and emotions. I would treasure these impressions for the rest of my life.

Everything I owned had had to go. In the end, only one box of my most precious gifts and memorabilia remained, safely tucked away at Dad's house. The rest of my possessions were in two bags. One awaited me in Rube's safekeeping on Kuredu. The other was with me at the airport as I checked in for my one-way flight towards a new life.

Making my way onto the plane, the wise words of my photography professor, Andreas, re-sounded in my mind as they had so many times over the years. He had cautioned how real freedom could only be achieved by always keeping a very low standard of living. Possessions inevitably ended up owning you, making sudden moves impossible. After many years of collecting furniture, movies, and books, my worldly possessions had now been reduced to a small pile that could easily fit in the belly of a Bottlenose dolphin. I smiled brightly, realizing I was finally following my mentor's advice to the letter. First shedding unwanted parts of my body, now giving up on all non-essential material possessions, I felt light as a feather – and free.

Not knowing where the road would lead was invigorating and delightful. The bars of the gilded cage I'd been living in retreated, offering a breathtaking vista of vast open oceans.

24

Indian Ocean

Sitting on an airplane bound for the Indian Ocean, with all relevant possessions in one bag and no return ticket in my pocket, I felt like an explorer about to make his greatest discovery. When would I take to the skies again? And where would I fly if I did? I had no idea, but anything seemed possible now.

Before leaving Switzerland, I had asked my doctor to write me a special prescription: thirty-six ampoules of testosterone. Not being able to produce enough of the male hormones on its own, my body needed a little help on a regular basis. My checked luggage now contained a two-year supply of testosterone injections, vials, and needles. My doctor had written a letter, attesting to the fact that my bodily functions would be severely disrupted without the medication I carried. Nevertheless, I was nervous. What if my stash was confiscated at Maldives customs? What would I do?

Maldives immigration was easy. I presented papers from my employer and within five minutes, my passport sported a big, new 'work visa' stamp.

Then came the hard part. Already sweating with apprehension, I collected my luggage and headed for customs. There, my heart skipped more than a few beats when my luggage was singled out for inspection. Vials and needles were easy to see on the bag scanner's screen. Even I could spot them, as I nervously snuck a peek over the customs officer's shoulder. Surprisingly, he waved me through. Just like that, maintaining my manhood was ensured for the immediate future.

An hour later, on the seaplane bound for Kuredu, I found myself grinning from ear to ear. Unlike my fellow travelers, I wouldn't be getting on a plane home. This time, the island paradise would *be* home. It felt as right as anything ever would. I was on my way to where I belonged.

Our seaplane touched down softly, just outside the turquoise lagoon of the amazing island sanctuary of Kuredu. Rube picked me up on the jetty and I was happy to see him. His eyebrows were in a relaxed horizontal state. His enthusiastic, muscular handshake almost cracked the bones in my small hand.

"Hi Liam, welcome back," he said. "The luggage you left with me is at the dive center. Let me bring you there now. You have today off to settle in, then tomorrow you'll plunge in and start work right away."

I had hoped to have at least a few days off, but I was also eager to get started. I nodded and gave him a big smile.

Just a two-minute walk from the jetty, Rube dropped me off at his office. "Just wait here. Someone will come by any minute to show you around. I need to dash off. See you here tomorrow at 8.45 a.m."

Reunited with my second bag, I happily gazed at the entirety of my possessions on the floor in front of me. I felt as free as a blue whale roaming the oceans. From now on, I promised myself to hold on to only a few keepsakes and limited memorabilia. Instead of amassing material possessions, I would dive much more passionately into collecting precious moments and people on my travels. Life, just like any theatrical stage, doesn't necessarily need many props to be meaningful. Rather, the genuine life experiences, the passion and soul of the actors are what breathes life into each production.

After only five minutes' wait, Judith, one of the senior instructors, walked into the office and welcomed me with a big hug.

"So great to have you back. Come on, I'll show you quickly around the staff blocks and then to your room."

Originally from Germany, Judith had been working abroad for a very long time. She was in her forties, a compassionate, calm person who was always up for any fun little bit of mischief. During my previous month as a divemaster, we had become good friends. I had loved her adventurous tales of exploring the planet.

Ever since I had started roaming the world myself, my greatest pleasure was meeting new people. I didn't care so much about partying with them, but would hang on every word of their stories. Like Judith, some of those new people became good friends. Others would remain in touch as acquaintances. I loved catching up with them periodically over the years, to see how their lives were developing, always curious if they had found what they had been searching for, and most of all, whether they had found happiness.

Following Judith now with my luggage in tow and listening to her anecdotes of every day island life, I felt us reconnecting as seamlessly as if I had never left.

The staff accommodation set-up was very amusing. I was reminded of Alcatraz as Judith showed me A-Block, B-Block, and C-Block. My "solitary confinement" would be located in C-Block, a long L-shaped building with many small doors leading into very small rooms. Mine was C-7.

Each of our rooms was only about sixty-five square feet, equipped with a bed, a small night table, and a wardrobe. Everything else needed to be bought and installed by the occupant. Judith and her partner Rowan had secured an air conditioning unit for my little home already.

"You might soon be able to buy a TV as well if you want," Judith said. "Departing staff are always eager to sell their sparse furnishings and decorations to the new arrivals."

Some dive center staff stayed for many years, but most seemed to leave after one, or maximum two, years. Living on one-square mile of sand isn't for everyone. Many enthusiastic dreamers would succumb to island fever and barely manage to finish their first contract year. They would pace the island's brilliant white beaches for months, like sunburned lab rats. When they were finally released, they didn't walk to the idling seaplane, they ran, with their sun-bleached hair spilling in tangles from their heads.

I wasn't worried about meeting a similar fate myself. I smiled at the sight of my humble abode. Curious about my new bathroom, I squeezed between the sparse furnishings and the walls to reach the bathroom door.

The bathroom was a cozy thirty-two square feet. The simple showerhead stuck out of the wall like a periscope. The toilet bowl and small sink looked like they had been recovered from an ancient shipwreck. Rough and crumbling walls looked as if they might cave in at any moment. A corrugated iron roof covered only half of the bathroom. The uncovered half was open to the equatorial sky. The ground had been left in its original, sandy state. A tropical tree grew inside my bathroom, opposite the narrow shower area. Its branches reached far above the C-Block roof. I was enchanted and felt instantly at home.

Reality would encroach on my idealism in the coming months. For instance, as idyllic as it may be to have a tree growing out of your bathroom, it was essentially a convenient natural ladder for assorted island wildlife. Surprise visits from lizards, snakes, rats, gigantic cockroaches, and birds became a regular part of my life. I would learn to open my bathroom door cautiously at night, ready to jump away from whatever critter was illuminated by the bathroom light. I would also learn to do my business in record time; who knew what might crawl over your feet or fly into your face as you sat contemplating the stars?

But as I hugged Judith goodbye that first day and dumped my bag into my new home, I was still blissfully unaware of these little details. I had come to the right place. Island fever would not become a major issue for me. I was sure of that. If I had a small favorite restaurant and a bar close by, ideally surrounded by lots of nature, then all bases were covered. After fourteen years of Swiss over-structuring, I longed for simplicity.

Later that afternoon, I strolled through the staff areas by myself for the first time. Kuredu had more than three hundred and fifty rooms with space for nine hundred guests. An equal number of employees took care of the customers' every need. The majority of employees were housed in dorm rooms within a walled-in area in the center of the island, called simply 'Staff Area'. Employee accommodation and canteens were strictly segregated into Maldivian, Asian, and Western. This segregation struck me as unnecessary. We were all squashed in this small environment together, surrounded by ocean as far as the eye could see. There was no choice but to mingle.

Apart from accommodations and staff canteens, the staff area housed a mosque, TV rooms, a basketball court, the guest restaurant kitchen areas, huge greenhouses where most vegetables for the guest menu were grown, a small desalinization plant for all shower and tap water, a garbage incinerator, carpentry workshops, and other essential infrastructure. It was impressive how much could be crammed into so little space.

I kept walking on through the guest areas. I had seen it all before but now, being an employee, I saw everything with new eyes and took stock. There were numerous sports grounds, ranging from a big soccer field, to tennis courts, from a golf putting range to beach volleyball courts.

The island watersport center was sizeable. Our dive center was the biggest one in the Maldives. It could accommodate up to two hundred divers at once. In high season, we were easily booked solid – which also made us the busiest dive center I would ever lay eyes on. The Kuredu dive center operated the island's medical clinic as well. The well-equipped facility housed a top-of-the-line decompression chamber, treating divers with decompression sickness from all surrounding atolls.

Six restaurants were available in the hotel. This included an Italian restaurant, fully-equipped with a pizza oven and Maldivian cooks who – surprisingly – whipped out pizzas that could easily compete with their original Italian counterparts. There were also several bars.

I would come to avoid the island nightlife. After socializing professionally with guests for up to twelve hours each day, I would opt for more tranquil surroundings.

Most tourists spent their entire vacation sunbathing on the pool deck or drinking at the pool bar. They craved comfort and alcohol. Consequently, there were many secluded areas where it was still possible to enjoy a piece of island paradise without stumbling over any drunks or sunbathers.

During my days as a tourist, my favorite spot had been at the very end of Kuredu jetty. It was too far away for most lazy vacationers, so someone seeking solitude to re-charge could sit relatively undisturbed, sipping beer and watching dolphins play on the horizon as the sun went down.

My first day on Kuredu ended with celebratory beers in Akiri Bar, right next to the hotel reception. The dive center staff would meet up in this small bar every evening, before heading over to their staff canteen in smaller or bigger groups. It was a chance to spend time with each other on a more private basis after work. It was also a chance for hotel guests to drop in and join us if they had questions, or just wanted to spend some more time with their favorite instructors.

As I sat in the bar, I felt as happy as a bee in a meadow of its favorite flowers. I was exhausted from the last four weeks of frantic organizing and goodbyes. Now I was looking forward to daily immersion in the Indian Ocean. Work would be hard, but also highly satisfying on a completely different level than my previous five years at McKinsey. I was back to following my passion. I had traded safety and comfort for a healthy body, and a life of emotional roller coasters and calculated risk.

As a snorkel guide, I started with a monthly salary of five hundred USD. Board and lodging were included, as was treatment for any medical problems that could be solved by the island physician. However, most other benefits were unheard of in this line of work. Before my arrival on

Kuredu, I had been immersed up to my ears in every kind of insurance while working at a very safe desk. Now, I had no insurance at all in a line of work that exposed me to the multiple and exotic dangers of the ocean on a daily basis. The miniscule paycheck made health insurance unaffordable. Thankfully, I had always been healthy enough – that is, if I chose to ignore my youthful spasticity, and my ongoing, mysterious, maybe heart-related, fainting spells, along with my life-long dependence on testosterone shots.

As strange as it may sound, I wasn't worried. All things considered, this isolated island was just as safe – if not safer – than anywhere else. Life was peaceful and slow. Everyone endeavored to forget modern civilization for the duration of their stay. Streets were non-existent and the hotel used only four trucks and vans to deliver baggage and other items all over the island.

I was thirty-four. I felt healthy and energetic, so I was happy to brave a less regulated life and found its many loose ends enchanting.

One thing I needed to take care of right away, though, was learning to inject myself with testosterone.

My body would never be able to produce enough testosterone on its own to maintain secondary male characteristics like an overall male build, a low voice and a beard. So, a jelly-like mass of the male hormone needed to be injected into my muscle tissue every twenty days, for the rest of my life. The jelly-store would slowly dissolve over a period of three weeks, supplying my almost-male body with much-needed hormones more or less evenly. Other options, like daily pills, were available on the market, but so far, injections had proven to be the simplest method for me.

While living in highly-civilized Switzerland, I had shied away from injecting myself. I hated getting any kind of shot. This would make the doctor's assistant, who administered them, laugh out loud. She would look at the extensive tattoos covering my chest, shoulders, back, and legs. She would then wave the huge needle in front of my face and ask, grinning, "Really, you're afraid of needles?" Absolutely! Especially the very thick and long variety used to inject the gelatinous testosterone fluid into my muscles.

And now here I was, stuck on an island far away from any familiar doctors. I didn't know much about the local culture and mentality. I only knew I was living in an extremely fundamentalist Muslim country and thus felt insecure, exposing myself to any local physicians.

Knowing Judith was a former nurse, I told her about my gender reassignment over a coffee.

"Would you mind teaching me how to inject myself?"

Luckily she was an amazingly open-minded, discrete human being.

"No problem, Liam, let's do it tonight."

We spent the evening in my room, poking needles into my thighs, with vials, needles and other paraphernalia spread out on my bed.

I spent a lot of time training myself to relax my thigh muscles, since they were cramped up in anticipation of pain. Relaxing them before injecting into them was important, to avoid increasing the pain. Overall, however, injecting myself was far easier than I had ever imagined it would be.

As a novice 'needle master', I did experience frequent moments of panic. For example, once I neglected to expel air from the syringe before injecting myself. Imagining a small pocket of air circulating through my blood stream towards my heart, I ran over the entire island trying to find Judith, fully expecting to drop dead at any moment. When I found her and breathlessly proceeded to tell her of my impending death, Judith smiled at me.

"Don't worry," she said. "A much larger amount of air would be needed to accomplish that. You have obviously seen way too many movies."

Having Judith as an ally made me feel safer. In addition to Rube, she could protect me if needed. In case of an accident, she would be there to intervene, making sure I wasn't exposed.

Once a week, each department on the island had to send one random person for drug testing. Rube and Judith always made sure I wasn't sent. Peeing without a penis into a plastic cup in front of dozens of zealously religious men was the last thing I needed.

In general, though, I felt very relaxed. During my first few days on Kuredu, a Swedish shopkeeper on the island shared her valuable advice.

"On a small, isolated island nothing stays private. The best thing you can do is to make sure you can stand up for all of your actions – because they *will* become public knowledge, one way or another."

It was good advice. In addition to the bored expat staff readily divulging and spreading any gossip-worthy material faster than a striking moray eel, the locals were fascinated by our strangeness, constantly hovering in the bushes, seeming to know what we were going to do before we knew ourselves. Privacy existed only inside my room with the doors firmly closed and curtains neatly drawn.

Island life raised social competence to a whole new level. Your teammates became your faithful shadows. No matter where you looked, there they were. On a typical day, I would get up in the morning to the sound of twenty different alarm clocks. The walls were so thin, I could hear someone whispering three doors down. Walking out the door, I would find my neighbors sitting outside, smiling a "Good morning" to me, following their polite greeting with, "Would you be so kind as to turn off your alarm clock a bit speedier in the future? And oh, do you feel all right this morning? You were throwing up in your bathroom for such a long time last night."

During breakfast, my work family would surround me, some people trying to make conversation, others grumpily trying to disappear into their cereal bowls to unearth a little bit of privacy. Straight after breakfast, everyone would meet yet again, wishing each other a good morning at the dive center as if they had never seen each other before.

Even before opening the big wooden dive center doors, hotel guests would already be poking their heads through our narrow windows and the "staff only" doors asking 'urgent' questions.

As soon as we opened the front doors, our entire team of thirty was busy for an hour, just with answering questions concerning issues above, on, or underwater. Some of us would be stuck with educating until 12:30 p.m., while others would head into the ocean with their divers.

For lunch break, we would all migrate to our small canteen together, inevitably talking about work, while replenishing our supply of carbohydrates. At 2 p.m., we would be back at the dive center for yet another round of enthusiastic divers and snorkelers, who were either learning, or eager to explore the Lhaviyani Atoll via one of our dive or snorkel boats.

As a snorkel guide, I wouldn't wrap up before 7 p.m. and was given only half a day off per week. Working hard was not unusual for me. But not having a weekend? That was a problem. I never got used to it. Sometimes my half-day off was in the morning. After sleeping in and having breakfast, my "weekend" was irretrievably lost and all that was left was the depressing thought of having to wait another six days before my next half-day.

Hotel guests hunted us down wherever we went. In their eyes, we led an existence equal to being on perpetual vacation. I contemplated buying a wig and very large sunglasses so I could get some peace.

Inevitably, hotel guests would stop us and say "Just a quick question…" It was impossible to say "no", due to the obliviousness of the average vacationer, as well as the fact that the entire island *was* the hotel and we were hotel employees, taking care of all the guests' questions and needs. Imagine you work in a bank, and wherever you go outside the bank building, people stop you with a delighted smile on their face, asking about how to best set up their account. Privacy on the island truly was the employees' most highly sought after commodity.

Some of the questions and issues raised by hotel guests were nothing short of amazing. I fondly remember complaints about palm trees not being green enough and there being just too much sand on the island.

One couple was convinced the ocean exhibited different tidal behavior, depending on which side of the island they stood on.

"We demand to be relocated to a bungalow at the beach with the lowest tide," they requested.

Other guests would seek us out in a panic in the middle of the night to remove a gecko from their pillow. Many hotel guests would swear they had seen rats climbing the palm trees. Indeed they had, but we assured them – as we had been asked to do by the hotel – that there was no such thing in the Maldives.

"Madam, Sir, this is impossible. You must have seen a palm squirrel."

It was harder to explain away the occurrence of snakes. They had the unfortunate habit of falling out of trees right in front of people's feet.

In one instance, I was serving customers in our equipment room. The beautiful building had a very high ceiling. As I stood filling out rental forms for the nice couple in front of me, something fell onto my left shoulder with a loud slap. As my customers started screaming, I realized a snake had fallen from the roof, hitting me on the way down. There was nothing I could say to pacify the panicking couple. I did the next best thing and engaged in energetic snake wrestling, brandishing a broom that leaned conveniently on the shelf right next to me. The snake retreated, most likely more scared by the experience than any of us.

My personal favorite amongst such comical hotel guest experiences features a young medical student who signed up for a guided snorkel tour along Kuredu's house reef.

She started screaming as soon as we entered the water. I rushed over to her, concerned she may have stepped on a poisonous scorpion fish or been stung by a jellyfish. She was jumping up and down. Her eyes almost popped from their sockets. Trying to get out, she slipped on the jetty steps. She fell back into the water, then frantically crawled back out on all fours, as if she was about to be swallowed up whole by *Bruce*, the shark from Steven Spielberg's *Jaws*.

"Can you please wait for a moment right there in the shallow water," I asked my group and ran after my panicked customer in case she needed assistance.

Forty feet further, when the young woman finally caught her breath, she angrily exclaimed, "No one told me this was salt water!"

For just a moment, I thought she was joking. She wasn't, judging from her angry expression. She stared at me expectantly. At a loss for words, I stuttered, "We are, as you know, on a Maldivian island. The water surrounding us on all sides *is* the Indian Ocean. One major characteristic of any body of water called 'ocean' is that it consists of salt water."

The young lady was not happy. Short of desalinating the Indian Ocean, there was no way I could satisfy this guest. She refused to go back into the water.

"I need to assure the safety of the rest of my group. Can you please head back to the dive center and sign yourself out? I'm very sorry. Have a good day."

I was barely able to contain my giggles. The rest of my snorkeling group that morning had far less self-control. They had overheard our conversation and had giggled throughout. The inconsolable young lady stalked off, leaving the rest of us to snorkel towards our reef adventure. My group broke out with laughter at odd moments for the rest of our snorkeling tour. After a while, I couldn't help myself any longer, set professionalism aside, and joined in the laughter.

Snorkeling was not one of my favorite past times. Heading out into that turquoise water stretching all the way to the horizon, on the other hand, was an experience I never tired of. We would enjoy our trips on beautiful, remodeled Maldivian fishing boats called dhonis. I loved to stand way up in the bow, feeling the waves under my feet and the salty mist in my mouth and eyes. I simply was. Past and future disappeared to make space for the invigorating moment. We seemed to be the only boat for miles, puttering slowly towards our heavenly – or rather "oceanly" – destination of the day. Watching the waves gently parting for our boat was always a sight of pure beauty. Flying fish and Spinner dolphins regularly accompanied us on the way to snorkeling sites across the atoll.

Countless snorkelers were afraid of water or fish. Some could barely swim and clung to me with a death grip, leaving dark blue bruises on my arms. Still, they won me over with their boundless enthusiasm. On days when I started to feel responsible for our more glamorous reef inhabitants not showing themselves, I was always able to elicit screams of excitement from snorkelers at the simple sight of a squirming sea cucumber or an immobile sea star.

On one particular morning, hundreds of crabs seemed to have decided to descend on us from the neighboring atoll. The little red fellas looked cute as they propelled themselves towards us, moving their appendages like baby martial artists. Everyone laughed at their clumsiness. The crabs seemed to be exhausted from their long swim across the channel. Upon reaching us, they clung to us to catch their breath, mistaking my poor snorkelers for driftwood. We were getting pinched all over. I controlled the urge to laugh about the outbreak of panic this caused in my guests. I calmed down screaming grandmas and children as best I could.

While working as a snorkel guide, I enthusiastically prepared to become a diving instructor. I went on dives on my lunch break or after work whenever I could manage it.

Sunset dives on Kuredu's reef just off the jetty, called Housereef, were a magical experience. Hovering silently next to a small shipwreck, we would see large dark shapes descending upon us as the sun went down. About a dozen Napoleon wrasse would congregate on the shipwreck to use it as their night sanctuary. An adult Napoleon wrasse can easily be five feet in length. Their heads are massive and their eyes rotate in their sockets to scan their surroundings. The skin of these fish displays a breathtaking range of green and blue shades. I was mesmerized amongst those giants, silently watching and feeling like the luckiest man alive as they hovered silently above the wreck openings, seeming to discuss between themselves who would get the coziest corner that night.

Back at C-7, I would study diving theory, and prepare for the upcoming instructor examinations.

My small island home was a personal space with a door that could be closed to the world. Apart from this undeniably practical factor, it was far from relaxing. But, unlike the sounds of civilization driving people crazy in the Western world, the assorted island sounds were rather comical, even when they kept us awake.

Every so often, a coconut would fall from one of the palm trees towering around us and smash onto the corrugated iron roofing. It was enough to get my heart racing, evoking worries of whether we had gone to war with a neighboring atoll.

Rats lived in the narrow spaces between ceiling and roof. It seemed as if they organized regular marathons up there. At all hours of the day, we could hear herds of rats stampeding over our heads from one end of C-Block to the other, as heavy-footed as elephants.

The usual human sounds were magnified due to the paper-thin walls. Unlike me, most staff members were between twenty and thirty, with a taste for boozing, partying, and nightly sexual adventures. Slamming doors and drunken socializing added another layer to the ruckus.

The island being one of the safest environments imaginable, most of us never locked our doors. One night after midnight, on my birthday, my door was ripped open by ten of my charming colleagues. They crowded inside my room, howling "Happy Birthday" at the top of their voices. I almost died of a heart attack right then and there, at the tender age of thirty-five.

Another night, my door was thrown open around 3 a.m. Lila, a fellow snorkel guide, stood in the doorway with a happy smile on her face. After getting over the initial shock, I realized Lila urgently needed to share something with me.

With the most enthusiastic smile, she said: "Liam look, isn't this the cutest iPod sock ever?" Not waiting for my answer, she happily slammed the door on her way out.

Of all nightly surprises, bizarre animal encounters of the ten-, eight-, and six-legged type, are amongst my fondest memories. Creative hermit crabs found the most surprising new homes after growing too big for their seashells. One night, stumbling home after too much beer, I detected movement from the corner of my eye. I stared, closed my eyes, stared again, pinched myself, and then stared once more. A coconut was leisurely crossing the street alongside me. Other memorable encounters included ambulatory pottery, as well as a very agile plastic 35mm film container hastily clambering towards the nearest foliage.

Spiders had a way of raising my adrenaline to uncomfortable levels. As embarrassing as it was, my phobia made it impossible for me to relocate them myself. My snorkeling colleague Lila, of iPod-sock fame, would heroically come to my aid more than once, removing the big, hairy creatures from my room and saving me from a sleepless night.

Cockroaches scuttled everywhere. There were none any less than two inches long. During the day, they would crawl into the grating encasing the air conditioning unit. I quickly learned to step aside before turning on the AC because as soon as the fan inside the unit started to turn fast enough, cockroaches of all sizes would get catapulted into the room. Lila and I formed a bond in our war against the six-legged deluge.

When either of our rooms got infested with our crawly friends, we would inevitably start spraying potent poisons, which led to surprising encounters. During one very memorable cockroach stand-off, Lila found five big specimens in her room after coming home from the bar in the middle of the night. She started spraying the resilient insects that then raced for the many cracks in her wall.

I was sitting on the toilet at the time, oblivious of the war raging next door, looking at the stars through the foliage of my bathroom tree, when one of Lila's panicked cockroaches flew straight into my face. In a matter of seconds cockroaches were everywhere, crawling through the cracks from her room into mine. I managed to control my panic, grabbed my spray can and started dousing the insects with poison.

After a few minutes, the noxious substance was having much more effect on me than it was having on the cockroaches. I felt as if I was suffocating while they still merrily hurried to and fro. Lila and I opened our doors at around the same time, to avoid dropping dead before the roaches did. Finally, the tough little critters succumbed to our attack, leaving Lila and me to collect their quite sizeable corpses. By around 3 a.m., our garbage can held more than thirty dead roaches. We were quivering from impossibly high levels of adrenaline, both unable to go back to sleep. So we seized the moment, brought out the champagne, and sat in front of our rooms, two friends celebrating our victory under a starry sky.

On land, I easily qualified as the clumsiest man alive but cockroaches brought out the best in my formerly-spastic self. One night, I was half-asleep when weird clicking sounds made my insect-paranoid ears perk up. Yep, those were definitely six little cockroach feet walking toward my pillow in the dark. I debated for a minute what to do, since reaching over to turn on the bedside lamp might also mean making contact with the enormous insect. Curiosity won out. I reached over and switched on the lamp. The poor cockroach must have had the shock of its life. It launched itself away from the bright light and straight into my face. What happened next, I don't really know. Within fractions of a second, I was standing upright at the foot end of my bed, brandishing a towel as a weapon. I must have launched myself into the air from a horizontal position, sticking the landing like a world-class gymnast, facing pillow and cockroach, ready for battle. I had unconsciously executed the perfect somersault, like some kind of seasoned circus performer. Unfortunately, I did not have much time to ponder the enormity of my acrobatic achievement. The panicked cockroach spun about like a damaged helicopter. I charged with towel in hand, managed to open my front door and – executing another athletic first – batted the unfortunate cockroach with my towel all the way across the vast C-Block courtyard into the underbrush.

Despite all these nightly interruptions, I was well prepared when the dive instructor examinations started. German course director Ulla shared her considerable wisdom and enthusiasm with me and the other four instructor candidates. For two weeks, we lived on another planet, thoroughly absorbed by lessons and exams on dry land and underwater. I loved every second of training. Ulla struck the perfect balance between fun and authority. Our time with her passed far too quickly. In the underwater realm, clumsy Liam once more turned into an elegant creature. I proudly managed perfect results in both practical exercises and theory. I was in my element. The instructor course surely rated among the top-ten best experiences of my life.

My struggles when learning to scuba dive in Malta, as well as my personal history of overcoming fear and other obstacles, predestined me to be a compassionate, patient teacher who was able to understand my students. I looked forward to helping them overcome their instinctual fears so they could dive in and enjoy an alternate universe few ever had the privilege of experiencing.

True to his word, Magnus moved me from snorkeling to diving straight after I completed my instructor examinations successfully. I was in heaven. As much as the snorkelers touched my heart with their appreciation for the ocean, I had never grown more fond of snorkeling or snorkel guiding. Scuba diving, as well as teaching, were my true passions. After a short leave, I would be ready to start my new duties.

Magnus insisted that we take a two-week vacation after six months, as well as a longer break of up to eight weeks after each contract year. Island fever was a force to be reckoned with, even for the most resilient of us. There was nothing to speak of that could close in on us, but somehow the brilliant blue all around us could become suffocating as well.

For my very first short break, I went diving in Indonesia. We were all addicted to the Big Blue, so "vacation" simply meant exploring the ocean elsewhere. I was nervous, exited, and happy.

Looking at my fellow travelers in the airports on my way to Indonesia and back, I felt amazingly privileged. Most of them were only traveling. I was living my dreams and living abroad, diving not just into the seas, but also into living conditions previously unknown to me, all the while collecting life experiences too valuable to ever be expressed in dollar signs.

Back on Kuredu, I felt refreshed and ready for the new challenge of teaching underwater. The team of diving instructors shared all diving-related responsibilities. Our daily schedule was designed to equally share tedious tasks, along with those everyone coveted.

To be assigned as dive guide to the morning two-tank dive boat was most desirable. It meant two enjoyable dives with experienced divers. The workday finished at 2 p.m., which felt, I admit, almost like being on vacation.

The least popular task was dive center duty. Most instructors longed to be out in the Indian Ocean, not inside battling paperwork. Dive center duty was closely followed in unpopularity by teaching the Discover Scuba Diving programs. These programs were tailor-made for people who wanted to experience scuba diving, but didn't want to invest the time to take a course first. Most days, taking care of these lazy divers felt as if we were trying to teach a flock of drowning sheep to appreciate aquatic surroundings.

Still, I was one of the few who appreciated this particular challenge and felt happy when, after their third Discover Scuba dive with me, the uprooted vacationers came to say goodbye with shining eyes.

"Thanks so much. We felt very safe with you as our guide. You made a dream come true for us."

What more satisfaction could I possibly wish for?

I did have some favorites and least favorites of my own. Least favorite was Divers Night, which happened each week in the largest island bar. We showed a slide show that never changed. After the overly-long slide show we had to stand around on stage and present a little dive center exhibition to interested hotel guests. We all had to stay until the last curious individual left the stage. Of course, there was always at least one diver who had to tell us all about his latest underwater encounters and just wouldn't leave. Meanwhile twenty dive center staff all around him struggled to smile, trying hard not to fall asleep.

The worst part about Divers Night, though, was having to wear a sarong. I never learned how to tie the fabric correctly. Since I lived in constant fear of ending up on stage in my underpants, I would tie the long cloth around my belly as creatively and tightly as I could. At the end of each Divers Night, I would spend a good ten minutes at home, trying to disentangle the mess.

My favorite activities were teaching courses and guiding boats over the vast expanse of the Indian Ocean.

When teaching a course, I was able to plan the week for my students independently. I loved being able to organize and knowing my schedule in advance for a short while was a luxury, a carry-over from the more regulated job in Switzerland, which I remembered and treasured in its own right.

Most of all I loved the variety. Each course was different because my students always brought their unique personalities and fears into the mix. I was blessed with an unerring intuition about what each of them needed in order to successfully meet their new challenge.

Guiding boats was pure pleasure. Being able to go out to sea on a dhoni with our Maldivian boat crews was a truly humbling experience. A single look told these experienced seafarers the strength and direction of currents. I was, and am to this day, awestruck by their feel for the ocean.

Some instructors were arrogant towards the local boat crews, ordering them about, but I was grateful to have them on board. I didn't have a clue about currents or other oceanic behavior patterns.

During training, I had inquired, "How can I know what the current is doing or will do later just by looking at it?"

One of my mentors had replied, "See those clouds over there? They are an elongated shape, fluffy and light. It means the channel underneath it will have a gentle current flowing to the north. Cloud formation will tell you all you need to know about the daily current conditions."

I stared at him, completely amazed, until he couldn't help himself any longer and started dissolving in hysterical laughter.

I did learn a few boatman skills over time. Still, without the amazing local boat crews, I would have been screwed. I respected and trusted them. When I made mistakes, I apologized and asked for advice. In return, the boat crews taught, respected, and trusted me as well. We had our language barriers, but much could be understood using the eyes, smiles, and gestures.

Maldivian culture, being firmly rooted in Islam, meant there was a whole contingent of Mohameds, Ibrahims and Abdullahs all over the island and on the boats. Some mornings, it took all my self-control to remain respectful and not burst out laughing while I introduced the boat crew to the divers.

"Good morning everyone! Meet our fantastic boat crew taking care of us today – Captain Mohamed, Mohamed, and Mohamed."

The most liberating element of island life was how walking in nothing but swim shorts all day helped me overcome the remainder of my body image challenges. After hardly being able to walk as a child, and battling my body every step of the way through early spasticity, frequent fainting spells, and gender misalignments, I was now teaching people how to scuba dive at one of the most beautiful destinations on Earth. I could hardly believe my good fortune. While the equatorial sun softly caressed my skin, I didn't think about my physical shortcomings, my scars, or my lack of penis anymore. I felt handsome, vibrant, and healthy. My self-confidence grew with each day. I found myself. And more than ever before, I was at peace with myself.

Rube, Magnus, Judith, and the few other dive center staff that knew about my gender history were wonderfully discrete. Maldivians were timid about undressing in public, due to their Muslim beliefs. This was very beneficial for me, since no one ever thought to question why I always chose a booth to pee, or disappeared into the bathroom to change after diving.

It was just as well that no one ever saw me completely naked. It was difficult to explain a missing penis to people. Explaining my chest scars was easier by far. Most people were too shy to ask, and I will never know what they thought, or said behind my back. Apprehensive at first, I slowly learned to not concern myself with what I didn't know or couldn't change.

Some fellow diving instructors or students asked me eventually, "I couldn't help but notice your scars. What happened to you?"

If only I could have explained the considerable scars across my chest with something as adventurous as, "Twin sharks attacked me, but I walked away from it a hero, and survived." Unfortunately, common sense dictated not resorting to this fantasy as an explanation. My scars were far too regular to have been caused by any natural occurrence. Many of our scuba divers were highly educated people who wouldn't be fooled easily. Many of them were doctors.

For years, I stumbled through bad explanations. Many a listener likely realized I was spouting utter nonsense but kindly didn't let on.

Rescue arrived in the form of a German family. Both mom and dad were doctors. After confiding in them, they informed me mastitis scars look very similar to mine. While mastitis is an infection of the chest tissue mainly afflicting nursing mothers, a rare 2% of the male world population is also plagued by it. From that moment onward, I had a plausible alternate answer.

Each time it came up, I would make a judgment call about how to respond. Depending on the situation and my level of trust in the questioner, my answer would be either mastitis, or the truth.

On one of my long breaks between contracts, I decided to try to align my body just a tiny bit more. I felt slightly foolish, but needed to see what might be possible. No matter how hard I trained, I never seemed to be able to achieve a six-pack. The flabby love handles on my hips stubbornly remained.

The other, much bigger, issue was that the scars on my chest were unbelievably thick. At the time my gender reassignment was done, plastic surgery had not been supported by German health insurance. Regular surgeons had done the best they could, with an emphasis on practicality rather than beauty. In the years after my surgery, the courts ruled that health insurances had to support their transgender patients in achieving optimal results, in order to minimize the trauma of their transition as much as possible. Unfortunately this ruling had come too late for me.

On a sunny morning in Switzerland, I went for an examination in a specialized clinic for plastic surgery.

"Oh my god, what butcher got a hold of you?" the plastic surgeon exclaimed upon looking at my chest.

Apart from the scars, my nipples were only shadows of their former selves. They had been hacked off and placed back into their roughly assumed locations, and it showed.

"Using laser surgery, I will be able to transform your thick scars into thin lines barely visible to the human eye, as well as obtain far better results with your nipples," the surgeon assured me.

As for the persistent fat around my midsection, she explained how female fat tissue differed greatly from male tissue.

"Males have thin skin. If they are athletic, they have only few fat reserves. Female bodies, on the other hand, come with thicker skin, due to directly connected fat deposits. No matter how athletic, females will also retain fat in strategic places like the thighs, hips and belly."

With the cumulative impact of regular testosterone injections on my body, over the years, my fat deposits would conform more to a male anatomy.

"But, with a little liposuction," I was told, "we can speed up your body's transformation process. Laser corrective surgery and the liposuction will take place during one morning only. You'll be able to go home straight after. The recuperation time won't extend beyond the duration of your vacation."

After careful consideration, I decided to take the plunge. Coming out of anesthesia, the surgeon visited me with a relieved expression on her face. Apparently my body had reacted adversely to the liposuction and I had come within inches of bleeding to death. Apart from this rather unsettling news, the scars across my chest were now barely noticeable. My belly looked flat, my nipples pristine. I knew I would have to deal with swelling and pain in my abdomen for a few weeks, but was happy my physical appearance had come a step farther along towards being male.

Imagine my surprise, when just two days later my scars began to swell and grow. At check-up one week later, my surgeon was shocked as well. My scars looked almost the same as they had before the surgery. Further tests revealed that my body reacted to injury by producing excessive scar tissue. In fact, my body produced ten times as much scar tissue as bodies normally did. In the end, there was nothing we could do.

My scars were still as noticeable as they had been since my initial top surgery. But I hadn't bled to death, and my belly was flat. All things considered, all was well. This latest endeavor of mine hadn't turned out exactly the way I had envisioned, but it could have turned out far worse. I had escaped death yet again.

25

South Ari Atoll

Back on Kuredu after my eight-week break, I proudly proceeded to tan my noticeably slimmer midsection. Everyone assumed I had worked out like crazy and dieted while away. Harboring my little secret with a smile, I delighted in looking more manly and athletic than ever before.

Being a diving instructor had all the perks of being a snorkel guide and then some. I still ventured out into the turquoise endlessness on a dhoni several times a week and encountered amazing ocean creatures in close proximity.

But where before I had gazed down upon the enchanting marine life from above, I now came face-to-gills with them. Hovering for seemingly endless minutes, I was able to savor all the minute details of the underwater world.

Teaching was more than a pleasure. It was a passion. I enjoyed every single course I taught. In the beginning of my career, my students struck me as being awkward and slow on the uptake. After about one year of teaching, it dawned on me that I had been the cause of their problems. My explanations had simply been too wordy and complicated. I evolved as an instructor and while I still talked a lot, I now kept the course content simple and concise. The results were amazing. My students aced their courses. I was proud and honored to sign their certification papers.

Many Kuredu hotel guests returned every year. I practically raised some of their children underwater. The eight-year old divers were fantastic. Contrary to their parents, most of them were fearless. When thrown into the water with a tank on their back, they would instinctively make all the right moves.

I could easily empathize with struggling adult students too, since I have a few phobias of my own – spiders and heights, mostly. In some cases, I needed to soothe nascent divers until their panic attacks subsided and they gradually relaxed. Most of my students overcame their fears and learned to enjoy exploring the ocean.

I will never forget one couple in their sixties. Margaret could not walk without the help of crutches. Wolfram, her husband, was physically fit yet mortally afraid of water. Being weightless underwater helped Margaret. After only a few days she passed her course with flying colors. Wolfram had barely made it through the exercises in shallow water. I certified his wife and asked Rube if he would mind me spending a few more days with Wolfram. Rube trusted my judgment and told me to take as much time as needed.

The next day, Wolfram and I set out towards Kuredu's house reef. Being alone together, he confided in me.

"I tried diving in Egypt, many years ago. At first it was all right, but then my instructor wanted to take me deeper and deeper. I shook my head at him. I wanted to ascend. Looking down, I felt so scared. But my instructor grabbed me and kept dragging me down to a depth of a hundred feet. Since then I've developed this problem. I just can't get a grip and start shaking uncontrollably as soon as I enter the water."

"Totally understandable," I said. "But we can reverse this together, Wolfram. Then you can go diving with your wife. There is nothing better than exploring the beauty of the underwater world with someone you trust with all your heart. Let's give it the best we've got, ok?"

He nodded, visibly composing himself like a ski jumper before his Olympic gold medal run.

After almost an hour, I managed to talk him into jumping off the jetty wall into the shallow lagoon. He panicked and seemed to lose all control of his limbs as soon as he hit the water. Holding onto him as tightly as I could, I pep-talked him like a football coach would his star player before the biggest game of the season. Slowly, I managed to calm him down enough to get him to deflate his buoyancy control device. I kept holding on to him as we slowly descended. To my big surprise, Wolfram relaxed as soon as we were completely submerged. His phobia seemed to manifest most strongly on the water surface.

Overnight, I pondered strategies to help my student overcome his fear. During the following couple of days, we dove together twice a day. As soon as Wolfram started panicking, I would grab him, put my arms around him, and hold him tight until he stopped shaking and kicking. We would then proceed to descend.

Wolfram's underwater skills were developing. Behind his mask, he wore one of the happiest grins I have ever seen. On the first day, it had taken almost thirty minutes of holding onto him with all my strength and waiting for his fits to subside before we were able to begin our dive. On the second day, it had taken only fifteen minutes. By the third day, I had only had to hold him for five minutes. On the morning of the fourth day, a very happy student completed his course without panicking once.

We celebrated in the afternoon by jumping into the deep blue once more – this time including his wife. They were over the moon. Their dream had come true: they would be able to go scuba diving together in the future. For a moment, I felt overwhelmed by sadness at the thought of how much I longed to have the same. But I quickly recovered, tears of happiness in my eyes. Seeing Margaret and Wolfram hold hands underwater like two infatuated teenagers was all the gratification I needed.

Not all of my experiences were positive, of course. Many husbands tried to force their spouses into diving. They dreamed of diving to world-famous wrecks and were determined their wives would be part of it. I made more than one enemy out of the husbands by talking with their crying wives. Some of the inconsolable ladies couldn't decide if they were more terrified of their husbands or the ocean. Being a non-judgmental listener, I helped some of these unhappy women find the strength to tell their angry spouses that although they loved them dearly, they would prefer mountain biking to ship wrecks.

As instructors, we experienced many near misses. Some people listened. Many, however, would become "experts" after only ten dives and ceased to take advice from anyone. Scuba diving is actually an extreme sport. Unfortunately, it does not advertise itself as such, since it feels incredibly relaxing whilst being dangerous. When breathing underwater, we are undeniably out of our element. Unequipped we would die. Considering the vast number of inexperienced, thickheaded divers trundling through our atoll, I often wondered if somehow, the turquoise Maldivian paradise attracted innumerable guardian mermaids to aid our oblivious divers.

Relations with fellow dive center employees were an emotional roller coaster, to say the least. In a regular city job, you don't have to socialize much with your coworkers. When conflicts arise, you either solve them or ride them out, avoiding each other for a while until it all blows over. On Kuredu, we lived in extreme proximity with our colleagues. As instructors, we had only one day off a week. Getting off the island and away from each other was impossible in such a short timeframe. Escape was not an option.

We all learned to deal with our differences by embracing them and dealing with any disagreements immediately. Leaving it for another day wasn't practical for the sake of the team. A good sense of humor helped – as it always does in life – to gain the emotional distance we needed to get along on our one-square-mile sandbox.

Considering how many nationalities, not to mention personalities, were thrown together on our little speck of sand, we managed incredibly well. Perspective was the key. No one made this clearer than Udo, a German diving instructor who joined us for a year. While all the rest of us were whining about having to live like so many sardines in a can, he was disappointed we weren't closer together.

Udo had just come from serving eight years in Afghanistan with the German army. He had shared mass quarters with hundreds of fellow soldiers, each man's cot only a few feet from the next. No walls. No doors to be closed. Now, the paper-thin walls separating him from his neighbors made him feel lonely, while the rest of us sometimes felt like Michael Douglas in *Falling Down*, ready to go on a rampage to eradicate all of our snoring, singing, alarm-clock-ignoring, coffee-making, door-banging neighbors.

Life on the island became especially difficult where intimate relations were concerned. At times, emotions flared high and couples would shout at each other, letting their tears flow freely.

Many of them broke up. Ultimately, being cooped up together in a room the size of a shoebox was too much for most of us spoiled Westerners. In addition, few could resist the temptation of engaging in sexual adventures with their often very attractive colleagues. Due to my gender history and shyness, I was one of the very few who did not plunge into multiple affairs.

But even though I led a quiet life, a touch of drama lurked behind every corner. Most conflicts occurred due to simple misunderstandings concerning differences in culture or personality, or due to staff members who had gotten up on the wrong side of the bed.

On rare occasions, people's behavior could get downright disturbing. Judith's partner Rowan's sunny smile, fantastic tales, and bear hugs were often the highlight of my day. He came across as a brilliant man with a touch of the crazy professor. We all knew he was prone to exaggeration, often spinning yarns worthy of old sailors. His frequent lies were smiled upon and attributed to his quirky character.

When Rowan and Judith separated but remained on the island, our big teddy bear started to slowly lose his mind. Her promotion to dive center manager didn't help the situation. Rowan confided in me and shared emails he had allegedly intercepted from our managers. Some of the emails he showed me were horrendous, betraying a blatant disrespect for human beings. I was shocked and concerned. For months, I didn't think of asking the most obvious question: how had Rowan come by this information?

As his actions became more paranoid, I grew more worried. I was deeply torn. Being Rowan's friend, I felt a deep loyalty towards him. On the other hand, my instincts screamed that we had long ago left the land of post-breakup instability and had now entered the realm of insanity.

Finally, I made a fateful decision. I approached Judith as a friend, as well as in her role as dive center manager, and confided in her. I explained how Rowan's ramblings and actions were reaching highly unsettling levels. Judith was shocked by my description of the emails Rowan had shown me. She insisted no emails of the sort had ever been sent. We agreed to not inform upper management yet, but instead confide in my old divemaster mentor and IT wizard, Friedrich.

Friedrich found keyloggers installed on most dive center staff's laptops. Many of us had entrusted our laptops to Rowan over the years. He had been known as a computer wizard and nerd who could fix anything. Through the keyloggers, Rowan had gained access to everyone's passwords and intercepted correspondence from management. Not only had he spied into confidential emails but also changed their content, inserting hideous statements that had never been uttered by the original senders.

Unfortunately, our discoveries meant we could not delay involving upper management – meaning Rube and Magnus – any longer.

Rube stayed calm, but took decisive action.

"I will call Rowan into my office tomorrow morning and fire him," Rube informed Friedrich, Judith and I.

A few hours later that evening I received a text from Rowan.

"Can you help me pack my stuff?"

I didn't respond. How had he found out? What could I possibly say? I felt horrible betraying my friend. At the same time, all information that had been unearthed over the last days had painted a very clear picture of severe, possibly schizophrenic, instability. Our research had uncovered far more shady and criminal activity than we had wanted to know. We had evidence of fraud, and theft from numerous hotel guests as well as dive center suppliers. Nothing Rowan had told us had been true. His imagination had created a life and persona that simply didn't exist. Our island community being as constrained as it was, there was no way we could allow Rowan to remain on the island. Trust had been broken on too many levels, with too many people.

True to his word, Rube called Rowan into his office the next morning. He presented all his tangible evidence and asked Rowan what had driven him to betray everyone he had come in contact with. Rowan answered with silence. He stared at Rube, unwilling, or perhaps unable to respond.

It was heartbreaking. Rowan and I had first become friends during my intensive month of divemaster training. Since then, three years had passed. I couldn't bring myself to say goodbye to him. My heart was in turmoil. I had loved Rowan like the older brother I'd never had. Losing him felt like losing family all over again.

On the other hand, I was angry with him for having deceived me for years. Part of my anger was directed at myself. I had taken everything at face value, never judging, never thinking things through, no matter how crazy or illegal Rowan's claims had seemed. Thus I felt partly responsible for his fate. I had endangered my friend, my brother, by not taking decisive action sooner. He wasn't a criminal but rather needed professional help.

My old friend spent his last night on the jetty, underneath a cloudy sky. He was alone, surrounded only by his bags. No one came to see him off and give him one last hug. The weekly luggage speedboat heading to Male, the capital island, took him away at first light.

For a few months those of us closest to Rowan – Judith, Rube, and myself – were shell-shocked. Part of our innocence had been lost forever. Could we trust our perception of people? How much of what we saw was real? How much of it was only what we wanted to see? Rube earned my deepest respect during this unglamorous part of our island history. He stayed calm. He never badmouthed Rowan to anyone. I was witness to admirable fairness and integrity.

Whatever happened in our dive center universe, the Maldivian staff watched in amusement from a distance. In their eyes, we were loud and emotional, rude and immoderate. Maldivians were soft-spoken in general, and very gentle. Most of them were tiny and slim. Apart from our emotional outbreaks and seemingly uncontrolled behavior, it was the wealthy – mostly European – hotel guests who shocked our Maldivian colleagues most often. Many vacationers were already drunk after breakfast. The majority of Western tourists were voluminous to a degree that must have seemed surreal to the delicate Maldivians.

I will never forget sipping tea with a group of Maldivian waiters and boatmen one afternoon. A very big, gleamingly-white British lady thundered rather than walked past our teahouse. All the Maldivians stopped eating. Their faces reflected puzzlement rather than judgment. As the obese lady slowly heaved herself out of sight, one Maldivian who was barely the size of a European child, softly exclaimed, "Wow, mega-structure!"

For our part, the many incidents we witnessed involving Maldivian staff left us just as perplexed. The locals lived on what we called Maldivian time. Everything was done very slowly. When one of our instructors complained her staff room window couldn't be locked, a locksmith finally arrived four weeks later, and installed a lock – on the outside.

Growing up in the middle of the Pacific Ocean, many Maldivians had no comprehension of the rest of the planet. A garbage bag floating past our boat would be regarded with a shrug of their shoulders. If I asked, "Can we please stop briefly to retrieve the bag?" the captain would stare at me in complete puzzlement, and ask, "Why would you want to do that? It's floating away!" Considering his very simple grasp of the English language and my non-existent Dhivehi, I was at a loss to explain global pollution.

All Muslim staff on our hotel island adhered to the rules of their religion. The artificial world of Western holiday seekers collided every day with the strict lives of predominantly Muslim hotel employees. Would my Maldivian friends tolerate a trans man amongst them, I often wondered?

Every now and then, island fever would hit me with a vengeance. I might have handled it better than most, but I still wasn't as immune as I had thought. When it did rush over me like a freight train running downhill with no breaks, all I would want to do was pack my few belongings and board the next seaplane.

Linda, a fellow instructor who left only a few months after I had arrived on the island, had left us a goodbye note. "In the end," she wrote, "no matter how tough it gets, you will remember only the good times you had during your stay on this small, secluded island. Enjoy every moment with all your heart. Most likely you will never be happier anywhere else."

Whenever I succumbed to island fever, I would recall her words and feel the truth of her sentiments resonating within me. Years later, in other places, doing other jobs, I would still remember her wisdom.

No matter how depressed I got at times, the moment I stepped off the jetty into the water or onto a dive dhoni, I immediately felt elated and immensely happy to be alive. Underwater, I was a different person – self-confident, relaxed, decisive, elegant and fearless.

To experience animal encounters on a daily basis made me feel richer than Aristotle Onassis. On the house reef, I was able to spot anything from jackfish hunting like a pack of wolves to relaxed sea turtles, from giant Napoleon wrasse to thousands of lively, colorful reef fish – all on just a one-mile swim. It was the only time in my life during which I enjoyed workouts with all my heart.

On the reefs, or even just in the shallow lagoons, unforgettable experiences, life-altering in their splendidness, were the norm rather than the exception. Manta rays could be seen all year around, with huge numbers congregating at specific sites during the last quarter of the year. Manta ray cleaning stations, usually a nondescript pile of coral blocks teeming with little cleaner wrasse, were a sight to behold. Providing I had divers who listened to my instructions and had the patience to lay low and wait, Manta rays would invariably come by for a good 'cleaning job', letting hundreds of cleaner fish swarm over their bodies and even inside their mouths and gills. The rays would glide over our heads with only inches to spare, most of them sporting a wingspan of up to ten feet.

I often hovered motionless and watched the coral reef for a while, contemplating reef fish behavior. Each organism was busy defending its way of life. Tiny fish would attack divers the moment we ventured too far into their territory. There were all kinds of characters: the camouflaged, the timid, the curious, the bullies, and the cowards. Some were defensive, others aggressive. As I watched the busy shuffling and posturing on the reef, I saw an intricate microcosmos, a perfect metaphor of human social life and daily struggles.

Odd ocean creatures enchanted me: sponge-like Frogfish breathing through their feet; leaf fish with eyes like fairytale mirrors, weaving in the current on wobbly fins; flatworms flying like tiny carpets, except Sindbad had fallen off somewhere along their journey.

The bigger ocean inhabitants were attractive in their own right. A fully-grown tuna accelerating behind me would generate a quasi-sonic boom as it hurtled past me towards its prey. Schools of eagle rays looked like ambassadors from another planet gliding past with eternal smiles on their likeable faces. Green sea turtles reached enormous proportions, some of them almost seven feet in length. They refused to let themselves be stressed by divers. If we hovered in front of their favorite overhang, they gently pushed us out of the way like a firm yet gentle parent.

Some dives remain forever etched into my memory.

Once I spotted a beautifully colored nudibranch (a sea slug) on the reef wall. It was barely a seventh of an inch long. As it slithered slowly along the outer edge of a coral block, it looked like a striped stocking on continuous tracks. We had just descended to a depth of eighty-two feet. I used my tank banger to get my divers' attention. They all ignored me and instead kept staring over my shoulder with shocked expressions on their faces. Frustrated, I turned around and came face-to-face with a Hammerhead shark. Dark eyes made contact with mine. As it slowly glided past me, the animal seemed to have no end. It must have been at least sixteen feet long. Very slowly, the massive sea creature turned away from us and disappeared into the deep blue sea. We were all spellbound. Surfacing after the dive, I asked if anyone had managed to capture the moment. Even though everyone had an underwater camera, sheepish grins said it all. They had been too immersed in their tense encounter with one of the biggest predators of the open seas to think of photos.

Hammerhead sharks were rare, but we encountered other sharks frequently. During one night dive, my group and I were able to watch a hunting Nurse shark. It was nine feet long, greyish-brown, with a wide, flat head and a beautiful, elongated caudal fin. The absence of claspers on its underside suggested the formidable hunter was a female. She was oblivious to our presence and spent five minutes dismantling a coral block right next to us, in an attempt to snatch whatever delicious prey lay hidden underneath.

After the first few years of working as a diving instructor I was frequently allowed to guide experienced divers during full-day dive trips. On one of these exciting days, I was taking care of my divers after our first dive. I was listening to their stories, helping to fix minor issues with equipment, and sipped a relaxing tea. Out of the corner of my eye, I spotted a member of the boat crew securing my equipment and automatically assumed he had changed my tank as well. At the same time, the boatman assumed I had already changed it myself.

After a one-hour break between dives, we got ready for our second dive of the day. As guide, I jumped first, without checking my pressure gauge to see the status of my tank. After only two minutes at ninety-eight feet, I realized breathing was becoming very laborious. My training kicked in and, angry at my carelessness, I recognized all the signs of a dwindling scuba tank. I knew I had ten seconds at the most before I would be completely out of air.

At lightning speed, I went through all options in my head. Ascending on my own wasn't possible in any of its varieties. I was out of time and too deep for that. If I attempted to surface, I would most likely sustain significant lung damage or, worst-case, my injuries would be severe enough to kill me. My only option was to immediately find another diver and share his air.

Being the guide, I didn't have a dive buddy. It was highly embarrassing to have to rely on my divers, but I managed to find a member of our group just as my air ran out. I calmed myself and signaled "out of air" to him. Wide-eyed, he complied instantly, offering me his alternate air source. We signaled his buddy to stay with another couple, then ascended together maintaining a very slow, controlled speed to avoid injury.

Arriving at the surface, I apologized profusely. The boat crew quickly changed my tank, and my savior and I were on our way back down to reunite with his partner and the rest of our group.

It was a wake-up call. I had become over-confident. Now I was reminded very clearly that, no matter how much experience I had, diving would always remain an extreme sport in which I explored an element not my own. I could easily get myself – or worse, others – killed if I got complacent. The experience humbled me and made me a better instructor. I became more alert and pushed my students to retain a healthy respect for the aquatic realm at all times.

Diving never lost its magic. Instead it became an inseparable part of my soul. In my recurring dreams of flying, I would manipulate my lung volume just as I did to maintain buoyancy underwater. I would take deep, long breaths and rise up in the air, enabling me to soar over the dreamscape. I would be able to lift off at any time, simply by filling my lungs with air, and in the end land gently wherever I liked by breathing out lengthy and steadily, becoming heavier as my lungs emptied.

As always, I was inquisitive and eager to learn more about my new profession. In my free time, I studied as much as I could, completing several courses over the years, enabling me to assist in training experienced divers to become diving instructors. Twice a year, I worked with Ulla, who had taught me all she knew. Only two years after she had certified me as an instructor, we were preparing our instructor candidates for their examinations. Each Instructor Development Course I assisted her with helped me grow even further in my profession. At the same time, I utterly enjoyed coaching our novice instructors.

Another advanced element of scuba diving I tackled was working in our hyperbaric chamber on Kuredu.

The chamber looked like a thick, white, sixteen by seven foot cigar. It was a hard-shelled steel pressure vessel with a hatch on one end and two plate-sized acrylic view ports on the front side. Squeezing through the small entry hatch, I felt like climbing into a small submarine. The first narrow partition, just big enough for one person to hunker down, led to another hatch, which opened into the main chamber. Here, two narrow steel cots were set up, leaving barely enough space to turn. The ceiling was too low for even a short man like me to stand up straight. Medical supplies, bedpans, and a dozen full water bottles were neatly stacked to the side. The smell of disinfectant was almost nauseating, the noise of a running chamber deafening. Depending on each case, patient and tender needed to brace themselves for five to nine hours of a singularly claustrophobic experience.

Rube organized courses for us to become certified operators and tenders. It was no small feat to operate the pressurized chamber. The smallest mistake could risk the lives of the people locked inside the metal tube.

Thankfully, we didn't need to use the chamber very often. But every few months, one of our divers, or a diver from one of the surrounding atolls, would succumb to decompression sickness and had to be treated. It wasn't so much that they had made mistakes during their dives: the bends would often strike scuba divers who were dehydrated from the equatorial sun and too many beers.

To stay healthy, it was necessary for the tender, as well as the patient, to drink several liters of water during the decompression treatment. Being decompressed adds to the bladder feeling full very often, so both patient and tender would have to relieve themselves every half hour at least.

I never told anyone how excruciating it was for me to serve as tender. It wasn't like I could risk revealing myself by pulling my pants down in front of the – often fundamentalist Muslim – strangers who were struggling to stay alive and had most likely never known a trans person in their life. I didn't want special treatment, so I kept my pants zipped. I would get through three to five hours of my bladder almost exploding by sheer will power until I was relieved by the next tender, and the chamber was opened. Then I would bolt for the bathroom under the amused stares of the doctor and my fellow hyperbaric chamber assistants. Needless to say, I greatly preferred running the chamber from the *outside*.

Our island physician, Dr. Albert, was a highly competent, eccentric individual. He was also a functioning alcoholic with a very peculiar sense of humor. During chamber treatments, Dr. Albert loved to play music for us, as well as for our patients inside the chamber. His favorite choice of musical inspiration was Andrea Bocelli, specifically the song *Time to Say Goodbye*, which he played over and over again at full volume. It made me cringe as well as laugh. Nothing beats a little dose of black humor during treatment to cheer a patient up.

Often, when Dr. Albert was drunk and needed to perform common procedures – clean a cut, say, or stitch a wound – he would play Eminem at full volume. As soon as he was done, he would elegantly remove his bloody gloves, ball them up in one practiced move, and shoot the bloody mess across the room into the rubbish bin.

Unfortunately, a depressing call from his ex-wife one night coincided with a patient being ferried over from another island for hyperbaric treatment. By the time the boat with the injured tourist arrived, it was 1 a.m. and our doctor had drunk himself into a stupor. He was far beyond being able to help anyone that night. On the way to his room, he fell and ended up with a nasty scalp laceration himself. He was fired the very next day and, as was customary on Kuredu, had to leave the island immediately. As drunk and eccentric as he had been, no one after him was ever able to match his brilliant medical skills and outrageous sense of humor. Andrea Bocelli was banished from chamber sessions henceforth, which I always deeply regretted.

Magnus, the owner of our dive center on Kuredu, was also the proud and lucky owner of two more dive centers on islands much smaller than ours. I had the pleasure of helping out on both tiny specks of sand for extended periods of time during my four years of working for Magnus's company.

It might sound strange, since Kuredu was already only three thousand feet long and nine-hundred feet wide at its widest point, but I felt much more comfortable on the smaller islands. Both smaller islands were six hundred fifty feet long and wide. The dive center teams on both islands consisted of only four people. One island was in the same atoll as ours. The other island was two hours south by seaplane, in the South Ari atoll.

I fell madly in love with the beautiful southern Maldivian island of Vakarufalhi. The hotel had not been renovated in some time. Staff accommodations, as well as hotel accommodations, had a refreshingly rustic flair. The Vakarufalhi dive center was located in the middle of the tiny island. Walking in either direction would bring you to the ocean in less than two minutes. On two different occasions, I spent three months working on Vakarufalhi. It was there in the South Ari Atoll that I had the three most magical experiences of all my time in the Maldives.

The first happened during a full moon night, around midnight. I witnessed green sea turtle babies hatch, for the first time. Over sixty hatchlings dug their way out of the soft Vakarufalhi sand. They were adorable, fragile little creatures, moving their tiny flippers like windup toys running on a tireless battery. We gently protected them and guided them away from the hotel lights towards the moonlight and the open sea. Hotel guests helped us, heeding our advice on how to handle the tiny animals, everyone respectful, in awe and truly touched by the memorable experience.

Another dream came true during an atoll outreef dive. I was guiding a small group of only six divers. We were nearing the end of our dive when the light around us grew suddenly darker. Looking up, it seemed as if an airplane were coming in for a landing above us, blotting out the sky with its impressive bulk. What we witnessed was far more astonishing though: an adult whale shark, easily forty feet long, slowly descended over our heads. He was incredibly close to us, oblivious to our presence, gliding towards the depths. As we looked up, his body kept moving past our eyes. After what seemed like minutes, we saw the end of his tail fin, then treasured the miraculous privilege of watching him disappear into the abyss. I was truly speechless. Closing my eyes, I took a picture with my heart. Opening my eyes, I looked at my group of divers. All were similarly awestruck, elation written all over their faces. An elderly French couple were diving with us that day. Neither spoke a word of English. The elderly gentleman was writing on his diving slate. I could see him struggling for the English words. When he finished writing, he turned his slate around for me to read. It said "Me dreeem." I was profoundly touched and grateful I had had the privilege to be their guide. We looked at each other underwater, experiencing pure joy.

The final magic was falling in love again. Her name was Ella. She captured my attention from the very first moment she sashayed into the hotel restaurant. Ella was pure charisma. She was a German theater actress. I tried to hide my feelings as best as I could due to the fact I had no idea what to do. She was on the island for two weeks. I would return to my home island of Kuredu; she would return to Germany – end of story. As the days passed, Ella fascinated me more and more. She wasn't a classic beauty, but I found her profoundly interesting. Ella dove with my group several times, proving to be a talented, enthusiastic scuba diver.

Three days before her return to Germany, Ella and I had a drink together, then a walk along the beach, which led to stargazing – and kissing.

"You know," she said, "I kept looking at you over the last two weeks but you never looked back. You have the most beautiful eyes. I'm fascinated by you and would *love* to get to know you better."

Smiling, I admitted, "I'm fascinated by you too. And I *did* look at you often when you weren't noticing. Problem is, I'm not sure where this can lead."

"Well," she said, "let's just find out."

I fell head over heels right then and there. Her adventurous spirit and good humor broke through the last of my defenses.

"Sounds great," I laughed, then immediately grew more serious. "In that case, I should be honest with you. I'm a transgender man. I was born female, and even though my reassignment surgeries went well, my body is far from perfect. I don't have a penis. I have ugly nipples, and huge scars. And I am a very clumsy lover."

Ella didn't miss a beat. "I've seen your nipples and scars on the boat, and wondered what might have happened. Thanks, I really appreciate your honesty. I'll be honest with you, too, Liam. Be aware. I'm a bitch."

"Thanks for the warning," I said, amused. "Don't worry, I can cope with it." My self-confidence was high, and my happiness at loving and being loved again made me feel invincible and incredibly alive.

Ella looked at me, oozing the dangerous sexiness of Sigourney Weaver in *Alien: Resurrection*.

"What do you say, should we find a quiet corner and see about that clumsiness of yours?"

I only grinned and followed her lead.

We were all over each other for three days, until the time came for Ella to depart the romantic island.

One week later, I returned from the South Ari Atoll to my duties on Kuredu as well.

Another month later, I was due for my long break. Months earlier, I had booked flights to Zurich and Auckland. The plan was to spend time with old friends at my favorite lakeside sanctuary and then scratch another item of my bucket list: a round trip through New Zealand.

Now I was wondering if I could fit a visit to Ella in Germany into my already busy schedule as well.

26

Philippine Sea

Ella and I stayed in touch, sending each other romantic, heartfelt emails. I offered to change my travel plans to Zurich and instead visit her for a week in Osterburg, Germany, where she worked at a small city theater. She readily agreed.

We would have spent the whole first week in bed, if she hadn't had to go to rehearsals periodically. Ella was by far the most experienced lover I had ever had. The bedframe shook like an earthquake from the raw power of our passion. To relax after, we would drink Irish coffee in bed while listening to audiobooks, or reading stories to each other.

When we finally got out of bed, I got to experience Ella's world of theater, which had always been one of my favorite places on earth. Since my days as a photography student in Zurich, I hadn't had the opportunity to spend longer periods of time backstage. I had missed it, even more so because of the dearth of cultural opportunities in the Maldives.

Ella's director allowed me to sit in at as many rehearsals as I wished. I felt right back at home in the magical darkness. I was in heaven, soaking up every syllable, every movement and gesture.

During our week in Germany, Ella casually mentioned one morning, "Maybe I can come over for a year, and work with you in the Maldives."

I was beside myself with joy. We seemed to be made for each other, even though her warning from Vakarufalhi lingered at the back of my mind, keeping me on edge. Nevertheless, I was far too happy to analyze that offhand comment about being a bitch too closely.

With my usual impulsiveness, I offered, "How about I cancel my trip to New Zealand? I'd be leaving in a week and be gone for five weeks. But if you're ready to drop everything you have here for a whole year to be with me, it seems only fair that I should sacrifice, too. I could stay a few weeks with you here now and get to know your world. That way, if you ever feel homesick over there, I'll understand what you're missing."

Ella smiled.

Thinking back to my long-distance relationships with both Heinrich and Alana, I dreaded the thought of Ella and I being apart for too long.

"Also, if I go to New Zealand now, it might be up to six months before you'll be able to join me over on Kuredu. You'll need to get a lot more dive experience first before they'll even consider hiring you. It'll be hard to be apart for so long. If I stay, we'll at least get some quality time together now. Then it might only be five months before we're reunited. I really want us to give this all we've got. I want to be with you."

Ella's smile faded. She seemed taken aback.

I, of course, didn't realize how much my sincerity and commitment scared her. Ella wasn't worried about long-distance. She was dreaming of noncommittal fun and adventure, with the off chance of our romantic affair maybe developing into something more substantial in the process. She saw me as a friend and lover, whereas I, desperately lonely and longing for a return of the consummate love I had experienced years earlier with Alana, had already married her in my mind.

Taking her quietness for earnestness, I kept on thinking, planning and talking. As excited as I was by Ella's offer to join me on Kuredu, I worried about her. She wasn't island material. Ella couldn't sit still for more than a few minutes and relished the excitement of cultural diversity. To give her a better idea what to expect, I talked openly about my often unglamorous island existence.

"Island fever is a force to be reckoned with and island life is not quite as romantic as it might seem from a tourist perspective. We'll need to be careful, look out for each other, and rather leave before we let anything break us apart. I've seen too many couples suffer over there already," I concluded.

Several unpleasant scenarios played themselves out in my mind, all inevitably leading to my losing her sooner rather than later. But, if I was aware of inherent dangers and battled them from the outset, it might just end well this time.

To a great extent, I had been shaped by many fateful surprises while growing up. They had often punched the breath out of me just as I recovered from a previous blow. As an adult, I was more compassionate than most because of my life experiences. On the other hand, I complicated life for myself, as well as for those around me by always analyzing what could go wrong. Instead of relaxing and trusting in life and my own capabilities, I tried to anticipate potential bombs long before they could go off.

My foresight and planning must have scared Ella to death. She had become very quiet and reserved. Still she seemed determined.

"I'd love to give it a try over there in the Maldives. As for now, I'll be pretty busy the next few weeks, but, ok, if you think it's the right thing to do and you won't regret cancelling New Zealand, let's spend some time together here at my place." She smiled, "You're crazy. I would never give up an awesome trip like that for anyone."

We hugged and I made a few phone calls to cancel plane tickets and hotel bookings.

Even as I hung up the phone, I could feel a change in the air. The aroma in Ella's apartment seemed to have gone from blooming roses to stale and dusty wasteland. I wasn't sure what to think. In bed that night, I felt her pulling away from me.

"Sorry Liam, I'm tired and tomorrow will be an early start. I've got rehearsals at 9 a.m. Good night."

The following weeks were fraught with problems.

Instead of exploring New Zealand, I spent an emotionally draining month with Ella in Germany, interspersed with brief moments of inspiration and happiness at the theater. Ella retreated to a safe distance, allowing me to be with her and long for her, yet controlling how close we could become.

I returned to Kuredu, lovesick and longing to rediscover the passionate, limitless woman I had met on Vakarufalhi. Even as Ella remained distant, she continued to profess her love for me. So I agreed to ask Rube and Judith if there was a job opening for Ella. They reluctantly agreed to employ my mysterious girlfriend as a snorkel guide.

In the few months before Ella was due to arrive on Kuredu, she completed multiple diving courses, all the way up to divemaster. My romantic heart wanted to believe she was working hard and was willing to give up everything she knew, for us. I told myself she was risking her success as an actress at the peak of her career to live with her boyfriend in the middle of the Indian Ocean, so it must be real love, right?

But during our Osterburg weeks, Ella had admitted to having needed a break in her career for a long time.

"Theater work isn't all it's cracked up to be. Don't get me wrong. I love what I do but, maybe, there is more out there. I've been longing to explore the world for a while now. I just needed someone to elope with. It turns out, it's meant to be you," she said with a mysterious smile.

Judith tried to warn me.

"I have seen it happening many times before, Liam. Ella might just want to use you to get her instructor license on Kuredu, and spend some time on a beautiful Maldivian island."

My friend meant well, but my lovestruck heart wasn't ready to heed her advice.

From the moment Ella arrived, I was painfully reminded of Eleanor's advice years earlier, when I had had trouble understanding her daughter Alana's behavior.

"Whenever you are in doubt about someone," she had said, "ignore their words and look at their actions instead."

Ella's words and actions didn't match.

She moved into my tiny room, because the hotel required couples to do so. We shared my queen-sized bed, yet Ella slept as far away from me as she could get. She would rather have hugged the cold stone wall than touch me. Every now and then, she would throw me a bone and allow me to hold her hand while we slept. Under no circumstances did she want to be seen holding hands with me in public, however.

Ella easily made friends on the island. She was funny and kind to everyone else, while avoiding any inkling of warmth that might make me too enthusiastic and hopeful about our relationship.

Ella kept telling me, "I really care for you Liam," which was all I needed to hear to keep bumbling after her like a blind little puppy hoping for a treat. My friends on Kuredu as well as those abroad witnessed my self-destructive behavior. They were worried sick and tried to talk some sense into me. I wouldn't listen.

My best friend on the island, Milo, had arrived one year after me. He was German and an amazing soul. Milo had a beautiful body and long blond hair, making him very popular with the single ladies vacationing on Kuredu. What made him one of a kind, though, was his keen people sense and his positive spirit, which was second to none. His good humor and naiveté often had us all in tears with laughter. Milo's English was very basic upon his arrival. When he started guiding snorkel boats, he would greet his snorkelers every morning with a heartfelt, "It's such a pity to see you today!" then misinterpret the roaring laughter of his snorkelers as pure delight. We enjoyed the show too much to inform him of his error.

Milo and I were soul mates. We spent many evenings outside on the front step of our rooms, drinking gin and cokes and gorging ourselves on ready-made cheese fondue brought all the way from Europe for us by returning guests. We traveled together several times in our breaks between contracts. We dreamed of exploring the world together, planning daring adventures for the years to come. I hadn't been blessed with such a deep friendship since my childhood. Milo was like the younger brother I never had. His friendship and unwavering loyalty meant the world to me. And yet I failed to heed Milo's advice as well. He got very angry with me.

"I can't bear watching you with Ella," he told me. "Where is your dignity? You are letting her abuse you emotionally. It breaks my heart to see you like this."

I knew he was right but was simply too terrified to lose her.

With my help, Ella reached her goal, and became a scuba instructor. Immediately after she did, it became obvious even to me: she had gotten what she came for, and I had reached the end of my usefulness. Still, she seemed oblivious to my pain. It seemed to be easier for her to become ever more distant, thus provoking me into ending it myself. Which I did, only four months after her arrival on the island.

"Ella, I can't go on. I can't let you treat me like this any longer. You're breaking my heart every single day."

She reacted with barely-concealed relief. "Maybe it's for the better. I guess it would be best for me to leave in two months, at the same time you go on your long break. We're still traveling together for those eight weeks, right?"

Milo and I had planned to backpack through the Philippines, Palau and Indonesia together during the upcoming break. We had invited Ella to come along some months earlier. I should have uninvited her now, instantly. Instead, clinging to the insane hope that things might change between us while on the road, I allowed Ella to remain part of our travel plans – adding one last bad decision to the most self-destructive year of my life.

"Yeah, sure," I said, "Why not have some final adventures together."

Ella looked happy at the thought. She had detached herself from me emotionally a long time before, and already saw this as simply going on a trip with friends.

Milo was angry and disappointed in me.

"Liam, are you out of your mind?"

I knew I was in the process of betraying him and making our vacation miserable. But I couldn't help myself, and Milo was too good a friend to set me straight. He grudgingly agreed to have Ella along.

"Fine then, it's your own funeral. Just let's try to have at least a little fun together, ok?"

When Ella needed to confront Judith about wanting to leave six months too early, she asked me to accompany her for support. Ever the understanding doormat, I held her proverbial hand through her talk with Judith, who was less than thrilled by Ella breaching her contract.

I was disgusted with myself. All my life, I had pondered why victims of abuse stayed with their partners. Now I realized that my fear of being alone again was greater than my sense of self-preservation and integrity. I was willing to subjugate myself to Ella's will, giving up my dignity if it meant there was a small chance she would keep loving me. My self-confidence had been almost completely destroyed by our disastrous relationship. I couldn't grasp that she had never truly loved me, and never would.

Finally, it was August 2008. Six months of hell on my beautiful island sanctuary came to an end. The last two had been the worst. Ella and I had had to keep sharing my room after breaking up. The atmosphere between us had dropped far below freezing. Sleeping in the same bed together had felt like being trapped in a phone booth with a contract killer. While I became a shadow of myself, Ella obviously enjoyed her last weeks on Kuredu before her departure. Clearly her self-preservation skills far surpassed her consideration for others.

Magnus caught me in front of the dive center the night before we were scheduled to leave for vacation. He rarely talked with me personally, so I was surprised when he asked, "Would you mind accompanying me to my office?"

I nodded and followed him along, assuming he needed to ask me something about our dive center website, which I updated regularly for the company.

"Close the door," he said with a serious expression.

He rummaged on his desk, then turned around, handing me an enormous wad of money. It turned out to be 500 USD in one-dollar bills – it was often impossible to get bigger bills on Kuredu.

"Thank you for all your help and tireless support. Enjoy your vacation!" Magnus said, as he pushed me out of his office with a big smile on his face.

Very touched, I managed to mumble my thanks before he disappeared behind the fast closing door.

Ella, Milo and I left together the next morning.

We headed to Manila and then onwards to Mindoro where we threw ourselves enthusiastically into the waves. Each time we submerged, Ella and I entered neutral territory. The ocean was as unpredictable as it was beautiful. As dive instructors, we knew it was imperative to put all personal differences aside in favor of safety.

Contrary to the gentle turquoise of our Maldivian waters, the Philippine Sea was dark and wild. Waves were high; stinging jellyfish were everywhere. The water ranged from a deep blue to a more brownish, greenish blue. Visibility was often poor. It felt like diving through a thick fog and left the doors of my imagination wide open. I envisioned all kinds of sea monsters waiting for us in the depths.

The water being colder, it is more nutritious, turning the Philippine Sea into a formidable wilderness. We encountered ocean life that resembled a colorful LSD trip more closely than it did reality. The ocean currents whipped us along, making us laugh out loud as we somersaulted our way along the coral reefs. I loved every second of it.

Ella stayed distant, shutting me out ever more with each passing day. Paradoxically Milo, Ella and I nevertheless experienced eight unforgettable weeks together. Milo was very relaxed, brightening each of our days like a school of bioluminescent fish gently gliding through the deep sea. In stark contrast to his serenity, Ella's manic energy and never-wavering sense of adventure, catapulted us into far more bizarre and beautiful encounters than we could have ever imagined. What's more, my frustrations and cravings for Ella spurred me to throw myself into as many exotic adventures as possible.

In Mindoro, we rode currents like rodeo champions. Every day, we saw sea creatures we had, until then, only admired in ocean encyclopedias. Sea slugs of all shapes slithered over corals like rainbow colored candies come alive, on a stroll through the aquatic wilderness. Flamboyant cuttlefish scuttled across the sand like walking discotheques, strobing kaleidoscopic colors as they moved past us. Then, on our last day, we were swallowed up by a vortex and plummeted from ten to sixty-five feet in seconds, fearing for our lives, surviving only through courage and calm teamwork.

In Palau, we stumbled upon a half-empty scuba diving safari boat. It was due to leave the next day and was still in need of three more passengers. As last-minute arrivals, we secured places onboard for a fraction of the regular price. Seven days of scuba diving on a beautiful sailing boat had been my dream for as long as I could remember. We hooked on to reefs, flying in currents far too strong to swim against. Massive sharks circled us effortlessly, hunting for their next meal. One day we moved far out into the open ocean where we came face to face with the oldest creature on our planet, unchanged since the late Triassic period – the nautilus. We circled the small group of cephalopods carefully, marveling at their delicately probing tentacles and elegant shells. Soon after, we watched them propel themselves ever deeper, to return to the abyss at one thousand feet where they have made their home for millennia. My heart felt ready to burst with happiness.

At Palau's famous Jellyfish Lake, we floated amongst millions of yellow jellyfish of all sizes. They had lost their ability to sting over time due to the lack of natural predators. The lake water was an eerie blue-green that perfectly complemented the milky yellow color of the countless floating jellyfish. Suspended in mid-water, softly breathing through our snorkels, all sound muted, I felt myself entering a fairytale world where everything – including me – was utterly calm and untouchable.

Upon our return to the Philippines, we embarked on an exploration of Palawan. Landing in Busuanga airport in 2008 felt like arriving in unchartered territory. The runway for our small airplane was a green meadow, the airport an unobtrusive, almost unnoticeable building.

Surrounded by jungle and the midnight blue Philippine Sea, we spent a few days exploring remote reefs and Japanese warships that had sunk in water shallow enough for compressed air divers to reach. On the dive boat, I met a man named Gregory, a carpenter from the United States.

Red dots were distributed all over the historical map of the world that had been tattooed on his back. I couldn't contain my curiosity and asked the charismatic fellow about the meaning of his tattoo. He had worked for Cirque du Soleil all his life, he explained, for both touring as well as resident shows. Each dot signified a town where his shows had performed. He was currently working for a Cirque du Soleil show in Macau, China.

During dinner, he suggested we check out the website of Cirque's competitor, Dragone Entertainment, since they were building a huge water show in Macau and would be looking for scuba instructors.

I hadn't the faintest idea where Macau was, yet the moment Gregory mentioned the unique opportunity, I felt goose bumps covering my entire body.

I raced to a computer station in the simple guesthouse, and found only an online teaser of the project, and an ad proclaiming diving technicians were needed for the most visionary theater project of all time. I was already hooked, and knew without a doubt: I would have to try to be a part of this project. It was located in the "City of Dreams" in Macau, which seemed a very good omen indeed.

To Ella's credit, she was very supportive and immediately understood my enthusiasm. I had never applied to a theater before and was absolutely clueless.

We had three more weeks of travel ahead of us when I mentioned, "I need to try getting into that project. I'll send an application as soon as I get back to Kuredu."

"Are you crazy?" Ella exclaimed. "If you really want this job, you need to send them an email *right now*! Tell them you're very interested but stuck in the middle of the jungle without access to your documents. Tell them you'll send them your full application as soon as you get back to civilization, and let them know when that'll be."

I was grateful for her advice and immediately wrote an email to the Dragone Entertainment Group.

Milo, Ella and I enjoyed our final weeks of adventure. We explored an underground river, and ate fruit bats and *tamilok* – woodworms, a local delicacy of Palawan. Judging by the faces of our hosts, the local specialty existed only to have fun with tourists.

Palawan offered many pristine, authentic areas. We could see a road being built – which most likely meant the beginning of tourist invasions and the end of romantic palm-leaf huts. We were lucky to have the privilege of exploring this part of the Philippines in its still almost undisturbed natural beauty.

The most memorable part of our journey was a trip from El Nido in the North of Palawan, to Sabang. Milo, Ella and I decided to experience the bus journey in true local spirit. Climbing onto the roof of our bus in El Nido, we maneuvered until we found places for our butts atop our luggage. We hoped this would cushion us from the thousands of local potholes we were bound to encounter along the way.

Balanced on top of a pile of baggage, wind and dust whipping into our faces, we held on for dear life as our bus plummeted along rarely-traveled mountain roads and on through countless valleys. Never before had my ass had to endure such a continuous beating. Even low hanging branches and power lines became a threat. Every so often, we would warn each other to duck, just in time to avoid being garroted or beheaded. Every minute was worth it, though – and infinitely better than sitting in the sweltering bus, fighting for space with local school children and chickens.

All three of us endured the entire nine hours atop the bus. I felt intensely alive. I savored the moment, secretly hoping our trip would never end. It was one of the best journeys of my life.

Sabang proved to be a little jewel hidden at the edge of the jungle, offering the most glorious natural beach I had ever laid eyes on. Clouds of saltwater mist hovered over powerful waves crashing onto the beach. The air around Sabang was energized, sunsets gaining an otherworldly quality as if viewing the world through a diamond. The ocean mist reflected iridescent, myriad colors. I spent every evening lying on a comfortable hammock, sipping a cold *San Miguel* beer and gazing through the multi-colored mist at the powerful Philippine Sea.

After doubling back to Manila, our eight adventurous weeks came to an end. Ella, Milo and I parted ways in the bustling Philippine capital. Ella headed towards Vietnam and continuing adventures before returning to Germany a few months later. Milo and I had to go back to Kuredu, to get ready for our next contract year.

I was sad to see Ella go. At the same time, I realized it was the best thing that could possibly happen to me. As good as our vacation had been, I had been given a better glimpse of her true self than ever before. She was a lone adventurer, incapable of commitment or compromise.

Our eight weeks of travel had helped me take a step back to gain perspective. I had been close to subservient for months. Now, I was rediscovering my strength and astonished at my ability to enjoy myself. At some point, on top of the bus, exhilarated, and laughing from the bottom of my heart at having evaded yet another low-hanging tree branch, I just knew: I was going to be fine without Ella.

Like a wrongly imprisoned man walking through the gates towards the brightest light, I remembered that I could indeed be lovable, soulful, fun, courageous and handsome. Following this realization, I moved on to inner freedom with the speed of a hunting tuna, nearly breaking the sound barrier as I went along.

I had suffered enough. It was time to reclaim my independence, get back on my feet and enjoy life again, even if it meant being alone.

27

Noonu Atoll

I hadn't forgotten about the visionary Dragone theater project in Macau. How could I? Featuring millions of gallons of water under a moveable stage, it was going to unite my two passions in the biggest show ever created. I sent my CV along with an enthusiastic application letter to the Dragone Entertainment Group on the very same day Milo and I got back to Kuredu.

I was about to start my fourth year of diving into turquoise bliss, sharing the waters with Manta rays, sharks, and millions of other marine organisms. My fascination for the ocean had grown with every passing year. I longed to immerse myself in it again and again, and never regretted my decision not to study marine biology in Seattle. Learning first-hand through daily experience seemed infinitely better, even if it meant never holding a degree in my hands.

I enjoyed having my tiny room to myself again. While others partied, I found sanctuary in my books. I would sit either in my cozy quarters, or on my doorstep, enjoying the equatorial deep blue sky and the bright sunlight. I would walk around the island, savoring the sight of juvenile stingrays in the shallow lagoon. They looked like tiny dinner plates with tails. Juvenile black-tip reef sharks tried hard to look menacing, but due to their small size looked utterly adorable.

Then, during Christmas dinner 2008, only four months after Ella, I fell in love quite suddenly and uncharacteristically soon.

I had never jumped from one relationship to the next. I simply wasn't the type. It would take me years to get over a lost love. The depth of my emotions sometimes scared me, and I needed time to process.

This time was different. Her name was Gabriella. She was Italian, born and raised in Germany, and worked as a tour guide on Kuredu. Gabriella looked like Sandra Bullock's twin, only younger. Apart from being breathtakingly beautiful, she exuded warmth as well as compassion. She fell for me, too, Cupid's arrow piercing us both at the same time.

I had become quite the hermit in the three months since my return to the island. But now I became a regular guest in Akiri bar where all the tour guides gathered to meet with their respective hotel guests. Gabriella and I spent many hours sitting in comfortable armchairs on the Akiri terrace, philosophizing about life and love.

I was aware Gabriella would have to return to Germany in only two months, and if I ever got a reply from the project in Macau, I might be headed in the opposite direction. This time, I would not cancel my plans for anyone, no matter how much I loved the person. I had learned at least that much from my disastrous experience with Ella.

I wondered if it even made sense for Gabriella and me to start anything? I could tell her roots were in Germany and she longed to go back. I, on the other hand, needed to keep roaming the planet. All worries aside, taking action was always preferable to cowering in a corner wondering what could have been. So I leaped over the careful boundaries Gabriella and I had erected, and confessed.

"I'm in love with you. Actually, it's love at first sight, ever since our first meeting at Christmas."

She was delighted. "I'm in love with you, too, Liam. I'm catching myself planning my day so you and I can 'accidentally' meet as often as possible."

"Ha," I said, "I'm doing the same thing."

We both laughed. Next, I outed myself as a transgender man.

Gabriella's face fell. She looked positively shell-shocked.

I was stumped. This was the very first time a woman who had fallen in love with me was troubled by my being trans.

Gabriella fought with her confusion.

"I was over the moon when you told me you loved me the other day," she told me when we met again a few days later. "But when you came out about your gender identity, it was like someone had hit me over the head with a scuba tank. You know, I was raised in a very conservative, Italian Catholic household. I can't help but wonder, would me being with you make me a lesbian? For me as a Catholic that is unthinkable. I really don't know what to do."

"Can you imagine giving us a chance? I think you'll find I'm as much a man as most other guys."

Gabriella's eyes still betrayed love, but she seemed seriously distraught.

"Yes, I suppose we can try. But Liam, I really don't know. I mean you don't even have a penis. That's a really big problem for me. I *like* penises."

This, too, was a first for me. In all the intimate relationships I had had since my transition, the women in my life had never missed a penis. For a short while, I almost lost myself all over again. I even considered whether she would be worth going through reconstructive penis surgery after all.

Then, I was struck by the insanity of wanting to risk the loss of all genital feeling for a woman who couldn't accept me as I was. A penis created artificially from the skin and bones of my thighs would not change anything. A malfunctioning monstrosity in my underpants would only make things worse. Gabriella would most likely not be able to overcome her conservative upbringing no matter what, and I would end up being worse off. Besides, I was happy with my body as it was. My four years spent under the sun, scuba diving and swimming extensively every day, had given me a lean, athletic figure. I was a handsome young man – penis or not.

Gabriella tried. We met for nightly walks on the beach. On one unforgettable evening, we lay together on a sun lounge, only feet away from the ocean, and lost ourselves in electrifying kisses. We never even noticed when it started raining and were completely soaked by the time we headed to our separate rooms. It was a perfect moment, one of those that warp time, rendering it irrelevant.

We tried to have sex several times. Gabriella couldn't help but recoil. She was helpless in the face of my gender identity. Even though we were in love, we broke up soon after Gabriella returned to Germany. A simple Skype call ended our short, but spirited, relationship.

Gabriella had been everything Ella wasn't. Gabriella possessed heart and consideration for the feeling of others. Nevertheless, we had been doomed from the start.

To be rejected once more, no matter how gently, so shortly after my last disastrous relationship, did nothing for my self-esteem. I realized I needed to stay away from women for a while. Over the years, I seemed to have become needy, forgetting how to be my own best company.

All the while, the Dragone Entertainment group did not reply to my application for Macau. I was determined and began regularly battering them with applications at four-week intervals. I had no clear idea what I was actually applying for, but it sounded exhilarating.

In late spring of 2009, they sent an email.

"Our project in Macau is delayed, due to the worldwide economic crisis. Your application is on the top of our pile. We are interested in interviewing you in the near future. Currently, however, we are unable to start the hiring process. Please stand by for further information."

I replied, "Thank you for getting in touch and letting me know you are interested. I will look forward to hearing from you again, soon."

In the meantime, the ocean continued to soothe my soul. Out in the Big Blue, it was impossible for me to be unhappy.

When my short break came up, I was at a loss of where to go. On a whim, I decided to visit friends in Rarotonga, Cook Islands.

For the first time on vacation, I didn't take the opportunity to experience a different ocean. Throughout the first half of my stay in Rarotonga, I was withdrawn. I couldn't help but still mourn both Ella and Gabriella, as well as the loss of much of my self-esteem.

Midway through my stay, I decided to follow the scenic road along the coast to walk once around the entire island. I had been told one day was enough to cover the entire distance.

I set out in my sandals early in the morning. After only one hour of walking, I knew I was in trouble. Blisters were already forming inside my unsuitable shoes. I contemplated going back to change into something more comfortable but decided to push on instead. After only a few hours, my feet were bleeding and I was in excruciating pain. As I kept on going, my entire body straightened with determination. It never once occurred to me to simply take off my shoes and continue barefoot.

Something inside me snapped that day. I needed to push through, no matter what. So I kept walking and bleeding. In some ways, my behavior was no different than when I had cut my arm with a sharp stone in Genoa many years earlier. I needed the physical pain to overcome the emotional pain that had lodged itself in my heart and soul. So I stumbled on until my feet were so raw, the slightest movement shot bolts of pain through my entire body.

It was twelve hours since I had set out and I couldn't move anymore. When I realized I had made it as far as was humanly possible for me on that day, I finally relented. I called my friends to please pick me up and give me a ride home to their place. As it turned out, I had almost made it. Only one more mile of stumbling, and I would have completed my task.

For the second half of my stay in Rarotonga, I was unable to do much of anything. My feet were a mess of deep, open wounds. As they were slowly healing, I realized it had been cathartic to face the physical pain. I felt relieved, almost cleansed. And I was ready for a new beginning.

In June 2009, I finally received a phone call asking me for a Skype interview with the head of Dragone human resources. The interview went very well. A follow up interview was set up with the manager of the Aquatics department who would be in charge of all the diving instructors working for the project. Neither individual was able to clearly describe the scope of work my position would entail. It still sounded intriguing however, as it seemed to encompass both working backstage in theater, as well as teaching scuba diving and being in the water on a daily basis. I couldn't see how combining two passions at the same time could be bad.

Good feelings being mutual, the Aquatics manager, Warner, and I both agreed enthusiastically to work together commencing October 2009.

I decided to leave Kuredu in August. By then, my accumulated time on the beautiful island sanctuary would be close to four years. Part of me wanted to stay on my turquoise island sanctuary forever. But the adventurous nomad in me needed to break free from living in an artificial hotel environment, no matter how enticing the lifestyle might be. Judith, Rube, and Magnus were supportive and happy about the amazing opportunity that had opened up for me. They agreed to let me finish my contract early. I would be able to leave beginning of August and enjoy some time off before facing the next challenge.

My last months in Kuredu were unmatched. Coincidentally, our staff quarters were being renovated and we were given regular beach villas for a few weeks. So I spent my last two months in island paradise, sharing a luxurious villa with Judith. Morning coffee on the porch was a delight. Our staff accommodations were in the middle of the island. This beautiful villa was at the edge of the lagoon, with an unrestricted view of juvenile black-tip reef sharks hunting in the gentle morning sun.

The time passed much too quickly, as it always does when something good is coming to an end. My sadness and excitement rose as I performed many duties for the last time. A week before my final day on Kuredu, I was scheduled for my final full-day dive boat, guiding divers in the neighboring Noonu atoll. All instructors coveted guiding this boat, since Noonu atoll offered breathtaking underwater vistas. I greatly appreciated being allowed to enjoy the privilege one last time.

All my divers that day were experienced and had visited Kuredu multiple times. We planned three dives. After two, we had a luxurious lunch on the boat, warming our bodies in the sun and preparing for the final dive of the day.

Esa, a very experienced Maldivian boatman, approached me quietly after lunch.

"Can you please start the third dive as soon as possible? A violent storm is on its way."

I looked up and saw only clear blue sky in all directions. I nodded, yet did nothing to speed up the process to begin our last dive.

Esa approached me once more before we started our dive and urged me gently, "Please make it fast and stay underwater for only half an hour."

Captain Ibrahim, Esa, and another Ibrahim all were looking very worried. But I still couldn't spot one single cloud in the sky, so I dismissed their worries. Also, it was an unwritten rule to never deny experienced, repeat customers the pleasure of a full, one-hour dive. Noonu atoll and especially this last dive of the day were always a special treat. The coral wall, covered in pink soft corals of all hues, was legendary. My group would never understand if I cut their dive short.

After forty-five minutes underwater, the world turned black as if we had entered into a full solar eclipse. From below, the surface seemed to be boiling violently. The invisible storm had arrived, becoming all too visible, all too quickly. After four years in the Maldives, it seemed I was as green as ever. I still didn't fully grasp the urgency of the situation, and let my divers finish their full hour. We surfaced into an inferno of black clouds, thunder, lightning, and massive waves.

Ibrahim 1, Ibrahim 2, and Esa shook their heads in unison, their eyes telling me what their politeness forbid them to say: "We told you so."

We clambered back onboard, which was no small feat, considering the heavy scuba equipment on our backs and the heaving deck. As we secured our equipment, Captain Ibrahim moved the boat towards the edge of the atoll. Maldivian dhonis aren't built to brave stormy seas. Their flat-bottomed keels are constructed to enable them to slip easily over shallow reefs.

"The heavy waves we are experiencing now, are nothing compared to what'll await us once we leave the shelter of the atoll," a resigned Esa explained.

In good weather, crossing the channel of deep ocean between the Noonu and Lhaviyani atoll usually took two hours. There was no telling how long it would take us in this tempest. We briefly considered waiting out the storm and taking shelter in a harbor right where we were. Then our captain made the decision to forge ahead.

The full seriousness of our situation finally hit me as I watched Captain Ibrahim clutch the steering wheel. In all my time on Kuredu, I had never seen a captain afraid. Captain Ibrahim was the best, utterly fearless and wise, way beyond his years. He now held on to the steering wheel for dear life, his body language radiating tension, his knuckles white from the strain.

Our small dhoni was lost in an ocean of giant waves. Either watery walls rose up before us, or deep troughs opened up behind us. Without our outstanding boat crew, our journey would have ended right then and there. Captain Ibrahim's instincts and competence brought us through four hours of navigating the roughest seas I had ever encountered, all the way home. While Captain Ibrahim was busy saving our lives, I performed standard tour guide duty. I chatted and joked with my divers in an effort to take their minds off the fact that our situation was exceptionally disquieting.

Sabrina, Judith's assistant dive center manager and a seasoned Maldivian tour guide, met us at Kuredu jetty. She had given me this final full day to Noonu atoll and had been terrified she might be responsible for our untimely deaths. We hugged, and she told me wind speeds had exceeded fifty miles an hour. Countless prayers had been sent to Allah, by Muslims and Christians together since no one could be sure if we would ever make it back.

Only one week before leaving them, I had let my boat crew down and made the rookie mistake of ignoring their advice. As a direct consequence,

I had gravely endangered all of our lives. The hotel guests would never know – but I did. I felt horrible.

After saying goodbye to my happy guests, I stayed behind to apologize to both Ibrahims as well as Esa, who were exhausted after our ordeal. Knowing apologizing alone wasn't enough, I first went into the hotel shop and bought an assortment of delicious cookies and chocolates. Short of buying them a souvenir shirt of their work place, these were the best gifts available. I then went back to the dhoni, arriving just as the boat crew finished securing the boat.

"I'm so sorry, guys. Please forgive me. You were right and I was stupid." Embarrassed out of my skin and wishing the soft Maldivian sand could swallow me, I offered the cookies as a symbol of my heartfelt appreciation. The fabulous three men forgave me way too easily, and gave me an understanding, gentle smile.

My last days continued in much calmer conditions. I was given boats all week, and enjoyed saying goodbye to my favorite dive sites and critters along the reefs. Dolphins followed our boat almost every day, their striking beauty and smiling faces making it harder with each passing day to imagine leaving this unique haven.

Dive center staff were usually organizing goodbye dinners amongst themselves. I had never seen anyone throw a goodbye party for our amazing boat crews. Apart from Ibrahim saving my life just a few days before, all the boat crews had saved my honor and good reputation as a guide many times over the years. Without them, I would have been as lost as a toddler in New York's Central Station.

I contacted the hotel. Would I be allowed to have a Maldivian buffet dinner for all boat crews in the local teahouse restaurant directly across from our dive center? Thankfully, the hotel management agreed to my unusual request. I asked our Maldivian instructors to please spread the word. I crafted invitation letters to all boat crew members, approximately forty remarkable individuals. With very few exceptions, like Ismail or Esa, they were all named Abdullah, Ibrahim, Ahmed, or Mohamed.

It was a glorious evening. Everyone was touched. Captain Ismail had whittled a beautiful scale-model dhoni for me, so I would never forget my life on the remodeled Maldivian fishing boats. Anecdotes were exchanged, most rather unfavorable of me – such as the full-day trip when I had decided to take a dump in the dhoni's head just as we stopped to pick up a group of divers. My turds had floated right by them, creating a memory to amuse boat crews for years to come.

After dinner, the boat crews broke out in song and carried me on their shoulders. For an instant, I was concerned they might be able to feel the absent penis between my legs. Then I told myself to stop being silly, relax, and enjoy the moment. After all, I had always been safe in their capable hands. We shared tea and ate more delicious reef fish, celebrating our mutual respect until very late.

Countless times, I had stood on Kuredu jetty, waving final goodbyes to yet another member of our team heading back out into the "real" world. Now it was my turn. Filled with hope and excitement for my unknown future, I turned towards my island family on the jetty.

After hugging everyone goodbye, I found myself on a seaplane with tears in my eyes yet again, staring out at my waving friends, wondering if I would ever return to this unique sanctuary of innumerable turquoise hues.

28

Belgian Pool

Four years on Kuredu had shaped me into a handsome man. I was thirty-eight years old, suntanned and more athletic then ever, with a newfound spring in my step. On a spiritual level, I had found myself many times over during those turquoise years. My life felt like a flowing mosaic, becoming clearer with each passing challenge.

Guiding scuba divers through the Indian Ocean wilderness, I had, in part at least, fulfilled my childhood dream of becoming a game warden. A contented smile spread over my face as I realized another dream was about to come full circle. Many years before, I had stood in a movie theater, watching as the cast and crew of Alegría celebrated their unity and creativity. Back then, as a silent observer in the darkness, the intensity, cultural diversity, and creative heart of such a group had brought tears of joy to my eyes. I had longed with all my heart to one day belong to a colorful show family. Now, ten years later, I was only weeks away from becoming part of the Dragone Entertainment family. I was moving from turquoise seas towards mysteriously black backstage waters – to join an aquatic circus.

Water had become the foundation of my existence. The amniotic fluid of my birth mother's womb had spilled into the strengthening, salty waves of the North Sea. From there, the briny elixir had meandered towards the Columbia River. Creative ripples had turned into an ever-growing stream, emptying only months later into Lake Zurich. Then, turbulent swells had stranded me on the painful shores of Genoa. But the tides had been kind. They had carried me back into the River Limmat from where a strong drift had continued to flow through several streams and oceans, only to bring me back to the mighty Columbia and, even further, to the awe-inspiring Pacific Ocean. Soon, white-crested, aquamarine-blue waves had carried me onwards into the turquoise Indian Ocean and its surrounding seas.

Now the currents pushed strongly towards an underwater life in the biggest indoor pool ever built, close to Hong Kong's exotic South China Sea.

My professional life had led me from art to business to adventure. Over the years, I had distilled many transferable skills from these activities. With all I knew – and didn't yet know – I was ready for my biggest challenge to date.

However, the theater in Macau was still under construction. Thus a large rehearsal studio had been constructed in Antwerp, Belgium, based entirely on the needs of our director. It contained a pool as well as expansive training space to prepare our performers for all aspects of their work in the show. To my utter delight, I had been picked from the large team of future Macau show divers to be one of only five instructors who would be sent ahead to Belgium, to take care of all underwater-based training.

Before plunging into the dark Belgian pool environment, I needed to feel the ocean once more as well as touch base with a precious friend. My buddy Milo had left Kuredu a few months before I did. We reunited in Quintana Ro, Mexico, and spent two adventurous weeks exploring underwater caverns and ancient Mayan ruins.

Soon after, in mid-August of 2009, I arrived back in Zurich, energetic and happy. The only downside: after four years of living barefoot, shoes and socks felt as if my feet were being crushed in *Spanish boots*.

Ignoring the surprisingly large amount of blisters on my toes, I immediately went about visiting all my Swiss friends. We would have a lot of catching up to do in the weeks before my next departure. Months earlier, when I had first announced I was leaving the Maldives, everyone had been delighted.

"Yes! You're finally coming home. It'll be great to have you back."

It wasn't easy to break the news to them now.

"I'm so sorry guys, but adventure beckons once more. I'm going to move even farther away than before – first to Belgium, then to China."

September 2009 was a blur of spending as much time as possible with my closest friends. We enjoyed open-air cinemas, concerts, and theater festivals together, sipped beer at Zurich's beautiful lakeside, and shared our hopes and dreams under a blue, late-summer sky.

Ten days before heading to Belgium, I visited my parents. For many years, I had been tough on Dad. Thankfully, him moving to the Swabian Ocean and thus closer to me had helped. Then, while in the Maldives, I had tried even more to put things in perspective. I knew I had every right to be angry about certain elements of our relationship, and sometimes I still was. Maybe I always would be. The more I thought about our difficulties, however, the better I understood that there was no other way but to forgive. No family would ever be perfect. Dad certainly wasn't, and neither was I. But in his own way, Dad had always been there for me, and always would be.

His eleven-year-old dog had died just a month prior to my arrival. I was glad to visit him at this time in his life. It was good to be able to support him and share his grief. We walked in the warm September sun, increasingly spent but content, speaking honestly about the past and the present, hardship and death.

Visiting Hildegard was far harder. Since her divorce from Dad and her subsequent moving out, I had made it a personal rule to see her at least once a year, even if I was forever at a loss of how to relax around her. But while my heart struggled with memories as well as her recurring episodes of neurotic behavior and mistrust, my mind knew my tormented mom was trying to be every bit as supportive as Dad.

She never forgot a special day. Each birthday, Easter, and Christmas, without fail, she would send me a card with at least one hundred Euros inside. The card would be decorated with dozens of tiny, bright red hearts and glimmering, golden stars.

She would call me every few weeks.

"You're so smart and beautiful. You can do anything. Keep your chin up," she would tell me whenever we talked.

During my visits of at least a day or two she was always visibly moved and grateful. The submissive way in which she resigned herself to this paltry amount of time I was mentally able to give her made me feel guilty and depressed. As odd as it may sound, our encounters reminded me of

King Kong and his demise at the end of the movie. Just like my mom, the beast had no concept of how much pain and destruction he was causing. He was good at heart but still, people had to hurt him in order to save themselves. I had no intentions of attacking my mom with tanks, fighter planes and machine guns, of course. Rather, I meant never to give up on her, no matter how unsettled I ended up feeling after each visit.

Twelve years after my transition, she still had to focus on getting her grammar concerning her daughter-turned-son right. I would be "Liam" and "he" – until her concentration slipped. Then she would use the pronoun "she" and I would revert to being "Stefanie". If we met my mom's acquaintances on the street, she would never introduce me. She only ever told them about her daughter and was at a loss of how to explain the presence of the young man at her side. So she didn't, and ignored their curious looks. No matter how understanding I tried to be, it hurt.

Knowing she would never truly be able to accept me wasn't the only problem. Hildegard's deep mistrust of everyone and everything still affected me as profoundly as it had in my childhood. My emotional walls had never grown high enough. Even my sense of humor wasn't strong enough yet to protect myself from the darkness Hildegard inevitably brought to our encounters. I continued to feel traumatized, and spending time with her was strangely reminiscent of an unarmed conservationist coming across a wounded rhinoceros. I loved her and I felt how deeply she needed me to save her. Nevertheless, no matter how hard she tried to reign in her irritation and paranoia, I couldn't help but expect to be eviscerated at any time. We were both defensive, carefully circling each other to find an opening, a way to settle close to each other, to be there for each other, without hurting too much.

Once home at my lakeside sanctuary, emotionally exhausted from seeing my parents, I turned to the people who had always been my true Swiss family – Naomi and Sienna.

Naomi had taken care of my mail and bank account for many years while I was abroad. Whenever I visited, we continued our tradition of sharing a latte macchiato together while we brought each other up to date on our lives and continued to support each other unconditionally.

Sienna and I had stayed close ever since our first graveside chocolate-sharing in Genoa. We still spent hours talking about our lives, photography, and the world. Additionally, it was Sienna's spare mattress I would use whenever the road led me back to my old home of Zurich.

I shared a strong spiritual bond with both women. No matter how many years passed between visits, my friendships with them only grew stronger.

Spending my last four days before running off to the circus exclusively with them felt like dancing in a warm summer rain after months of drought.

Several days, macchiatos, and animated discussions later, the dust in my soul was washed off enough to feel confident about moving on to the Dragone Entertainment universe. The swing in my step that I had brought over from the Maldives returned.

By the beginning of October 2009, I was off to Brussels. My new company had spared no expense. A professional driver met me at Brussels International Airport. He escorted me to Antwerp, where all of those working on the Training & Formation phase of the Macau show were stationed.

Our team leader welcomed me at our hotel. Lauren had joined us all the way from Las Vegas, the birthplace of the very first water shows on the planet, *O* and *Le Rêve*.

My new profession was incredibly rare. At the time I joined the game, there were only sixty show divers worldwide. The first water show had opened in 1998. Lauren had been one of the pioneers. During the previous months she had been in charge of training the small contingent of new show divers in Belgium, sharing trade secrets from her eleven years of experience. I was the last of her team to arrive.

"Settle in and get your bearings," she said as she handed me my room key. "You'll start work tomorrow. We'll need to catch you up with the Belgian divers as soon as possible, so you'll be ready to come to Macau with us in four months. Our team will have the honor and tough responsibility to train the other guys in Macau. That's twenty-five future show divers who as of now have never handled or supported a performer underwater. I'll count on you as one of my team to teach them all you know when the time comes. And by then, you better be brilliant!"

As she clapped me on the back and hustled towards her car to head to the studio, I felt intimidated as well as hyped and enthusiastic.

A first look at Antwerp curbed my mettle somewhat. My new surroundings presented a harsh contrast to my turquoise Maldivian paradise. The city of Antwerp is the quintessential urban desert – flat, brown, and grey, with no nature in sight for many miles. In keeping with the prevailing theme of dreariness, my hotel room overlooked the highway and was decorated in varying shades of grey. I did my very best to transform the space with photographs and colorful personal items. Overall, I was in no position to complain. Dragone Entertainment generously provided a hotel studio apartment for each of us. I had not experienced such a high level of civilized comfort in a very long time.

The next morning saw me awakening early and drinking far too much coffee. Our company had designated two rental cars for us five divers. As we would every morning for the next months, we met at 8 a.m. to face the excruciating one-hour commute. Slower than any slug known to man, we crept towards our training facility through one traffic jam after another.

The training studio itself was an amazing structure, providing all necessary infrastructure we could possibly require. Most of the performers were housed in small apartments on the top floor of the studio. The building provided a gym, showers, a professional kitchen, office space, a beautiful terrace on the top floor, as well as a luxurious break room with dining tables, huge flat screen TVs, a pool table, coffee machines, and a cozy couch corner. Everything looked surprisingly warm and welcoming.

As the door to the actual training space opened, I was rendered speechless. The enormous space was seventy-two feet high, two-hundred feet long and a hundred feet wide. The cathedral-like hall was divided into a dry area featuring professional rigging and a soft training floor on one side, and a hundred-foot-long and eighty-two-foot wide swimming pool on the other side. The pool was twelve feet deep. It was painted jet black to get us all used to the backstage conditions we would eventually encounter in our theater in Macau. A training zone covering one third of the pool area simulated the actual theater conditions as closely as possible. In effect, we had our own customized dive center.

I had never seen an athlete or acrobatic performer close-up before. While I was still standing in the open door to my cavernous new work environment, all performers seemed like well-muscled giants. Astonishingly, as I closed the distance between us they seemed to shrink before my very eyes.

The experience was comical, as well as unsettling. It dawned on me that I was seeing a mirage of sorts. My brain was used to an average person's proportions. These young men and women had impossibly muscular bodies, their chests and shoulders bulging under their tight shirts. Their width had led to an illusion of height. As I got closer, it became evident that many performers were, in fact, shorter than me. I had always been one of the shortest guys around, at only five foot six. Here, I seemed to be taller than most. It made perfect sense. In order to fly through the air and perform death-defying, graceful acts in all sorts of positions, performers had to be small. The more mass they had, the harder it would become for them to support their own weight and make their movements graceful and seemingly effortless.

I was mesmerized and immensely curious to learn as much as I could in this fascinating training environment. As I was given a tour of the facilities, people were flying over my head, catapulting through the air, and executing complicated somersaults while jumping from a high dive tower into the dark pool. The atmosphere was charged with creative energy, focused and filled with joyful anticipation.

Each training day would start at 9 a.m., with an excruciating one-hour warm up for the performers. The rest of the day would be filled with alternately practicing everything from high-level acrobatics to dance choreography and underwater skill development – until 7 p.m. I couldn't help but laugh uncontrollably when, at the end of my first day, I witnessed the performers exclaiming their relief at the training day being over while running straight to the gym for another few hours of rigorous, private workout. These people were certainly beyond dedicated – as well as slightly insane.

My first day was rough. Lauren knew I had just come from teaching divers of all experience levels. She nevertheless required me to demonstrate how to retrieve my regulator and clear my mask underwater, a task usually asked only of novices. I felt humiliated, and found myself reacting with utter nervousness over motor skills I would usually be able to perform in my sleep. Needless to say, my performance was disappointing, humiliating me even further.

Getting introduced to my teammates, I could feel it clearly: this team had gelled long before my arrival. Training had commenced six months earlier. I was replacing another Las Vegas show veteran who was being transferred to help with the technical preparations in Macau. As I looked around me, I saw eighty performers and thirty technicians, everyone comfortably settled into their daily routine. Facing Lauren and the three scuba instructors immediately in front of me, I felt as if I was entering a train compartment under the hostile, territorial stares of travelers who had already claimed their space and gotten acquainted.

The three Belgian divers, Gary, Albert, and Jacques were native French speakers. Over the coming months, I had to continuously remind them to switch to English when discussing work-related issues. I seemed to be faced either with a language I couldn't understand well enough, or a secret code between Lauren and my three colleagues.

Instead of putting my foot down, I remained agreeable and patient, feeling lonelier with every passing day. I regressed to behavior patterns of long-forgotten schoolyards, and caught myself trying too hard.

My situation was exacerbated by the fact that our managers in Macau, Warner and Owen, weren't interested in my arrival in Belgium. Far away, on the other side of the world, they neglected to come up with a plan to integrate me into the existing team.

I was left in Lauren's hands. On one hand, she was a very competent instructor. On the other hand, she treated every situation as if we were warriors in the process of infiltrating a hostile country. Lauren's father was a US career soldier with an anger management problem (who had allegedly inspired the main character in Sylvester Stallone's *Rambo*). He had given her a childhood comparable to military boot camp.

Lauren was proud of her upbringing.

"I'm glad my daddy taught me right," she would say. "It's a tough world out there, man. You've gotta be tough and prepared for every eventuality. At home in Vegas, I always sleep with a gun under my pillow."

I could only imagine.

While we crept through endless traffic jams every morning, she was all slogan and catch-phrases.

"We are the best divers in the world!" she would say. "Where we go one, we go all!" and "Just suck it up, man!"

I was all for team work and loyalty, and definitely applauded anyone who could take care of themselves, but all of these clichéd exclamations raised my hackles. I wondered which Hollywood action drama I was stranded in and how long it would be before US Navy Seals stormed our training facility to take out anyone not fiercely loyal to the cause.

One of our daily duties was floating for hours in the pool, while performers catapulted each other from a device called a 'Russian Swing'.

Each swing was a solid monster about ten-feet high. The platform that pushers and fliers stood on was approximately three-feet wide and five-feet long. Made of very heavy, solid metal, it could easily behead someone. One or two pushers would stand on the back, one flier in front. It took an almost incomprehensible level of synchronicity, delicacy, and motor skills for the flier to be catapulted into the air at precisely the right moment, to fly high and far. From the moment the flier was airborne, he would execute complex maneuvers in the air. So as not to break any bones on the hard water surface, he would need to remember where he was relative to the water surface, stay in control, and then finally plunge in just right.

As I observed the performers practice, clumsily fall, survive hard landings, fine-tune, succeed, then continue to fine-tune and work on their tricks again and again, I understood how easily one of them could get killed or paralyzed at any given moment.

My teammates and I floated patiently and calmly in the mysteriously dark pool, far enough away to not impede the proceedings yet close enough to be able to respond within a matter of seconds. We were the response team who, in a worst-case scenario, would make sure a performer ended up "only" paralyzed instead of dead or drowned. The level of responsibility on our shoulders was terrifying.

During my very first week on the job, one of our Russian Swing fliers hesitated for just an instant, lost his precious balance, and fell off the swing at its point of highest energy. He landed directly under the swing. I was nine feet away, floating on the water surface. I watched helplessly as the massive swing platform swung back up and away from the fallen flier, then hurtled back down towards him like a guillotine with the momentum of a freight train. The performer was dazed from the impact of his fall. He lifted his head. The descending platform bore down on him. At the very last instant, another performer managed to push him out of the way. The swing platform missed the fallen flier by inches, hitting the rescuer's arm instead.

That very same day, a performer had died during Russian Swing training at Cirque du Soleil. I was shocked, suddenly understanding fully what I had gotten myself into. A tenth of a second difference and our flier would have died that day, too.

Lauren responded to my emotions after the accident with her usual, "Suck it up man!"

I fully intended to do just that, yet didn't need someone tossing clichés at me at that precise moment. I was a complete novice in the show industry. I needed help in better understanding the incident.

On my way through the grey cityscape towards my even greyer hotel room, I bumped into our high diving coach, Tadek. He had just visited the injured performers at the hospital.

"Don't worry," he said. "Derek is fine. The lucky bastard only chipped his tooth instead of getting decapitated. His rescuer's arm is injured, but it's nothing serious either. We got very lucky."

I was grateful to Tadek for sharing his news and relieved beyond measure.

Clapping me on the back, he said, "You'll be fine. It's a lot to take in at first and sometimes the horizon seems to be as dark as our pool. But trust me, you'll have just as many days when what felt forbidding a day earlier will feel exhilarating and incredibly rewarding. Hang in there."

"Thanks Tadek." I said, feeling much better already.

We hugged and went our separate ways.

Looking past Lauren's posturing, I had to admit she was highly knowledgeable. She taught me many essentials about being a show diver and performer handler. As was often the case in my life, facing someone's continuing disapproval drove me to accomplishments way beyond what I had believed possible. I used her bullying to my advantage, letting it drive me forward, for my own sake and the sake of the performers, instead of letting it destroy me.

One point I agreed with wholeheartedly: we carried an enormous responsibility and needed to do our utmost to ensure performers could trust us with their lives. In order to do their job well, they needed to be sure that, no matter what happened, we would be right by their side when needed, responding instantly even if it meant risking our own lives.

To catch up on six-months' worth of training, I spent every free minute practicing. I forced myself through the underwater obstacle course over and over, training breath-hold techniques, discovering and developing stamina and strength I never knew I possessed. After only a few weeks, Lauren had to grudgingly let me design training sessions for our performers.

"Ok, show me what you can do," she said. "I'll never allow anything though, unless you can expertly demonstrate to me what you want to ask our performers to accomplish."

"Fine by me," I said, and made sure to ace every single exercise we confronted our performers with. Even though I soon performed all tasks required of my position, Warner and Owen steadfastly refused to recognize me officially as a performer trainer.

They answered none of my questions as to why. I went ahead and studied all necessary theory in my off time. I took matters into my own hands and, with the help of local dive centers, obtained all necessary credentials without support from my superiors. Training was why I had signed up for this job in the first place. I was a coach with all my heart and soul. Helping others explore their strengths, giving them support to overcome whatever challenges lay before them, was my greatest passion.

But even though the performers came to trust me implicitly, Warner and Owen emailed me from across the planet, "You will *not* join your Belgian teammates in becoming a trainer for our divers and performers in Macau as planned. You will be an underwater stage hand."

To their credit, my Belgian colleagues also failed to understand why I was being sidelined. It had been a long time since I had felt this lonely and unappreciated. And yet I pushed on.

Our small team had to perform hard physical labor underwater, moving heavy objects or transporting up to four performers on our backs at once. Due to not having a genetically male body, my physical strength had never been quite the same as other men's. Should I tell people about my gender history? No. If I wasn't able to perform my duties like any other man on the team, I would be a liability for my teammates as well as for our performers. I could not let that happen. I gritted my teeth, thought of Lauren's condescending attitude towards me, and pushed myself even harder.

For the first time in my life, I developed bulging biceps and was almost able to see my stomach muscles. Sometimes, I felt as if I might faint underwater and drown, but I never complained or gave up. In our Belgian pool, I grew stronger, tougher, and better with each passing day. I promised myself there and then: I would be the last man standing. I would be damned before I would let Lauren run me off the premises.

Working with our performers was an experience too amazing to pass up without a fight. They were a delightful group of eighty individuals from thirty different countries. Most of them were refreshingly non-judgmental. They challenged me underwater, testing if they could truly count on me to save them, if necessary. I didn't mind and plunged into our daily training sessions without fear.

One exercise had me waiting underwater to catch a performer after he dove in. I would grab him, hand him a mask and my spare regulator then swim him to the edge of the pool, to safety. Besides my own regulator, my equipment featured two alternate air sources for performers in need. The exercise was designed to catch performers one at a time.

One day, six of them jumped at the same time. A second later, they were all floating mid-water, with big grins on their faces. They held out their hands to receive a regulator. I was at a loss how to save them all at the same time. We surfaced, laughing. No one thought less of me for not succeeding on the first attempt.

When all six performers jumped in a second time, I grabbed one on each side of me, handing them one of my alternate air sources. They held onto my shoulder and reached out to their buddies who were still holding their breath beside them. Three performers ended up sharing one regulator on each side of me. They all held on to each other, handing the alternate air source to their buddy after taking a long breath. As they calmly circulated the regulator between themselves, I slowly swam them thirty feet underwater to the edge of the pool. We had successfully managed a six-person rescue with only one diver and two regulators. It was a stunning example of what coordinated teamwork can accomplish.

As I looked out at the dark expanse of water after that session, I felt some of the exhilaration and instant gratification Tadek had promised me would become part of our daily endeavors. I was smiling, my back straight and proud, as pearls of pool water ran over my lean body like thousands of tiny, caressing hands. At that moment, I felt strong and confident enough to tackle an Ironman competition.

The performers' bodies glowed with body heat because their muscles were continuously forming. Their biceps bulged so hard, sometimes my small hands bounced off of their muscles as I tried to get a firm hold to guide them through the water.

No matter how many years they had trained their bodies to do the inconceivable or how death-defying their acrobatic accomplishments on land, though, our performers battled the same fears underwater as everyone else. Unlike other students I had taught however, our artists never gave up. At times they were terrified and hot tears would flow behind their dive masks, but I could see them pull themselves together. They would stop crying, swallow hard, and try again until they learned each skill they needed to master to perfection.

Some of them came to us unable to even swim. Within only a few months, they not only learned to swim better than I ever would, but also learned to scuba dive, free dive, execute costume changes underwater, and rescue each other if necessary.

In one advanced rescue scenario during which we anticipated the cave-like underwater backstage environment in the Macau theater, we asked them to find their way poolside while traveling upside down and one of them guiding the other who is blind-folded. Hookahs – regulators hanging from the ceiling – were spaced in six-foot intervals to provide them with air during this exercise.

Close to panic at first, the performers would learn to calm themselves with regular breathing from an air source at their starting position. The blindfolded one would climb onto the other's back, holding on with all his might. He would place one hand on his guide's shoulder to be able to give him squeeze signals when needed. Then they would set off together, hanging upside down on handrails underneath scaffolding that blocked their way to the surface – just like the ceilings and lifts would in the future. The hookahs were installed along the entire sixty-five-foot distance they needed to cover.

The guiding performer would travel hand-over-hand until he reached the next hookah. He would then take two long breaths. Squeezing his partner once, to let him know he would put the regulator into his mouth a moment later, he would then gently supply his partner with air. Until they felt calm enough to continue being on their way, both the guide and his blindfolded buddy would take turns breathing. As soon as they felt ready, they would give each other a double-squeeze and set off again.

In the space between the hookahs, the performers would need to move relaxed and slow, while continuously releasing small bubbles of air from their lungs so as to not hold their breath underwater and avoid lung-overexpansion injuries.

It was an agonizingly slow process, yet all performers eventually managed to guide as well as be guided the entire distance. The amount of teamwork and trust needed to accomplish this feat for both participants was astronomical. Especially being blindfolded required every ounce of courage, tenacity, calmness, and trust a performer could muster. To not have a continuous air supply strapped to their backs; lose all sense of orientation, time and distance; and not know when the next breath will become available, terrified every single one of them.

Preparing the exercise, I had, of course, gone through the scenario of being blindfolded myself. I had managed, my heart racing, hanging onto my guide and teammate Gary like a baby orangutan to his mother. Each distance between hookahs had felt like a mile for my starving lungs.

Our performers inspired me on a daily basis. Never had I been around a group of people with more passion and dedication to their goal. I had never seen people work harder before in my life. As a direct result of their efforts, they mastered their skills exceptionally well. I felt like a proud father, watching his children literally struggle and bleed, only to emerge better and stronger than ever before. Whenever I faltered, whenever loneliness ate me up, whenever I wanted to scream obscenities at Lauren, I just looked at all the hard-working artists around me. They had pushed the envelope since childhood. No matter how hard it got, they never, ever gave up. Watching them reminded me of my own inherent tenacity and strengthened my resolve.

Being able to observe bodies and souls grow right in front of my eyes, sustained me. At first the performers' bodies and minds were soft, since many of them had not been part of a huge show before. They learned to cope with the harshness of a corporate environment, however, as we all did. As their skin and muscles grew harder, so did their mental stamina. Less blood and fewer tears flowed with each passing day.

Whenever I had a free minute, I would talk with artists and coaches. I would watch as many rehearsals as possible. Straps were a particular favorite of mine. The artists would hang on to long cotton straps with just their hands and arms, flowing through the air in a display of pure poetry in motion. I was in awe. My body had always been an obstacle. Now here I was, surrounded by eighty people for whom the human body was an open portal leading to the top of the world – until, either because of age or multiple injuries, their aches and pains became unbearable and they were forced to retire.

Through daily perseverance, our gymnasts, dancers, high divers, and acrobats had perfected their bodies to a breathtaking extent. As mesmerized as I was by the beauty all around me, I was also confronted on a daily basis with what I could never have. This caused me a deep existential angst. Was it wise to remain in this environment? Instinct told me to persevere and remember my own physical grace and beauty, discovered while gliding through the Indian Ocean.

Tadek, the high-diving coach, became a good friend. The flamboyantly gay, Polish-American was one of only a small handful of people who knew I was trans. Tadek was with me every step of the way without pitying me. We shared our emotional life. He had been a performer as well as an Olympic high-diving champion. His heart knew no boundaries. His sense of humor swept us all away and brightened our days. I loved listening to him coach. Tadek effortlessly managed to combine compassion, good humor, and toughness. If necessary, he could be incredibly strict. He could just as easily hug someone with such intense love that their pain ceased to matter. Tadek knew his performers well. He knew what every single person needed to push them forward.

One day, he caught Eliza in a moment of self-criticism after failing a complicated dive. No one was harder on her than herself.

Tadek looked at her with emphatically raised eyebrows and asked, "Do you know where the train station is?"

Eliza bawled, "I don't want to leave!"

To which Tadek replied, "Well, you can throw yourself in front of a train and end your misery."

Eliza was totally shocked. Then, understanding dawned in her eyes. A small failure was irrelevant. What mattered was to get up and keep going. Tears still streaming from her eyes, she smiled. Tadek had shocked her into moving on. It was tough love, but it worked. It put things in perspective for her, and helped her achieve feats other people could only dream about.

Even though Lauren's approach of constant rebukes was far less motivating, I grew as a diver as well as instructor.

I was still clumsy and stiff on land. But once in the water, I matched the performers' elegance and perfection.

Like Tadek, I was the performers' coach, their biggest supporter, and a shoulder to cry on. They trusted me beyond reproach. It was a hard-earned trust. I worked diligently every single day to gain and preserve it.

Once again, water became a catalyst for a new beginning, a means to transcend boundaries. Working for one of the biggest shows on Earth, I stretched my physical and mental limits more with every passing day.

Still feeling unwanted in Aquatics, I enquired about my performance, honestly looking for pointers. What could I do to improve my skills further?

"I love you, man. I wouldn't trade you for a million bucks," Lauren responded.

Nevertheless, Lauren, Warner and Owen still made no effort to integrate me into the existing team. Despite the performers' unwavering trust in me, our Aquatics management remained firm in their earlier decision of removing me from the team of trainers as soon as we reached Macau.

"You won't be allowed to continue teaching like your teammates. Just suck it up man," Lauren said with an indifferent shrug of her shoulders.

Depression and loneliness began to overwhelm me. Quitting never seriously crossed my mind, though I couldn't help but wonder if, despite all the positives, I had landed on the wrong planet. Warner was ex-US-military. So was Lauren in a manner of speaking. There were no women on the team in Belgium, and the only women on the team in Macau would eventually be a female Israeli soldier and a butch Corsican.

During our carpools, Lauren irritated me to no end. She kept trying to indoctrinate me with her ideas of who I should become. She explained why she felt I wouldn't quite make the cut.

"Liam, you're too soft-spoken. It's a tough gang over there in Macau. Good hearts though. Still, they won't respect you if you don't toughen up. They won't listen to you if you don't talk louder."

To keep the peace, I let her ramble on, and enlighten me with stories of how she had rescued people in the Nevada wilderness and stood up to guys much tougher than her. What I saw in her was a judgmental bully. Needless to say, I didn't bother telling her anything about my history. I thought of saying, "Yes, I'm soft-spoken and gentle, but I'm far from weak. Our performers trust me precisely because of who I am." But it seemed a waste of time to defend myself.

I tried being immune to all she said, but have to admit I wasn't strong enough. The more time passed, the more Lauren got to me. I reached the point of being scared shitless and fearing the worst for Macau. It seemed I had plunged into my deepest stereotypical nightmare, and despite my passion for coaching our performers and my admiration for our show, my instincts screamed at me: "Get out. Now. You are headed for military boot camp – or something painfully close to it."

To make matters worse, once in Macau, we would be provided with a communal shower and locker room. I had never been in one before. Like many years earlier when I had panicked and given up on my chance at becoming a zoo animal handler, the thought of having to share a locker room with dozens of boisterous bio-males made me cringe.

In our Belgian training facilities, I was able to avoid the locker rooms most of the time. I used a dark corner of our dive center to quickly change clothes and only took showers in my hotel room. In the Maldives, the prudishness of the religion practiced all around me had protected me. In showers and locker rooms without doors or shower curtains, where everyone happily mingled in their muscular nakedness, I would have no choice but to be the odd one out who seeks the privacy of a toilet cubicle to get changed. I couldn't possibly drop my pants and stand there exposed and soaping away, revealing my penislessness to the world. I wasn't sure if I was ready for a coming out of that magnitude – or if my colleagues were, for that matter.

My mind started to become so overwhelmed with worry, I decided to seek professional help. I found a therapist in Antwerp. Talking to her helped. She couldn't provide solutions, but at least she listened non-judgmentally. I could let all my anxiousness flow out freely and deal with it.

My concern wasn't so much with the performers. They seemed genuinely open-minded towards anything. I was concerned with my, allegedly very rough, fellow technicians in Aquatics. The locker room situation I could deal with, but what if they were all as soldier-like during every day life and work as Lauren had suggested? How would we communicate with each other? I had always been an artist and philosopher at heart, not a fighter. As much as I loved water, this time it seemed I might end up in an environment detrimental to my overall wellbeing.

Imminent departure loomed in January 2010, when suddenly, to my utter delight – and everyone else's disappointment – it was announced that our departure had to be delayed due to technical difficulties.

Our project was one of the most daring in the history of performance. An enormous theater was being custom-built, featuring an auditorium with two thousand seats, a one-hundred-and-sixty-five-foot high ceiling and the biggest circular pool in the world, holding five million gallons of water.

Chinese work crews had been busy building this behemoth of a theater for months. When the creators deemed the construction concluded, they ordered the pool to be filled with water for the first time and all lifts moved up and down to test range of motion. Water displacement in this huge body of water was enormous, and thus a major design-flaw was discovered: no one had thought of building gutters able to handle the thousands of gallons of overflowing water displaced by the lifts.

To everyone's horror, the entire basement had been flooded, destroying major electrical systems. Parts of the pool system needed to be re-designed, leaving us stranded in Belgium for another three months.

As disastrous as it may have been for Dragone Entertainment, for me, the delay meant a precious extension, giving me a chance to train even further, making sure I mastered all skills perfectly so I could stand up to scrutiny in Macau, soft-spoken or not. I also planned to invest considerable time in relaxing and making myself happy.

I had always stood back politely, letting my Belgian colleagues use our rental cars. Now, I began asking for the car every two weeks.

I hadn't driven a car in over seven years, ever since I had opted for selling my vehicle in favor of buying more plane tickets for Alana and me. In the Maldives, there weren't any cars, let alone any traffic.

In Northern Europe, streets are icy in January. On the first weekend my teammates left me the car, I waited until 2 a.m. before I dared take it for a ride. I started battling with clutch and gears in the hotel parking lot, making the car look more like a bucking kangaroo then a Volkswagen. After half an hour of exhuming forgotten motor skills, I started to rediscover the perfect balance between clutch and gas.

I set off into the Antwerp night, driving around the deserted town for hours until the first wave of a sleepy work force started populating the streets. Utterly exhausted, I fell into bed that morning and slept way into the afternoon. Teaching myself how to drive again had been liberating beyond measure. I could almost taste the freedom of exploring European highways, a task I needed to tackle before it was too late.

Back at the studio after my weekend, I renewed my resolution to focus on the good things in my life.

For many reasons, lunch used to be my favorite time in the training studio. It was a time of mingling together amiably, without the pressure of having to be at the top of our game.

The kitchen chef, Lyna, was an irreplaceable presence in all our lives. She always knew who needed to be comforted and who would benefit from an extra snack to soothe their soul.

Lyna and I became friends, offering each other what no one else could give us during the harsh training days. We took every opportunity to meet for delicious breakfasts in local bakeries, pouring our hearts out and helping each other cope with that day's company politics.

Even though I was well liked amongst the performers it took a long time to build any close friendships. Everyone was far too busy with their own lives. So it was a pleasant surprise when I hit it off with two performers, Naya and Noel.

Naya was a dancer, Noel an acrobat. Both were closer to my age than most of the other artists. Noel had scared me at first. He was a muscular giant from former Eastern Germany who had grunted at me every now and then in passing. Naya was a refreshingly unpretentious soul, breathtakingly gorgeous, with no awareness of her beauty.

Naya suffered through many problems during our underwater training. She experienced frequent panic attacks ending inevitably in tears. I decided to sacrifice my lunch breaks to help her. With the pressure of her fellow performers waiting in line behind her removed, she visibly relaxed. We practiced relaxing breath-hold techniques to help her slowly gain confidence in her abilities.

Our successful sessions brought us closer and we started to spend our off time together. Naya would bring Noel along. Surprisingly, the muscular giant turned out to be a sensitive man who was able to talk about his feelings and had a charming, dry sense of humor to boot. Noel, Naya and I began spending countless hours relaxing in movie theaters, clowning around in our 3-D glasses, and munching popcorn. Being with them gave me the beautiful sense of belonging I had craved ever since I had thrown myself into the new universe at Dragone Entertainment.

When Naya needed to bring her cats from her former home in Paris to Belgium, she was told she wouldn't be allowed to have animals in her small apartment at the training studio. Being a fervent animal lover, I instantly offered to take care of her cats in my hotel apartment until we departed.

Suddenly, two gray cats populated my gray accommodation. Other than fitting the hotel décor in color, they were far from dreary. Their charming, joyful bounding around made me intensely happy. It felt good to be needed.

In addition to going to therapy, caring for the cats and cultivating my friendships, I went on several long-distance weekend road trips, visiting Dad, and exploring France, Northern Germany, Holland and Luxemburg to soothe my disquieted mind.

Since I was feeling more fulfilled, the three months until our March departure passed astonishingly quickly.

Belgian Aquatics was scheduled to fly out first. The performers and most other technicians would follow together on a flight three days later.

Our flight to Hong Kong was uneventful. My teammates, Lauren, and I quietly hurtled towards our destination. Slouched in my seat, I tried to raise my spirits by watching one in-flight movie after another. I wanted to experience Macau but at the same time still dreaded it with all my heart. My optimism took over halfway into the flight. I had never been to Southeast Asia and felt excited to explore new territory.

As we descended into Hong Kong, I stared out the window, mostly ignoring the looming skyscrapers while instead absorbing the beautiful sight of hundreds of small, green islands surrounded by the dark blue water of the South China Sea.

From the airport, we boarded a speed ferry to Macau. Racing over the ocean, my heart filled with happiness. This subsided somewhat as the blue ocean water turned an earthy, impenetrable brown, the closer we got to Macau. The blue Hong Kong skies gave way to a hazy, grey-brown sky. I felt intrigued and disquieted at the same time.

Upon our arrival at the Macau ferry terminal, Warner, Owen, and five team leaders greeted us. The initial hugs and friendly handshakes gave me hope. Maybe this wouldn't be so bad?

Unfortunately, as soon as we sat down for welcoming drinks, Warner opened his mouth.

"You need to understand, I'm an asshole and I'll make your life here as difficult as possible. As long as you do exactly what you're told, you should be just fine."

Instead of turning on my heel, I renewed my vow from months earlier: I would outlast them all and remain the last man standing. I loved my new profession and would overcome whatever obstacles might materialize in front of me.

Dragone Entertainment had booked hotel rooms for ten days. I spent the first three days exploring town and looking for apartments.

Macau was incredibly ugly and grey, filled with casinos and a lingering stench of pollution. Nevertheless, the small street markets and vendors selling local hot pot meals smelled enchanting. I had missed the Asian potpourri of scents and chaotic noises.

Naya, Noel and I had discussed sharing an apartment together. It gave me comfort to have friends with me who would give me the strength to survive this brave new world.

On the early evening of the third day, my last booster shot arrived at the hotel in the form of two fully packed buses. As the bus doors opened, our performers tumbled out and I found myself with tears in my eyes. I had missed this highly energetic, charismatic group of people from all over the world. I realized how much they had taken a hold of my heart during the intensive training sessions of the last six months.

Now that they had arrived, Macau seemed far less drab and forbidding. The sun seemed to shine more warmly that evening. My worried heart started to feel the first stabs of excitement and wonder. The biggest water show on Earth, its creation, premiere, and operation – many unknowns lay ahead of us.

The nomad and adventurer in me couldn't help but feel intensely alive. I began to smile and finally enjoyed the glorious moment of arriving in an entirely new culture and work environment.

29

Pearl River Delta

On the evening of the arrival of our performers, my friends Noel, Naya and I celebrated our reunion with a delicious dinner. The next day was going to be my first official work day in the Dragone Theater. As I fought off waves of uneasiness, I held onto their friendship like a drowning man to a buoy in a stormy ocean.

Early the following morning, my Belgian Aquatics colleagues and I took a cab to the Cotai Strip where the "City of Dreams" casino complex was located. We were shell-shocked about the way we had been welcomed by our head of department, Warner, and huddled close together on our way to the theater like a group of new boys on their way to a spooky schoolyard.

Nothing we had seen on photographs prepared us for the dimensions of the Dragone Entertainment Theater. It was a purpose-built venue that had been five years in the planning. Everything in it was larger than life. The auditorium featured two thousand seats. The stage was such a large expanse, it would be hard to fill it with the eighty performers we currently had. The dry stage consisted of eight lifts that could each move independently, enabling us to in the future open the stage and unveil a large body of water. At thirty feet deep and one hundred and sixty-five feet across, it would be like a dark miniature ocean. Filtering systems for a pool this size had to be invented. The pumps to operate the lifts had been taken from aircraft carriers. The sealant used for the underwater lighting bubbles had been acquired from the US Navy who used it for their submarines. The lifts could carry up to sixty tons, which was fortunate, since our show would feature an enormous pirate ship weighing roughly thirty tons. The grid above the stage was one hundred and sixty-five feet high and stacked with the best rigging, automation, lighting, sound, and special effects equipment money could buy. Two hundred and fifty million US dollars had already been spent on the development of our colossus, and we weren't even performing yet.

Our first day started with a tour through the theater. The stage pool was empty. Without performers and water to give this vast space a soul, the circular theater looked eerily like a smaller version of Star Wars' *Death Star*.

Most of the aftermath of the flood that had delayed our arrival had been repaired. But we were still a few months away from starting rehearsals in our theater. All technicians, us clueless newcomers included, would be given crash courses in carpentry and metal work so we would be able to pitch in with whatever pool repairs and reconstruction remained.

Our small Belgian Aquatics contingent stood on the immense stage surrounded by state-of-the-art technology, and stared into the almost incomprehensible space. We were given schedules, hard hats, steel-toed boots and thick leather gloves. Our boss, former GI Warner, seemed to enjoy our discomfort. As the day came to a close, he joyously barked into the technological void, announcing our early morning starting times for the next day's operations.

In Belgium, the inspiring camaraderie within the group of performers had sustained me. We had all worked together in one large room. No matter what their relationships had been in private, while on the job the performers had given each other feedback and support. If a new trick worked after weeks of hard work, they clapped and cheered for each other. Belgium reminded me of the show family I had dreamed of years earlier when standing behind a dark curtain, watching the cast and crew of Cirque du Soleil's Alegría in the movie theater.

While still training in Belgium, our artistic director had told the excited performers, "You will make your mark. You will infuse your soul into the very walls of the building you perform in."

Looking at the vastness of space we would now inhabit, with its ten floors segregating departments and people that had, up until then, worked together in closest proximity, I wondered how strong our souls would need to be to breach technology and space of this magnitude. Our venue in Macau was gigantic, beautiful and visionary, challenging the boundaries of every limitation known to theater professionals. By its very nature, it also challenged the collaborative effort that lies at the heart of theater.

Since construction was still ongoing, our performers were sent away for vacation. The ensuing weeks were a nightmare. As we labored on in the bowels of what was supposed to become a home to fairy tales and magic, I felt bereft of the enchanting people who gave this entire enterprise its essence and meaning.

Naya and Noel were only away for a few days of vacation. Still, due to my schedule, we hardly saw each other. I missed having more time with them. As we searched for apartments during our first week in Macau, it proved hard to find places suitable for the three of us. In addition to the challenge of one hundred Dragone employees searching for the same thing at the same time in a small housing market, most apartments featured only a single master bedroom. All other rooms were just big enough for a bed and I dreaded being so limited in my personal space. I opted for independence and rented a small studio apartment in Coloane, the green lung of Macau.

I still needed Naya and Noel, though. I felt so lost, I couldn't imagine coping without their friendship. Thankfully both were loyal companions and Macau distances were short and easy to overcome.

The realm of Aquatics was on the first basement level. It was a dungeon beyond measure. Warner, being an ex-soldier, had hired thirty people who would have been more suited as mercenaries fighting a war in some remote jungle. It was a rough gang of commercial divers, ex-soldiers, and instructors, just as Lauren had predicted.

Just before we had left Belgium, Warner and the main trainer, Owen had threatened to fire me because I had asked too many questions and seemed too soft for their taste. I had been pushed far into the defensive and was now way too tense and self-conscious.

I soon realized I wasn't the only person wary of my surroundings. Warner had driven his Macau team with a hard hand for months, instilling an unhealthy level of aggression and competitiveness in his divers. Like abused children, everyone cramped up as soon as Warner and Owen raised their voices. Lauren knew both men from Las Vegas and her tough-chick attitude went a long way. The rest of us Belgian divers were speechless as well as severely disenchanted.

We were split into six teams. The hierarchy was very much like a military operation with senior officers, junior officers and common foot soldiers. I was assigned to Blue Team as a common foot soldier, which almost led me to look for a new favorite color.

Imagine the worst schoolyard bully of your childhood. Now multiply it by three and top it off with a conflict-averse team leader. My team was at each other's throats – usually mine – over the tiniest of occurrences. Our team leader was a relaxed Southern American individual who had already worked at water shows in Las Vegas. Under different circumstances he would have been my favorite superior. Stuck together in Blue Team hell, I wished he would stop being so non-confrontational, take charge and put an end to the obvious bullying and aggression which above all had no place in a theater backstage environment.

An aggressive bitch from Corsica who seemed to take emancipation to a whole new level; a female soldier from the Israeli army who was not only psychopathically confrontational but also very young and immature; and last but not least, an overweight British tough guy with anger management issues – these were the characters that ruled Team Blue. I couldn't wait for the pool to be filled with water; at least once submerged, they would have to shut up.

Years later, I met the assistant head of department who had survived only the first few months of our operation.

"Warner wanted you gone," he admitted. "He figured the easiest way to get rid of a sensitive guy like you would be to stick you into his most dysfunctional and aggressive team."

As for the rest of the Aquatics team at the time, I found no one I could confide in. My three Belgian colleagues were as traumatized as I was but were by far the better politicians, as well as being accustomed to roughhousing with other guys. An Aquatics military consultant who seemed at first very caring turned out to be interested in my state of mind only for the purpose of gathering inside intelligence about the emotional state of our performers. When I refused to deliver, he retreated into the shadows.

Everyone was busy being as tough as they could be. Since we weren't in a war zone but in a theater, I failed to see the point. The head of rigging summed the situation up quite nicely by wearing a hard hat adorned with jungle leaves, plastic frogs, and a sign bearing the message "Art is not an Emergency". I couldn't have agreed more.

Warner, Owen, Lauren, and all the other bullies failed to understand the true meaning of strength. Ever since I had started in Belgium, I had been told over and over again I wasn't tough enough, wasn't man enough. What did it mean to be a man? Was it even important? I honestly didn't think so. As for courage and toughness, I knew I had only come so far because endurance, tenacity, and courage had been faithful partners throughout my journey.

I had never been able to identify with military minds. Now in the face of our homophobic underwater soldiers at theater boot camp, I couldn't help but provoke them just a bit by throwing in the odd comment of wanting to adorn my locker with pink flowers and thinking of painting some of the bare walls of our department in bright rainbow colors. It amused me to put them off-balance. It was a subtle way to get under their skin without reciprocating their aggressive behavior. I was going to be better than that.

So I invested a lot of energy in being bright and cheerful, no matter how ugly some confrontations were. I refused to let them see how much they got to me. Maybe I should have turned around right then, but my own breed of warrior's heart refused to give up so easily. They may not know about true integrity and passion, but I did. I would outlive them all.

Our locker room was small and crowded, harboring twenty-five men. It was gloomy and forbidding. I wasn't only joking when I talked about decorating. We desperately needed a little color in our lives to cheer everyone up. In an attempt to start a positive trend, I decorated my locker with pictures of colorful reef fish. Minutes later, I had Warner leaning over me and breathing into my face.

"No pictures allowed. I remember saying that quite clearly. I'll give you exactly ten seconds to get rid of this crap, boy!"

I grudgingly did it in fifteen.

The locker room became a daily thorn in my side. Now thirty-nine years of age, I found it hard to share such a personal space and adapt to the overall new experience.

I obviously hadn't missed much. It was all boobs, beer, lady-boy remarks and homophobic jokes. I knew the guys were half as bad as they sounded but it was still hard for me to get past the talk. Banter was an acquired taste, as it turned out. The guys loved posturing and playfully having a go at each other. Not having any practice, I simply couldn't tell the jokes apart from the insults. I couldn't help but feel lost and threatened most of the time.

The Aquatics team ended up helping with theater construction for three months. The initial, local work crews had not only forgotten gutters and caused a flood, but also seemed to have missed the fact that they were building a pool. All the metal they had used needed replacing with stainless steel.

Pipes with a two-foot diameter would eventually have water pumped through them at high speed. They had been installed without buffers to help soften the violent vibrations and keep the pipes from slamming into the pool's concrete walls. To avoid disasters during our future shows, we needed to place padding between the pipes and the walls all around the pool.

Our construction months were spent welding, cutting Chemgrate for the pool floor, and replacing thousands of already-rusted, small metal parts. Several divers got injured. Cutting Chemgrate was the worst. As we were cutting, the flimsy carpentry protection masks couldn't keep the fine, abrasive fiberglass dust from entering our lungs. Some divers were cutting for hours and ended up coughing blood for weeks afterward.

Working at height was an especially terrifying experience for me. Our semi-militaristic management did not allow for weakness of any kind. Admitting to fear would brand someone forever, opening them up to further harassment. Clenching my fists, I forced myself through every minute of working at the edge of an abyss.

We arrived at the end of construction and the moment of truth: the re-filling of the theater pool with five million gallons of water. This time we hoped there would be no nasty surprises.

The show opening was set for September 2010, exactly one year later than originally planned. Our artists were now all back from sun-tanning on Philippine beaches and were brimming with impatience. Our director was due to arrive any minute to start the process of what in the show world is called "creation" – the bringing together of all post-production planning, creative input, technology, and human talent during months of rehearsals to shape a magnificent collaborative work of art on stage.

The monstrous pumps in the deep basement of our theater worked at full power for six hours, filling the large body of water to the brim. The *Death Star* disappeared, becoming a soulful, black, indoor ocean. For the first time, I got a sense of why I was here. Surrounded by the cheerful anticipation of our performers and the fresh scent of water, I relaxed and felt more at home in this rough world of metal beams and grids.

Technicians swarmed around the pool and stage while others checked for flooding in the basement, but we had indeed arrived at our final destination. This time, when the lifts were moved up and down the entire depth of the pool, the gutters caught all overflowing water with a cheerful gurgle. Water temperature was set for eighty-six degrees Fahrenheit. Within hours, our Aquatics basement became a tropical comfort zone. Steel-toed boots and sweaters were exchanged for flip-flops and t-shirts.

It was time to get wet. The divers looked at the dark, forbidding water, containing only chemicals and pipes, with a deep longing in their eyes that could only be brought on by months of being swallowed up in the dry belly of a monster. Diving into the biggest pool in the world would easily wash off the Chemgrate residue, sawdust, motor oil, and blood of the previous months.

We had seen computer animations of what awaited us in the cave that was to be our underwater theater environment. Nothing prepared me for the unique power and beauty beneath the ceilings, pipes, and lifts, though. As the lighting changed in the theater, the color of the water changed into a million hues of myriad colors. Billions of tiny bubbles referred to as "masking" transformed the dark water into a living entity. The moving lifts stunned us with their stealth while at the same time creating powerful currents. The water was crystal clear, enabling us to see the entire distance across one hundred and sixty-five feet to the opposite side of the circular pool.

The end of construction ended some of our pain. But we remained entangled in the power games exquisitely played by our managers, Warner and Owen. Bringing their experience from Las Vegas they, including Lauren, were the only people who truly knew what needed to be done underwater. Consequently, no one controlled them. No one from upper theater management set foot into the basement to see what was going on in Aquatics.

Owen was the perfectionistic master of underwater performer handling. Unfortunately, he did not possess the character to deal humbly with his achievement of being a show pioneer. Instead he became obsessive, possessive, and abusive towards we novice show divers who were entering the dark realm of an underwater backstage for the first time in our lives.

Our enthusiasm and willingness to look up to as well as learn from him were rewarded with imperious contempt. Incapable of trusting anyone but himself, Owen hardly slept and looked increasingly like an apparition.

Warner had been a show diver and special effects technician in Las Vegas. When offered the challenge to become the head of department for Aquatics in a project ten times the size of the world's first water shows, Warner had gladly accepted. With every passing month, he became more overwhelmed by his responsibilities and the subtle tap dance of corporate politics. At first, he struck me as a demented monster. Later I realized that, much like me, he detested the dishonest maneuverings necessary for survival in our shark-infested, corporate show waters. Both Warner and Owen's nerves were frayed to the point of breaking. Much of their aggression towards us was rooted in their being in over their heads.

With the imminent arrival of Alexander, the creator of our show, everyone in management was like a crazed squirrel who had chugged far too many Red Bulls. Stories of Alexander were spread through the house, warning artists and technicians alike in much the same manner children would be kept in line with stories of the bogeyman.

Warner and Owen prepared for Alexander's arrival by conducting frantic pool training sessions with performers as well as show divers, to ready them for the coming challenges. I was left at the sidelines during these sessions, forced to watch my three Belgian colleagues conduct the training while the performers, oblivious to the dark political games, still found every opportunity to come to me for underwater advice.

I decided to keep the performers' best interest at the forefront of my mind. After all, my main responsibility was to them. I would keep quiet and follow orders unless an artist specifically asked me to help or I witnessed actions endangering performer safety. I had the deepest respect for these people who would jump daily into the unknown, out of breath from exertion on stage. Blind without a mask underwater and starving for air, they entrusted us with their lives, counting on one of us to be there to catch them and bring them out of the water to safety backstage.

Apart from training each other and the performers, we spent many hours familiarizing ourselves with the underwater theater environment.

We needed to set props on lifts within seconds, then get clear of the lifts as swiftly as possible to allow for them to come up to surface level, revealing to the audience whatever the next scene would hold – a giant pirate ship, a pagoda, a bridge, or Russian swings. The ship weighed thirty tons and was equipped with telescopic masts that moved with hydraulic pressure and could be raised to a height of thirty-six feet. Other props were lighter but could still trap a diver and severely injure him if he was caught unaware.

Warner and Owen became ever more overwrought, pushing their divers to their limits. I reacted to their continuing unwillingness to include me in anything of substance by volunteering for everything. Since I was often one of only few volunteers, they had no choice but to let me run with it.

On one particularly horrific day of preparing for Alexander's arrival, my fellow Blue Team diver Mark, and I came in on our day off and helped to move and test all underwater props. We spent eleven hours underwater without being granted a single break. We changed scuba tanks every two hours and went straight back to the bottom of the pool at thirty feet down, pulling heavy equipment, setting and striking props.

After eight hours, I was reaching my physical limits. It was one of the few moments during which Mark overcame his anger issues and became supportive. During a brief rest on the backstage water surface, he urged me on.

"Don't give them the satisfaction. They'll see it as a weakness if you take a break now."

I pushed on and together with Mark made it all the way to the end of the eleventh hour with no break and no food or drink. When we came out of the water, I could see a hint of grudging respect in Warner and Owen's features. I was beyond caring what they were thinking though, as well as beyond letting them turn my life in this beautiful theater into a living hell. I had been gripped by the magic of backstage, had been enchanted by the beautiful trust and wide range of positive human emotions I experienced every day while working with the artists. To survive, I needed to focus on the beauty, greatness, perseverance, dedication and passion all around me. While my body worked in the dark basement, my soul needed to stay accessible to light, to motivation and inspiration.

Warner was unpredictable. From one moment to the next, he would turn from nice uncle to choleric psychopath. During pirate boat rehearsals one day, Celeste, one of our performers asked if I could bring her some tape she needed for wrist protection. I grabbed a roll and swam the short distance from the edge of the stage towards the boat.

"Boy, get your ass back here right now, " roared Warner.

Both Celeste and I stared at him in shock and confusion. Stunned, I opened my mouth and started to say, "Yes, I'll be right back…"

But Warner was beside himself, face turning red.

"You shut your mouth or I'll shut it for you," he continued to roar. "You get right back here to the side of the pool. No one here goes anywhere without my permission."

I am sure he was worried about my safety on stage, yet the delivery of his message was disheartening to say the least.

Even after very long workdays, Warner would insist on one-hour meetings late at night to go over the day's events. One evening, someone must have gotten bored listening to our boss and created a small doodle on the daily sign-in sheet.

The next morning, Warner went into a mindless rage.

"I'll have to hand this piece of paper to human resources at some point and won't be made a fool! If you insist on acting like children, then that's how I'll treat you. Get your asses over here right now, all of you!"

During the following five minutes, Warner and Owen towered over us and forced us to get in an orderly line outside the Aquatics office. Then we were ordered inside one-by-one to re-sign a fresh sign-in sheet. What planet was I on again? I couldn't remember. Never had I experienced more absurd or humiliating actions.

Every day brought with it other degrading incidents. Had I signed up to become a Navy Seal, I would have expected this type of behavior by my superiors to be part of the process. In a theater, however, where a beautiful creation would soon be underway, I found myself at a loss for words.

It took all my energy to stay hopeful and positive. Performers remained my inspiration. They never gave up, no matter how hard it got for them. I had to look after them, and wouldn't be able to do so while wallowing in despair. For their sake, I needed to keep going, with all the positive power I could muster. During their training, they needed to feel safe. A simple smile from one of us on a hard day could make all the difference for their performance on stage. I was determined to be their rock in the heavy surf of our indoor ocean.

Macau's eternal brownish haze did not help our general disposition in the very limited time we were granted off. Everything was brown. Pollution reached us from Mainland China, making it impossible to see very far on even the clearest of days. The Macau hills disappeared underneath a dirty brown veil and the air felt as hard to breathe as the Chemgrate dust during pool construction. The water surrounding the tiny, self-administrative Region of Macau reminded me more of a gigantic cup of hot chocolate than an ocean, but without the cozy cheerfulness. The ironically-named Pearl River Delta enveloping the small landmass of Macau was a toxic, ocean/river of sludge. Taking a swim off of one of Macau's beaches never even crossed my mind.

But I still found walking along the coastline and gazing out at the un-pearly Delta reassuring. One day, I even came upon a pod of Chinese white dolphins that were hunting for fish.

From then on, I spent as much of my free time walking along Macau's dirty beaches as possible. As I looked out over the water, I wondered what other treasures were hidden underneath the murky waves.

Often, I would spend my mornings as pleasantly as possible with breakfast on the rooftop, enjoying the wide brown yonder. I would convince myself that the meager Macau forests were beautiful and that the Pearl River Delta was far better than having no ocean at all.

On the streets, I would convince myself that the grumpy, introverted nature of the general Macau populace was in fact only my faulty perception due to misunderstanding their culture.

Once in the theater, I would connect with the people I cared about and every so often, whenever I was close to slamming the door behind myself and never setting foot in our behemoth of a building again, I would walk out into the auditorium of our magnificent theater before work, inhaling its beauty and promising myself it would all be worth it.

The small studio apartment I had rented was delightful. It had been beautifully renovated and was one of six apartments in a village house, which had been painted a dreamy light blue. The other five apartments were populated with fellow artists and technicians from our show. In the evenings, we would meet casually on the rooftop and enjoy the romantic view across the river to Mainland China, while sipping on relaxing red wine.

To find a sense of belonging and peace, I adopted half of Macau's shelter occupants. I adopted a cat and her two kittens and named them Boo, Bocelli, and Lara. Unfortunately Lara died soon after from a neurological disorder. An aquarium of colorful fish and clumsy turtles were next. The first pair of turtles were named Bonnie and Clyde due to their murderous tendencies towards my aquarium fish. The second pair of turtles, when held together, curiously resembled a walnut, which made naming them Wal and Nut an obvious choice. There were days I wished I could plunge into the colorful little water world in that small tank to escape the treacherous tank full of corporate sharks at work.

On our days off, Naya, Noel and I often walked across the border into the neighboring Chinese town of Zhuhai. I could find nothing enticing about the bustling Chinese metropolis, except cheap, black market DVDs and colorful street markets.

In one street market, I happened to find a pet store. Curiosity led me inside, where I was faced with sick parrots chained to small perches as well as other small animals languishing in cages way too small for their bodies. A young Red-lored Amazon parrot batted his eyes at me. The little green bird snuggled onto my shoulder and refused to leave. I contemplated for an hour, well aware that owning a parrot meant a seventy-year commitment in most cases. His natural charm won me over, though, and I bought him.

I was presented with a small technical problem: it was illegal to bring animals across the border from Mainland China to Macau. The street vendor assured me it would be easy to smuggle my little friend. We pulled a hood over the parrot's head and restricted his movements by placing him inside a soft pouch. Little Onion, as I decided to call him because of his already apparent countless layers of personality, stayed stock still and quiet. We then placed the pouch complete with bird inside a crude shopping bag I casually swung at my side. At the border, I was processed swiftly and cursorily. Onion didn't let out a peep and thus entered the colorful casino world of our gambling Mecca in a dirty plastic bag.

My little zoo kept me sane throughout my years in Macau. Whenever I felt close to my breaking point, all I needed to put life back into perspective was an evening and morning at home, surrounded by my lively menagerie.

I converted an entire room of my apartment into an aviary for Onion. No matter how hard I was working, I always took him out for several hours each day so he could be with me. He purred and sat on my shoulder, snuggling as close to my neck as he could. But the older he got, the more apparent it became that he was bored and needed much more company than I was able to give. Onion became increasingly frustrated and aggressive.

As his attacks on me intensified, my nerves became increasingly frayed. The immense pressure at work brought me to my limits each and every day. At home, I needed balance and tranquility. I was heartbroken to have to let go of my little green friend, yet also relieved when friends of mine adopted Onion and gave him the home of a parrot's dreams. In turn, with just the cats quietly snuggling with me on the couch, the peacefulness I so desperately needed in order to survive my Macauan adventure was restored.

30

Macau Pool

June 2010 was the start of a new era at the Macau theater. Our infamous creator, Alexander, arrived. Three hundred cast and crew were bracing themselves for four months of working with an obsessed genius.

From day one, Alexander required all cast and crew to be on standby for up to fourteen hours a day. It turned out that, on most days, the show divers were not needed. We spent our time confined in the aqua coulisses, which was the name for the main entry points to the underwater realm. All-in-all, there were four, one from each backstage section.

I found myself cooped up in a space the size of a closet with my less-than-delightful Blue Team members. Their levels of aggression were blooming to new heights now that the pressure of proving their worth to the great Alexander was upon them. After only a few days of their constant negativity and aggression, I was ready to pull my hair out.

Three vomitories, narrow, partially-hidden passages, led from backstage onto the stage. My team leader grudgingly allowed me to slip out of my scuba gear during standby and wait in the vomitory closest to our aqua coulisse. As soon as we were called, it would take me only seconds to run the thirty feet back to my hyper-aggressive team, slip into my gear, and submerge for whatever action Alexander needed us to perform.

Thus followed four of the most intense months of my life. We worked six days a week, fourteen hours a day. Whereas others quietly sat drooling in a corner waiting for their next call, I spent every free minute on the vomitory, watching Alexander's creation process first-hand from outside his line of sight. Witnessing the artistic endeavors on stage gave me all the inspiration I needed to weather through whatever indignities Warner, Lauren, Owen, or any other of the soldier boys and girls decided to throw at me.

Halfway through creation, our artistic director, Manuel, joined almost one hundred performers at our house, for a rooftop barbecue.

During a tour through my apartment, seeing how much he loved it, I surprised myself by offering, "It's yours, if you want it."

Manuel was shocked. "Why? What's going on, Liam?"

I was deeply unhappy in the Aquatics boot camp atmosphere and had reached a point where the daily indignities far outweighed the worthwhile moments. I realized that to save myself, I needed to set a limit of how much I was willing to endure for a profession – no matter how glamorous and intriguing it might be.

I told Manuel everything: our working conditions at Aquatics; my gender identity; my terror of being found out by the wrong people; and my realization of having ended up with a group of people in our theater with whom I shared nothing but a love for water. I was a passionate artist at heart, a romantic, a dreamer, and a humanitarian. But even though I felt isolated from my fellow divers, I loved working with our performers and loved our show and the overwhelming presence of water in it. The creativity and the bold vision of it all touched my heart. I was at a loss of what to do.

Manuel understood. "I'm glad you confided in me, Liam. Of course the decision is yours, but give it a little longer. Don't give up. I'll be there for you whenever you need me."

My resolve was strengthened by his compassion as well as by the magical night on our rooftop. I could feel the soul and the essence of what kept me involved in the show. Towards midnight, fifty artists performed impromptu body percussion under the stars, conducted by Manuel. Macau's Coloane village erupted with the choreographed thunder of clapping, stomping, and other unique noises I would never have believed the human body capable of producing. I cried tears of happiness and gratefully soaked up the positive energy all around me.

One week later, Dragone Entertainment fired Warner. A month after that, our sublime head trainer Owen suffered a nervous breakdown and fled to recuperate in a psychiatric hospital in Thailand. Some weeks later, Lauren went back to Las Vegas – thankfully. Suddenly, we were an army without any officers.

An African-American named Max took over our department. Intriguingly, Max had been one of the divers Warner and Owen had most disrespected. Massive rumors surrounded Warner's demise and Max's rise to power. Some said Warner had been a violent racist on top of being a choleric tyrant, and had made Max's life almost unbearable. Others said, Max had skillfully waged an intricate political war against Warner during the preceding months and had finally won. I didn't care one way or the other. I just felt immense relief at the absence of constant aggression in the form of a nervous Owen and a raging Warner.

And, I was glad. The bullies had, in fact, *not* made it. I had ended up outlasting them all and it hadn't even taken very long.

Following these events, our team neatly divided into two factions: the brainwashed soldier boys who missed Warner versus the relieved idealists who hoped life under Max would turn out to be better.

Max worked hard to break through the psychological barriers that had been erected. Tension and paranoia had been instilled in the diving team from the moment Warner had taken charge. Almost a year had passed since then. Now Max aimed to create a harmonious team atmosphere. It was a slow process. Most divers were still at each other's throats.

"Warner is gone. No more bullies, no more aggression, no more blame, no more finger pointing. We need to trust each other and work together, guys." Max emphasized time and again.

It sounded great.

For some, Max was too soft. Others, like me, blossomed in the newfound freedom and the atmosphere of mutual respect. After I had languished on the bench for months like a shunned quarterback, Max now put me into the game. He was appalled that, even though I had been part of Blue Team for more than six months, I had not been allowed to handle any of the props. Overnight, he literally showered me with show diving responsibilities as well as reinstated me as a performer trainer – the part of my profession as a show diver I felt most passionate about.

I stayed out of the Aquatics locker room as well as out of the Blue Team aqua coulisse as much as possible. I kept doing what I had done all along, except now with renewed hope. I focused on delivering superior work quality during every waking moment.

Seeing that I was now being given opportunities, my Blue Team colleagues redoubled their bullying efforts. I finally had enough of it. After several horrific confrontations, I went to see Max.

"Can you please remove me from Blue Team?"

Max understood and nodded. "Liam, things will be fine. Give me a little time and I'll sort it out."

A week later, he transferred me to Green Team on the other side of the pool.

After three months of creation, everyone was exhausted to the bone. Backstage on standby looked like a homeless shelter with performers as well as technicians passed out all over the floor, covered with towels to keep themselves warm. Meanwhile, I still spent every free minute on the vomitory, absorbing as much of the creative process as possible.

At first Alexander only played with lighting and special effects. He then proceeded to set the stage with props. This was followed by choreographing the actual acts and attempting to balance the stage with the eighty performers he had at his disposal.

Most performers could barely stand anymore and were relieved when one day Alexander asked them in his strong Belgian-French accent, "All of you, please lie down and cover the stage with your bodies as evenly as you can. Try to look exhausted."

There was no trying involved.

Alexander asked his performers to stay in this position for hours, while he tested lights and special effects all around them. Then, finally, he said, "Ok, this is it. Clear the stage."

At first nobody moved. Most had to be kicked in the ribs because they had fallen into a deep sleep.

During one particular week, Alexander was placing hundreds of mirror balls. It took days. He would tweak each of them inch by inch, seeking to deduce the perfect positioning for optimal light effects. Drunk with fatigue, the technicians made many jokes about Alexander and his balls while the cast giggled uncontrollably backstage.

The divers were asked to remain underwater in case Alexander had an epiphany and needed us to instantly set props. For many hours during that week we held on to handrails on the ceiling of our underwater domain, waiting to be called. It never happened. Instead, towards the end of the week, I learned it was possible to fall asleep underwater. Staring out into the black void, I drifted off into a state of relaxed slumber. When I opened my eyes, still breathing from my regulator, I wondered if I could have drowned. How much time had passed? Minutes? Hours? Suspended in the infinite liquid darkness, it was impossible to tell.

Most of the time, creation kept me wide-awake. As I stood watching, speechless, or while I took an active part in its creation, Alexander's story took a clearer shape with each passing day.

Our show was going to be called *The House of Dancing Water*. Geysers shot sixty-five feet high and could catapult a person into the air, if they happened to stand in the wrong spot at the wrong time. Jets and rain were additional attractions augmenting the – in itself breathtaking – pool which was hidden under eight hydraulic lifts. They could be moved at any time to reveal either a flat surface, or a body of water, alive with bubbles.

Imagine you are sitting in a theater-in-the-round, the size of a football field. A sixty-five foot long and thirty-seven foot high pirate ship rises up on the lifts, out of the depths of the circular stage pool. All of a sudden, thirty scary pirates surface and jump onto the edge of the stage. They face you, muscular, menacing, and dripping with water. The music ramps up and the pirates climb the boat, performing tricks and jumping from great heights over and over again. These tortured souls have been trapped in the dark depths of the ocean for a very long time. They have now been freed for just a moment and rejoice with daredevil acts. At the end of the six-minute act, the pirate ship, shrouded in fog, sinks back into the depths, disappearing forever.

Thunder rolls, lightning strikes. A torrent of rain plummets from the almost incomprehensibly high ceiling of the theater, pushing the fog aside on its way down. The dense wave of fog rolls over your head, revealing a shipwrecked sailor, all alone, lost on the vast ocean.

Unbeknownst to you, the telescopic masts of the boat are being retracted underwater and the ship driven off stage to a large aquatic backstage area hidden under the auditorium.

Moments later, the shipwrecked sailor finds himself beached on a dry stage.

You and the rest of the audience gasp at witnessing the sudden appearance of solid ground where only moments before there had been a life-sized pirate ship and then nothing but water and a struggling survivor swimming for his life.

This is only the beginning of the magnificence to come.

The view of the stage from our underwater positions, too, was a sight to behold. When masking came on, it meant hundreds of pods at the bottom of the pool would release billions of tiny air bubbles. These bubble configurations released from thirty feet under bloomed like giant sparkling mushrooms, growing wider in diameter the closer they came to the surface.

No matter what difficulties I battled backstage, as soon as I entered the world of water, I felt confident and at peace. Imagine doing anything from being a stagehand to a stage manager taking care of performers during the shows, to a props technician, to a coach who would train and prepare the artists for rehearsals and shows. Now imagine doing all of that underwater. That's the life of a show diver.

During the creation process everyone evolved – on a professional as well as personal level. As a side effect of this collective learning experience, some conflict was inevitable, as were accidents.

Aquatics was responsible for moving a large bamboo boat, under which heavy water tanks had been installed for stability. The space between the ballast tanks was just big enough to allow a diver to squeeze between them. While the storyline of our show progressed, incorrect cues were sometimes given, leading to lifts being moved at the wrong time. One of my colleagues was muscling the boat across the stage pool when suddenly the lift underneath him was moved. In his moment of surprise he lost his air source just before his arms were pinned underneath the ballast tanks.

Alexander noticed the boat rising out of the water and, understanding the danger to the diver, had the presence of mind to shout, "Stop!" through his microphone, saving my colleague's arms from being crushed.

Everything stopped while the automation technician frantically tried to reprogram the sequence to reverse lift movements and free the diver.

Alexander pointed to the boat beached in two feet of water.

"Get him out from under there *right now*."

Over twenty artists raced over to the boat, lifting the seven hundred pound object off my colleague's body so fast, the automation technician never needed to finish his digital rescue. My colleague could easily have drowned yet escaped with only a few bruises.

I got trapped underneath the same boat once but, with my regulator in place, it was a relatively innocuous, if claustrophobic, experience.

The lifts moved without a sound. Additionally, once submerged in masking bubbles during full stage lighting, a lift was impossible to hear or see – a sensation much like driving through dense fog on full beam.

So another time, while I was traversing the stage in a cloud of bubbles, a lift came up in front of me and trapped my head between the front of the ballast tanks and the edge of the lift, nearly breaking my neck. I never saw it coming and was saved only by a quick-acting colleague who sounded an alarm, stopping all lifts immediately. All guardian angels seemed to be working overtime right along with us. No one was ever seriously hurt.

The bamboo boat did have its advantages. My biceps and thighs grew exponentially from propelling its mass across the stage. I loved my body. This was the fittest, most muscular and masculine I had ever been.

I kept volunteering whenever I could. If new show elements were tested, I was curious to be involved in the process. I didn't mind the danger but rather preferred it to the monotony of being trapped in the same process for too long.

My entire world was taken over by creation.

Many parts of our show featured dancers. All dance music is counted in "sets of eight," which, thematically, is like a "sentence" of music. "1-2-3-4-5-6-7-8" became our mantra. After witnessing thousands of choreography rehearsals, it was hard to do anything without catching yourself doing eight counts – even going to the bathroom.

And I couldn't stop working, even in bed. I once dreamed of checking the stage just minutes before a full run-through of the show. To my surprise, the stage was covered in my clothes. Embarrassed, I ran in circles, collecting an entire wardrobe's worth of clothing. But then, all lifts, except one, began to submerge. My clothes were floating everywhere on the surface of the now almost circular stage pool revealed by the lifts. With superhuman speed, I managed to retrieve all my clothes before they got sucked under and caused the lift mechanisms to malfunction. At the end of my dream, I proudly stood on the one remaining dry lift, next to my clothes that were stacked neatly into a pyramid. A few hours later, I woke up, rubbing my eyes. To my utter amazement, the entire contents of my wardrobe were piled up next to the bed in exactly the same manner they had been in my dream.

Looking back on creation, I see an endless blur of pool water, exhaustion, sleep, and cup o' noodles. At the end of the fourth month of that process, I was so drained I managed to fall asleep instantly in any position. I became the master of five-minute power naps.

Alexander was an abusive director, frequently screaming down the house. I remember one moment in particular when he became frustrated with the speed of preparation for a rehearsal and ended up yelling through the microphone, "Fuck you! Fuck you all! Ten minutes break!"

At the end of the day he apologized profusely, emphasizing the preciousness of teamwork and respect, only to launch into another uncontrollable rant the next day.

Once, I barely avoided direct verbal abuse by Alexander during the rehearsal of a scene involving a princess getting drowned in a cage. Normally, safety divers were stationed underwater surrounding the cage as it plummeted into the water and stopped just under the water surface. The divers then had a maximum of six seconds to release the princess from her cage before it was pulled back out of the water. To future audiences, the princess would seem to magically disappear while, in reality, divers were providing her with compressed air and escorting her underwater to a backstage exit.

Max misunderstood Alexander during this rehearsal and sent me out onto the dry stage in full scuba gear, to meet with the artists before rehearsal of the scene was to commence. The lights on stage were impossibly bright. I couldn't see anything but blackness in the shadows of the vomitory. As my eyes adjusted, I could make out Max and his assistant frantically waving me back.

At the same moment, an irritated Alexander leaned over the banister in front of his director's chair in the auditorium. Loudly, anger beginning to creep into his voice, he asked, "Why is there a diver on my stage?"

In my dark backstage scuba gear and fins on my feet, there was no way of swiftly and gracefully escaping. My face turning very red with embarrassment, I slowly waddled out of his sight like a big, black duck on oversized webbed feet, back through the vomitory, thus ending my one-minute debut on stage.

We knew that opening night was creeping closer yet somehow, it still managed to surprise us when it finally arrived. As tired as all members of cast and crew were, we were electrified – our show was becoming a reality!

The premiere on September 16, 2010 was an undisputed success. It was the first time I had been a part of such a dazzling endeavor. Premiere parties seemed to go on for days, everyone clapping each other on the back and drinking champagne, happy to have reached their goal.

I was somewhat disillusioned after having met Alexander personally at the end of creation. I had been bubbling over with enthusiasm, having just witnessed his genius from the shadows of the vomitory for the previous four months. While I stammered, trying to express my gratitude for taking part in his visionary project, our director had seemed decidedly bored with me, and strolled onward to more important individuals.

Over the years, we continuously performed ten shows a week for a sold-out auditorium. *The House of Dancing Water* still dazzles its audiences. It is sold-out every night and most likely becoming immortal, slowly approaching cult status in Mainland China and India. The water, as well as the super-sized stage, state-of-the-art technology and top-quality performances, guarantee a level of excitement even the most distracted audiences find hard to resist. Artists and technicians are swept along by the euphoria just like anyone else.

I loved my job. In fact, I loved my job too much.

Caught in the maelstrom of in-house politics, I was trapped like a suitor in an unrequited love affair – but only on a corporate level. Thankfully, all was fine on the personal front. The strong relationship of trust and respect connecting me to our performers brightened my every day. The open smiles and hugs of this group of creative, driven people made me feel at home and accepted as exactly the romantic fool I was.

In the past, I had often been stared at and asked about the sizeable scars on my chest. At *The House of Dancing Water*, no one asked. My fellow divers seemed curious, but no one ever approached me. As for our performers, I knew they had seen so many scars in their lives, they had stopped asking each other for such details a long time ago.

Our moto riders once saluted me as a fellow surfer, after seeing me bare-chested in the theater basement. I had stared at them, uncomprehending.

"Many professional surfers surgically remove their nipples to avoid the agony caused by abrasions," they explained to my astonishment.

Apparently, I had surfer's nipples. Who knew?

Whenever the daily trivialities inside our concrete cube got me down, I would take a day off and go to watch our show from the audience's perspective. Each time, I watched *The House of Dancing Water*, it would touch me and leave me with tears in my eyes.

Alexander had essentially managed the impossible and choreographed a masterpiece uniting people of all ages, genders and cultures, artfully weaving together Chinese and Western symbolism.

He created a timeless story: a beautiful princess endowed with magical powers has been locked away by an evil, power-hungry queen. Then a stranger appears from a shipwreck, freeing the princess with the help of a mysterious tribe. A fast-paced battle of good against evil ensues, keeping audience members at the edge of their seats for ninety minutes. Of course, there is a very romantic, happy ending.

Children and adults alike find themselves reminiscing of being read to sleep by their mothers. But this is no bedtime story. Moto riders catapult so far over the audience's heads, they almost seem to touch the ceiling. Cliff divers jump from unbelievable heights, presenting death-defying stunts. Dancers and acrobats fly through the air and dance over the surface of the water.

The size of our stage made it impossible to process all the detail during one show, turning every single one of my visits to the auditorium into a brand new experience. Like many others, I came close to sensory overload. The lifts make our stage come alive as if it was a breathing land-and-seascape. Earthquakes shake the ground while geysers erupt with a loud hiss. Props and artists magically appear and disappear under the water surface.

Sometimes, all lifts descend as one, colorful lighting from underwater and above turning the now gigantic pool into oceans of different colors, signifying our journey through life. Dazzling lights, rain, jets and fountains aid the story with their grand visual and sensory impact, leaving an unforgettable impression in the hearts of all audiences.

While seeing the great performance as just another member of the audience, I also experienced the joys of a coach seeing his charges rise to never-imagined heights – and, in our special water environment, depths. Like a father watching his children grow from their first clumsy steps to charismatic perfection, my heart almost burst with feelings of love and pride.

As the beauty on stage mesmerized me, I would forget the ugliness still abundant backstage, and remember why I worked there in the first place: because I believed in the vision, and the beauty of it all. Mind and heart refreshed, I would dive back underwater, performing my daily duties with dedication and passion.

My favorite work moments were the small rituals and encounters with our artists. During a part of the show called the "Fountain Dance", a group of swans would appear out of the dark blue depths of the stage pool to bring the lost princess and her savior together in a moment of budding romance. In order to magically appear out of nowhere, a group of fifteen dancers, dressed in tutus as swans, would need to get across an expanse of water. But once saturated, the dancers' tutus were too heavy to swim in. So they pulled themselves along a rope that led from a dry backstage area across the water surface to a set of stairs hidden at the edge of the stage, just out of view of the audience. Ready in case of an emergency, I would watch the swans hovering underwater as they pulled themselves slowly towards the stage. At the last moment, just before their cue to appear in front of the audience, I would kick up to the surface and the swans would wave to me, laugh happily, blow me kisses and we would splash each other with water. I would delight in watching the first minute of their performance from behind a dark curtain, before I needed to continue to my next cue.

Another highlight for me was the moment when performers would first come underwater at the beginning of each show. We would all share complicated handshakes and fist bumps in greeting or play a round of rock-paper-scissors. Some of the artists were only half-dressed and finished donning their costumes underwater, in full control of their movements even while immersed.

I loved being responsible for reveals or catches. During a catch, the artist would jump into the water, relying on me to catch him and give him air within a split second. I would then swim him underwater to the nearest pool exit backstage, or towards his next cue, so he could magically re-appear on stage. For a reveal, I would simply swim the performer to his cue position. Hovering just underneath the water surface, I would hold him, then, at a signal, let him go up for his cue on the water surface.

One of my favorite catches would happen just off the edge of one of the lifts. Thirty seconds before our catch, I would swim out to where the performer was standing. The pool water was crystal clear, so I could see his toes hanging over the edge of the lift and gently squeeze them, letting him know of my arrival. In turn he would wriggle them, saying hello to me, his invisible rescuer. Moments later, he would enter the water. I would grab him in one practiced, swiping move and swim him, as fast as possible, to safety. The audience would never be the wiser.

If I had to wait with a performer underwater, we would entertain each other with elaborate good-luck handshakes, snap our fingers to see who could get the loudest sound, blow air rings, and genuinely enjoy each other's company for a few seconds before the music told us the time for action had come.

During small breaks on the aqua coulisse surface backstage, I would talk to some of the artists while watching others playfully somersault their way towards their next costume quick-change. We would chat about our lives, our feelings, our hopes and dreams. I came to treasure these short moments together.

One of the acrobatic dancers, Todd, hugged me one day and exclaimed, "Liam, what a tragedy you're not gay. You're exactly the man I'd love to spend the rest of my life with."

What a beautiful compliment.

We continued talking about our day and other less romantic topics. I was still smiling hours later.

The next day, I found Todd in our theater green room and hugged him with all my strength.

"Thanks Todd, I might not be gay but your compliment totally made my day. It's most likely one of the sweetest ones of my life. Thanks. I'll never forget it."

As a show diver, my foremost duty was to guarantee the performers' safety, while at the same time always remaining invisible. I treasured the bursts of activity resulting from this conundrum. For example, two artists would be submerged in a sinking pagoda. We would have to wait for the lifts to be far enough down to hide us from view of the audience before we would be able to rush out in a flurry of fin strokes to get to the performers who were holding their breath and waiting for us inside the pagoda. We would reach them within three seconds, regulator in hand. This rescue was exhilarating no matter how often I did it. The sinking pagoda created a vortex, whereas rain fell from above, creating turbulence. Additionally, the sinking lifts created a strong drift. It was like navigating through a washing machine. I loved pushing myself to the limit, going ever faster, steadier, and stronger.

The audience never saw the divers. The masking bubbles made sure we remained well-hidden during crucial moments. Unfortunately, they also distorted both sound and vision to the extreme. I learned to become supremely self-assured in all my movements, yet fight complacency at all times. Anything could happen, at any given moment. Not being fully alert could easily cost someone his life.

Keeping calm was essential. Panic was not an option in our line of work. Thankfully, I had been blessed with abundant willpower. One evening, crossing under moving stage lifts to get into a strategic position for my next cue, a high-pressure line burst right underneath me. Within seconds, I was enveloped in a turbulent tornado of water and bubbles. I couldn't see. Which way was south? Which way north? Swimming the wrong way would expose me to dangerous scissor lifts that could easily snap my body in half.

I had no choice but to stay put, keep panic at bay, and wait until someone turned off the compromised system. Pressure waves surged through the water unabated, slamming me into the many pipes and protruding edges located just underneath the lifts. I felt like an infant at the whim of a raging giant. After two minutes that seemed like an eternity, the water calmed. I found myself only a few feet away from where I had been initially. Battered and bruised, hurting in places I didn't even know existed, and shaking from shock and adrenaline, I swam to safety. After catching my breath, I gave my team leader the standard diver sign for "ok" (thumb and index finger coming together to create a circle) and continued with my responsibilities for the rest of the night.

Whether we were recuperating from emergencies or just from a regular, exhausting day, the green room was a safe haven. Here, in the traditional theater break room, I could rest and mingle with like-minded souls. We always had a warm hug and a smile for each other. Half an hour's break amongst the relaxing artists was enough to get me through the rest of my day.

31

The Mangal

Every week, we had a cast meeting called 'Tapis Rouge'. (This term was originally coined by Cirque du Soleil and refers to the rehearsal room's plush red carpet.) The meeting was open to all cast and crew, yet I was one of only few technicians who grabbed the opportunity and sat in on a regular basis.

Tapis Rouge became one of my major sources of motivation. It was during these meetings that I felt the soul we had infused our theater's walls with, just as our artistic director Manuel had predicted during Training & Formation in Belgium. It was a pleasure to witness artists officially recognizing each other's achievements, openly speaking about their concerns, and carrying each other on their shoulders – literally as well as figuratively.

Moreover, these inspirational, honest meetings helped me admit a sad truth to myself: life in the Aquatics basement had not improved under Max's management as we had hoped.

Over time, it became apparent that we had exchanged one dictator for another, even though their dictatorship differed in style. Where Warner had been brutal in an unsettlingly straightforward and uninhibited manner, Max was all passive-aggressive smiles and hugs. He had never managed a big team before, nor had he had to balance the needs of his team with corporate pressures. Much like Warner before him, Max was in way over his head. Yet he was the perfect politician, a master of perception and manipulation. He did exactly what he wanted while telling everyone what they needed to hear. As time progressed, I was eerily reminded of

Rowan on Kuredu Island, who had won us all over with his dazzling charm while betraying us.

After all that Warner had inflicted on us, I was surprised to find myself missing him. If I had to work for a dictator, I greatly preferred an honest, overt one to an unpredictable, manipulative one.

While Max did care about trust and team, he was unable to delegate. When it came down to it, the only person he really trusted was himself. He needed to control every aspect of Aquatics life and rarely took a day off, which left him in a position of permanent exhaustion. He ended up forgetting his promises and responsibilities. Conversations would slip his mind only minutes after he had them.

Training was a permanent feature of our theater existence. Existing performers needed to fine-tune their skills, whereas new performers needed to be brought up to speed. All training needed to happen in the morning, before rehearsals and our two shows of the day.

Max insisted he needed his trainers all day. On course days, we would start training performers in the morning and then continue working until the end of our second daily show, late at night. On days such as these, we would easily spend ten hours in and underwater. It was obvious to anyone but Max that in the long run these kinds of hours were unsustainable. To make matters worse, he steadfastly refused to give any of his trainers special recognition or extra pay.

Within a year after operations began, all the Aquatics trainers quit – except me. I should have protested and quit as well. Max would have been forced to reconsider and find better ways of integrating performer training into our daily workload.

Instead, my passion once again became my Achilles' heel. I loved coaching with all my heart. I couldn't bring myself to cease training our performers. For months, I had given this part of my work all my remaining energy. I came in long before any other show divers and met with new performers to conduct their training from 9 a.m. to noon. When I became the only experienced trainer Max had left, I was at least able to bargain for a two-hour lunch break, during which I would try to power-nap in the very loud and overcrowded green room. Then, barely rested, I would go straight back to work at 2 p.m. for another eight hours of rehearsals and shows.

Max would pep-talk and hug me.

"Liam, you are my number one diver. You're awesome, buddy. Look at what you're accomplishing. You and I are going to go a long way together."

For a long time, I naively fell for his campaign, assuming he was just being overly American in his optimism and exuberance. Basking in his praise, I enthusiastically began taking over even more work in addition to my already backbreaking workload. I began to revise and conduct training for our new divers, designed performer training sessions better tailored to our pool environment, and I started to write training documentation.

In all discussion about training content, Max would push issues onto a personal level as soon as he wasn't able to deal with a problem professionally. At a loss for valid arguments, he would resort to physical and emotional blackmail. Working in Aquatics became a matter of trust and love. Max met uncomfortable questions with displays of emotion, a helpless waving of arms, and the frequent exclamation, "Don't you love me? Don't you trust me?"

Even as a hopeless romantic, I realized Max was navigating a perilous road.

My enthusiasm for training may never have wavered but I still understood all was not well in the House of Max. Even after two years of hard work as underwater trainer, Max continued refusing to recognize me officially as *The House of Dancing Water* Aquatics trainer. My work hours far exceeded anyone else's in our department, yet Max never considered adjusting my pay accordingly. He used me and, to my eternal shame, I must confess I allowed it. I understood the position I was in. I suffered from it. But I couldn't bring myself to let go of my beloved training role.

After a while I at least managed to find an assistant trainer Max agreed with. Dan taught with me for a period of half a year, suffering through the same rigorous schedule I had already had to put up with for many months. As I watched my buddy wither away, looking increasingly spent, I decided to up the ante and became more forceful in my dealings with Max.

"Can we please find ways to amend our schedule?" I asked over and over again. "Look at Dan. He is exhausted. So am I. I'm not sure how much longer he and I can continue alone without sufficient rest. We need to find more trainers, Max. But none of the existing team will be interested to help us unless you change the current setup. Maybe we can come to an agreement that trainers will not need to dive shows on course days? Or how about you let them compensate their overtime and get their strength back after each course by giving them a three-day weekend. This will allow them to recuperate from the added strain?"

My proposals didn't lead anywhere. Max reacted like a stubborn mule, unwilling to walk a new path through his home turf. After several confrontations, I went as far as to complain about him to general management – to no avail.

Then one day, Dan came into the locker room, his eyes sparkling brighter than ever before.

"Liam, I need to talk to you."

"Ok Dan, what's up?"

"You know, everything is clear to me now. We've got it all wrong. We're so stressed out because we don't have enough faith. Love will solve anything, man. It's not like the scientologists say. We use more than enough of our brain, but we don't use enough of our heart."

Even though he seemed to be onto something fundamental, his euphoric state began freaking me out.

"Trust me, Liam, love is all we need. Literally. If you believe enough, then you can go months without sleep. Love will sustain you. And that scuba tank over there – you won't need a compressor to fill it anymore. Love will do the job for you. Let's get together for a beer sometime, and I'll tell you all about it."

He bounced rather than walked off towards his locker. I was rooted to the spot, dumbfounded.

"Sounds great, how about tomorrow night?" I said, at a loss of how to respond and not wanting to hurt his feelings.

"Cool, let's get together at the Old Taipa Tavern after work."

"You got it!" I said, my heart constricting with worry at his beatific expression.

There was nothing I could do at that moment. I was already running late.

"Ladies and Gentlemen of the Dragone company: five minutes, I repeat, five minutes until top of show," our show caller announced through backstage speakers.

I hurried towards the Green aqua coulisse to get ready for my first cue. There must be a harmless explanation to Dan's odd behavior, I told myself. Maybe he had fallen in love, or finally caught up on some much needed sleep.

The next day, during that evening's first performance, Dan began playing with bubbles like a toddler in the bathtub. When the tricky cage rescue came up, he abandoned his position in favor of practicing underwater somersaults.

Max and Albert, Dan's White Team leader, took him aside between shows.

"Dan, what on earth is going on with you? You missed your cue during cage rescue. Are you sick? Do you need the rest of the evening off? We need to know you're on top of your game."

"I'm fine," Dan said, smiling. "I'm sorry, guys. It won't happen again."

Ten minutes into diving the second show, Dan aborted one of his cues and signaled "out of air". Thankfully, Albert saw him and rushed to his side. Dan was close to panic. He had to be escorted out of the pool by another diver.

The next day, Dan was sent to a psychiatrist in Hong Kong. We never saw him again. Allegedly, he had suffered a complete nervous breakdown and had been put on a plane back home to his mother in Canada.

During our months of training performers together, Dan's presence had become invaluable. Even though Max assigned divers to help me with the courses after Dan's departure, I felt the loss of my trusted colleague and friend.

For weeks I hoped his fate might at least raise some questions amongst upper Dragone management. But the incident was never investigated.

To please the artistic department, Max became more reckless with every passing month. Many of his training decisions heightened the risk of performer injury during performance. While my colleagues shook their heads at my continued involvement, I stayed on in an attempt to battle Max's decisions with tenacious diplomacy. I felt responsible and remembered my vow to let no harm come to our artists. What better way to do that than to try as hard as I could to make sure they were adequately trained?

As our situation in Aquatics became ever more dire, the team of divers grew more loyal towards each other. Unfortunately, I still felt quite disconnected from most of them.

I had never gotten used to working in the rough, testosterone-dominated environment. I still dreaded any minute spent in the Aquatics locker room as much as I had on the very first day. Still, after all this time, no curtains or room dividers of any kind had been installed in our private space. After work each night, I rushed to the locker room before everyone else and left without taking a shower, just as the other guys started coming in.

After listening to all their talk about homos and lady boys over the years, I couldn't possibly imagine showering with them and revealing myself. I would never be able to undress in front of these men, even if most likely many of them would turn out to be totally accepting of me. In effect, it was probably me who needed to learn to be less prejudiced and more accepting towards them and their ways. Some of my colleagues were very interesting men with diverse backgrounds and a charming sense of humor. They could have become good friends under different circumstances. But the chance of being able to be myself in the Aquatics basement had come and gone a long time ago.

As the protests of my workmates concerning my early departure every night became louder, I wondered what to do. To them it seemed as if I was letting down the team by avoiding cleanup duty. They didn't know I changed clothes quickly under a flimsy towel in case one of them came in early. And they were unaware of the cleanup work I did every evening after rushing out of the locker room, while they delighted in relaxing, communally-naked banter. I was too proud to defend myself in front of my suspicious teammates, however. I felt I had no choice but to confide in Max about my gender identity. I needed to at least have my boss understand why I ran out of the pool faster than most.

Max and I met one night after work. I told him about being a transgender man and explained how I felt when it came to changing clothes or showering in the locker room.

"It's a bit like being little *Nemo*, when he finds himself surrounded by sharks."

Max surprised me by being very understanding. He hugged me as hard as he could.

"Now I admire you even more than before. You are such a strong, amazing, and special person!"

I was utterly confused by Max at this point and didn't know what to make of him anymore. Was he friend or foe?

The harder it became for Max to gain the trust of his team, the more he used his tall body as a tool of dominance. He would lean over people, massaging their necks and ears whenever he wanted to make a point.

Over time, his behavior escalated. Max would twist our nipples. During social occasions, he would grab our crotches. His language became ever more lewd and salacious. He would deliver remarks as a joke in his booming voice, yet he was beyond funny. Rather, he bordered on creepy.

Performers as well as show divers began to complain to upper management about sexual harassment. I was unsure about getting involved at first, until Max crotch-grabbed me during a party. His knowing there was no penis to be found didn't make the moment any less awkward. The increasing number of nipple twists per workday also became too much to explain away by Max being an over-exuberant American.

When Emily, an English teacher and good friend from McKinsey, visited Macau, I invited her to join me at an Aquatics barbecue. Halfway through the evening, Max was well into nipple-twisting his employees when he suddenly decided to come after Emily. Using suggestive language, he went from harmless hugs to simply being too close for comfort. Emily was a very self-assured woman who had no troubles telling Max to keep his distance. I could tell she felt uncomfortable though.

Max was my superior. He was also in the process of acting highly inappropriately. I needed to protect my friend but was at a complete loss of what to do. One of my Green team colleagues came to our rescue. The barbecue was being held at his building. Being the official host, he pointed towards the door.

"Max, it's time to leave."

To my surprise, our boss turned around and indeed left quietly and immediately. I was disgusted by the entire episode. But more than with Max, I was disgusted with myself for not having taken action.

The next day, I handed in my own sexual harassment complaint. By now Dragone Entertainment had received at least a dozen complaints against Max, coming from all departments of the theater. A company executive as well as the human resources manager flew in to Macau from Belgium and interviewed all of us separately.

I explained my experiences. Deeply ashamed, I closed my statement with, "I can't help but feel violated and what makes it worse is that I don't know how to react to Max's daily advances without endangering my position at work."

The company executive was having none of it. He told every single one of us, "It's your responsibility to set the boundaries for Max. And – let me be straightforward about this – we have no intentions of taking any action against him."

It became clear to all of us in Aquatics that we had been left to our own devices. No one would come to our rescue. No one was interested in getting to the bottom of why it was the divers more than any other employees who quit their jobs within only a short time of being hired.

The blatant disregard of dozens of serious sexual harassment allegations remained hard for us to wrap our heads around. To his credit, the company executive must have at least had a very serious talk with our head of department. Max's physical transgressions became less frequent after the executive returned to headquarters. Unfortunately, the emotional blackmail as well as the appalling incompetence continued.

Still stubbornly in love with our show as well as with our performers, my heart and mind started searching for solutions. Naturally, I wondered if there might be a possibility of changing departments. I took one vacation day each month to do mini-internships with other departments. It was an invaluable and exhilarating experience as I began to understand our visionary endeavor on a far more comprehensive scale. I spent several days with stage management, fueling my hope of being part of their team one day.

Well-meaning senior theater staff, including our artistic director Manuel, warned me early on.

"Don't get your hopes up. Most likely, you won't be given the chance to become a stage manager. The general stage manager likes to have her kind of people around her. She'll only hire people she knows from prior jobs or from her home country."

"Thanks, I'll keep that in mind," I said, powering on.

Experience had shown me how important it is to give it your very best shot even if everyone says you will fail.

I never confided in anyone about my continuing personal trauma at Aquatics. I didn't want any pity or special treatment due to my gender identity. Instead, I focused on acquiring ever more knowledge about the inner workings of our theater.

Annabelle, the general stage manager, seemed interested as well as supportive at first. As we started to become friends, I made the mistake of confiding in her about my deep unhappiness working in the Aquatics department. Annabelle's instincts must have screamed, "No!" She needed someone clear-headed and impartial who had a grip on his emotions.

Almost a year later, when the moment came and someone resigned in stage management, Annabelle *did* accept my application for the position. She took weeks to get back to me, most likely battling with the dilemma of having to hurt me as a friend.

Finally, I sat opposite Annabelle in her office. Her rejection hit me like a train wreck. I stayed calm while my hopes of being able to continue being a part of this amazing show died an irrevocable death. I could barely breathe as I got up and left Annabelle's office.

I was close to folding right then and there. What I wanted most was to leave through the stage door and never return. Since I still had a one-hour break before show call, I *did* leave the building, and headed towards the Taipa Houses Museum just across from our casino complex.

Between this museum and the Cotai Strip where all the latest and grandest casinos were located, was a small lake called The Mangal. Only a ten-minute walk from our concrete monstrosity, it was a natural haven. Whenever my lunch break was long enough, I would try to come here instead of staying in the lustrous palaces of materialism flanking our theater.

The small lake with a marshy shoreline was covered with thousands of lotus flowers. The trees framing this vista were home to a surprising array of birdlife. My favorites were hundreds of white herons. They seemed sprinkled onto the small oasis like coconut flakes on top of a chocolate cake with jungle-green frosting. The romantic wetlands were Taipa's only refuge for migratory birds – and me.

As I pondered my talk with Annabelle, the extreme humidity and heat had an almost apocalyptic quality. I sat down at the lakeshore anyway. I let my gaze rest on the murky, green water while sweat ran over every inch of my body. Frogs quacked, mosquitoes buzzed, and birds sang. The otherworldly quality of the sea of lotus flowers had a calming effect on me. Half an hour of this and my mind was made up. I was still heartbroken by Annabelle's rejection, but I would undoubtedly return to our theater – for now.

In another venue, at another time, I might have made a fabulous stage manager. But in hindsight, I understand that being desperate to get out of my current situation was a dodgy motivation for changing departments. I wouldn't have been able to be cool-headed about anything at the time. Too much had happened and I was very close to burnout.

The weeks following my rejection passed in an emotional blur. I barely kept it together, battling with conflicting emotions.

"Liam, you need to let go," my friends told me. "You need to leave this job. You obviously love it too much, to the point of being obsessed."

Tadek, our exuberant high-diving coach and by now a very good friend, came back to give three weeks of intensive performer training. I found myself whining in his office countless times.

"Shut the fuck up," he finally snapped at me.

I was shocked and stared at my friend with wide eyes, not comprehending his harshness. I could see kindness in his eyes, yet his voice was firm, allowing no dispute.

"You need to stop this, Liam. You're turning in circles, and have been for quite some time now. This place and its politics will never change. Max will never change. You need to make a clear decision. Can you live with this situation? If you can, you need to shut up and simply get on with doing what you love. If you can't, you need to get out of here as fast as possible."

Tadek was right of course. I had known it all along. Hearing a friend spell it out for me so clearly was what I needed. I was deeply thankful for his trust in our friendship and for his amazing honesty.

It was time to take charge of my life again.

I tried approaching Annabelle one more time, inquiring if I could run tracks for stage management during my off time. She looked at me steadily.

"I don't think so. You're too hard to manage because you don't play the corporate game well enough."

I wanted to rip Annabelle's head off at the time, yet here was one more friend trying to tell me honestly, in her own cryptic way, that I was not made for the corporate world of *The House of Dancing Water*, or any other corporate world for that matter.

Only years later did I realize what a blessing it was to have been rejected. I was no politician and never would be. My entire face and persona could easily be read like the Encyclopedia Britannica.

Throughout my life, I had always put the individual first. As a photographer, I had failed in becoming a journalist because I wasn't able to go beyond the person in front of me to get to the story. I couldn't bring myself to take the picture if I had the option of dedicating my full attention to the actual person instead. I needed to be directly involved with the lives of others to maybe eventually tell a different kind of story.

At Dragone Entertainment, I was most passionate about helping others. I was the quintessential coach, making time for everyone, letting them know I understood them on a very personal level and would be there for them, to save their lives if necessary, or just to have a coffee and listen to their dreams. I loved to see people grow, loved to assist in the process. Sharing in their personal stories gave me strength and happiness.

Looking back at most of our show administrators now, I was a different kind of animal entirely. My heart would have broken many times over had I gotten involved in management. I wouldn't have been able to support the political decisions that needed to be made for a show of this magnitude.

Too much money was involved in Alexander's larger-than-life endeavor. Tough decisions needed to be made on a daily basis. Some of them couldn't be made without looking the other way and moving on. People involved in show management needed to keep their professional relationships alive no matter how much they might disagree with the person in front of them. Issues could not be made personal for, in the end, all that mattered was the continued, successful survival of the show.

Alexander wasn't concerned with the feelings of his employees. He never set foot in the Aquatics department. On one occasion, he invited us for drinks to thank us personally for our efforts. The Aquatics team arrived on time, waiting for hours for the creator of their beloved show who never bothered to honor the invitation he himself had extended.

Being absorbed by our show, stranded in a country whose culture and people we didn't have the time to understand or learn to appreciate, it was just us: an island of three hundred people from thirty different countries, all locked up in an oversized concrete cube without windows. These were years filled with passion as well as defiance. Work was extraordinary in every respect, while the in-house politics were disheartening and destructive.

Never did I experience more ugliness and beauty in the same place. It was *Jekyll and Hyde* many times over. Working for one of the biggest shows in the world brought out the best and the worst in people. Much like living on an actual island, nothing stayed hidden, nothing was private. It was just another large family. People took care of each other as well as breaking each other's hearts. And sometimes, beautiful things happened.

I vividly remember one conversation I had with our artistic director. We were discussing the negativity and blame culture prevalent throughout our ten-floor venue.

"I believe everyone is under too much pressure," I said. "Besides, we live in a bubble. We are too overworked to make local friends. And Macau is small. You can't go out of your apartment without meeting at least a dozen people from work. When you're on the edge, with nowhere to turn for balance, things get ugly."

"You might be right," Manuel conceded. "One main thing I notice is that people are too readily blaming others for anything. No one ever stops to ask themselves *why* someone has done or said something. Let me tell you a story.

In our first year here, Robert from moto was becoming a real problem. He wouldn't listen, wouldn't adapt, and was becoming ever more aggressive toward his fellow moto riders as well as the stage managers. Everyone in management began discussing if we might need to get rid of him. But I kept wondering what was going on.

So one day, I went to the moto riders' outdoor training space and spent the morning watching those guys do their incredible stunts. As always, it struck me how much they risk during every second of flying through the air on their bikes.

After practice, I found Robert behind a trailer and said, 'Hey buddy, it was a pleasure watching you. Can I talk to you for a second?'

He looked as if his famous temper might flare up but then said, 'Ok.'

I asked, 'You seem to get into a lot of trouble lately. What's going on? Are you alright? Is there anything I can do for you?'

He seemed taken aback by my question and looked at me for a while as if he was trying to gage my sincerity. Then he said, 'Oh man, I am just dying with pain. My tooth is killing me. It's been killing me for months.'

'What?' I said, flabbergasted. 'So what were you going to do? Just wait for it to heal itself or fall out?'

He just shrugged and then told me more about his life before coming to our show.

It turned out Robert had grown up in a trailer park in the US. His family had been so poor, they couldn't afford going to the doctor. All his life, he had known no other way but to live with pain until it went away again. But his tooth had been decaying in his mouth for months, the agony making it almost impossible for him to think. Still he had managed to come to rehearsals and ride two shows every day.

I sent him to the dentist straight after our talk. Once his tooth was taken care of, he was a changed man. He visibly relaxed. And look at him now. He is taking care of the younger moto riders and has become a real role model for them.

Instead of getting angry and jumping to conclusions when someone says or does something rubbing us the wrong way, we need to ask questions and think that, maybe, they have a reason that has nothing to do with us personally."

I was amazed and thankful to have met someone like Manuel on my journey. His words have stayed with me ever since. Whenever someone gets in my face, whenever I feel threatened by someone's behavior, I try to remind myself of Manuel's wisdom.

What I learned above all during those years was to channel and focus my passion, to harness its power rather than give it free rein. I learned from the artists. No matter what happened in their lives, whether it was the death of a loved one; a mom thousands of miles away who perished after years of battling cancer; a partner who betrayed them but kept working and flirting in the same show alongside them; broken promises; getting worn out by a multitude of intrigues and maneuvers; or enduring other, more work-related blows to the heart and ego, like being downsized by their company, whatever it was they didn't allow it to distract them. The performers would keep on training, keep on growing, even if they were ready to jump from one of our non-existent windows. They kept their goal in sight, focused on their passion, channeling it to sweep them past the unpleasantness towards higher goals.

Wondering what to do in my third year with the company, I considered Annabelle and Tadek's advice and realized I wasn't yet ready to leave.

With every year of being entangled in the great backstage drama of our company, I grew tougher, more disciplined and more focused. Dragone Entertainment constituted one of the hardest experiences of my life, positively traumatizing. Yet I grew far beyond my former limitations. People continued to inspire me through greatness, or through their lack of it, on a daily basis.

I needed to stick it out just a little further, endure and overcome. I needed to find another level of balance far beyond The Mangal, cuddly pets, sunsets, and a cozy apartment. I needed to transcend the Macau theater environment and look for new horizons. I needed to give myself the chance to leave with hope rather than bitterness in my heart, to leave with strength and a sense of accomplishment.

For almost a year, I had worked on a training manual for underwater performer training in our theater. Max seemed enthusiastic and asked me to continue yet denied me all resources I needed to successfully finish what was becoming a book. I vowed to finish the underwater training manual on my own, without Max's resources. I would not resign before leaving a sound legacy for future show divers as well as performers.

But I also needed to think of myself. Many lunch breaks and late nights after work saw me walking towards the overgrown shoreline of The Mangal. Sitting on the swampy shore of my small Taipa lake sanctuary, I began pondering my future.

During my mini-internships at *The House of Dancing Water*, I had realized without a doubt that theater in its essence was something I yearned to be further involved in. Arriving at home each night from the shores of The Mangal, after enjoying a relaxing after-work beer alone or a *Botellón* with my Spanish friends, I began researching study opportunities on the Internet.

Countless sleepless nights spent in front of my laptop brought me across the South China Sea to the Hong Kong Academy for Performing Arts. I found my way to Lea, the head of the Theater, Arts, and Events Management Department, and voiced my passion for theater as well as my wish to study and learn more than I could during my daily work in Macau.

Lea, a dedicated and seasoned theater professional, was delighted and offered me to join their Academy for a professional diploma in Theater, Arts, and Events Management.

"Thank you, I'm honored," I said, "but I'm unable to cut down on my hours at work. I *am* willing, however, to invest all my off-time in my studies. I have some mornings off and our theater is closed for two days each week, Tuesday and Wednesday."

Lea surprised me with a swift and proactive approach. Within days, she managed to design a study schedule for me that involved two full days of school during each of my weekends, as well as self-study in the mornings before work.

I had done it before, working and studying, and painfully remembered the absence of free time. Like a mother after giving birth, however, the pain was a distant memory.

I dove right in and signed up for my next adventure. For two and a half years, my entire life had revolved exclusively around our show and the wellbeing of our performers. Taking a step outside the box, across the deep water of the South China Sea, I already felt my world shifting. I was ready to give it my all. In my experience, true change only happened if I worked hard for it.

32

South China Sea

In only three months' time, I would begin my studies. Thinking about my expanding horizons made me feel as high as if my blood had turned into pure Espresso. I entered the Aquatics basement with renewed vigor – not that I had ever slowed down – and hope.

My dad called me every week. Once he realized that I was once again obsessively working myself to death, a hint of worry entered his voice. Meanwhile, my cats, turtles and fish saw me only at night and in the early mornings. I treasured their soothing presence, as well as their patience with whatever little time I was able to give them.

Show life wasn't restricted to within the theater walls. Being part of a show family like ours meant working and living in a tight circle that absorbed all else like a giant black hole. With three hundred cast and crew, it was always someone's birthday, farewell, or arrival party. "Work hard, party hard" was the performers' motto. Consequently, our company weekends were an exercise in breathlessness with multiple events lined up like so many tempting chocolates on a platter.

I had never been much of a party person but in order to stay connected, it was important to take part and throw myself into the crowd. I felt like a puppy chasing after a whole armada of rubber balls bouncing in multiple directions – excited, swamped, exhausted, and loving it.

Under these circumstances, my fortieth birthday became an unforgettable experience. As a joke, I had sent an invitation to my friend Naomi in Switzerland.

I was dumbstruck when she emailed me two days later.

"Thanks for the invite. I'm coming. Tickets are already booked."

Her dedication to our friendship and her overall beautiful, giving nature humbled me beyond measure.

I invited the entire company to a barbecue on Macau's largest beach. We secured our favorite corner of the beach barbecue area and started piling up food and beverages early in the afternoon. Naya and Noel had left months before. My closest friends were now a small group of Spanish and Polish performers. They were honest, boisterous, and caring.

My friends arrived early to help Naomi and me set up the feast. Since there was no way of knowing how many people would show up for the occasion, I had practically emptied the frozen meat sections of what few Macauan supermarkets there were. My car suspension had nearly collapsed under the weight of the meat, hundreds of cans of beer, and many bottles of wine. One hundred and fifty people stopped by over the course of the day, bringing even more food and drink. We kept the bonfires going well into the night, consuming quantities of food and drink more suitable for a starved army.

Naomi and I were both exhausted at the end of the long day and night. I was overwhelmed by the attendance. The amazing displays of friendship and loyalty left me in awe. We had celebrated not only my birthday but also our show family, and our love for braving the limits of both body and mind together each and every day.

But no one left me more dazzled than Naomi. She had flown in for just two days to be with me for the occasion. Jetlagged, she had helped with all preparations and made the entire event even more special by being there. I returned the favor a few months later by flying into Switzerland for a couple of days to celebrate her wedding in the romantic Swiss Alps.

Time flew. Weeks turned into months. My first semester at the Hong Kong Academy for Performing Arts snuck up on me. There it was, looming on the horizon. The next thing I knew, it was my first Tuesday at college. It was time to start my props making, scenic arts, stage management and many other theater related classes.

As I struggled out of bed that morning, I wondered what on earth I was doing to myself. In order to make it in time for my 9 a.m. class, I needed to get up at 5:30 a.m., catch the 7 a.m. ferry across the South China Sea to Hong Kong, and then hustle through town on the subway to the Academy.

From that morning on, a barely-conscious, scruffy-looking student could be seen in the Academy park every Tuesday morning, nibbling on a muffin and forcing a caramel latte down his sleep-constricted throat. Thankfully, my study weekends would start with a props making class. Wielding dangerous carpentry tools and welding equipment has a tendency to snap a person wide-awake.

Entering the bustling metropolis of Hong Kong for my study weekends never failed to amaze me. On the one hand, the local population seemed friendlier and more service-oriented than their Macau contemporaries. I wasn't elbowed out of the way as frequently, and would go days without someone spitting on my shoes. On the other hand, the sheer size and continuous noise level of Hong Kong took me aback. As always in large, noisy cities, the country boy in me felt overwhelmed.

Not that I saw much of the bountiful city life. I never found the time to venture beyond well-trodden paths. Each week, it was the same.

I would take public transportation straight to the Academy, spend twelve hours attending classes, and then venture past bars and nightclubs in the late evening towards whatever hostel I had managed to book a room in. The rest of my night would be spent studying until I passed out. Wednesday mornings would see me trotting back to the Academy for another day of classes.

I would get back to Macau at 9 p.m. on Wednesday nights, usually passing out from exhaustion as soon as I arrived home, with my cats piled on top of me. Thursday morning would bring the beginning of a new workweek at the Dragone theater.

For a year and a half, I had hardly a minute to spare. Most mornings, I would crawl out of bed at 8 a.m. to spend a few hours bent over my books before heading to the theater.

Ever since my arrival in Macau years earlier, my theater weekends had helped me regain my balance. By throwing myself into an active social life on my off days, meeting cast and crew on a personal level, I was able to build a group of friends who helped ground me at work. Now I found barely enough time to cuddle with my cats, watch movies and read books. I longed for my friends and felt out of touch with the rest of the world.

During the first three months of studying, I felt worse than ever before in Macau and seriously considered leaving for greener – or rather, more turquoise – pastures. But gradually, I regained my balance and started to enjoy the added elements of my daily schedule. Being such a fundamentally different activity, studying started to energize rather than tire me. I had less time than ever before, yet my energy levels reached new heights. My professors were delighted at having a mature student in their classes. They genuinely enjoyed my input, showering me with positive feedback and praise.

Slowly, it dawned on me to what extent I had selflessly given all of my energy to everyone in our theater. Most performers had started training when they were barely old enough to walk. Many had no hobbies unrelated to their line of work. Whenever we met, conversations would invariably drift towards their work, their lives, their training, and their injuries. They were focused to the extreme – and thus self-absorbed – leaving little space for someone who wasn't engaged in the same activities. No matter how much I had socialized and loved living amongst them, I was lonely. I had only been able to connect on a more personal level with a very small handful of people. I missed and treasured talking about subjects beyond acrobatics and show business.

Yet again, I had let my passion whisk me away. My enthusiasm had been an inspiration for many of my Macauan coworkers for years, but what about me? I had allowed most of my energy to be sucked up by other people's lives, careers, and dreams, without ever planting both of my feet on the ground and demanding space for my own life, my own hopes and dreams. Studying reminded me that there was more to life than our show. There was a whole world out there, beyond our windowless sphere, still waiting to be discovered. I had almost completely forgotten.

Everyone in *The House of Dancing Water* thrived on exploiting human perception. People's livelihoods were built upon it.

Max wagered his entire career on its powers, successfully keeping people from looking behind the illusion of competence he created by boisterously enveloping them in his arms, making sure to speak faster, louder and with more confidence than others.

Our performers spent their lives selling their beauty and exceptional fitness. Even their employee evaluations were largely based on superficialities: well-rehearsed smiles, a well-groomed physique, and carefully maintained body weight and muscle mass. No matter how talented they were, they had to dazzle, to play with appearances if they wanted to make it as a performer.

As my world expanded, I rediscovered a life in which appearances weren't everything. At the Academy in Hong Kong, a fresh, unpretentious wind blew through my life, gradually gaining momentum.

Due to the considerable language barrier, I wasn't able to talk much with my fellow students. Instead, I enjoyed talking with my professors. We spent hours exchanging life experiences. It turned out I wasn't the only one who found the level of politics and bedazzlement involved in our mega-show life unattractive.

Annabelle and others from *The House of Dancing Water* had led me to believe I was unsuitable as a stage manager. My goal had seemed unattainable. At the Academy, I watched in pleasant surprise as all around me twenty-year-old teenagers did a fabulous job calling shows and stage-managing behind the scenes. It was simply a matter of keeping a cool head, having an eye for details, and conscientiously organizing as well as documenting the goings-on during rehearsals and shows. In a theater that had retained its collaborative spirit, I would have been able to make a home. As opportunity beckoned, I was able to take a deep, revitalizing breath for the first time in years.

Meanwhile, in Aquatics, Max was relieving me of my responsibilities in stages. Overnight, the underwater training for new show divers was handed over to another member of our team. Max never explained his reasons. Characteristically, he simply hugged me with a big smile, shaking his head at my lack of trust when I asked for an explanation.

I in turn shook my head, clearing it of corporate spider webs, and focused on the positives: my studies, along with the responsibilities Max still allowed me to have.

My love of underwater show life was undiminished. Just as I had on the first day, I marveled at the myriad colors and the gracefully suspended performers enveloped by a vortex of bubbles and light. I was still allowed to train our performers as well. I focused on enjoying shows and training while it lasted.

Months passed in a blur of activity, interrupted only by exhaustion or pollution-induced illnesses.

I had not blacked out from my – possibly heart-related – health condition in years. Then one night in my apartment, I got up for a glass of water and passed out in my kitchen. I awoke minutes later, in an ocean of glass shards, water, and pee. Needless to say, being reminded that my mysterious illness still lurked in the shadows was less than thrilling.

Additionally, Macau's discolored, polluted air resulted in bouts of bronchitis, as well as multiple eye infections. The stifling humidity in the theater basement as well as outdoors led to skin infections I wasn't even aware existed.

The amount of pollution coming from Mainland China was incredible. During the Olympic games in Beijing, when most Chinese factories were ordered to take a one-week break, the Macau sky cleared within hours and shone in a dazzling, iridescent blue never before witnessed in this area. As soon as the Olympic games were over, all provinces affected by Beijing's manic industrial life were once more forced to live under a filthy, opaque veil.

As my first semester at the Academy came to an end, Max surprised me.

"Hey buddy, how would you like to be involved in the first cast changeover for *The House of Dancing Water*?"

My heart picked up a beat.

"I'd absolutely love to be a part of that. Thanks for asking"

"Awesome, I'm glad you're on board. We'll do this every year from now on, but for this year, twenty performers decided not to renew their two-year contracts. So you should have twenty new kids in the pool in Belgium. Training duration will be approximately three months."

Luckily, my summer semester break at the Academy coincided with this time frame. Max's new assistant, who had no training experience to speak of, would be in charge of our three-man team in Belgium. I swallowed my resentment and promised myself to enjoy getting away from it all. I was going to rejoice being a full-time performer coach once more – maybe for the last time.

So, in summer of 2012, I returned to the training studio in Belgium and began preparing a new generation of performers to join our show in Macau.

My second stint in this studio was outstanding in every respect. Without Lauren's military regime, training sessions were fun for trainers as well as performers. Max's assistant was happy to have escaped scrutiny for a while and spent the majority of his time sleeping on a mattress in a hidden corner of the Aquatics office. My other colleague just showed up to assist me in the sessions. It was I who, unofficially, designed all training sessions for this new group of artists. Others would get the credit for my work but still, I reveled in having a profound, positive impact.

The small group of cast and crew were quickly forged into a caring family in which everyone watched each other's back. I rediscovered the joys of jumping out of bed in the morning, looking forward to starting work each day.

In only three months, many performers' bodies underwent a radical change from relatively fit to unbelievably fit. Watching our first generation of performers in Macau for so many years had made everything seem easy. Here, the learning process started all over again. Many activities that had begun to seem safe over time and with experience began to look potentially dangerous again. We redoubled our safety efforts during most of the water-based training.

I was struck anew by the courage and dedication it took to keep getting up to try again and again until the first small signs of progress shyly peeked out on the horizon. Tears and blood flowed in abundance, just as they had three years earlier. It was hard to see my new charges bleeding. I had forgotten how long it took for their skin to harden. Everyone was in constant pain. Whatever healing power liniments, potions and salves exerted overnight was quickly undone by the first hour of training the next morning.

This new group of performers seemed even more dedicated than their predecessors. This time it was just work, no play.

Chef Lyna had been hired once more to take care of all our culinary needs. I delighted in being reunited with my friend.

After the first week, Lyna looked at me with a warm smile.

"Unlike many of the other original cast and crew, you've not become arrogant. As a matter of fact, you were way too nice before. Macau seems to have toughened you up. It suits you well."

I was surprised and also proud to have grown in a positive way.

During lunches in Antwerp, I rediscovered the joys of sharing meals at the studio. We would eat together in our bathrobes while looking out at the Belgian countryside. This time, I saw green meadows and sunshine instead of the grey clouds and snow that had been prevalent during Training & Formation in the winter of 2009/10.

I fondly remembered receiving my very first backstage bathrobe upon arrival years earlier. Dragone Entertainment's logo was stitched on the front. My name was stitched in red on the back. Back then, I had been hopeful and thought everything would be fantastic. I had been so proud of finally having managed to run off to join the circus. The wiser Liam now couldn't help but smile at my past naiveté.

Another friend, the high-dive coach Tadek, was back as well. How I loved sitting next to him again for high-dive training sessions, chatting but ready to pounce should someone need assistance in the water. My friend still had a boundlessly good and joyful heart.

My soul rejoiced during this Belgian summer. During our weekends, I would engage in one of my favorite pastimes, visit friends in Germany and Switzerland, and enjoy racing along proper highways. In the geographically-restricted Macau, I had missed stepping on the gas and hurtling towards my destination at one hundred and thirty miles an hour like a well-aimed missile. Drivers in Macau were chronically scared of everything, rarely venturing beyond twenty miles an hour. Having grown up with well-organized German traffic, the chaotic behavior of Macauan drivers had me struggling with road rage.

A Canadian friend from our show had me rolling on the floor with laughter one day when she said, "Liam, you are such a gentle person most of the time, but when you are driving, you are *so* German!"

Three months were gone in the blink of an eye. In August 2012, twenty thoroughly-trained new performers and a good handful of mentally-refreshed theater technicians headed back to Macau.

Upon entering their theater, the eyes of our new generation of performers grew wide with wonder, like children tasting cotton candy for the very first time. Seeing their excitement helped the rest of us remember the immensity and beauty of what we were privileged to be a part of.

"You did a great job over there," Max complimented me.

Unfortunately, it took less than a week for reality to come back with a vengeance.

"I am taking performer training away from you." Max announced. "Albert and Miriam will take over."

"Why?" I asked, bewildered.

But Max just walked away, refusing to provide any explanation. I wasn't allowed to conduct a professional handover to the new trainers either, even though they had never before coached in theater underwater.

Remembering Tadek's advice, I tried to breathe deeply and accept things as they were until the time came to leave the continuous, often bizarre, roller coaster of Dragone Entertainment politics.

It wasn't only the backstage power games of our larger-than-life endeavor that were exasperating. After over three years of daily use, our theater was starting to show signs of wear and tear. More and more often, we experienced failing parts inside our massive forest of technology.

Every so often, a small valve in our lifts would malfunction, causing a hydraulic hose to rupture, releasing hundreds of liters of oil into our theater pool. We would hear a noise like a cannon shot. Instantly, millions of pretty yellow bubbles would float before our eyes – a yellow mushroom cloud spreading through the entire pool. But what looked very romantic at first would turn into a disaster of epic proportions. Several shows would have to be cancelled while we waded through vegetable oil trying to keep damage to a minimum.

Technicians would work inside the empty pool around the clock, cleaning every surface with chemicals and soap, until we were able to resume operations. Not a drop of the viscous liquid could remain. Nobody needed the nightmare of a fatal accident caused by performers slipping on oil while performing life-threatening stunts in front of an audience of two thousand people.

Every equipment failure added to our weekly workload, exacerbating our perpetual state of exhaustion.

To make matters worse, my second semester at the Academy across the South China Sea was off to a bad start.

Whereas I had mostly had Western lecturers before, I was now faced with mostly locals who only grudgingly agreed to speak English. I would be mentally drained after trying to follow the many Cantonese lectures.

Despite language barriers, I greatly enjoyed my stage management and show caller (the person responsible to give cues to all backstage personnel during a performance) classes with a young lecturer. She radiated an inspiring passion for her profession.

Early on in the semester, I noticed a young woman who quietly sat there, two rows back, class after class, seemingly lost in her own universe.

A few weeks into the new semester my mentor Lea suggested taking me out of a lighting class taught in Cantonese and instead organize separate lessons in English. To my delight, I was told there would be only three of us: another student who couldn't understand Cantonese, the lighting designer, and me.

Delight turned to disappointment the morning we met for the first time. My fellow student turned out to be Helena, the very quiet young woman I had noticed in my stage management class. As we discussed our semester schedule, Helena again barely said a word. I was struck by how utterly dull and lifeless she seemed.

Our lighting class was to be held every Wednesday morning, in a studio on another campus.

"Can you meet with Helena next Wednesday morning to show her how to find Bethany campus?" our lecturer asked. "As I recall, you already had a sound class there last semester?"

I was less than thrilled, but nodded.

"No problem."

Turning to Helena, I said, "How about we meet at Pacific Coffee for breakfast? We can take a cab up to Bethany after."

"Thank you," she said, her face lighting up with a shy smile for the very first time since our paths had crossed.

The following Wednesday, we enjoyed an early breakfast together. I was amazed by my misconception: Helena was far from dull. Quite the contrary, she was lively, charming, and intelligent. We had an energizing conversation over a caffé latte, reaching our lighting class stoked on caffeine and in good spirits.

A one-off event turned into a joyful weekly occasion. Throughout the remainder of my second semester, our Wednesday breakfasts brightened my life. We philosophized extensively. Helena was twenty-six years old, yet her maturity impressed me. Before long, I cared far more for our mornings than for any other part of my Academy schedule. It had been a long time since I had felt so comfortable with another human being.

At *The House of Dancing Water*, I had never felt comfortable looking for romance. The female technicians often tried too hard to be more masculine, witty, and nonchalant than their male counterparts. As for the female performers, they seemed to dance and somersault everywhere they went, and then partied until they fell over. Nightlife began at midnight for most of our artists – just when I would be ready to pass out. They were adrenaline junkies who lived for anything fast-paced and exciting.

Their life would never match mine. I danced to a whole separate set of eight-counts in my private life. To feel comfortable going out onto life's dance floor together, I would need a dance partner who matched my rhythm.

I was also intimidated by the performers' beauty. One of the hardest everyday things at *The House of Dancing Water* was looking at hundreds of Adonises and Aphrodites. They were all perfect and graceful physical specimens. No matter how comfortable I had grown in my own skin, seeing their amazing, half-naked bodies every day only highlighted my own physical imperfections further. Watching over artists whose bodies put Michelangelo's *David* to shame, I couldn't help but dream of what might have been, had I been born in the right body.

I didn't want to feel the same pressure in my private life, and couldn't imagine any of our female performers finding a long-term interest in someone with an incomplete body like mine who also sucked at small talk, who came up with the right comeback hours, sometimes days, later, and adored anything slow-paced. I loved gliding through the ocean with a scuba tank strapped to my back; walking through romantic meadows; swimming through turquoise lagoons; reading on my couch; watching movies on that same couch; drawing and painting and daydreaming – once again on the same couch.

I had always seen the world differently from others. My world was slower, iridescent, and more detailed.

After coming back from my year in the US, I was one of many students interviewed by a local journalist. I remember how stunned she was as she listened to my account. My tales were about the breathtaking natural beauty of the desert and the eerie resemblance of American high school life to exactly what we knew from the movies. I spoke of spanning cultural distances and transcending boundaries between religions and mentalities that couldn't be further removed from each other.

Unlike other exchange students, I had never partied, drunk, or smoked a joint.

When saying goodbye, the journalist smiled at me and said, "It seems the US you explored is an entirely different country to the one other exchange students experienced."

So even though we all shared abundant passion, I had yet to meet a performer who would be comfortable in my quiet, philosophical world.

With Helena, on the other hand, I felt admired and challenged at the same time. Listening to her opinions, I wondered if I had discovered a soul mate. As we got to know each other better, I felt subtle changes in balance between us. Helena became ever more self-confident and lively. The air between us seemed to be charged with positive energy.

But for the first time in my life, instead of forging ahead, I was very careful. My last relationships with Ella and then with Gabriella had thrown my self-esteem all the way back to the Stone Age. After years of struggling with loneliness, I had come to enjoy single life again. I had way too much on my plate, what with school and trying to survive the rest of my time at Dragone Entertainment with dignity and integrity both intact.

The fact that Helena's parents were Christian missionaries didn't raise my enthusiasm any further. Fundamentalism in any form sent shivers up my spine and triggered a fight-or-flight response. Helena seemed open-minded enough. But then, how open-minded could you be, growing up in a missionary household? I decided to not pursue the relationship and enjoyed the unique sensation of really letting go for the first time in my life, content with enjoying the precious moment, not expecting anything.

Meanwhile, at *The House of Dancing Water*, life in Aquatics took another turn for the worse. Max was on a mission to relieve me of as many of my few remaining duties as he could without firing me entirely.

After leaving the abominable Blue Team, I had found a steady home in Green Team on the other side of the pool. Green Team was one of the main reasons why I had managed to hold on for so long. It remained an island of sanity and integrity, a good team, with a good leader and experienced show divers I was honored to be associated with.

John, our Green Team leader, had been with us since the beginning. He was a grumpy American who closely resembled *Tintin*. Over the years, John protected me from the worst of Max's incompetence. We trusted each other and silently weathered each new political development. As show divers came and went, John and I kept each other company. He was my moody, yet solid rock in our treacherous shark-infested waters. Every single day, we would strive for perfection. Max on the other hand, encouraged mediocrity.

In the Maldives, I had learned that, to understand a dive site, you can't view it exclusively from an underwater perspective. Only when you understand exactly where everything is in correlation to the surface are you able to use the current conditions in a way that enable your group to have the optimal experience.

The House of Dancing Water was no different. Everyone could run cues underwater or swim a performer to his cue position. Just like a mediocre guide in my turquoise paradise, they could do a decent job. But was "decent" enough, in an environment as large-scale, dangerous, and magical as the Indian Ocean, or our show?

A mediocre diver was like an artist attempting to form a mosaic without having all the pieces. An excellent show diver had all the pieces, and weighed and used them wisely. He understood the timing, the soul, the rhythm, as well as the intentions of our director, the minute differences between each performer, and the perspective of the audience at any given moment. Thus he was able to deliver a subtlety in timing that allowed for smooth transitions and perfect beauty on stage.

The new generation of divers showed little interest in what went on above the water surface. John and I were powerless, looking on as Max hired more and more people who would blindly follow his orders instead of cultivating a mind of their own.

Seeing how he had effectively put me on ice like a salmon waiting to be devoured on the next festive occasion, I had no doubt that Max longed to replace me with a more moldable individual. Though exasperated, I kept holding on.

My yearly evaluation was, contrary to what Max's actions suggested, excellent as usual.

"I'm so proud of you, buddy," he concluded. "We're glad to have you on the team."

By then, I had given up on making sense of his behavior and just smiled, nodded, and shrugged inwardly.

That year, artistic direction surprised us by deciding to reveal our second anniversary show as a truly collaborative effort. The final bow would be re-choreographed especially for the occasion.

On the day of the anniversary show, on September 16, 2012, our hearts were thudding in anticipation even though we had rehearsed for several hours the day before. On cue, we swam as fast as we could to the center lift, arranging ourselves in a wide circle. As the lift ascended, we slowly rose from the depths onto the stage. At the same time, all other indispensible backstage technicians ran on stage together with our performers, who were still out of breath from their performance. Three hundred cast and crew joined together that night, revealing the human element behind the magic.

The audience went wild. As we bowed as one towards all cardinal points in turn, two thousand spectators rose for a standing ovation.

Applause thundered through our monumental theater like never before. We bowed and applauded in turn for several minutes, our hearts filled with awe and wonder, then all technicians but the show divers exited the stage along with our performers, waving as they went.

During their exit, the center lift we were standing on in full dive gear began descending. We waved, ready to disappear once more into the mythical depths. But water displacement triggered an emergency switch and stopped all lifts.

Left alone on stage, in water up to our waists, we faced an audience still on their feet, happily waving and clapping.

Nothing moved, so I started waving back. As I looked into the love-struck eyes of the spectators closest to my position, I felt like a dolphin riding the crests of the highest waves. I laughed and cheered with all my heart. While my fellow divers shyly waved, I blew kisses in all directions.

Then, after the two longest but also most extraordinary minutes of our lives, the pumps restarted, allowing us to exit the stage beneath the surface of the biggest pool in the world.

33

Lake Minnewanka

Every person in our life leaves their mark. Max was my nemesis at *The House of Dancing Water* and, as many obstacles do, he spurred me to outlast and transcend. So I poured my heart and soul into my studies and was doing incredibly well as a result.

As conditions in the Aquatics basement worsened, I continued to invest my full energy in keeping our artists safe. I plowed on, helping to deliver a show that literally rocked the stage.

I would get home to my small apartment late at night, downtrodden and exhausted. Snuggling with my cats on the couch quickly revived me.

In the mornings I would get up early and study at my desk, looking out at the river separating Mainland China from Coloane. I would work on my semester papers and build theater models while the turtles, Wal and Nut, looked on in wonder and my cats, Boo and Bocelli, tried to help out – by flattening my newly-erected set models with their soft but slightly overweight butts.

In November 2012, Helena was still brightening my Academy life. I invited her to Macau on a Monday evening to experience *The House of Dancing Water* backstage. After the show, we went to my home in the village.

We watched the James Bond classic *Octopussy* on my comfy couch with Boo and Bocelli. Suddenly, inspired by Sean Connery and Maud Adams, we kissed. After resting in the soft embrace of each other's arms overnight, we left early the next morning for my usual Tuesday morning ferry to Hong Kong. I was happy.

Coming home after my Academy weekend, I realized Boo and Bocelli had understood, far more deeply than I, how that kiss had changed my life. As I opened the apartment door, I was greeted by an unbelievable stench. Boo and Boccelli had spent their two days alone in righteous indignation over my betrayal, making a statement by using their favorite armchair as a litter box. Thirty degrees Celsius plus liters of poo and pee – I am sure you can do the math.

I was amused by this loving display of uncontrolled jealousy. My armchair was beyond salvaging, however. To prevent further disasters, I stocked up on feline pheromone spray. On Helena's next visit, I doused her from head to toe in the allegedly potent spray, and instructed her to fawn over Boo and Boccelli during every waking minute. It worked. My four-legged companions relented and refrained from further fecal attacks.

It had been years since someone had adored me and intimately loved me for exactly who I was. For the first time in my life, however, I wasn't blown away by passion. Yes, I was falling in love. Yet it felt slow, rooted in reality, and peaceful this time. Surprisingly, I still felt no need to push, no need to expect anything. I was going to let our blooming romance play out peacefully, whichever way it was meant to go.

In the beginning of my third and last semester at the Hong Kong Academy for Performing Arts, it was mandatory for me to complete a four-week internship. Most students turned to Hong Kong's Disneyland as their place of training. I asked my mentor Lea for permission to go out of the country and went in search of theaters and shows around the world.

Aidan, a good Canadian friend from Macau who had worked at Cirque du Soleil, offered me a position as the first internship student at The Banff Centre, high up in the Canadian Rocky Mountains. I had never heard of Banff before and was astonished to hear it was not only one of the prime areas in the country for outdoor sports but also a beautiful National Park that happened to feature one of the best-known arts centers in Canada.

The Banff Centre sounded great as an institution but truthfully it was the fantastic tales of elk, mountain lions, and grizzly bears that piqued my interest and had me raring to go.

Max signed off on my request for four weeks of unpaid leave in early 2013. Before leaving for the internship, he surprised me immensely by asking, "Are you available for another cast changeover in Belgium this summer? Most likely it'll be between June and August like it was last year."

"Yes, sure. My studies at the Academy will be finished by then."

We shook hands and Max assured me, "You're still my No. 1 performer trainer. I'm delighted to have you onboard in Belgium again!"

With butterflies in my stomach, I boarded the airplane to Canada. Pristine mountain air was precisely what my lungs and I needed. Shortly before leaving, I had suffered from another Macau-induced bronchitis. It stubbornly persisted with the incessant pollution.

Banff was everything Aidan had promised it to be. My lungs were as happy as I was. My self-esteem returned with vigor as my depression and bronchitis lifted.

I couldn't get enough of sipping coffees at The Banff Centre café. Gazing out at the snowy wonderland of the Rocky Mountains, I wished I could stay longer than just one month. Mule deer crossed our path between theater buildings. Campus security had to be called when a gigantic moose lost its way and blundered onto the campus.

My peek into theater and events management at the creative mountain arts center was refreshing, reminding me that a collaborative work environment and calm mutual respect still existed in the world of entertainment. I gave public talks and shadowed theater professionals who had seen it all.

Aidan set me up in the private residence of one of Banff's theater technicians. Myles and his partner, Kate, spent many evenings with me in their cozy living room watching *Bones*, enjoying each other's company and openly discussing our lives and emotions. Their cat and two enormous Rottweilers completed one of the most perfect months of my life.

Aware of my connection with water, Kate offered to take me to a glacial lake only about three miles northeast of Banff. It is called Lake Minnewanka, which in Nakoda means *Water of the Spirits*. The drive up through winding mountain roads was a treat in itself. When we arrived, I felt as if we had reached the top of heaven. Kate and I were the only people for miles around. A vista of snowy peaks and the almost completely frozen lake spread out before us.

"You should come here in summer one day," Kate said. "In 1941, they built a dam which raised the lake by a hundred feet. A small village was submerged in the process. The ruins are very popular with scuba divers."

We had come in at the far side. The dam or any other manmade structures were nowhere in sight. Gazing longingly at the frozen water surface, I wished I could jump in for just a moment to unite with the spirits residing beneath and purge my body of any remnants of Macauan exhaustion.

When Kate and I left the shoreline of the enchanted waters a few hours later, I felt as if I had indeed been freed of a heavy load. Furthermore, scuba diving through a ghostly underwater village on top of the Rocky Mountains sounded very appealing. I was fascinated, and vowed to come back one day.

During my last weeks at the Banff Centre as well as in the surrounding town and national park, I felt myself heal more with every passing day. Working with a true theater family, walking through mountain forests, inhaling my daily dose of mountain air, enjoying micro-brewed beer and bison steaks in the picturesque mountain village, it became abundantly clear that I had spent more than enough time enduring the Macauan environment, both inside and outside our theater.

I left Banff in early March, as energized as if I had undergone an exclusive high-dosage-vitamin-wellness diet for the duration of my internship.

Once back in Macau, I contemplated staying with my job until the end of the year, to finish my studies, and train performers in Belgium once more as agreed with Max, before slowly preparing to leave while still able to do so on good terms.

Seeing Helena again only days after my return from Banff was like glimpsing one of the world's natural wonders. Taking her into my arms, my entire world seemed to light up with millions of candles. It felt like coming home. The loneliness I had felt throughout the last four years with our colorful show family had completely disappeared.

Helena had frequently come over to my apartment during my absence to take care of my menagerie. Now, reunited on my couch and enjoying a glass of wine, her expression became very serious.

"I've been thinking. Would you mind if I move in with you?"

I had been waiting for her to ask, not wanting to push her into anything.

"I wouldn't mind at all. Quite the contrary, I'd love to have you around. Also, if we want to stay together, it might be a good idea to live together now, instead of one of us dragging the other halfway around the world only to find out we don't like each other well enough after all."

Two days later, Helena was due to arrive late in the evening with all of her possessions. I was worried, expecting large suitcases filled with hundreds of shoes and other possessions, wondering where we would put it all.

The doorbell rang. When I opened the door, Helena stood before me with a small backpack and a large carry-on case.

"Where did you leave the rest of your luggage?"

She smiled.

"This is all I have."

Happiness flooded me. I had definitely found my soul mate.

Only two weeks after my return from Canada, Max and his assistant summoned me for another evaluation. As always, Max was full of praise and assured me that Aquatics management held me in the highest regard.

I handed over the Aquatics training handbook I had worked on over the last one and a half years. While in Banff, inspired by the spirit of respect and joy that surrounded me, I had completed the essential encyclopedia of training techniques for an underwater theater environment. Max thanked me and accepted the handbook with a happy smile.

During our meeting, all my inquiries on broadening my horizons within Dragone Aquatics were answered with nothing but a friendly smile. Max and I had long ago ceased trusting each other and had been warily circling each other ever since. After one hour of amiable diplomacy on both our sides, we got up and shook hands. As I went to leave, Max cleared his throat.

"Oh, one more thing."

I turned, "Yes?"

"I've decided *not* to send you to Belgium this year, Liam."

"Why on earth would you do that?"

He thought for a moment then looked directly into my eyes. "I'm uncomfortable with how much our performers trust you."

I just stared at him, then shook my head and walked away, at a complete loss of what to say.

Later the same day, I broke down in tears during one of my breaks. In one fell swoop I had been removed from all remaining training. Max's reasoning was beyond me. Obviously, the most important element of my position *was* to gain the performers' trust. Why was Max uncomfortable with that? Did he fear losing control if someone else's relationship with the performers was stronger than his? Did he need them to come to him instead of someone else? Whatever lay behind his cryptic statement, it was the final drop in the bucket of my frustration. Utterly thunderstruck, it took me days to fully understand the implications of what had happened.

I knew what I had to do but, still too passionately involved with the show, I agonized over actually doing it for two weeks. Thankfully I wasn't alone. Helena's presence provided me with the strength I needed to finally let go.

Three weeks after the evaluation, I walked into the Aquatics office, resignation letter in hand. My last day of work would coincide almost precisely with my last day at the Academy in Hong Kong. I had three months more to go.

As the first wave of relief settled over me, my anger drove me to work harder than ever, both at work and at school. As stubborn as ever, I invested all my remaining energy into a last push to make a difference. I would be leaving with profound life experiences, precious friendships, and a college diploma. No one would be able to take those away from me.

During the final months at *The House of Dancing Water*, my work at the Academy as well as my relationship with Helena bolstered my self-esteem and helped me stay almost super-humanly focused and positive. As I prepared for my departure, I knew, without a shadow of a doubt that the people who really mattered, the people whose lives I had held in my hands each day for four years, did not want me to leave. Even though my mind was made up, their vote of confidence meant the world to me.

During my last week of work at our theater, the Hong Kong Academy cordially invited me to their annual awards ceremony to officially receive an Award of Excellence. Apart from feeling incredibly honored, I knew accepting my Cantonese hosts' invitation would be interpreted as a sign of respect. I went to see Max and his assistant, Frank and showed them the invitation.

"I don't want to cause any inconvenience, and I know this invitation has unfortunately been sent to me very short notice, but can I possibly have a day off tomorrow to go over to Hong Kong and attend the ceremony?"

Max and Frank scanned the invitation.

"No way. We can't let you go."

"This is a once-in-a-lifetime kind of thing. Are you sure you can't do without me for those two shows? Please?"

"There's no way. Sorry Liam."

The team would be able to cover all the cues without me. I knew it without a doubt. I had checked the roster. Our show diver team was chronically over-staffed at that point, allowing us to have up to five divers on leave at any given time. On the day of the ceremony, only three divers would be missing, counting me.

Considering the circumstances, I suspected Max had ulterior motives. It turned out I wasn't the only one thinking along those lines. A beautiful side effect of Max's last strike in our work relationship was that, in this final week, after four long years in Dragone Aquatics, his betrayal brought me closer to some of my fellow show divers. Strong friendships were forged as people voiced their open support. They unanimously urged me to simply go against his orders.

"You have nothing to lose. You are leaving in one week anyway."

In my heart, I knew this was not an option. I would be damned if I would let Max destroy the good memory of my work. I had been forthright and reliable all these years and would not let him provoke me into lying, defying his decision and disrespecting him only days before leaving. Smiling to myself, and realizing, as usual, that I had most likely watched too many Hollywood movies, I decided to do the honorable thing and dive straight and true until the very end.

I calmly confronted Max and Frank.

"I respect your decision but I don't agree. I owe it to myself to go above your heads to our general manager to ask for his help. Should this fail, I promise you, I'll show up for work on the day of the awards ceremony."

Max and Frank stared at me and grudgingly nodded.

"Go ahead."

Clayton, the general manager, had time to see me one day before the ceremony. I presented my dilemma.

"Let me see what I can do. Can you come back to my office between shows? I'll have an answer for you then."

Minutes later, our general manager was on his way to hold an impromptu meeting with the artistic director and Max.

As I stumbled into Clayton's office in my work bathrobe a few hours later, I could tell his attempt to come to my aid had been unsuccessful.

"I'm sorry I couldn't be of more help. Max admitted that it'll be possible to do the shows without you tomorrow. But he still adamantly refused to let you go. He said there's always a chance some divers will fall ill overnight. While I can give Max suggestions, the final decision is his."

We looked at each other and both understood the nature of the game that was being played.

Keeping eye contact, Clayton said, "I can't tell you what to do. If you decide not to come to work tomorrow, there's nothing we can do about it. Your last day of work will be in four days anyhow. However, I ask you to do what you've always done. Give your very best for the sake of our performers. They need you."

He never broke eye contact, his gaze now gentle and searching.

No pondering was required from my side.

"I've never worked for Alexander, for *The House of Dancing Water*, for Aquatics, or for Max. I've always worked for myself. And I'll continue being honest no matter what anyone else decides to do. I've given most of my time and energy to our performers and won't desert them just a few days before my final exit. The awards ceremony will have to be held without me. I'll honor the decision Max made, regardless of right or wrong."

Clayton smiled. As we shook hands, I realized our respect for each other had grown.

When I arrived at work the next day, the divers as well as many other technicians and performers who had heard about the drama of the previous day were shocked to see me getting ready to dive the first show.

"What on earth are you doing here?" they asked with sad expressions.

As much as I understood their sentiments and appreciated their support, I knew without a shred of doubt I had made the right decision.

Encouraged, dreaming of a better future, I did what I still loved doing and navigated *The House of Dancing Water*'s underwater realm without missing a beat.

At last, my final moment in Aquatics arrived. I was grateful that Max refrained from giving a speech. Honest disdain was preferable to open lies.

My teammates, on the other hand, surprised me with a heartfelt gift. In old Las Vegas show diver tradition, our most trusted veterans had secretly rotated a pair of work fins throughout the theater, collecting signatures and mementos on it from all performers and divers.

The general manager organized tickets for Helena and me to see the show one last time from the audience. He bravely joined us in the first row.

Like a mischievous teenager, Clayton had informed all performers where we would be seated during the show. I couldn't stop smiling as I watched my friends defy the laws of gravity with their usual breathtaking gracefulness. Many waved, winked, or imperceptibly nodded their heads towards us. At every opportunity, they dove as close to us as they could, causing waves to crash over the glass barrier separating the auditorium from the watery stage. Performers materialized in front of us, cupping water in their hands, or even hiding it in their mouths. We got drenched many times over.

As Clayton, Helena and I ducked and dodged, we laughed, cried, and felt intensely alive. My show family was sending me off in style. Water became life once more that evening as I fondly remembered periods of our long journey together. *The House of Dancing Water* had been a growth milestone for us all.

Before leaving, I wanted to give our phenomenal artists one final token of appreciation. I organized a short group trip to my turquoise home in the Maldives for anyone who wanted to come. Fifteen performers and my partner Helena embarked on this memorable one-week vacation. What better way to complement our four years of sharing underwater training and show life than by joining three of my families in an endeavor that united the dark backstage underwater world with equatorial turquoise bliss?

On our own boat for the week, we explored the Lhaviyani Atoll above water and below. In the evenings we relaxed under palm trees and stars.

Helena ventured into the underwater universe for the first time. To my utter delight, she discovered she loved diving as much as I did.

Back in Macau, it was time to officially graduate. Commuting across the South China Sea on all of my days off, I had persevered and finished my diploma. Through many years of dedication and hard work, Helena had finished her Masters in Theater, Arts and Events Management.

The graduation was set for the 27th of June 2013. Leung Chun-Ying, Chief Executive of the self-administrative region of Hong Kong had the honor to present the degrees to the graduating students. He had been appointed by Mainland China and was notoriously unpopular in Hong Kong.

Decked out in traditional graduation attire, Helena and I were happy to be able to experience this defining moment together. After a long day of rehearsals, the actual ceremony began. TV crews started appearing through every theater entrance. Helena and I looked on in astonishment as our graduation ceremony turned into a revolution.

Two hundred and thirty three students graduated from the Academy that day. The majority of graduates seized the moment to display anger at the presence of the undemocratic Chinese impostor. Instead of bowing to Leung Chun-Ying as had been rehearsed, they shook their fists at him, screamed political slogans, gave him their backs or even their butts, or walked past without recognizing his presence. Entire groups of students presented banners while seated in the auditorium waiting for their turn on stage.

Due to the Chinese cultural restrictions of saving face, Leung Chun-Ying could not interrupt the proceedings. He weathered the rush of humiliations, smiling gently as he announced each graduate's accomplishments.

Being neutral observers, Helena and I followed the proceedings with unease and fascination. We were witnessing history in the making, our hearts beating faster with each act of nonviolent protest, wondering if there would be any consequences for these young artists.

During our academy classes, many of the local students had seemed shy and withdrawn. Seeing them now, vehemently defending their freedom of speech and mind in front of the national press, I was deeply touched by their courage. Helena and I were in the presence of true bravery. I cheered them on, wondering what I should do when I would be called on stage to receive my diploma? I had never concerned myself with Hong Kong politics and while I felt deeply sympathetic for and proud of my fellow graduates, I felt their fight was not mine.

Three hundred students later, when it was my turn, I faced the Chief Executive and bowed. As he read out my accomplishments, the nondescript smile he had worn all along never changed.

34

Xijiang River

My final days under Macau's oppressive brown haze were spent saying goodbye to the people I had grown very close to during our years together. Time passed in a flurry of goodbye breakfasts, brunches, lunches, and dinners. Many of these were savored on my rooftop, under a murky sky, overlooking Coloane village and the muddy Xijiang River.

This village had once been a haven for pirates. Here, between Macau and the Chinese mainland, their ships had hidden from sight before venturing out to face their next battles. I had done much the same. Each night, I had returned to my home at the banks of the Xijiang River from my daily struggles at the theater, often sipping a glass of wine while looking out over the peaceful stream. It had raised my spirits and even sparkled gracefully under the starry sky. Then in the mornings, I had sailed out once more to throw myself into the fray.

I longed to leave Macau behind me. Over the years, I had passed through many foreign countries. Some had found a place in my heart. Others had become a true home. But Macau had always felt suffocating. Still, I *did* make a home there for three years – not within the self-administrative region itself, but rather in my small hideaway on the banks of the Xijiang River, and in the isolated bubble of our Dragone theater family.

Only one Macau-Chinese person outside our theater community became a lasting, positive memory.

There was a frail old man who worked in the parking garage of my favorite supermarket, *Park'n Shop*. He would sit in the dreary garage all day,

...his big toothless smile. His little table was in front of t...

...ne manually validated parking stubs for shoppers before th...

...rds into the gaudily-decorated grocery paradise. Sometimes, I wc...

...h the old man taking a nap, but he would snap awake at the sound o...

...ny steps, greeting me with a beaming smile. I would try to leave him a tip on my way back from shopping. But he would always totter after me, insisting I take the small amount of change back. So I resorted to bringing him chocolates on a regular basis.

He wanted me to teach him a few words of English every so often. I will never forget the day he excitedly pointed at a slogan on a dirty plastic bag spread out on the table in front of him. He kept pointing and asking, "Nīgo dím duhk a?" (How do you pronounce that?)

I ended up spending twenty minutes in the stuffy garage with my eager student, teaching him the sentence, "I am a plastic bag. Please use me responsibly." When I took my leave, he happily bowed a few times. Charmed, I waved and said with a – most likely – horrible accent, "Mhgòi sai. Bāaibaai." (Thank you. Goodbye.) It was about as far as my Cantonese stretched.

This amiable old man had made me look forward to every shopping trip. But generally speaking, the locals vexed me. Macau, more than any other place I traveled through over the years, made me realize how much we are shaped by our upbringing and our roots – even someone as rootless as myself.

Asia had always been a favorite destination of mine, due to the amazing charm and friendliness of its people. Balinese, Thai, and Philippine people did things in a pleasant manner, even when they were scamming you. Here in Southeast Asia, for once, I never had to watch out for scams. But the unsmiling sea of faces all around me made me miss the chaotic appeal of other Asian mentalities.

No matter how good my mood was at the beginning of the day, no matter how strong my resolve to stay positive, the walls of indifferent Chinese stoicism turned me into an irritated old grump by the end of most days. I found myself preferring workdays to days off. At least inside the theater I was able to enjoy the vibrant diversity of thirty different cultures.

Walking through Macauan streets made me want to study Kung Fu. The Chinese populace seemed to have no spatial awareness and stoically used whatever appendage was necessary to bump passersby out of the way. I delighted in imagining this unresponsive sea of people flying off in all directions after they connected with my impressive martial arts moves a la *The Matrix*. Instead, I would get elbowed out of the way by elderly Chinese ladies.

Local walking patterns felt erratic to my European mind. I couldn't help but accidentally bump into other people myself. They would stop right in front of me without warning, or would suddenly cut across the sidewalk without any consideration for their fellow pedestrians. To make matters worse, many locals would hawk and spit enthusiastically while walking.

Whenever a bus arrived at a stop, it seemed as though it were the last bus on earth. Everyone would grapple to get on first. Wide shoulders or extreme contortion skills came in handy during these exasperating encounters. Amazingly, people never turned toward each other after colliding. No one apologized. People simply moved on and attacked the next wave of pedestrians that rolled towards them. For someone who had grown up in Central Europe, this behavior was unthinkable.

I would wake up each morning to villagers exchanging the latest gossip on the small plaza in front of my apartment. They would be standing right next to each other yet somehow manage to hold their conversations so loudly, everyone within a quarter mile radius would become an involuntary participant. Thankfully, during the rest of the day, my remote village apartment was a haven of tranquility – unlike the rest of Macau, where constant shouting, door slamming, and power drilling were the rule rather than the exception.

Most likely, the locals were as exasperated with me as I was with them. Intellectually, I knew there were valid reasons for all these behavior patterns, starting with the over-crowdedness of Chinese metropolitan life. But the longer I lived in Macau, the more I struggled with my perception of the rudeness of this society. I expected to adapt as I had always done before, but I couldn't. Their way of life simply made me too unhappy.

Above all, I hated who I became in this environment. To claim my space, I had to bump and shove just like everyone else. To cut through the stoic passivity of store clerks, I would have to insist until their initial persistent "no" turned into a "yes". I felt like a pushy asshole and disliked the irritable, quick to anger, road-raging expat who stared back at me in the mirror.

After years of living a worldwide nomadic existence, I realized I was inherently European and always would be. I also understood I did not have to accept everything I encountered. Some cultures and places simply didn't agree with my personality and that was just fine. It was a big planet after all. It was time to seek healthier pastures. I had endured this one long enough.

Towards the end of my Macau experiences, I met a Native American shaman who traveled the world to share his wisdom with those in need of guidance. Since I had always admired North American indigenous cultures, I was curious to hear his philosophy on life and briefly considered approaching him.

Coincidentally, we both ended up being invited to a boat party in Hong Kong. The shaman made his rounds amongst the partying Dragone performers, imparting wisdoms left and right. Not keen on getting self-help advice during a social gathering, I stayed away.

Suddenly, the shaman was at my side and looked me over.

"You should stop being so needy. Of course no one wants to love you. You're too dependent on people. You lean on them. All of this is made clear by your slouched shoulders."

My eyebrows must have been raised as steeply as Rube's in the Maldives. Even though I *had* been needy in some of my intimate relationships, I was by far the opposite on a daily basis with my friends and acquaintances.

His condescension saddened me. Being well aware of my posture and its cause, I felt no need to argue with his misconceptions about my body language. I had spent a good ten years of my life deliberately slouching to hide my enormous breasts. Later, after my breasts had been removed and normalcy restored to my universe, I realized reversing my slouch completely would be nearly impossible. My bad posture had become permanent.

He was only one of thousands of shamans, yet the young boy in me who had devoured any book on Native American spiritualism couldn't help but feel the heroes of his childhood evaporate into the polluted Hong Kong air. Irritated by his judgmental invasion of my privacy, I walked away without a word. What gave him the right to nonchalantly dismantle my personality without asking me a single question?

I ticked the experience off as just one more drop in my Macauan bucket.

Despite this encounter, my last days in town were happy and unforgettable. My show family wrapped me in its loving embrace.

Robbie, one of my fellow show divers, hugged me and broke into tears as we said goodbye.

"You know, when I first saw you, with your closely shaved head and tattoos, I was a bit scared of you. Then you opened your mouth and proved to be one of the gentlest, most compassionate people I've ever met. You always stayed strong and personal. And you never stopped trying to look beyond the politics. Thanks for inspiring me. I'll really miss you, Liam."

Squeezing him one more time, I struggled with some tears of my own.

The learning curve of my Macau years had been exponential. While listening to coaches and performers over the years, what had struck me the most was their decision-making process. The key to executing a stunt perfectly, and more importantly, safely, was commitment.

During Russian Swing for example, pushers and fliers would push together in perfect harmony, bringing the swing higher with each concerted effort. The swing needed to be high enough. At the same time, too much momentum meant loss of control. It was the flier who needed to feel for the perfect moment, to enable him to soar through the air in the most magnificent arc while remaining in control. When the flier felt this moment arrive, he would loudly call, "Up!"

Both pushers and the flier would put everything they had into one last, strong, synchronized push. Only a few seconds later, the flier would let go and get catapulted high and wide, performing a series of spins and turns. In the end, he would land gracefully in the water.

Acrobatics is characterized by many such moments of no return. In this example, the flier needs to commit. More than anything, he needs to believe in himself without any doubt. Once he shouts, "Up!" he cannot change his mind. The momentum of the swing has grown too powerful to resist. Stopping the swing at this point can mean injury, or even death.

From the very first day of my exposure to acrobatics and coaching, I saw them as a metaphor of life. Once you commit to something, you need to forge ahead with confidence. And, more often than not, going forward is far better then turning back.

Many acrobatics acts also require diligent teamwork and a trust so deep, you literally put your life into someone else's hands. No matter how confident you are, without pushers who are just as committed as you, dedicated to a common cause, you will not fly far. But even a solo act is never truly solo. If no pushers are visible, then the successful performance of the acrobat rests in the hands of the technicians who have prepared his equipment and assisted him behind the scenes.

I treasured such insights with all my heart. Working in close proximity to individuals who risked their very lives for their profession on a daily basis, made me appreciate more than ever how important it is to believe in ourselves. We need to be clear in our intentions, make our decisions with conviction, and overcome fear. We need to trust others, too. They're out there, the pushers with common goals, just as we can become pushers for someone who needs us. And whatever our circumstances, we need to live life to the fullest. No doubts. No regrets.

At my goodbye party, I had a last chat, hug, and kiss with each of our passionate performers and some of the technicians. Looking at everyone around me made me fully realize that I had, in fact, beaten the odds and made a difference by believing in myself, and giving myself wholeheartedly to this venture for the past four years. I had stayed genuine, kind, and honest in an overwhelmingly political, corporate environment.

Battling with the impact of the locker room, surrounded by Adonises, entangled in a web of politics and incompetence, I had come close to sacrificing my physical health as well as my happiness to our proud endeavor at Dragone Entertainment. Whereas many other technicians simply came to work and managed to keep an emotional distance, I had allowed myself to be swept away by my passion, committing myself fully to the task of keeping our performers safe at all times. Far from being needy, as the shaman had suggested, I had given everyone around me all I had.

Alexander kept pushing the physical boundaries of the entertainment industry. He had the courage to go where no one had gone before. He took risks beyond other people's wildest dreams and had the creative genius to boot.

Like me, Alexander believed anything was possible and immediately questioned if someone told him something couldn't be done. During creation in 2010, he spent two weeks working on the *Moto Act*. It was the only part of our show that didn't involve any water, but rather was on a dry stage with three ramps and up to eight motorcycle riders, who flew through the air as if their bikes had sprouted wings.

Aiming to find the fastest transition between acts, Alexander wanted to drive the two smaller ramps onto our circular stage through the narrow cast and west vomitories, instead of bringing all moto ramps one by one through the wider north passage underneath the raised backdrop.

"Do we have enough space backstage for the ramp vehicles to turn the sharp curve onto the vomitories?" he asked his head of carpentry. "I wonder if this'll allow us to bring them from their backstage parking spots to their stage positions in less than a minute?"

"No way. It's too narrow," was the instant response.

Alexander kept asking.

"No. Impossible," the head of carpentry insisted.

Then one day, Alexander stopped asking.

Instead, he walked backstage during a rehearsal break, stopwatch in hand, and approached a carpenter.

"Hey, you. Get in that truck and drive it onstage through one of the vomitories. Do it as fast as you can."

Shocked into instant action by seeing the infamous Alexander only an arms length away, the carpenter hustled and managed to drive the little ramp truck into its position within thirty seconds.

After the break, Franco called all technicians on stage for a meeting.

"I can't build this show without you. In order to achieve greatness, I need you to be with me every step of the way. You're here to make whatever I need happen. If it's not yet possible, make it possible."

Then he started to shout.

"You lazy bastards. Who do you think you are? I've been asking for days if we can bring those ramps through the vomitories. You couldn't even be bothered to try? If this ever happens again, there will be serious consequences. I can easily replace each and every one of you within minutes. I *never* want to hear the word 'impossible' again. Is that clear? Nothing is impossible. If we can't do it one way, we find another way. I need positive people who can make things happen. Nothing of this magnitude has ever been done before. We're all part of something incredible. I need you to be proactive and bold."

I was shocked by his outburst, but couldn't help but be inspired as well.

"Why are you still standing around here? Get back to work! And bring me those damn solutions when I ask for something."

We all escaped from under his furious glare, almost falling over each other to get to our positions.

Just like Alexander, and any of our performers or technicians, I did not regret a single minute of being a small part of creating and operating what was the biggest show on Earth at the time.

Like a sailor in a storm, I had clung to the mast as the waves of my passion swept me higher and plunged me deeper than ever before. I could have left the ship at the next possible harbor. Like I had so often during the course of my life, though, I had braved the waves instead of seeking safety and opted to climb all the way to the top of the mast while my ship raged on the black ocean of our theater waters.

Instead of drinking myself into a stupor in the evenings, or abruptly walking off the job, I had chosen to work even harder for *The House of Dancing Water* and learn as much as I could in the process.

Then I went a step further and decided to build on my existing knowledge by studying theater at the Academy. These choices had saved me. I had survived once again, emerging stronger and wiser, if a little burned out and greyer at the temples.

35

Untersee

Had I not decided to endure and stubbornly keep with it against all odds at *The House of Dancing Water*, I would never have met Helena.

Ours was a slow-moving love affair, fraught with difficulties. I was a European, transgender man brought up in a very liberal German household, who spent his early years far from churches on open-minded, nudist beaches. Helena was a woman born into a Christian missionary household in conservative Korea who then moved far off the beaten path with her family, so her father could bring enlightenment to the people of Kyrgyzstan and Afghanistan. Such a union seemed doomed from the start.

Yet, as different as our lives seemed at first glance, we shared a similar homelessness, rebelliousness, artistic passion and spiritual belief. Helena was the partner I had envisioned: self-reliant, proud, gentle, beautiful, compassionate, adventurous, supportive, nonjudgmental and open to growth. I could only hope to be able to live up to her amazingly high moral standards.

All my life I had wondered if maybe I was too odd and too serious for a long-term relationship. Rarely had I felt adequate. Instead, I had felt the pressure of having to make up for not being interesting, cool, or manly enough. Having also spent too many years at odds with my body, I had retained a certain level of physical reticence.

My past partners had told me they were satisfied, yet I couldn't help feeling that I was a boring lover. I could barely bring myself to remember one position in bed and felt too inhibited to expand my sexual horizons.

I never craved drugs, parties, clubs, or anything too outgoing. Quite the opposite – I was content to remain surrounded by water, open plains, forests, wildlife, pets, books, and movies.

I remembered the frantic, unsettling pace of my former relationships. My intense passion and longing had often put too much pressure on my partners. At the same time, I knew now, I had felt no real sense of being safe with any of them.

With Helena, it was different. I felt as safe and unhurried as if I was strolling along my favorite beach without a care in the world.

Helena loved me entirely as I was, body and soul, the entire package, good and bad, grumpy, boring in bed, impatient, impulsive, and penniless.

Of course we also had had to work for our happiness. We had fought, cried, hurt and misunderstood each other, gradually overcoming the obvious as well as subtle differences in our cultures, mentalities, and characters. Our relationship had grown like a table coral – and still did. Tree-like, it fanned out, each tiny branch connecting to others to build a magnificent structure – tough and brittle at the same time.

Both of us knew how easily such a delicate formation could break. For the first time, however, I was confident to have found a partner who was as committed to our common cause as I was. Helena and I were different in so many ways, yet together our universe expanded. We challenged and supported each other in equal measure. And we both felt it, without a doubt: we were soul mates. We had found the person of our dreams.

The beginning of July 2013 saw Helena and me happily smiling above the clouds. We were leaving Macau and heading towards Europe. My two faithful, four-legged companions, Boo and Bocelli were on their way as well, flying in the cargo hold towards the same destination.

Dad's house, located on the tranquil shore of the Untersee, was to become our home base for a six-week period of recuperation. The Untersee branches out from Lake Constance's main body. Only half a mile from Dad's half-timber home, the lake narrows even further and flows into the river Rhine.

Boo and Bocelli took the fortress by storm. My dad, who had formerly not been a cat person, fell in love, as did the kitties. They adopted each other faster than Helena and I could blink. This was just as well, since we had no real concept of where life might lead over the following months, and we feared having to leave them behind.

We explored the wealth of European culture and traveled through Switzerland, Germany, France, Spain, and Italy. We savored open air concerts, festivals, opera, theater, and an assortment of medieval fortresses. We marveled at the deliciousness of German bread, the sensual qualities of Swiss cheese fondue, the delightful aromas of Southern European wines. Above all, Helena and I were mesmerized by the azure blue of summer skies, and were even more deeply enchanted by the royal blue Mediterranean Sea off the Cote d'Azure in the South of France. After the polluted, turbid Pearl River Delta, I couldn't get enough of the crystal clear water with its powerful, salty taste.

It felt good to spend time with my dad as well. Over the years, we had bridged the gap. I had learned from our past and forgiven all there was to forgive. After drifting apart, we had come back together with a more profound understanding of one another. I was still more impatient with him than with most people, but he knew I didn't mean any harm when I cut him short or groaned at yet another one of his long-winded monologues on history, politics, or the stock market.

My relationship with Hildegard was still fragile yet we were slowly growing closer. The treacherous swampland of our past relationship steadily evolved into firmer ground. In her own convoluted way, Mom had done her part in helping me grow. Despite numerous paranoias and neuroses, she had been with me every step of the way and meant me no harm. While struggling with her demons, she loved me very much.

I was more relaxed now when I met with my mom, and could feel her relaxing in turn. We even laughed together. We would sit together, eating *Fleischkaese* and potato salad, followed by many cakes and coffees. To my utter surprise, Helena and Mom hit it off. They accepted and valued each other. Helena's presence helped both of us enjoy the moment rather than holding on to painful memories of the past. Conversation began to flow more easily.

Whenever we saw each other, I made sure to fold Mom into my arms and hold her for a long time. Whereas she would feel stiff as a board when we said "hello", she would let herself fall into my embrace by the time we needed to say "goodbye".

"It was so good to see you," she would say each time. "I feel so much better now, so happy and full of hope and cheer. Come back soon, my dear Liam."

"I will, Mom. Take good care of yourself. I love you."

Being able to make her happy felt as right as the sun rising and setting each day. I finally understood that I needed to love my mom the way she is, no matter how much pain we might have caused each other in the past. I needed to stop asking "why" and purely appreciate her for who she is and what she is able to give.

When Helena and I left Mom that summer, we drove off with a smile. For the first time in many years, I felt no anxiousness after our reunion and looked forward to seeing her again on our next visit to Germany.

While in Europe, I touched base with many of my closest friends as I always did, marveling at the strength of our connection. Helena joined Naomi and me for our traditional latte macchiato. Sienna and I picked up where we had left off years earlier and philosophized for hours.

My Serbian friends from Cinema Metropol kept feeding me until I felt like an over-inflated balloon and had to use the only Serbian phrase I knew to get them to stop.

"Ja imam problema sa stomakom." (I have an upset stomach.)

On a beautiful Zurich morning, my former photography lecturer, Lars, and I shared spirited stories of our latest worldwide adventures while sipping a strong, Swiss coffee.

My best buddy Milo met us for beer and bratwurst in one of Bavaria's finest beer gardens. Incidentally, Judith and another friend from the Maldives were in Nuremberg on the same day. So was Naya, my dear friend from the early days in Belgium and Macau. They all joined us underneath a canopy of tall maple trees. Every now and then, sunlight broke through the dense foliage, and softly caressed our bodies. Devouring one bratwurst after another, we laughed and shared many fond memories until late that evening.

No matter how far away I wandered or how long I stayed, my closest friends remained. Our doors were always open for each other. Reminiscing, I was struck by the beauty of being allowed to touch lives and be touched in turn, the pleasure of remaining a small part of someone's life for many years, or even having the privilege of guiding and inspiring them.

We all have so much to give. As our lives intersect, our actions matter. Some lives we touch by elaborate deeds, some with a simple smile or by giving a minute of our time. Some we touch for just one precious moment, others over a period of many years. I am deeply humbled by the impact we can have on other people's lives. It is a responsibility to be treasured, and never to be taken lightly.

Having felt homeless for most of my life, I valued my friends a great deal. Home became wherever I felt loved and able to give love in return.

That summer, I met with my sister Petra as well. We had met a few times, but up until then, we had carefully avoided discussing any personal topics. While we drank cold beer under a clear Munich summer sky, nibbling on tasty *Obatzter* and *Currywurst*, we talked for the first time about our shared birth mother, our respective histories, our fears and dreams. The last walls between us crumbled, revealing only trust and closeness.

Petra confided in me that our mother, Sandra, was dying of lung cancer. Apparently, she had strongly expressed not wanting to see me. Even though both revelations shocked me, I took them in stride. What else could I do but respect my birth mom's wishes, while at the same time making sure to be there for my fabulous sister?

Part of my "Tour de Europe" was to touch base with relatives I hadn't seen in almost twenty years. My oma and I had visited them only a dozen times during my early childhood, yet they had left a lasting impression on me. My dad's cousin, Hubert, and his wife Trudy had inspired me throughout my life.

Hubert was the elder of two sons. As German tradition would have it at the time, he was obligated to take over his father's business. Hubert hated the idea of having to own it even more than he hated working there. But he followed in his father's footsteps with grace, integrity, and an immense sense of responsibility.

Over the years, Hubert managed to strike the perfect balance by following his dreams in his off time. My dad would shake his head at his cousin's dangerous leisure activities, which involved paragliding, dirt bike racing, and many other risky endeavors.

Meanwhile, I would cheer Hubert and Trudy on from a distance. Every weekend, they were on the move, in search of adventure. Later in life, Hubert showed still more strength of character by setting his sons free. He allowed them to follow their hearts twenty-four-seven. During adolescence, my dad's cousin's story had influenced me more than any other. Hubert had shown me it was possible to combine responsibility and integrity with following your heart.

Amazingly, when Helena and I arrived at Trudy and Hubert's home in the summer of 2013, the twenty years apart simply evaporated. Trudy ended up inviting the closest members of their family for an unforgettable dinner. We all felt instantly comfortable with each other. Aunts, uncles, and cousins shared their lives and mouth-watering German delicacies until late into the night. I was immensely proud to be a part of such an open-minded, inspiring family.

As I listened to the life stories of my charming relatives, having the chance to inspire them with tales of my adventures as well, I loved life more than ever.

By the end of August 2013, Helena and I needed to return to Hong Kong. Following my studies, I was offered the opportunity to work as a production manager for an events management company.

As exciting as it sounded, both Helena and I felt unsettled at the thought of having to return to Hong Kong. We had both become increasingly uncomfortable with Hong Kong-Chinese culture over the years.

To make matters worse, whilst in Europe, Clive, the manager of the events management company I was soon to join, had contacted me with unsettling news. In the six weeks since my interview, Serious Events had been taken over by another company called WRG. The individuals who were supposed to become my mentors had resigned. I felt profoundly uneasy about this development, but nevertheless decided to give life and work in the bustling metropolis a chance.

Before going anywhere, I needed to stock up on drugs and supplies. Over the course of my nomadic years, I had made regular pit stops at my trusted doctor's clinic in Zurich to renew my prescription of male hormones. My doctor usually gave me a two-year supply, with needles and syringes "to go". I was astonished, but so far no border officer had ever stopped me to ask why there was a large canvas bag filled with needles, syringes, and injectable drugs in my suitcase.

Carrying my new stash, I was as ready as I was ever going to be. Helena and I wrapped my dad and our cats into our arms one last time and took to the skies once again. When our airplane approached Hong Kong, we had tears in our eyes. We would have much preferred turning around right then and there.

As soon as I arrived at my new company, I knew I had landed on the wrong planet. It was, quite frankly, a disaster. Apart from my mentors being gone and the Hong Kong-Chinese employees of the company refusing to collaborate with me, I strongly felt the lingering *House of Dancing Water* burnout. I felt nowhere near ready to throw myself into the next working experience with fourteen-hour days and zero personal time.

As the weeks wore on, I tried very hard to feel excitement for our projects. But I discovered almost instantly that I was too much of a creative romantic to get excited about cocktail parties for luxury brands.

Being a production manager turned out to be the wrong end of the stick as well. I was fascinated with the creative, organizational side of our work, not with the technical side I was meant to execute.

Within weeks, I felt more desperate than I had after four years of living in a state of constant exhaustion at Dragone Entertainment. My Hong Kong-Chinese teammates kept sabotaging my every effort to become a functional part of their team. They withheld all information concerning our projects, making it impossible for me to do my job properly. Clive and I were at a loss as to how to proceed.

At the same time, Hong Kong assaulted my senses. During my time at the Academy, I had spent almost two years commuting to Hong Kong on a regular basis. I had loved the break from my Macau routine. Staying in Hong Kong as a full-time resident now, I found the city to be fascinating as much as unnerving. Wherever I looked, there was no space, no privacy, and no peace. People had just as little spatial awareness as the average Macau citizen. The volume and density of pedestrian traffic were almost unbearable and made me want to become a monk, isolated deep in the Amazonian rain forest.

Cell phones were everywhere. With each passing day, I understood better why Hong Kong citizens were inseparable from their wireless electronic devices: the small, glowing screens gave them privacy amidst the ceaseless flow of people. Whilst shuffling through the city crowd, or being crammed into the confines of a subway train like sardines, each person blocked the onslaught of a world that was all too real and constricted. They escaped into the intimate, spacious world of virtual reality.

Leaving Macau had seemed like a step into a better future. But I now found myself unable to adapt and get comfortable in Hong Kong's even more aggressive and artificial environment.

Thankfully, Helena and I found a cozy studio apartment on the green and quiet Lamma Island, just twenty-five minutes by ferry from Hong Kong Central. The daily commute across the ocean quieted my mind enough to hang on for the time being.

Long before resigning from *The House of Dancing Water*, I had begun thinking of ticking off yet another item on my bucket list. This one had been a lifelong dream: writing a book. For a long time, I had envisioned writing my memoirs and maybe inspiring people on a broader scale by sharing my unique story with the world.

Towards the end of my time in Macau, I had been imagining taking a few months off and renting a little room in the Philippine jungle, to spend time thinking and writing my heart out. My plans had changed after meeting Helena and being offered the job opportunity in Hong Kong.

As I now sat drooling at my desk, I knew my situation at the events management company was unsalvageable. I was at the wrong place at the wrong time in the wrong position with the wrong team. I wasn't going to endure anymore, like I had done so many times in the past. It was time to move on – in more ways than one.

So I took a stand and made the decision to take my remaining inconsequential savings as well as all of my courage, and say "no", sooner rather than later. At the same time, I said "yes" to writing my memoirs.

In the beginning of October 2013, after six weeks of struggling in my new company, I handed in my letter of resignation and left the same day. Immeasurable relief flooded me. I felt like I had been climbing Mount Everest in flip-flops and had suddenly found a way to parachute onto golden, sandy beaches.

Helena and I were now both unemployed, but I knew without a doubt I had made the right decision. Helena was amazing, supporting me in following my heart.

I needed a tranquil spot on the planet to begin the journey into the vast ocean of my memories. Quiet Lamma Island seemed as good a place as any. Our house was at the edge of the jungle, surrounded by lush foliage. Orchids, holding on to tree trunks with only a few of their obstinate roots, would bloom periodically.

Besides a small police car, a miniature fire truck and a dozen tiny delivery trucks, no motor vehicles were allowed on the island. Still, it wasn't quiet.

The constant hum of dehumidifiers and ACs was complemented by a deafening concerto of birds, frogs and cicadas. Still, compared to the rest of Hong Kong this was bliss. Away from city life, I found my equilibrium. As my mind began buzzing with positive energy once more, my fingers began dancing over the keyboard.

Helena and I adopted two puppies and settled into a life that saw me mostly sitting on our couch or kitchen table, bent over my laptop, while Helena and our two dogs gave me lots of love and space to tackle my daily word count.

Looking out our kitchen window, diving into peaceful shades of green while trying to objectively remember so many aspects of my own history was exhilarating. Only a few minutes of walking brought me to a deserted beach facing the South China Sea. I could listen to the waves and dream of what might lay below the surface while writing notes for my book.

Over the months, I kept a rigorous schedule. I would write up to forty hours each week, then recharge my batteries by spending many loving hours with Helena, or by seeking solitude in the green hills of Lamma Island, accompanied only by thousands of mosquitoes, spiders, frogs, birds, the odd snake, and Buzzy and Ricky, our ever-growing puppies.

In mid-August 2014, after eleven months of writing, I came to wit's end concerning the local customs, as well as the end of my savings, the end of my rental contract, and the end of my third draft.

Helena and I had trusted and supported each other over the course of a year that had proven to be far from easy despite its many virtues.

Following her Masters, Helena had had high hopes of finding employment in the town where she had graduated. Yet after a year of searching and writing more than three hundred applications, she had still not been given a chance by anyone.

I had battled pneumonia.

My sister Petra and I had suffered the loss of our mother, who had finally succumbed to lung cancer. To the very end, my birth mom Sandra had refused to let me see her. She had given us no chance of reconciliation.

Last but not least, Helena and I had tried our very best but had both become ever more exasperated with the intensely self-centered, rude and often unkind behavior of the local Hong Kong populace. I had felt too many elbows in my ribs, and had been batted aside by too many pedestrians with umbrellas. Questions for help or public service had been met by too many empty stares, passive aggression, or outright refusal to engage with the unwelcome "gweilo" (the disparaging Cantonese word for foreigners.)

So, Helena and I decided to move on.

With no funds left at our disposal and no home or job to go to, we were faced with a tough decision. We couldn't possibly continue taking care of Buzzy and Ricky.

The now one-year-old puppies had become an irreplaceable part of our little family. They had blessed us with abundant trust and love. Leaving them behind was unthinkable. As we came ever closer to a point where we wouldn't be able to buy food for them anymore, much less pay for their air transport to another country, we took courage in hand and began searching for a new family for our furry companions. Luckily, a Chinese couple from another island fell in love with them and decided to adopt them.

The day we had to bring Buzzy and Ricky to their new home was one of the saddest days of my life. When the moment came for us to say goodbye, our puppies followed us to the garden gate of their beautiful, spacious new home. We asked them to "sit" and "stay." With unfailing obedience, their big eyes trustingly meeting ours, they did. We closed the gate between us and walked away as fast as we could. Our hearts broke. Unable to keep walking, Helena and I immediately found a park bench, sank into each other's arms, and cried for a long time.

Arriving back at our apartment on Lamma Island, every cozy corner of it felt cold and forbidding. For three days in a row, we couldn't stop crying. Our hearts were as heavy as if we had lost our children.

After a few days, the sadness became more bearable. Helena and I focused on packing our few belongings and saying goodbye to our friends in Hong Kong and Macau.

All in all, despite all hardships and failure to connect with the locals, my year in Hong Kong had been one of the happiest of my life. With every sentence I had written, I had grown. I had gained an even better understanding of myself. I had rejoiced in the privilege of being able to funnel my entire creative energy into a personal project. I had felt the love and support of friends and family like never before.

At one point I had even launched a crowd-funding campaign for my book, to be able to cover editing and publishing-related costs. I was amazed when at the end of my fifty-six day campaign over one hundred former work colleagues, acquaintances, friends, and family donated ten thousand one hundred and seventeen US dollars. Even people I knew to be completely broke did not want to miss the chance to help. The children of friends gave me part of their pocket money, and some of my closest friends made more than one donation online. Just like the equatorial sun had lit up the white Maldivian beaches with its warmth and almost ethereal glow, the overwhelming support and trust had brightened my every day.

August 26th, 2014 was the big day. My book was not quite finished yet, but I was already well into my third draft. Leaving our green oasis with only three suitcases, we made our way to Hong Kong International Airport. We couldn't wait to leave.

My dad had rented us a cozy little vacation home in his village, with a direct view of the lake. We would be able to stay there until – hopefully – our path forward became clear.

We had looked at options with Dad.

"I trust you," he had said. "You've always been a hard worker. Take the time to finish your book. I can support you and Helena until then."

I had been immensely grateful and accepted his offer.

"Thanks for believing in me, Dad. I'll continue working forty to fifty hours per week as soon as we hit the ground in Germany. It should only take me another three months and I'll be done with my manuscript. We'll be out of your hair as quickly as possible."

I would spend those first three months in the soothing quiet of our temporary haven, on the lush, green shores of the Untersee, writing a fourth, fifth and then sixth draft. Then the hunt for an agent, a publisher, and hopefully a new job would begin in earnest.

Helena wanted to immediately start looking for jobs. Neither of us had any idea what to expect. So we agreed to try not to expect anything. We would wait and see who would discover an inspiring opportunity first. The other would simply follow and trust in finding something in the same location.

It felt good to let go, and for the first time in my life, to not be paranoid about what potential booby traps life might have set for me. I had escaped death and depression too many times to be scared anymore. I felt free, loved, and energized. I had survived more than most, and felt intensely happy. I had so much to give.

Helena and I kissed deeply before boarding our airplane at Hong Kong International Airport's gate sixty-five. Once on board, we celebrated the new beginning with a glass of champagne. We had no money and no concrete plans. But we had love and hope. We had the romantic heart of true nomads. It was all we needed.

75% – an Epilogue

All my life I have been a fighter, a survivor. I have longed for home, exploring the world in search for it. Growing up, I felt homeless in body, family, and country. I knew early on that fate had led me to inhabit the wrong body. Long after emerging from my mother's amniotic fluid, I had discovered my family was not my own. And I had learned I was a product of not just one country, but three. Over the years, my homelessness seemed a curse as much as a blessing. I was profoundly lonely, yet free.

The last remnants of my feelings of homelessness dissolve as I am telling my story. I now realize, I was never really homeless. As imperfect as my body is, not ever fully male, it is part of who I am, and it is what I have been given.

My adoptive parents will always be my true parents. In their own imperfect way, Dad and Hildegard, my dear, struggling mom, love me. They have never judged me. No matter how much the way I lived scared the crap out of them, no matter how far I strayed from the path of the safely anchored bank teller they had envisioned for me, they were always by my side. They believed in me and supported me as exactly who I was, not as who they wanted me to be. I hadn't comprehended this as a confused, transgender teenager. But I see it now.

My sister Petra – found, then lost, then found again – expands my family universe. Many irreplaceable characters I met along the way have given me a sense of belonging. They are my extended family and always will be.

Helena and I continue to make each other happy. There are no guarantees, of course. But right now, each time we look at each other, we both feel we've arrived in a safe harbor. Hopefully, in time, we'll forge our own family.

As for countries, I no longer see the need to belong to a specific one. The world is my country. The bodies of water spread all over its surface are my true home – the one place where I feel complete in body and soul, not at odds with anything, serene, elegant, and handsome.

A multitude of life experiences have helped me grow into the man I am today. Sometimes it felt as if life pushed me into a dark underground river. I got shaken through and through as I hurtled through unforeseeable rapids. Other times, seeing no other way, I jumped in voluntarily, testing the limits of my endurance. Eventually, I always glimpsed a bioluminescent creature on the bottom of this stream of life. Like a *Tinkerbelle* of the deep, the dancing speck of brightness in front of my weary eyes helped me find my way back to the surface every time.

Whatever the reason for my hardships, they have supplied me with abundant strength and compassion. I am sure the torrents will take me again. It is inevitable. Be that as it may, I am looking forward to continuing my journey. And I wonder, where will the water take Helena and me next? It *is* "we" now, and I am awed by the enormity of that transition.

As a professional scuba diver, I know it is pointless to struggle against a strong current. You need to learn to ride it, embrace it, love it, follow the flow and let its power work for you. We are prepared to follow the current.

The oceans make up 71% of our planet's surface. Counting all other bodies of water, a good 75% of our world is immersed in hues of turquoise and blue. It's a vast home offering infinite possibilities. Anything can happen.

Acknowledgements

A friend once told me, "Behind every name on a book cover are at least five people without whom writing the book would never have been possible." In my case there were far more than five, but let me start with eight magic individuals who supported, guided, and guarded me.

Grandma, I will never forget you. You are always with me. You helped me find my strength, my soul, and tenacity when I was young. Wherever you are, you will never be forgotten. I will always be searching for your false teeth just to find them in the most unlikely places, and will forever gaze up at the moon together with you. You made me smile. You found humor in the saddest of moments. You made me feel that the world is a beautiful place. I am forever grateful and love you with all my heart.

Dad, you are an amazing kind soul with a very big heart. When it really mattered, you were always right there. You supported me and loved me no matter what. When I dropped everything else to finally write this book, you believed in me.

Helena, my irreplaceable, beautiful, soulful partner: how could I ever have been so lucky as to meet you? You never doubted me. You believed in me and stood by me, even though when I started writing this book our outlook was scary and we didn't know if we would end up sleeping under a bridge.

Naomi and Sienna, you are my true Swiss home. No matter how far away my travels take me, I can always come home to you, and always count on you.

Milo, my best buddy and adventurous soul mate: you supported me with all your heart. You always cared and were ready to help in case I needed you.

Lars and Hubert, you showed me we can be caring, dedicating our lives to helping others, while at the same time seeking adventures and living to our heart's content.

Apart from these major sources of inspiration and support, I would like to thank all the great characters I was destined to come across so far. You all taught me, helped me grow, helped me find my voice. No moment in our life is meaningless, no encounter worthless. Everything and everyone contributes to our very own odyssey and shapes us into who we are meant to be.

Publishing this book would not have been possible without the very real, overwhelming moral as well as financial support I received through a crowd-funding campaign. My contributors are all inextricably connected to the soul of my journey. Let me list all of them to thank them with all my heart: Lena Lee, Amy Jost, Johnny Kim, Andrew G. Smith, Michaela Roehrig, Annette Fournet, Marshall Nelson, Nicole Depping, Felix Jost, Colin Hoffmann, Natalie Hirt, David Filshie, Jessie Ksanznak, Passage Reisen, Laura Graham, Andreas Zingg, Nancy and Thomas Duerrenberger, Andrew Stansfield, April Bailey, Bronwyn Claasen, Josep Clota, Rosa Brau, Danica Groehlich, Jonathan Liengme, Patricia Persano, Maggie Tischhauser, Jennifer Meier, Susana Farr, Frank Wannenwetsch, Alice Chan, Ralph Siegfried, Sally Bowden, David Dittrich, Jenny Gudlat, Susan Hofmann, Annemieke de Groot, Racheal Cogan, Lasse Andersson, Claudia Bombach, Mags Webster, Andrea Mosch, May Au, Ana Arroyo, Moira O'Hagan, Armin Juenemann, Katrin Beckedorf, Gaby Hafner, Oliver Guggisberg, Susanne Stauss, Krzysztof Holowenko, Tomasz Kapuscinski, Jacinta Wu, Antje Stieber, Stefan Keller, Malia Jones, Patrick John Ross, Christiane Hilty-Fetsch, Tanja Gerber-Fries, Roger Ehrensberger, Nicole Herrmann, Nicholas Piercy, Claudia Piercy, Emily Putzer, Philipp Rickenbacher, Lut de Clercq, Petra Hellmann, Stefan Haslab, Rex Lockyer, Jean-Marie Tholl, Barbara Boscardin, Lori Ballantyne, Kate Allert, Dorina Truniger-Hambsch, Nico Karsdorf, Ralf Wannenwetsch, Sacha Storto, Wolf Nitschke, Hans Ruedi Eppelsheimer, Ute Frlec, Francine Dodson, Sabine Mosch, Angie Brooks, Jay Brooks, Jo Evans, Dr. Markus Deeken, Ursula Wannenwetsch, Travis Hickey, Eva Andrea, Jutta Baecker, Tom Hodge, Zoe Hodge, Anna Bader, Glenn Larson, Jan Larson, Geordie Yip, Eve Bernier, Jessica Baker, Suchan Vodoor, Gabriella Vitto, Silvia Graf, Melissa Reed, Gregg Van Loock, Catherine Fessler, Heather Rose-Chase, Michael Chase, Nathan Chase, Benjamin Chase, Tobias Staerk, Elke Sandmann.

During the months I dedicated to writing my story, the many acts of kindness and support have humbled me. Friends volunteered to become actively involved in designing and marketing my book long before my manuscript was finished. I was given an overwhelming amount of good advice. People believed in me and gave me strength through their unerring faith in my abilities.

Many special thanks to Nicole for entrusting me with a large loan; to Axel for his help with videos and early marketing; to Racheal for helping to find a great editor; to Monica Meneghetti for her superb editing skills and overall overwhelming support; to Helena for her help in finding the right title and book cover design; to Sienna for the perfect cover and professional press photos.

Finally, deeply felt thanks to my publisher for giving me this opportunity to speak up and give something back to the world.